Debating the A Priori

Timothy Williamson is the Wykeham Professor of Logic at the University of Oxford and a Fellow of New College Oxford. He was previously Professor of Logic and Metaphysics at the University of Edinburgh, and has also taught at Trinity College Dublin, and as a visitor at MIT, Princeton, the Australian National University, the Chinese University of Hong Kong, and elsewhere. He has published *Identity and Discrimination* (Wiley-Blackwell, 1990), *Vagueness* (Routledge, 1994), *Knowledge and its Limits* (Clarendon Press, 2000), *The Philosophy of Philosophy* (Wiley-Blackwell, 2007), *Modal Logic as Metaphysics* (OUP, 2013), *Tetralogue: I'm Right, You're Wrong* (OUP, 2015), and many articles on logic and philosophy.

Paul Boghossian is Silver Professor of Philosophy at New York University and the director of the New York Institute of Philosophy. He has also taught at Michigan, Princeton, Birmingham and the Ecole Normale Superieure. His research interests are primarily in epistemology and the philosophy of mind, although he has written on a wide range of topics, including: color, rule-following, naturalism, self-knowledge, a priori knowledge, analytic truth, realism, relativism, the aesthetics of music and the concept of genocide. He is the author of *Fear of Knowledge* (2006) and *Content and Justification* (2008). He was elected to the American Academy of Arts and Sciences in 2012.

Debating the A Priori

Paul Boghossian and
Timothy Williamson

OXFORD
UNIVERSITY PRESS

OXFORD

UNIVERSITY PRESS

Great Clarendon Street, Oxford, OX2 6DP,
United Kingdom

Oxford University Press is a department of the University of Oxford.
It furthers the University's objective of excellence in research, scholarship,
and education by publishing worldwide. Oxford is a registered trade mark of
Oxford University Press in the UK and in certain other countries

First published 2020
First published in paperback 2022

Published in the United States of America by Oxford University Press
198 Madison Avenue, New York, NY 10016, United States of America

British Library Cataloguing in Publication Data
Data available

Library of Congress Cataloging in Publication Data
Data available

ISBN 978–0–19–885170–7 (Hbk.)
ISBN 978–0–19–288221–9 (Pbk.)

PB: To my daughter Octavia
TW: To my sister Bridget and my brother Toby

Contents

Preface

This book records a series of animated and productive philosophical exchanges between its authors, amounting to a debate extended over more than fifteen years. It has revolved around the questions, How and what can one learn by sheer *thinking*? In more elevated language, its subject matter is the nature and scope of reason, especially human reason. A central case at issue has been basic logical knowledge, and the justification for basic deductive inferences, but the arguments have ranged far more widely, at stake the distinctions between analytic and synthetic, and between a priori and a posteriori. They naturally involved problems about the conditions for linguistic understanding and competence, and what it might be to grasp a concept or to have an intuition. Whatever reason is, we take it to be central to philosophical method, so there are associated implications for how philosophy itself works, or should work. In particular, we found ourselves raising fundamental concerns about how to approach epistemology.

The exchanges do not make up a *convergent* series. Although the matters in dispute have been clarified, the result has not been a dissolution of our differences. Rather, as the debate evolved through twists and turns, the depth and breadth of our philosophical disagreements were revealed as greater than at first appeared. There is no comfort here for the idea that philosophical disputes are at bottom merely verbal. Nevertheless, we hope that the book provides evidence that an adversarial methodology is not opposed to a more general conception of philosophy as a cooperative enterprise, but instead illustrates ways in which sharp disputation can advance a shared overall project. It is not a zero-sum game. Through mutual criticism, each of us has been prodded into developing, extending, and sharpening his views much further than might otherwise have happened. Motivation is crucial to inquiry, as to every other human activity, and a view's opponents are better motivated than its proponents to find and spotlight its weaknesses. Each of us owes much to the other. Indeed, our friendship has not so much survived the exchanges as been created by them.

Although we are no nearer to agreeing philosophically than we were at the beginning of the process, neither of us has the sense of having reached deadlock. Instead, there are two opposed research programmes, each in its early stages. What is needed is not to convert those who support the other programme but to develop one's own. In the long run, like other research programmes, they will be judged by their fruits.

We hope that readers will find the clear contrasts on many points between our approaches helpful in defining their own views and taking them further, in agreement with one of us or with neither. There is so much still to be understood.

The series was initiated in 2002, when Paul was invited to present a paper, and Tim to reply, at the Joint Session of the Aristotelian Society and the Mind Association at Queen's University Belfast in July 2003. That became our symposium on 'Blind Reasoning', published in the 2003 supplementary volume of *Proceedings of the*

Aristotelian Society. The chairman was Crispin Wright; we both owe him an apology, since it was almost impossible for him to get a word in edgeways. Paul's paper represented a stage in a line of thought about analyticity and knowledge of logic that he had been pursuing for some years previously, and on which he had already published several articles. Tim had written much less directly on these matters, but was glad of the opportunity provided by a sharp foil against which to clarify, develop, and articulate his views on them. His contribution to the symposium, 'Understanding and Inference', drew him into a new line of research on analyticity and the methodology and nature of philosophy, which led to his 2005 Blackwell Brown lectures at Brown University and his resulting 2007 book *The Philosophy of Philosophy* (Blackwell). Paul was then invited to contribute to a symposium on the book in *Philosophy and Phenomenological Research*, published in 2011, with Tim replying as author. Paul's contribution was 'Williamson on the *A Priori* and the Analytic'. That exchange was a natural follow-up to the one in Belfast.

A further round followed soon after. We were both invited to speak at a memorial conference in Milan in April 2011 for the leading Italian analytic philosopher Paolo Casalegno, whose views on many issues in the philosophy of logic and language were similar to Tim's, though reached independently and by different arguments. Paul's paper was 'Inferentialism and the Epistemology of Logic: Reflections on Casalegno and Williamson'. Given how much he agreed with Casalegno, Tim chose to make his contributions to the conference be replies in defence of Casalegno to Paul and to Crispin Wright, who also contributed a paper critical of Casalegno. His response to Paul was 'Boghossian and Casalegno on Understanding and Inference'. The proceedings of the conference, including our papers, were published as the June 2012 issue of *dialectica*.

Meanwhile, Tim had been invited to contribute by Albert Casullo and Joshua Thurow to a collection of papers they were editing, *The A Priori in Philosophy* (Oxford University Press), published in 2013. He took the opportunity to develop some sceptical remarks in *The Philosophy of Philosophy* about the significance of the a priori–a posteriori distinction into a more detailed critique, in the paper 'How Deep is the Distinction between A Priori and A Posteriori Knowledge?' In June 2013, we were both speakers at a conference on the a priori that was held in New York University's Villa La Pietra in Florence. Paul presented an early version of his response to the above-named paper, which had been available pre-publication. Tim responded informally.

Herman Cappelen had already suggested to Paul the idea of a volume based on our exchanges, with some further rounds. Paul mentioned it to Tim in January 2013, and we agreed to try out the idea on Oxford University Press. Peter Momtchiloff and several anonymous referees were supportive, so we went ahead. Since then we have been working towards this volume, though slowed down by many other commitments; each of us has had to balance the needs of various different writing projects. We have also had several more public exchanges of ideas since then. Paul presented a paper on intuition and the a priori to the Oxford Philosophical Society in June 2016, with Tim in the audience, and 'Understanding, Intuition and the A Priori' to a conference on Conceptual Truth, Analyticity, and Conceptual Competence at the University of Oslo, to which Tim replied, in June 2017.

We are reprinting our previously published contributions in almost exactly the form in which they originally appeared, except for some slight tidying of notation and correction of misprints, and the addition of a few footnotes, indicated by square brackets. Although this entails a few repetitions, we prefer to let readers see how the exchanges actually unfolded, with no rewriting of history. We have also included some other previously published papers, which were not directly involved in the exchanges but amplify and clarify our views on the questions at issue. The final third of the book consists of previously unpublished material.

Acknowledgements appear in footnotes to individual chapters. In addition, Paul would like to acknowledge a special debt of thanks to Yu Guo for his incisive and subtle comments and for his meticulous editorial help in preparing the typescript for publication.

Paul Boghossian and Timothy Williamson

Publisher's Acknowledgements

We are grateful for permission to include the following copyright material in this book.

Chapter 1 is reprinted from Paul Artin Boghossian, 'Analyticity Reconsidered', *Noûs*, Volume 30, Issue 3, pp. 360–91, Copyright © 1996 Wiley, by permission of Wiley, doi: 10.2307/2216275.

Chapter 2 is reproduced from Paul Boghossian, 'Blind Reasoning', *The Aristotelian Society Supplementary Volume*, Volume 77, Issue 1, pp. 225–48, Copyright © 2003, doi: 10.1111/1467-8349.00110. Reprinted by courtesy of the Editor of the Aristotelian Society: © 2003, https://academic.oup.com/aristoteliansupp. Chapter 3 is reproduced from Timothy Williamson, 'Understanding and Inference', *The Aristotelian Society Supplementary Volume*, Volume 77, Issue 1, pp. 249–93, Copyright © 2003, doi: 10.1111/1467-8349.00111. Reprinted by courtesy of the Editor of the Aristotelian Society: © 2003, https://academic.oup.com/aristoteliansupp.

Chapter 4 is reprinted from Paul Boghossian, 'Williamson on the A Priori and the Analytic', *Philosophy and Phenomenological Research*, Volume 82, Issue 2, pp. 488–97, Copyright © 2010 Philosophy and Phenomenological Research, LLC, by permission of Wiley, doi: 10.1111/j.1933-1592.2010.00395.x.

Chapter 5 is reprinted from Timothy Williamson, 'Reply to Boghossian', *Philosophy and Phenomenological Research*, Volume 82, Issue 2, pp. 498–506, Copyright © 2010 Philosophy and Phenomenological Research, LLC, by permission of Wiley, doi: 10.1111/j.1933-1592.2010.00400.x.

Chapter 6 is reprinted from Paul Boghossian, 'Inferentialism and the Epistemology of Logic: Reflections on Casalegno and Williamson', *dialectica*, Volume 66, Issue 2, pp. 221–36, Copyright © 2012, by permission of Wiley, doi: 10.1111/j.1746-8361.2012.01303.x.

Chapter 7 is reprinted from Timothy Williamson, 'Boghossian and Casalegno on Understanding and Inference', *dialectica*, Volume 66, Issue 2, pp. 237–47, Copyright © 2012, by permission of Wiley, doi: 10.1111/j.1746-8361.2012.01295.x.

Chapter 8 was first published as Timothy Williamson, 'How Deep is the Distinction between A Priori and A Posteriori Knowledge?', in Albert Casullo and Joshua Thurow (eds.), *The A Priori in Philosophy*, pp. 291–312, Copyright © 2013, and is reprinted here by permission of Oxford University Press (https://global.oup.com).

Chapter 12 was first published as Timothy Williamson, 'Knowing by Imagining', in Amy Kind and Peter Kung (eds.), *Knowledge through Imagination*, pp. 113–23, Copyright © 2016, and is reprinted here by permission of Oxford University Press (https://global.oup.com).

The publisher and authors have made every effort to trace and contact all copyright holders before publication. If notified, the publisher will be pleased to rectify any errors or omissions at the earliest opportunity.

1

Analyticity Reconsidered[1]

Paul Boghossian

1

This is what many philosophers believe today about the analytic–synthetic distinction: In his classic early writings on analyticity—in particular, in 'Truth by Convention', 'Two Dogmas of Empiricism', and 'Carnap and Logical Truth'—Quine showed that there can be no distinction between sentences that are true purely by virtue of their meaning and those that are not. In so doing, Quine devastated the philosophical programs that depend upon a notion of analyticity—specifically, the linguistic theory of necessary truth, and the analytic theory of a priori knowledge.

Quine himself, so the story continues, went on to espouse far more radical views about meaning, including such theses as meaning-indeterminacy and meaning-skepticism. However, it is not necessary, and certainly not appealing, to follow him on this trajectory. As realists about meaning, we may treat Quine's self-contained discussion in the early papers as the basis for a profound *insight* into the nature of meaning-facts, rather than any sort of rejection of them. We may discard the notions of the analytic and the a priori without thereby buying in on any sort of unpalatable skepticism about meaning.

Now, I don't know precisely how many philosophers believe all of the above, but I think it would be fair to say that it is the prevailing view. Philosophers with radically differing commitments—including radically differing commitments about the nature of meaning itself—subscribe to it: whatever precisely the correct construal of meaning, so they seem to think, Quine has shown that it will not sustain a distinction between the analytic and the synthetic. Listen, for example, to Bill Lycan:

It has been nearly forty years since the publication of 'Two Dogmas of Empiricism.' Despite some vigorous rebuttals during that period, Quine's rejection of analyticity still prevails—in that philosophers en masse have either joined Quine in repudiating the 'analytic/synthetic' distinction or remained (however mutinously) silent and made no claims of analyticity.

This comprehensive capitulation is somewhat surprising, in light of the radical nature of Quine's views on linguistic meaning generally. In particular, I doubt that many philosophers accept his doctrine of the indeterminacy of translation...

Lycan goes on to promise that in his paper, he is going to

make a Quinean case against analyticity, without relying on the indeterminacy doctrine. For I join the majority in denying both analyticity and indeterminacy...[2]

Debating the A Priori. Paul Boghossian and Timothy Williamson, Oxford University Press (2020).
© Paul Boghossian and Timothy Williamson.
DOI: 10.1093/oso/9780198851707.001.0001

Now, my disagreement with the prevailing view is not total. There is *a* notion of 'truth by virtue of meaning'—what I shall call the metaphysical notion—that *is* undermined by a set of indeterminacy-independent considerations. Since this notion is presupposed by the linguistic theory of necessity, that project fails and must be abandoned.

However, I disagree with the prevailing view's assumption that those very same considerations also undermine the analytic explanation of the a priori. For it seems to me that an entirely distinct notion of analyticity underlies that explanation, a notion that is epistemic in character. And in contrast with the metaphysical notion, the epistemic notion can be defended, I think, provided that even a minimal realism about meaning is true. I'm inclined to hold, therefore, that there can be no effective Quinean critique of the a priori that does not ultimately depend on Quine's radical thesis of the indeterminacy of meaning, a thesis that, as I've stressed, many philosophers continue to reject.

All of this is what I propose to argue in this paper. I should emphasize right at the outset, however, that I am not a historian and my interest here is not historical. Think of me rather as asking, on behalf of all those who continue to reject Quine's later skepticism about meaning, Can something like the analytic explanation of the a priori be salvaged from the wreckage of the linguistic theory of necessity?

Belief, apriority, and indeterminacy

We need to begin with some understanding—however brief and informal—of what it is to believe something and of what it is for a belief to count as a priori knowledge.

Let's work with a picture of belief that is as hospitable as possible to Quine's basic outlook. According to this 'linguistic' picture, the objects of belief are not propositions, but rather interpreted sentences: for a person T to believe that p is for T to hold true a sentence S which means that p in T's idiolect.[3]

Against this rough and ready background, we may say that for T to know that p is for T to justifiably hold S true, with a strength sufficient for knowledge, and for S to be true. And to say that T knows p a priori is to say that T's warrant for holding S true is independent of outer, sensory experience.[4] The interesting question in the analysis of the concept of apriority concerns this notion of warrant: What is it for a belief to be justified independently of outer sensory experience?

On a minimalist reading, to say that the warrant for a given belief is a priori is just to say that it is justified, with a strength sufficient for knowledge, without appeal to empirical evidence.[5] On a stronger reading, it is to say that *and* that the justification in question is not defeasible by any future empirical evidence.[6] Which of these two notions is at issue in the present debate?

My own view is that the minimal notion forms the core of the idea of apriority and, hence, that it would be achievement enough to demonstrate its possibility. However, in this paper I will aim to provide the materials with which to substantiate the claim that, under the appropriate circumstances, the notion of analyticity can help explain how we might have a priori knowledge even in the strong sense. A defense of the strong notion is particularly relevant in the present context, for Quine seems to have been most skeptical of the idea of empirical indefeasibility.

Before proceeding, we should also touch briefly on the notion of meaning-indeterminacy. In chapter 2 of *Word and Object*, Quine argued that, for any language, it is possible to find two incompatible translation manuals that nevertheless perfectly conform to the totality of the evidence that constrains translation. This is the famous doctrine of the indeterminacy of translation. Since Quine was further-more prepared to assume that there could not be facts about meaning that are not captured in the constraints on best translation, he concluded that meaning-facts themselves are indeterminate—that there is, strictly speaking, no determinate fact of the matter as to what a given expression in a language means. This is the doctrine that I have called the thesis of the indeterminacy of meaning.

An *acceptance* of meaning-indeterminacy can lead to a variety of *other* views about meaning. For instance, it might lead to an outright eliminativism about meaning. Or it might be taken as a reason to base the theory of meaning on the notion of likeness of meaning, rather than on that of sameness of meaning.[7] In this paper, I am not concerned with the question what moral should be drawn from the indeterminacy thesis, on the assumption that it is true; nor am I concerned with whether the indeterminacy thesis is true. I am only concerned to show that a skepticism about epistemic analyticity cannot stop short of the indeterminacy thesis, a thesis that, as I have stressed, most philosophers agree in rejecting.

Analyticity: Metaphysical or epistemological?

Traditionally, three classes of statement have been thought to be the objects of a priori knowledge: logical statements, mathematical statements, and such 'conceptual truths' as, for example, that all squares are four-sided. The problem has always been to explain what could justify us in holding such statements true on a priori grounds.

The history of philosophy has known a number of answers to this problem, among which the following has had considerable influence: We are equipped with a special evidence-gathering faculty of *intuition*, distinct from the standard five senses; by exercising this faculty, we are able to know a priori such truths as those of mathematics and logic.

The central impetus behind the *analytic* explanation of the a priori is a desire to explain the possibility of a priori knowledge without having to postulate such a special faculty, one that has never been described in satisfactory terms. The question is, How could a factual statement S be known a priori by T, without the help of a special evidence-gathering faculty?

Here, it would seem, is one way: *If mere grasp of S's meaning by T sufficed for T's being justified in holding S true.* If S were analytic in this sense, then, clearly, its apriority would be explainable without appeal to a special faculty of intuition: mere grasp of its meaning by T would suffice for explaining T's justification for holding S true. On this understanding, then, 'analyticity' is an overtly *epistemological* notion: a statement is 'true by virtue of its meaning' provided that grasp of its meaning alone suffices for justified belief in its truth.

Another, far more *metaphysical* reading of the phrase 'true by virtue of meaning' is also available, however, according to which a statement is analytic provided that, in some appropriate sense, it *owes its truth value completely to its meaning*, and not at all to 'the facts'.

Which of these two possible notions has been at stake in the dispute over analyticity? There has been a serious unclarity on the matter. Quine himself tends to label the doctrine of analyticity an epistemological doctrine, as for example in the following passage from 'Carnap and Logical Truth':

> the linguistic doctrine of logical truth, which is an epistemological doctrine, goes on to say that logical truths are true purely by virtue of the intended meanings, or intended usage, of the logical words.[8]

However, his most biting criticisms seem often to be directed at what I have called the metaphysical notion. Consider, for example, the object of disapproval in the following famous passage, a passage that concludes the official discussion of analyticity in 'Two Dogmas':

> It is obvious that truth in general depends on both language and extralinguistic fact. The statement 'Brutus killed Caesar' would be false if the world had been different in certain ways, but it would also be false if the word 'killed' happened rather to have the sense of 'begat'. Thus one is tempted to suppose in general that the truth of a statement is somehow analyzable into a linguistic component and a factual component. Given this supposition it next seems reasonable that in some statements the factual component should be null; and these are the analytic statements. But for all its a priori reasonableness, a boundary between analytic and synthetic statements simply has not been drawn. That there is such a distinction to be drawn at all is an unempirical dogma of empiricists, a metaphysical article of faith.[9]

Now, I think that there is no doubt that many of the proponents of the analytic theory of the a priori, among them especially its positivist proponents, intended the notion of analyticity to be understood in this metaphysical sense; very shortly I shall look at why.

Before doing that, however, I want to register my wholehearted agreement with Quine that the metaphysical notion is of dubious explanatory value and possibly also of dubious coherence. Fortunately for the analytic theory of the a priori, it can be shown that it need have nothing to do with this discredited idea.

The metaphysical concept

What could it possibly mean to say that the truth of a statement is fixed exclusively by its meaning and not by the facts? Isn't it in general true—indeed, isn't it in general a truism—that for any statement S,

S is true if for some p, S means that p and p?

How could the *mere* fact that S means that p make it the case that S is true? Doesn't it also have to be the case that p? As Harman has usefully put it (he is discussing the sentence 'Copper is copper'),

> what is to prevent us from saying that the truth expressed by 'Copper is copper' depends in part on a general feature of the way the world is, namely that everything is self-identical?[10]

The proponent of the metaphysical notion does have a comeback, one that has perhaps not been sufficiently addressed. If he is wise, he won't want to deny the meaning-truth truism. What he will want to say instead is that, in some appropriate sense, our meaning p by S *makes it the case that p.*

But this line is itself fraught with difficulty. For how can we make sense of the idea that something is made true by our meaning something by a sentence?

Consider a sentence of the form 'Either p or not p'. It is easy, of course, to understand how the fact that we mean what we do by the ingredient terms fixes what is expressed by the sentence as a whole; and it is easy to understand, in consequence, how the fact that we mean what we do by the sentence determines whether the sentence expresses something true or false. But as Quine points out, that is just the normal dependence of truth on meaning. What is far more mysterious is the claim that the *truth of what the sentence expresses* depends on the fact that it is expressed by that sentence, so that we can say that what is expressed wouldn't have been true at all had it not been for the fact that it is expressed by that sentence. Are we really to suppose that, prior to our stipulating a meaning for the sentence,

Either snow is white or it isn't

it wasn't the case that either snow was white or it wasn't? Isn't it overwhelmingly obvious that this claim was true *before* such an act of meaning, and that it would have been true even if no one had thought about it, or chosen it to be expressed by one of our sentences?

Why, if this idea is as problematic as I have claimed it to be, did it figure so prominently in positivist thinking about analyticity?

Much of the answer derives from the fact that the positivists didn't merely want to provide a theory of a priori knowledge; they also wanted to provide a reductive theory of necessity. The motivation was not purely epistemological, but metaphysical as well. Guided by the fear that objective, language-independent necessary connections would be both metaphysically and epistemologically odd, they attempted to show that all necessities could be understood to consist in linguistic necessities, in the shadows cast by conventional decisions concerning the meanings of words. Conventional linguistic meaning, by itself, was supposed to generate necessary truth; a fortiori, conventional linguistic meaning, by itself, was supposed to generate truth. Hence the play with the metaphysical concept of analyticity.

But this is, I believe, a futile project. In general, I have no idea what would constitute a better answer to the question, What is responsible for generating the truth of a given class of statements? than something bland like 'the world' or 'the facts'; and, for reasons that I have just been outlining, I cannot see how a good answer might be framed in terms of meaning, or convention, in particular.

So I have no sympathy with the linguistic theory of necessity or with its attendant Conventionalism. Unfortunately, the impression appears to be widespread that there is no way to disentangle that view from the analytic theory of the a priori; or, at a minimum, that there is no way to embrace the epistemic concept of analyticity without also embracing its metaphysical counterpart. I don't know whether Gil Harman believes something of the sort; he certainly gives the impression of doing so in his frequent suggestions that anyone deploying the notion of analyticity would have to be deploying both of its available readings simultaneously:

It turned out that someone could be taught to make the analytic–synthetic distinction only by being taught a rather substantial theory, a theory including such principles as that meaning can make something true and that knowledge of meaning can give knowledge of truth.[11]

One of the main points of the present paper is that these two notions of analyticity are distinct and that the analytic theory of the a priori needs only the epistemological notion and has no use whatsoever for the metaphysical one. We can have an analytic theory of the a priori without in any way subscribing to a Conventionalism about anything. It is with the extended defense of this claim that much of the present essay is concerned.

The epistemological concept

Turning, then, to the epistemic notion of analyticity, we immediately confront a serious puzzle: How could any sentence be analytic in this sense? How could mere grasp of a sentence's meaning justify someone in holding it true?

Clearly, the answer to this question has to be *semantical*: something about the sentence's meaning, or about the way that meaning is fixed, must explain how its truth is knowable in this special way. What could this explanation be?

In the history of the subject, two different sorts of explanation have been especially important. Although these, too, have often been conflated, it is crucial to distinguish between them.

One idea was first formulated in full generality by Gottlob Frege. According to Frege, a statement's analyticity (in my epistemological sense) is to be explained by the fact that it is *transformable into a logical truth by the substitution of synonyms for synonyms*. When a statement satisfies this semantic condition, I shall say that it is 'Frege-analytic'.[12]

Now, it should be obvious that Frege-analyticity is at best an *incomplete* explanation of a statement's epistemic analyticity and, hence, of its apriority. For suppose that a given sentence S is Frege-analytic. How might this fact explain its analyticity? Clearly, two further assumptions are needed. First, that facts about synonymy are knowable a priori; and second, that the truths of logic are. Under the terms of these further assumptions, a satisfying explanation goes through. Given its Frege-analyticity, S is transformable into a logical truth by the substitution of synonyms for synonyms. Facts about synonymy are a priori, so it's a priori that S is so transform-able. Furthermore, the sentence into which it is transformable is one whose truth is itself knowable a priori. Hence, S's truth is knowable a priori.

Frege tended not to worry about these further assumptions, for two reasons. First, Frege thought it obviously constitutive of the idea of meaning that meaning is transparent—that any competent user of two words would have to be able to know a priori whether or not they meant the same. Second, Frege also thought it obvious that there could be no substantive epistemology for logic—a fortiori, not one that could explain its apriority. As a consequence, he was happy to take logic's apriority for granted. For both of these reasons, he didn't worry about the fact that an explanation of apriority in terms of Frege-analyticity simply leaned on these further assumptions without explaining them.

I think the jury is still out on whether Frege was right to take these further assumptions for granted. There is certainly a very strong case to be made for the transparency of meaning.[13] And there are well-known difficulties providing a sub-stantive epistemology for something as basic as logic, difficulties we shall have occasion to further review below. Nevertheless, because we cannot simply assume that Frege was right, we have to ask how a complete theory of the a priori would go about filling in the gaps left by the concept of Frege-analyticity.

I shall have very little to say about the first gap. The question whether facts about the sameness and difference of meaning are a priori cannot be discussed independently of the question what meaning is, and that is not an issue that I want to prejudge in the present context. On some views of meaning—for example, on certain conceptual-role views—the apriority of synonymy is simply a by-product of the very nature of meaning facts, so that no substantive epistemology for synonymy is necessary or, indeed, possible. On other views—for example, on most externalist views of meaning—synonymy is not a priori, so there is no question of a sentence's Frege-analyticity fully explaining its epistemic analyticity.

Since this issue about the apriority of synonymy turns on questions that are currently unresolved, I propose to leave it for now. As we shall see, none of the analyticity skeptical considerations we shall consider exploit it in any way. (Quine never argues that the trouble with Frege-analyticity is that synonymies are a posteriori.)

Putting aside, then, skepticism about the apriority of synonymy, and, for the moment anyway, skepticism about the very existence of Frege-analytic sentences, let us ask quite generally, What class of a priori statement would an account based on the notion of Frege-analyticity *fail* to explain?

Two classes come to mind. On the one hand, a priori statements that are not transformable into logical truths by the substitution of synonyms for synonyms; and, on the other hand, a priori statements that are trivially so transformable.

Taking the first class first, there do appear to be a significant number of a priori statements that are not Frege-analytic. For example:

Whatever is red all over is not blue.
Whatever is colored is extended.
If x is warmer than y, then y is not warmer than x.

These statements appear not to be transformable into logical truths by the appropriate substitutions: the ingredient descriptive terms seem not to be decomposable in the appropriate way.

The second class of recalcitrant statements consists precisely of the truths of logic. The truths of logic satisfy, of course, the conditions on Frege-analyticity. But they satisfy them trivially. And it seems obvious that we can't hope to explain our warrant for belief in the truths of logic by appealing to their analyticity in this sense: knowledge of Frege-analyticity presupposes knowledge of logical truth and so can't explain it.

How, then, is the epistemic analyticity of these recalcitrant truths to be explained? As we shall see below, the solution proposed by Carnap and the middle Wittgenstein turns on the suggestion that they are to be viewed as *implicit definitions* of their ingredient terms. When a statement satisfies this semantical condition, I shall sometimes say that it is 'Carnap-analytic'. However, before proceeding to a discussion of Carnap-analyticity, I want to reexamine Quine's famous rejection of the much weaker concept of Frege-analyticity.[14]

2

'Two Dogmas' and the rejection of Frege-analyticity

For all its apparent limitations, the concept of Frege-analyticity is not without interest. Even though Quine made it fashionable to claim otherwise, the sentence 'All bachelors are male' *does* seem to be transformable into a logical truth by the substitution of synonyms for synonyms and that fact *does* seem to have something important to do with its apriority. If, then, appearances are not misleading here, and a significant range of a priori statements are Frege-analytic, then the problem of their apriority is *reduced* to that of the apriority of logic and synonymy and, in this way, a significant economy in explanatory burden is achieved.

It was, therefore, an important threat to the analytic theory of the a priori to find Quine arguing, in one of the most celebrated articles of this century, that the apriority of no sentence could be explained by appeal to its Frege-analyticity, because no sentence of a natural language could *be* Frege-analytic.

It has not been sufficiently appreciated, it seems to me, that 'Two Dogmas' is exclusively concerned with this weaker notion of Frege-analyticity, and not at all with the more demanding project of explaining the apriority of logic. But this is made very clear by Quine:

Statements which are analytic by general philosophical acclaim are not, indeed, far to seek. They fall into two classes. Those of the first class, which may be called *logically true*, are typified by:

(1)   No unmarried man is married.

The relevant feature of this example is that it is not merely true as it stands, but remains true under any and all reinterpretations of 'man' and 'married'. If we suppose a prior inventory of *logical* particles... then in general a logical truth is a statement that remains true under all reinterpretations of its components other than the logical particles.

But there is also a second class of analytic statements, typified by:

(2)   No bachelor is married.

The characteristic of such a statement is that it can be turned into a logical truth by putting synonyms for synonyms.   ('Two Dogmas' (TD), pp. 22–3)

Quine goes on to say very clearly,

Our problem... is analyticity; and here the major difficulty lies not in the first class of analytic statements, the logical truths, but rather in the second class, which depends on the notion of synonymy.   (TD, p. 24)

Most of the rest of TD is devoted to arguing that no good sense can be made of such analyticities of the 'second class'.

None of this would make any sense unless Quine were intending in 'Two Dogmas' to be restricting himself solely to the notion of Frege-analyticity. Of course, it is the point of two other important papers of his—'Truth by Convention' and 'Carnap and Logical Truth'—to argue that there is no non-trivial sense in which *logic* is analytic. We will turn to that issue in due course. Relative to the Fregean notion, however, the logical truths are trivially analytic; and so, given his apparent desire to restrict his attention to that notion in TD, he simply concedes their 'analyticity' in the only sense he takes to be under discussion. What he wishes to resist in TD, he insists, is merely the claim that there are any *nontrivial instances of Frege-analyticity*.[15]

Skeptical theses about analyticity

What form does Quine's resistance take? We may agree that the result being advertised isn't anything modest, of the form: There are fewer analyticities than we had previously thought. Or, there are some analytic truths, but they are not important for the purposes of science. Or anything else of a similar ilk. Rather, as a very large number of Quine's remarks make clear, the sought-after result is something ambitious to the effect that the notion of Frege-analyticity is, somehow or other, not cogent. TD's many admirers have divided on whether to read this as the claim that the notion of Frege-analyticity does not have a well-defined, determinate factual content, or whether to read it merely as claiming that, although it has an intelligible content, it is necessarily uninstantiated. I'll call the first claim a *Non-Factualism* about analyticity:

> (NF)   No coherent, determinate property is expressed by the predicate 'is analytic' (or, since these are correlative terms, the predicate 'is synthetic'); consequently, no coherent factual claim is expressed by sentences of the form 'S is analytic' and 'S is synthetic'.

And the second an *Error Thesis* about analyticity:

> (ET)   There is a coherent, determinate property expressed by 'is analytic', but it is necessarily uninstantiated; consequently, all sentences of the form 'S is analytic' are necessarily false.[16]

Regardless, however, of how TD's skepticism about Frege-analyticity is understood, I don't see how either thesis can plausibly stop short of a radical indeterminacy about meaning.

Non-factualism about Frege-analyticity

Let's begin with the non-factualist version. To say that there is no such property as the property of Frege-analyticity is essentially to say that, for *any* sentence, there is no fact of the matter as to whether it is transformable into a logical truth by the substitution of synonyms for synonyms. Presumably, this itself is possible only if, either there is no fact of the matter as to what counts as a logical truth, or no fact of the matter as to when two expressions are synonymous. Since the factuality of logic is not in dispute, the only option is a non-factualism about synonymy.

But, now, how can there fail to be facts about whether any two expressions mean the same—even where these are drawn from within a *single* speaker's idiolect, so that no questions of interlinguistic synonymy arise? Wouldn't this have to entail that there are no facts about what each expression means individually? Putting the question the other way, Could there be a fact of the matter about what each expression means, but no fact of the matter about whether they mean the same?[17]

Let's consider this question first against the background of an un-Quinean relational construal of meaning, according to which an expression's meaning something is a relation M between it and its meaning, the meaning C. Someone who held that a non-factualism about synonymy could co-exist with a determinacy about meaning would have to hold that, although it might be true that some specific word—say, 'cow'—bears some specific relation M to some specific meaning C, there is no fact of the matter about whether some *other* word—some other orthographically identified particular—bears precisely the same relation to precisely the same meaning.

But how could this be? How could it conceivably turn out that it is intelligible and true to say that 'cow' bears M to C, and not merely false but *non-factual* to say that some other word—'vache' as it may be—also does? What could be so special about the letters 'c', 'o', 'w'?

The answer, of course, is that there is nothing special about them. If it is factual that one word bears M to C, it is surely factual that some other word does. Especially on a relational construal of meaning, it makes no sense to suppose that a determinacy about meaning could coexist with a non-factualism about synonymy.

The question naturally arises whether this result is forthcoming *only* against the background of a relational construal of meaning. I think it's quite clear that the answer is 'No'. To see why, suppose that instead of construing meaning-facts as involving relations to meanings we construe them thus: 'cow' means *cow* just in case 'cow' has the monadic property R—a history of use, a disposition, or whatever your favorite candidate may be. Precisely the same arguments go through: it remains equally difficult to see how, given that 'cow' has property R, it could fail to be factual whether some other word does.

The error thesis about Frege-analyticity

I think, then, that if a plausible skepticism about Frege-analyticity is to be sustained, it cannot take the form of a non-factualism. Does an error thesis fare any better? According to this view, although there are determinate facts about which sentences are transformable into logical truths by the appropriate manipulations of synonymy, this property is necessarily uninstantiated: it is nomically impossible for there to be any Frege-analytic sentences. Our question is, Does at least this form of skepticism about Frege-analyticity avoid collapse into the indeterminacy doctrine?

Well, I suppose that if we are being very strict about it, we may have to admit that it is barely *logically possible* to combine a denial of indeterminacy with an error thesis about synonymy, so that we can say that although there are determinate facts about what means what, it is impossible for any two things to mean the same thing. But is such a view plausible? Do we have any reason for believing it? I think not.

Let's begin with the fact that even Quine has to admit that it is possible for two *tokens of the same orthographic type* to be synonymous, for that much is presupposed by his own account of logical truth.[18]

What about two tokens of different types? Here again, our own argument can proceed from Quine's own admissions. For even Quine concedes that two expressions can mean the same thing, provided that they are explicitly stipulated to mean the same thing.[19] So his skepticism about synonymy has to boil down to the following somewhat peculiar claim: Although there is such a thing as the property of synonymy; and although it can be instantiated by pairs of tokens of the same orthographic type; and although it can be instantiated by pairs of tokens of distinct orthographic types, provided that they are related to each other by way of an explicit stipulation; it is, nevertheless, in principle impossible to generate instances of this property in some other way, via some other mechanism. For example, it is impossible that two expressions that were introduced independently of each other into the language should have been introduced with exactly the same meanings.

But what conceivable rationale could there be for such a claim? As far as I am able to tell, there is precisely one argument in the literature that is supposed to provide support for it. It may be represented as follows:

Premise: Meaning is radically holistic in the sense that: 'What our words mean depends on *everything* we believe, on *all* the assumptions we are making.'[20]

Therefore,

Conclusion: It is very unlikely that, in any given language, there will be two words of distinct types that mean exactly the same thing.

I am inclined to agree that this argument (properly spelled out) is valid, and so, that if a radical holism about meaning were true, then synonymies between expressions of different types would be rare.

However, I note that 'rare' does not mean the same as 'impossible', which is the result we were promised. And, much more importantly, I am completely inclined to disagree that TD provides any sort of cogent argument for meaning-holism in the first place.

It's easy to see why, if such a radical meaning-holism were true, synonymies might be hard to come by. For although it is not unimaginable, it is unlikely that two words of distinct types will participate in *all* of the same beliefs and inferences. Presumably there will always be some beliefs that will discriminate between them—beliefs about their respective shapes, for example.

But what reason do we have for believing that *all* of a word's uses are constitutive of its meaning?

Many Quineans seem to hold that the crucial argument for this intuitively implausible view is to be found in the concluding sections of TD. In those concluding sections, Quine argues powerfully for the epistemological claim that has come to be known as the Quine–Duhem thesis: confirmation is holistic in that the warrant for any given sentence depends on the warrant for every other sentence. In those concluding sections, Quine also assumes a Verificationist theory of meaning, according to which the meaning of a sentence is fixed by its method of confirmation. Putting these two theses together, one can speedily arrive at the view that a word's meaning depends on *all* of its inferential links to other words, and hence at the thesis of meaning-holism.[21]

This, however, is not a very convincing train of thought. First, and not all that importantly, this couldn't have been the argument that *Quine* intended against Frege-analyticity, for this argument for meaning-holism is to be found in the very last pages of TD, well after the rejection of Frege-analyticity is taken to have been established.

Second, and more importantly, the argument is not very compelling because it depends crucially on a verificationism about meaning, a view that we have every good reason to reject, and which has in fact been rejected by most contemporary philosophers.

Finally, and perhaps most importantly, any such holism-based argument against the possibility of synonymy would need to be supported by something that no one has ever provided—a reason for believing that yielding such an intuitively implausible result about synonymy isn't itself simply a *reductio* of meaning-holism.[22]

3

The analyticity of logic

If the preceding considerations are correct, then there is no principled objection to the existence of Frege-analyticities, and, hence, no principled objection to the existence of statements that are knowable a priori if logical truth is.[23]

But what about logical truth? Is it knowable a priori? And, if so, how?[24]

In the case of some logical truths, the explanation for how we have come to know them will be clear: we will have deduced them from others. So our question concerns only the most elementary laws of sentential or first-order logic. How do we know a priori, for example, that all the instances of the law of noncontradiction are true, or that all the instances of modus ponens are valid?

As I noted above, Frege thought it obvious that there could be no substantive answer to such questions; he was inclined, therefore, to take appearances at face value and to simply *assume* the apriority of logic.

What Frege probably had in mind is the following worry. 'Explaining our knowledge of logic' presumably involves finding some *other* thing that we know, on the basis of which our knowledge of logic is to be explained. However, regardless of what that other thing is taken to be, it's hard to see how the use of logic is to be avoided in moving from knowledge of that thing to knowledge of the relevant logical truth. And so it can come to seem as if any account of how we know logic will have to end up being vacuous, presupposing that we have the very capacity that's to be explained.

Michael Dummett has disputed the existence of a real problem here. As he has pointed out, the sort of circularity that's at issue isn't the gross circularity of an argument that consists of including the conclusion that's to be reached among the premises. Rather, we have an argument that purports to prove the validity of a given logical law, at least one of whose inferential steps must be taken in accordance with that law. Dummett calls this a 'pragmatic' circularity. He goes on to claim that a pragmatic circularity of this sort will be damaging only to a justificatory argument that

is addressed to someone who genuinely doubts whether the law is valid, and is intended to persuade him that it is....If, on the other hand, it is intended to satisfy the philosopher's perplexity about our entitlement to reason in accordance with such a law, it may well do so.[25]

The question whether Dummett's distinction fully allays Frege's worry is a large one, and I can't possibly hope to settle it here. If something along these general lines can't be made to work, then *any* explanation of logic's apriority—or aposteriority, for that matter—is bound to be futile, and the Fregean attitude will have been vindicated.

However, the question that particularly interests me in the present essay is this: Assuming that the very enterprise of explaining our knowledge of logic isn't shown to be hopeless by Frege's straightforward argument, is there any *special* reason for doubting an explanation based on the notion of analyticity? Quine's enormously influential claim was that there is. I shall try to argue that there isn't—that, in an important sense to be specified later on, our grasp of the meaning of logical claims can explain our a priori warrant for holding them true (provided that the Fregean worry doesn't defeat all such explanations in the first place).

The classical view and Implicit Definition

It's important to understand, it seems to me, that the analytic theory of the apriority of logic arose indirectly, as a by-product of the attempt to explain in what a grasp of the meaning of the logical constants consists. Alberto Coffa lays this story out very nicely in his recent book.[26]

What account are we to give of our grasp of the logical constants, given that they are not to explicitly definable in terms of *other* concepts? Had they been explicitly definable, of course, we would have been able to say—however plausibly—that we grasp them by grasping their definitions. But as practically anybody who has thought about the matter has recognized, the logical constants are not explicitly definable in terms of other concepts, and so we are barred from giving that account. The question is, what account are we to give?

Historically, many philosophers were content to suggest that the state of grasping these constants was somehow primitive, not subject to further explanation. In particular, such a grasp of the meaning of, say, 'not', was to be thought of as prior to, and independent of, a decision on our part as to which of the various sentences involving 'not' to count as true. We may call this view, following Wittgenstein's lead, the doctrine of

Flash-Grasping: We grasp the meaning of, say, 'not' 'in a flash'—prior to, and independently of, deciding which of the sentences involving 'not' are true.

On this historically influential picture, Flash-Grasping was combined with the doctrine of Intuition to generate an epistemology for logic:

Intuition: This grasp of the concept of, say, negation, along with our intuition of its logical properties, explains and justifies our logical beliefs involving negation— e.g., that 'If not not p, then p' is true.

As Coffa shows, this picture began to come under severe strain with the development of alternative geometries. Naturally enough, an analogous set of views had been used to explain the apriority of geometry. In particular, a flash-grasp of the indefinables of geometry, along with intuitions concerning their necessary properties, was said to explain and justify belief in the axioms of Euclidean geometry.

However, with the development of alternative geometries, such a view faced an unpleasant dilemma. Occupying one horn was the option of saying that Euclidean and non-Euclidean geometries are talking about the *same* geometrical properties, but disagreeing about what is true of them. But this option threatens the thesis of Intuition: If in fact we learn geometrical truths by intuition, how could this faculty have misled us for so long?

Occupying the other horn was the option of saying that Euclidean and non-Euclidean geometries are talking about *different* geometrical properties—attaching different meanings to, say, 'distance'—and so not disagreeing after all. But this option threatens the doctrine of Flash-Grasping. Suppose we grant that a Euclidean and a non-Euclidean geometer attach different meanings to 'distance'. In what does the difference in the respective psychological states consist? Officially, of course, the view is that one primitive state constitutes grasp of Euclidean distance, and another that of non-Euclidean distance. But absent some further detail about how to tell such states apart and the criteria that govern their attribution, this would appear to be a hopelessly ad hoc and non-explanatory maneuver.

The important upshot of these considerations was to make plausible the idea that grasp of the indefinables of geometry consists precisely in the adoption of one set of truths involving them, as opposed to another. Applied to the case of logic, it generates the semantical thesis that I shall call

Implicit Definition: It is by arbitrarily stipulating that certain sentences of logic are to be true, or that certain inferences are to be valid, that we attach a meaning to the logical constants. More specifically, a particular constant means that logical object, if any, which makes valid a specified set of sentences and/or inferences involving it.

Now, the transition from this sort of Implicit Definition account of grasp, to the analytic theory of the apriority of logic, can seem pretty immediate. For it would seem that the following sort of argument is now in place:

1. If logical constant C is to mean what it does, then argument-form A has to be valid, for C means whatever logical object in fact makes A valid.
2. C means what it does.
   Therefore,
3. A is valid.

I will return to various questions regarding this form of justification below.[27] For now I want to worry about the fact that neither Carnap nor Wittgenstein was content merely to replace Flash-Grasping with Implicit Definition. Typically, both writers went on to embrace some form of antirealism about logic. Intuitively, the statements of logic appear to be fully factual statements, expressing objective truths about the world, even if necessary ones, and even if (on occasion) highly obvious ones. Both Carnap and Wittgenstein, however, seemed inclined to deny such an intuitive realism about logic, affirming in its place either the thesis of logical Non-Factualism or the thesis of logical Conventionalism, or, on occasion, both theses at once.

By *logical* Non-Factualism,[28] I mean the view that the sentences of logic that implicitly define the logical primitives do not express factual claims and, hence, are not capable of genuine truth or falsity. How, on such a view, are we to think of their semantic function? On the most popular version, we are to think of it as prescriptive, as a way of expressing a rule concerning the correct use of logical expressions. By contrast, logical Conventionalism is the view that, although the sentences of logic are factual—although they can express truths—their truth values are not objective, but are rather determined by our conventions.

Despite this important difference between them, there is an interesting sense in which the upshot of both views is the same, a fact that probably explains why they were often used interchangeably and why they often turn up simultaneously in the analytic theory of logic. For what both views imply is that, as between two different sets of decisions regarding which sentences of logic to hold true, there can be no epistemic fact of the matter. In short, both views imply an epistemic relativism about logic. Conventionalism implies this because it says that the truth in logic is up to us, so no substantive disagreement is possible; and Non-Factualism implies this because it says that there are no truths in logic, hence nothing to disagree about.

Nevertheless, for all this affinity of upshot, it should be quite plain that the two views are very different from each other—indeed, incompatible with each other. Conventionalism is a factualist view: it presupposes that the sentences of logic have truth values. It differs from a realist view of logic in its conception of the *source* of those truth values, not on their existence. Therefore, although it is possible, as I have noted, to find texts in which a rule-prescriptivism about logic is combined with Conventionalism, that can only be a confusion.

The important question is, Why did the proponents of Implicit Definition feel the need to go beyond it all the way to the far more radical doctrines of Non-Factualism and/or Conventionalism? Whatever problems it may eventually be discovered to harbor, Implicit Definition seems like a plausible candidate for explaining our grasp of the logical constants, especially in view of the difficulties encountered by its classical rival. But there would appear to be little that prima facie recommends either Non-Factualism or Conventionalism. So why combine these dubious doctrines with what looks to be a plausible theory of meaning?

Apparently, both Carnap and Wittgenstein seem to have thought that the issue was forced, that Implicit Definition entailed one or the other antirealist thesis. It seems quite clear that Carnap, for example, believed that Implicit Definition brought Conventionalism immediately in its wake; and Quine seems to have agreed. What separated them was their attitude towards Conventionalism. Carnap embraced it; Quine, by contrast, seems to have been prepared to reject any premiss that led to it; hence his assault on the doctrine of Implicit Definition.

But if this is in fact the correct account of Quine's motivations, then they are based, I believe, on a false assumption, for neither form of antirealism about logic follows from the thesis of Implicit Definition.

I will proceed as follows. First, I will argue that Implicit Definition, properly understood, is completely independent of any form of antirealism about logic. Second, I will defend the thesis of Implicit Definition against Quine's criticisms. Finally, I will examine the sort of account of the apriority of logic that this doctrine is able to provide.

Implicit Definition and Non-Factualism

Does Implicit Definition entail Non-Factualism? It is certainly very common to come across the claim that it does. Coffa, for instance, writes that from the new perspective afforded by the doctrine of Implicit Definition, the basic claims of logic are our access to certain meanings, definitions in disguise, devices that allow us to implement an explicit or tacit decision to constitute certain concepts.... From this standpoint, necessary claims do not tell us anything that is the case both in the world and in many others, as Leibniz thought, or anything that is the case for *formal* reasons, whatever that might mean, or anything that one is forced to believe due to features of our mind. They do not tell us anything that is the case; so they had better not be called claims or propositions. Since their role is to constitute meanings and since (apparently) we are free to endorse them or not, it is better to abandon the old terminology (a priori 'principles', 'laws', etc.) that misleadingly suggests a propositional status and to refer to them as 'rules'. (*The Semantic Tradition*, pp. 265–6)

I have no desire to engage the exegetical issues here; as far as I can tell, the middle Wittgenstein seems very much to have been a Non-Factualist about the implicit definers of logic, just as Coffa says. What I dispute is that it *follows* from the fact that a given sentence Q is being used to implicitly define one of its ingredient terms, that Q is not a factual sentence, not a sentence that 'tells us anything that is the case'. These two claims seem to me to be entirely independent of each other.

To help us think about this, consider Kripke's example of the introduction of the term 'meter'. As Kripke imagines it, someone introduces the term into his vocabulary by stipulating that the following sentence is to be true:

[1]   Stick S is a meter long at t.

Suppose that stick S exists and is a certain length at t. Then it follows that 'meter' names that length and hence that [1] says that stick S is that length at t, and since it is that length at t, [1] is true.

Knowing all this may not be much of an epistemic achievement, but that isn't the point. The point is that there appears to be no inconsistency whatsoever between claiming that a given sentence serves to implicitly define an ingredient term and claiming that that very sentence expresses something factual.

Similarly, I don't see that there is any inconsistency between supposing that a given logical principle—for instance, the law of excluded middle—serves to implicitly define an ingredient logical constant, and supposing that that very sentence expresses a factual statement capable of genuine truth and falsity.[29]

Implicit Definition and Conventionalism

So far I have argued that it is consistent with a sentence's serving as an implicit definer that that very sentence come to express a fully factual claim, capable of genuine truth and falsity. Perhaps, however, when implicit definition is at issue, the truth of the claim that is thereby fixed has to be thought of as conventionally determined. Does at least Conventionalism follow from Implicit Definition?[30]

It is easy to see, I suppose, why these two ideas might have been run together. For according to Implicit Definition, 'if, then', for example, comes to mean the conditional precisely by my assigning the truth value True to certain basic sentences involving it, for example, to

If, if p then q, and p, then q.

And in an important sense, my assigning this sentence the value True is arbitrary. Prior to my assigning it that truth value, it didn't have a complete meaning, for one of its ingredient terms didn't have a meaning at all. The process of assigning it the value True is simply part of what fixes its meaning. Had I assigned it the value False, the sentence would then have had a *different* meaning. So, prior to the assignment there couldn't have been a substantive question regarding its truth value. And after the assignment there couldn't be a substantive question as to whether that assignment was correct. In this sense, then, the sentence's truth value is arbitrary and conventional. Doesn't it follow, then, that Implicit Definition entails Conventionalism?

Not at all. All that is involved in the thesis of Implicit Definition is the claim that the conventional assignment of truth to a sentence determines what claim that sentence expresses (if any); such a view is entirely silent about what (if anything) determines the truth of the claim that is thereby expressed—a fortiori, it is silent about whether our conventions determine it.

Think here again of Kripke's meter stick. If the stick exists and has such-and-so length at t, then it is conventional that 'meter' names that length and, therefore, conventional that [1] expresses the proposition stick S *has such-and-so length at t*. However, that stick S has that length at t is hardly a fact generated by convention; it presumably had that length prior to the convention, and may continue to have it well after the convention has lapsed.[31]

I anticipate the complaint that the entailment between Implicit Definition and Conventionalism is blocked only through the tacit use of a distinction between a sentence and the proposition it expresses, a distinction that neither Carnap nor Quine would have approved.

Such a complaint would be mistaken, however. The argument I gave relies not so much on a distinction between a sentence and a proposition in the technical sense disapproved of by Quine, as on a distinction between a sentence and *what it expresses*. And it is hard to see how any adequate philosophy of language is to get by without some such distinction.[32] Even on a deflationary view of truth, there is presumably a distinction between the *sentence* 'Snow is white' and that which makes the sentence true, namely, snow's being white. And the essential point for my purposes is that it is one thing to say that 'Snow is white' comes to express the claim that snow is white as a result of being conventionally assigned the truth value True; and quite another to say that snow comes to be white as a result of our conventions. The first claim is Implicit Definition (however implausibly applied in this case); and the other is Conventionalism. Neither one seems to me to entail the other.

Quine against Implicit Definition: Regress

As I noted above, I am inclined to believe that erroneous opinion on this score has played an enormous role in the history of this subject. I conjecture that had Quine felt more confident that Implicit Definition could be sharply distinguished from Conventionalism, he might not have felt so strongly against it.

In any event, though, whatever the correct explanation of Quine's animus, we are indebted to him for a series of powerful critiques of the thesis of Implicit Definition, critiques that have persuaded many that that thesis, and with it any explanation of the apriority of logic that it might be able to ground, are fundamentally flawed. We must now confront Quine's arguments.

According to Implicit Definition, the logical constants come to have a particular meaning in our vocabulary by our conventionally stipulating that certain sentences (or inferences) involving them are to be true. For instance, let us assume that the meaning for 'and' is fixed by our stipulating that the following inferences involving it are to be valid:

[2] $\dfrac{\text{A and B}}{\text{A}}$ $\dfrac{\text{A and B}}{\text{B}}$ $\dfrac{\text{A, B}}{\text{A and B}}$

Now, Quine's first important criticism of this idea occurs in his early paper 'Truth by Convention'.[33] As Quine there pointed out, there are an infinite number of instances of schema [2]. Consequently, the inferences of this infinitary collection could not have been conventionally stipulated to be valid singly, one by one. Rather, Quine argued, if there is anything at all to this idea, it must be something along the following lines: We adopt certain general conventions from which it follows that all the sentences of the infinitary collection are assigned the value Valid. Such a general convention would presumably look like this:

Let all results of putting a statement for 'p' and a statement for 'q' in 'p and q implies p' be valid.

However, the trouble is that in order to state such a general convention we have had, unavoidably, to use all sorts of logical terms—'every', 'and', and so on. So the claim, essential to the proposal under consideration, that all our logical constants acquire their meaning via the adoption of such explicitly formulated conventional assignments of validity, must fail. Logical constants whose meaning is not fixed in this way are presupposed by the model itself.[34]

This argument of Quine's has been very influential; and I think that there is no doubt that it works against its target as specified. However, it is arguable that its target as specified isn't the view that needs defeating.

For, surely, it isn't compulsory to think of someone's following a rule **R** with respect to an expression **e** as consisting in his *explicitly stating* that rule in so many words in the way that Quine's argument presupposes. On the contrary, it seems far more plausible to construe **x**'s following rule **R** with respect to **e** as consisting in some sort of fact about **x**'s *behavior* with **e**.

In what would such a fact consist? Here there are at least a couple of options. According to a currently popular idea, following rule **R** with respect to **e** may consist in our being disposed to conform to rule **R** in our employment of **e**, under certain circumstances. On this version, the notion of rule-following would have been *reduced* to a certain sort of dispositional fact. Alternatively, one might wish to appeal to the notion of following a given rule, while resisting the claim that it can be reduced to a set of naturalistically acceptable dispositional facts. On such a non-reductionist version, there would be facts about what rule one is following, even if these are not cashable into facts about one's behavioral dispositions, however optimal.

For myself, I am inclined to think that the reductionist version won't work, that we will have to employ the notion of following a rule unreduced.[35] But because it is more familiar, and because nothing substantive hangs on it in the present context, I will work with the reductionist version of rule-following. Applied to the case we are considering, it issues in what is widely known in the literature as a 'conceptual-role semantics'.

According to this view, then, the logical constants mean what they do by virtue of figuring in certain inferences and/or sentences involving them and not in others. If some expressions mean what they do by virtue of figuring in certain inferences and sentences, then some inferences and sentences are *constitutive* of an expression's meaning what it does, and others aren't. And any CRS must find a systematic way of saying which are which, of answering the question, What properties must an inference or sentence involving a constant C have, if that inference or sentence is to be constitutive of C's meaning?

Quine against Implicit Definition: Constitutive truth

Now, Quine's second objection to Implicit Definition can be put by saying that there will be no way of doing what I said any CRS must do—namely, systematically specify the meaning-constituting inferences. Quine formulated this point in a number of places. Here is a version that appears in 'Carnap and Logical Truth':

> if we try to warp the linguistic doctrine of logical truth into something like an experimental thesis, perhaps a first approximation will run thus: *Deductively irresoluble disagreement as to a logical truth is evidence of deviation in usage (or meanings) of words....* [However,] the obviousness or potential obviousness of elementary logic can be seen to present an insuperable obstacle to our assigning any experimental meaning to the linguistic doctrine of elementary logical truth.... For, that theory now seems to imply nothing that is not already implied by the fact that elementary logic is obvious or can be resolved into obvious steps.[36]

Elsewhere, Quine explained his use of the word 'obvious' in this connection thus:

> In 'Carnap and Logical Truth' I claimed that Carnap's arguments for the linguistic doctrine of logical truth boiled down to saying no more than that they were obvious, or potentially obvious—that is, generable from obvieties by obvious steps. I had been at pains to select the word 'obvious' from the vernacular, intending it as I did in the vernacular sense. A sentence is obvious if (a) it is true and (b) any speaker of the language is prepared, for any reason or none, to assent to it without hesitation, unless put off by being asked so obvious a question.[37]

Quine's important point here is that there will be no substantive way of distinguishing between a highly obvious, non-defining sentence and a sentence that is an implicit definer. Both types of sentence—if in fact both types exist—will have the feature that any speaker of the language will be prepared to assent to instances of them, 'for any reason or none'. So in what does the alleged difference between them consist? How is distinctive content to be given to the doctrine of Implicit Definition?[38]

Now, there is no doubt that this is a very good question; and the impression that it has no good answer has contributed greatly to the rejection of the doctrine of Implicit Definition. Jerry Fodor and Ernie Lepore, for example, base the entirety of their recent argument against a conceptual-role semantics on their assumption that Quine showed this question to be unanswerable.[39]

If Quine's challenge is allowed to remain unanswered, then the threat to the analytic theory of the a priori is fairly straightforward. For if there is no fact of the matter as to whether S is a sentence that I must hold true if S is to mean what it does, then there is no basis on which to argue that I am entitled to hold S true without evidence.

But that would seem to be the least of our troubles, if Quine's argument is allowed to stand. For what's threatened is not only the apriority of logical truths but, far more extremely, the *determinacy* of what they claim. For as I've already pointed out, and as many philosophers are anyway inclined to believe, a conceptual-role semantics seems to be the *only* plausible view about how the meaning of the logical constants is fixed. It follows, therefore, that if there is no fact of the matter as to which of the various inferences involving a constant are meaning-constituting, then there is also no fact of the matter as to what the logical constants themselves mean. And that, again, is just the dreaded indeterminacy of meaning on which the critique of analyticity was supposed not to depend.

The simple point here is that if the only view available about how the logical constants acquire their meaning is in terms of the inferences and/or sentences that they participate in, then any indeterminacy in what those meaning-constituting sentences and inferences are will translate into an indeterminacy about the meanings of the expressions themselves. This realization should give pause to any philosopher who thinks he can buy in on Quine's critique of implicit definition without following him all the way to the far headier doctrine of meaning-indeterminacy.

There has been a curious tendency to miss this relatively simple point. Jerry Fodor seems a particularly puzzling case. For Fodor holds all three of the following views. (1) He rejects indeterminacy, arguing forcefully against it. (2) He follows Quine in rejecting the notion of a meaning-constituting inference. (3) He holds a conceptual-role view of the meanings of the logical constants. As far as I am able to judge, however, this combination of views is not consistent.[40]

Part of the explanation for this curious blindness derives from a tendency to view Quine's argument as issuing not in an indeterminacy about meaning, but, rather, in a *holism* about it. In fact, according to Fodor and Lepore, the master argument for meaning-holism in the literature runs as follows:

A.   Some of an expression's inferential liaisons are relevant to fixing its meaning.
B.   There is no principled distinction between those inferential liaisons that are constitutive and those that aren't. (The Quinean result.)

Therefore,

C.   All of an expression's inferential liaisons are relevant to fixing its meaning. (Meaning-holism)

Fearing this argument's validity, and seeing no way to answer Quine's challenge, they spend their whole book trying to undermine the argument's first premiss, namely, the very plausible claim that at least *some* of an expression's inferential liaisons are relevant to fixing its meaning.[41]

But they needn't have bothered, for I don't see how the master argument could be valid in the first place. The claim that *all* of an expression's inferential liaisons are constitutive of it cannot cogently follow from the claim that it is *indeterminate* what the constitutive inferences are. If it's *indeterminate* what the constitutive inferences are, then it's genuinely *unsettled* what they are. And that is inconsistent with saying that they are *all* constitutive, and inconsistent with saying that *none* is constitutive and inconsistent with saying that some specified subset is constitutive.

Fodor and Lepore are not alone in not seeing the problem here. Let me cite just one more example. In his comments on an earlier version of the present paper, Gil Harman says,

Can one accept Quine's argument against analyticity without being committed to the indeterminacy of meaning? Yes and no. By the 'indeterminacy of meaning' might be meant an indeterminacy as to which of the principles one accepts determine the meanings of one's terms and which simply reflect one's opinions about the facts. Clearly, Quine's argument against analyticity is committed to that sort of indeterminacy. [However,] that by itself does not imply full indeterminacy in the sense of chapter 2 of *Word and Object*.[42]

As Harman correctly says, Quine has to deny that there is a fact of the matter as to which of T's principles determine the meanings of his terms and which simply reflect T's opinions about the facts—that, after all, is just what it is to deny that there are facts about constitutivity. However, Harman insists, this denial in no way leads to the indeterminacy thesis of chapter 2 of *Word and Object*.

But this is very puzzling. Against the background of a conceptual-role semantics, according to which the meaning of T's term C is determined precisely by a certain subset of the principles involving C that T accepts, an indeterminacy in what the meaning-determining principles are will automatically lead to an indeterminacy in what the meaning is—in the full sense of chapter 2 of *Word and Object*. If a subset (not necessarily proper) of accepted principles is supposed to determine meaning; and if there is no fact of the matter as to which subset that is; then there is, to that extent, no fact of the matter as to what meaning has been determined.

I think there is really no avoiding the severe conclusion that meaning is indeterminate, if the Quinean challenge to constitutivity is allowed to remain unanswered. I'm inclined to think, therefore, that anyone who rejects radical indeterminacy of meaning must believe that a distinction between the meaning-constituting and the non-meaning-constituting can be drawn. The only question is how.

Well, that is not the task of the present paper. Although there are some good ideas about this, I don't have a fully thought-through proposal to present just now.[43] My main aim here is not to *solve* the fundamental problem for a conceptual-role semantics for the logical constants; rather, as I have stressed, it is to show that, against the background of a rejection of indeterminacy, its insolubility cannot be conceded.

Pending the discovery of other problems, then, it seems open to us to suppose that a plausible theory of meaning for the logical constants is given by something like the following:

A logical constant C expresses that logical object, if any, that makes valid its meaning-constituting inferences.

Implicit Definition, justification, and entitlement

Now, how does any of this help vindicate the analytic theory of the apriority of logic, the idea that logic is epistemically analytic? Let us consider a particular inference form, A, in a particular thinker's (T) repertoire; and let's suppose that that inference form is constitutive of the meaning of one of its ingredient constants, C. How, exactly, might these facts help explain the epistemic analyticity of A for T?

To say that A is epistemically analytic for T is to say that T's knowledge of A's meaning alone suffices for T's justification for A, so that empirical support is not required. And it does seem that a conceptual-role semantics can provide us with a model of how that might be so. For given the relevant facts, we would appear to be able to argue as follows:

1. If C is to mean what it does, then A has to be valid, for C means whatever logical object in fact makes A valid.
2. C means what it does.

Therefore,

3. A is valid.

Now, it is true that this is tantamount to a fairly broad use of the phrase 'knowledge of the meaning of A', for this knowledge includes not merely knowledge of what A means, strictly so-called, but also knowledge of how that meaning is fixed. But this is, of course, both predictable and unavoidable: there was never any real prospect of explaining apriority merely on the basis of a knowledge of propositional content. Even Carnap realized that one needed to know that a given inference or sentence had the status of a 'meaning-postulate'.

But isn't it required, if this account is to genuinely explain T's a priori justification for the basic truths of logic, that T know the premisses a priori as well? Yet, it hasn't been shown that T can know the premisses a priori.

It is quite correct that I have not attempted to show that the relevant facts about meaning cited in the premisses are knowable a priori, although I believe that it is intuitively quite clear that they are. I have purposely avoided discussing all issues relating to knowledge of meaning-facts. My brief here has been to defend epistemic analyticity; and this requires showing only that certain sentences are such that, *if* someone knows the relevant facts about their meaning, *then* that person will be in a position to form a justified belief about their truth. It does not require showing that the knowledge of those meaning-facts is itself a priori (although, I repeat, it seems quite clear to me that it will be).[44]

Isn't it a problem for the aspirations of the present account that a thinker would have to use modus ponens to get from the premisses to the desired conclusion?

Not if Dummett's distinction between pragmatic and vicious circularity is credited with opening a space for an epistemology for logic, as discussed above.

Finally, how could such an account possibly hope to explain the man in the street's justification for believing in the truths of logic? For such a person, not only would the relevant meaning-facts be quite opaque, he probably wouldn't even be capable of framing them. Yet such a person is obviously quite justified in believing the elementary truths of logic. Thus, so our objector might continue, this sort of account cannot explain our ordinary warrant for believing in logic; at best, it can explain the warrant that sophisticates have.

I think that, strictly speaking, this objection is correct, but only in a sense that strips it of real bite. Philosophers are often in the position of articulating a warrant for an ordinary belief that the man in the street would not understand. If we insist that a person counts as justified only if they are aware of the reason that warrants their belief, then we will simply have to find another term for the kind of warrant that ordinary folk often have and that philosophers seek to articulate. Tyler Burge has called it an 'entitlement':

> The distinction between justification and entitlement is this. Although both have positive force in rationally supporting a propositional attitude or cognitive practice, and in constituting an epistemic right to it, entitlements are epistemic rights or warrants that need not be understood by or even be accessible to the subject.... The unsophisticated are entitled to rely on their perceptual beliefs. Philosophers may articulate these entitlements. But being entitled does not require being able to justify reliance on these resources, or even to conceive such a justification. Justifications, in the narrow sense, involve reasons that people have and have access to.[45]

When someone is entitled, all the facts relevant to the person's justification are already in place, so to speak; what's missing is the reflection that would reveal them.

Just so in the case at hand. If a conceptual-role semantics is true, and if A is indeed constitutive of C's meaning what it does, then those facts by themselves constitute a warrant for A; empirical support is not necessary. A can only be false by meaning something other than what it means. But these facts need not be known by the ordinary person. They suffice for his entitlement, even if not for his full-blown justification. This full-blown justification can be had only by knowing the relevant facts about meaning.

Conclusion

Quine helped us see the vacuity of the metaphysical concept of analyticity and, with it, the futility of the project it was supposed to underwrite—the linguistic theory of necessity. But I don't see that those arguments affect the epistemic notion of analyticity that is needed for the purposes of the theory of a priori knowledge. Indeed, it seems to me that epistemic analyticity can be defended quite vigorously, especially against the background of a realism about meaning.

On the assumption that our warrant for believing in elementary logical truths cannot be explained, the outstanding problem is to explain our a priori knowledge of conceptual truths. For this purpose, the crucial semantical notion is that of Frege-analyticity. I have argued that this notion is bound to be in good standing for a meaning-realist.

If the project of explaining logic is not ruled hopeless, then I have tried to show how the doctrine that appears to offer the most promising account of how we grasp the meanings of the logical constants—namely, Implicit Definition—can explain the epistemic analyticity of our logical beliefs and, hence, our a priori warrant for believing them. As long as we are not prepared to countenance radical indeterminacy, we should have every confidence that this form of explanation can be made to work.[46]

Notes

1. [This chapter was first published as 'Analyticity Reconsidered', *Noûs*, 30(3) (1996): 360–91. It is a shorter, and somewhat modified, version of a paper entitled 'Analyticity', which appeared in Crispin Wright and Bob Hale (eds.), *A Companion to the Philosophy of Language* (Oxford: Blackwell, 1997). Boghossian (2017), published in the second edition of the *Companion*, is a postscript to the longer version.]

2. 'Definition in a Quinean World', in J. Fetzer, D. Shatz, and G. Schlesinger (eds.), *Definitions and Definability: Philosophical Perspectives* (Dordrecht: Kluwer, 1991), pp. 111–31.

3. As I say, I am going to work with this linguistic picture out of deference to my opponents. I would prefer to work with a propositionalist picture of belief, according to which the objects of belief are propositions in the technical sense—mind- and language-independent, abstract objects which have their truth conditions essentially. Most of the crucial notions developed in this paper, and much of the argument involving them, can be translated, with suitable modifications, into this propositionalist framework.

4. The inclusion of the word 'outer' here is partly stipulative. I have always found it natural to regard a priori knowledge as encompassing both knowledge that is based on no experience as well as knowledge that is based purely on *inner* experience.

5. In the interests of brevity, I shall henceforth take it as understood that 'justification' means 'justification with a strength sufficient for knowledge'.

6. Even this strong notion is not as demanding as many have supposed. For instance, it is consistent with a belief's being a priori in the strong sense that we should have *pragmatic* reasons for dropping it from our best overall theory. For illuminating discussion of the modesty of the notion of the a priori see Crispin Wright: 'Inventing Logical Necessity', in Jeremy Butterfield (ed.), *Language, Mind and Logic* (Cambridge: Cambridge University Press, 1986) and Bob Hale, *Abstract Objects* (Oxford: Blackwell, 1987), ch. 6.

7. See Gilbert Harman, *Thought* (Princeton: Princeton University Press, 1973).

8. W. V. Quine, *The Ways of Paradox* (Cambridge, MA: Harvard University Press, 1976), p. 103.

9. W. V. Quine, *From a Logical Point of View* (Cambridge, MA: Harvard University Press, 1953), pp. 36–7.

10. Gilbert Harman, 'Quine on Meaning and Existence I', *Review of Metaphysics* 21 (1967): 124–51, p. 128. I am grateful to Paul Horwich for emphasizing the importance of this point.

11. 'Doubts about Conceptual Analysis', MS, p. 5 [Harman (1994a)]. See also his 'Quine on Meaning and Existence I'.

12. See G. Frege (Austin, trans.), *The Foundations of Arithmetic* (Oxford: Blackwell, 1950), sec. 3. (Some may regard the attribution of precisely this notion to Frege controversial. What matters to me is not who came up with the idea, but rather the philosophical role it has played.)

My use of the term 'analytic' in connection with Frege's *semantical* notion as well as with the preceding epistemic and metaphysical concepts may be thought ill-advised. But I do so deliberately, to highlight the fact that the term has been used in the literature in general, and in Quine in particular, to stand for all three different sorts of notion, often without any acknowledgement of that fact. This terminological promiscuity has undoubtedly contributed to the confusion surrounding discussions of this issue.

13. For some discussion see my 'The Transparency of Mental Content', in *Philosophical Perspectives*, vol. 8, 1994b, pp. 33–50.

14. What follows is a compressed discussion of Frege-analyticity. For a fuller treatment see my 'Analyticity'.

15. Exegetically, this does leave us with a few puzzles. First, TD does contain a brief discussion of the implicit definition idea, under the guise of the notion of a 'semantical rule'. Given that, why does Quine insist that he intends only to discuss the notion of Frege-analyticity? Second, the notion of a semantical rule is discussed only in connection with non-logical truths; since, however, the deployment of this idea would be exactly the same in the logical case, why is the analyticity of logic expressly excluded? Third, given that the analyticity of

logic is expressly excluded, on what basis does Quine allow himself to draw morals about logic's revisability towards the end of TD? I think there is no avoiding the conclusion that, on this and other related issues (see below), TD is confused. It would, in fact, have been surprising if these rather tricky problems had all been in clear focus in Quine's pioneering papers.

16. In this context, nothing fancy is meant by the use of such expressions as 'property' and 'proposition'. For present purposes they may be understood in a thoroughly deflationary manner. I have sometimes been asked why I consider just this particular weakening of a non-factualist thesis, one that involves, problematically from Quine's official point of view, a modal notion. Why not rather attribute to him the following *Very Weak Thesis*?

> (VWT)   There is a coherent, determinate property expressed by 'is analytic', but *as a matter of fact*, it has never been instantiated; consequently, all tokens of the sentence 'S is analytic' have been false up to now.

There are two reasons. First, the VWT is not a philosophically interesting thesis and, second, it could not have been argued for on the basis of a *philosophy* paper—i.e., on the sorts of a priori grounds that Quine offers. So although Quine may not be entitled to precisely the ET, I am going to ignore that and not hold it against him.

17. This question was first asked by Grice and Strawson in their 'In Defense of a Dogma', reprinted in Grice: *Studies in the Way of Words* (Cambridge, MA: Harvard University Press, 1989). Grice and Strawson didn't sufficiently stress, however, that Quine was committed to a skepticism even about *intra*linguistic synonymy, and not just about *inter*linguistic synonymy, for the theory of apriority doesn't care about the interlinguistic case.

18. See Peter Strawson, *Logico-Linguistic Papers* (London: Methuen, 1971), p. 117.

19. See the discussion of stipulative definitions in TD. For further discussion see my 'Analyticity'.

20. Harman, *Thought*, p. 14, emphasis in the original.

21. Recent formulations of this argument may be found in Jerry A. Fodor, *Psychosemantics* (Cambridge, MA: MIT Press, 1987), pp 62ff.; Jerry A. Fodor and Ernest Lepore, *Holism: A Shopper's Guide* (Oxford: Blackwell, 1991), pp. 37ff.; Michael Devitt, *Coming to Our Senses* (New York: Cambridge University Press, 1995), p. 17. None of the authors mentioned approves of the argument.

22. A further TD-based argument for meaning-holism, this time invalid, will be considered further below, in connection with the discussion of the thesis of Implicit Definition.

23. As before, subject to the proviso about the apriority of synonymy.

24. I am ignoring for now the class of a priori truths that are neither logical nor Frege-analytic. As we shall see, the very same strategy—Implicit Definition—that can be applied to explain our knowledge of logic can be applied to them as well.

25. Michael Dummett, *The Logical Basis of Metaphysics* (Cambridge, MA: Harvard University Press, 1991), p. 202.

26. A. Coffa, *The Semantic Tradition* (Cambridge: Cambridge University Press, 1991), ch. 14. In the next three paragraphs, I follow the general contours of the account that Coffa puts forward. However, the formulations are mine and they differ in important respects from Coffa's, as we shall see further on.

27. Readers who are acquainted with a paper of mine of mine entitled 'Inferential Role Semantics and the Analytic/Synthetic Distinction', *Philosophical Studies* (Spring 1994a): 109–22, will be aware that I used to worry that Implicit Definition could not generate a priori knowledge because of the falsity of something I called 'The Principle'. The Principle is the thesis that it follows from a sentence's being an implicit definer that that sentence is true. This is a tangled issue that I cannot fully discuss here. I will have to settle for a few brief

remarks. I stand by the letter of what I said in the earlier paper. However, *part* of the problem there highlighted for the theory of the a priori is taken care of here by a reformulation of the thesis of Implicit Definition; another part is taken care of by a reformulation of the relation between Implicit Definition and the a priori; and, finally, a residual problem, not discussed in this paper, is met by the section entitled 'A Pragmatic Solution' in my 'Analyticity'. Readers for whom this footnote reads darkly may ignore it in its entirety.

28. Not to be confused with the Non-Factualism about Frege-analyticity discussed earlier in the paper.

29. Someone may object that the two cases are not relevantly analogous. For the meter case is supposed to be a case of the *fixation of reference*, but the logical case an instance of the fixation of meaning. Doesn't this difference between them block the argument I gave?

     I don't see that it does. First, the two cases really are disanalogous only if there is an important difference between meaning and reference; yet, as is well known, there are many philosophers of language who are inclined to think that there isn't an important such difference. Second, it seems to me that even if we allowed for a robust distinction between meaning and reference, the point would remain entirely unaffected. Whether we think of an implicit definer as fixing a term's reference directly, or we think of it as first fixing its meaning, which then in turn fixes its reference, seems to me entirely irrelevant to the claim that Implicit Definition does not entail Non-Factualism. As long as both processes are consistent with the fixation of a factual claim for the sentence at issue—as they very much seem to be—the important point stands.

30. Certainly many philosophers seem to have thought so. Richard Creath, for example, sympathetically expounds Carnap's view that the basic axioms of logic implicitly define the ingredient logical terms by saying that on this view 'the postulates (together with the other conventions) create the truths that they, the postulates express'. See his 'Carnap's Conventionalism', *Synthese* 93 (1992): 141–65, p. 147.

31. This point is also forcefully made by Nathan Salmon in 'Analyticity and Apriority', *Philosophical Perspectives* (1993), and by Stephen Yablo in his review of Sidelle, *Philosophical Review* (1992).

32. Notice that conventionalists themselves need to make crucial use of such a distinction when they describe their own position, as in the passage cited above from Creath: 'the postulates (together with the other conventions) create the truths that they, the postulates, express'. As Hilary Putnam pointed out some time ago, it's hard to see how distinctive content is to be given to Conventionalism without the use of some such distinction. For a conventionalism merely about linguistic expressions is trivial. A real issue is joined only when the view is formulated as a claim about the truths expressed. See Hilary Putnam, 'The Refutation of Conventionalism', in his *Mind, Language and Reality: Philosophical Papers*, vol. 2 (New York: Cambridge University Press, 1975a).

33. Quine's argument here is officially directed against a Conventionalism about logical truth, that is, against the idea that logical truth is determined by our conventions. This idea we have already rejected in our discussion of the metaphysical concept of analyticity. However, Quine attacks Conventionalism *by* attacking the semantical thesis of Implicit Definition. Hence, the need for the present discussion.

34. Quine claims that this argument may also be put as follows: The claim that the sentences of logic lack assignment of truth value until they are conventionally assigned such values must fail. For logic is needed in order to infer from a formulated general convention that the infinitely many instances of a given schema are true. Hence, sentences of logic whose truth value is not fixed as the model requires, are presupposed by the model itself.

     It's unclear to me that this is a formulation of precisely the same argument. However, to the extent that it is distinct, it is also addressed by the proposal I put forth below.

Now, however, we need to ask how such a justified belief in the validity of all arguments of the form MPP could help a thinker be justified in performing any *particular* MPP inference, for example, the Argerich inference with which we began.

To bring this knowledge to bear on the justifiability of that inference will, it would seem, require the thinker first to establish its relevance to that inference, by reasoning as follows:

(i) Any inference of the form MPP is valid.
(ii) This particular inference, from (1) and (2) to (3) is of MPP form.

Therefore,

(iii) This particular inference from (1) and (2) to (3) is valid.[13]

Rational insight, we are conceding, gets us as far as the general propositional knowledge that all arguments of MPP form are valid. However, to bring this knowledge to bear on the justifiability of any particular inference will require the thinker to be able justifiably to infer the validity of that particular inference from the validity of all arguments of MPP form. And this will require him to be able to reason according to MPP justifiably.

Now, however a fatal circularity looms. To infer from (1) and (2) to (3) justifiably, I must be able justifiably to believe that the inference from (1) and (2) to (3) is valid. To be able justifiably to believe that this inference is valid, I must be able justifiably to infer that it is valid from the general proposition that all inferences of its form are valid. To be able justifiably to infer that it is valid from the general proposition that all inferences of its form are valid, I must be able justifiably to infer according to MPP. So, on the picture on offer, my inference from (1) and (2) to (3) will count as justifying only if I am already able to infer according to MPP justifiably. The very ability we are trying to explicate is presupposed by the internalist account on offer.

At this point, an internalist might be tempted by the following thought. So long as we are being so concessive about rational insight, why can't we grant thinkers rational insight into the validity of *specific* inferences, and not require that this be derived from some general knowledge of the validity of all inferences of the form MPP? Perhaps this more general knowledge could be arrived at later, by using the knowledge gained through these acts of individual insight.

It's important to appreciate that this maneuver will not help overcome Simple Inferential Internalism's difficulties with the problem of circularity. For, once again, we can ask how my knowledge of the validity of the inference from (1) and (2) to (3) is supposed to bear on my warrant to infer (3).

According to Simple Inferential Internalism, this inference will be justified only if I am able justifiably to believe that that my premises provide me with a good reason for drawing the conclusion. But it is very hard to see, once again, how my putatively justified judgment that my premises entail my conclusion could bear on my entitlement to draw the conclusion in anything other than inferential form, thus:

(iv) This particular inference from (1) and (2) to (3) is valid.
(v) If an inference is valid, then anyone who is justified in believing its premises and knows of its validity is justified in inferring its conclusion.

Therefore,

    (vi)   Anyone who is justified in believing the premises of this inference is justified in inferring its conclusion.

    (vii)   I am justified in believing the premises (1) and (2).

Therefore,

    (viii)   I am justified in inferring (3).[14]

Even if we conceded, then, that we have rational insight into the validity of specific inferences, we do not escape the threat of circularity that afflicts the internalist account. Once again, an ability to infer justifiably according to MPP is presupposed.

Commenting on an earlier presentation of this argument, Crispin Wright observes,

> It is clear how the simple internalist must reply to Boghossian. To staunch her view against all threat of Carrollian regress, she must insist that recognition of the validity of a specific inference whose premises are known provides a warrant to accept a conclusion not by providing additional information from which the truth or warrantedness of the conclusion may be inferred, but in a direct manner... In effect, and paradoxically, her view must be that warrants acquired by inference are, in a way, a subspecies of noninferential warrant in general: that an appreciation that a conclusion follows from warranted premises confers, when it does, a warrant for an acceptance of that conclusion in no less direct a fashion than that in which a visual appreciation of the colour of the sky confers warrant for the belief that it is blue.[15]

I agree with Wright that this represents the only escape route available to the simple internalist. Wright himself does not endorse it, or even present it as an especially attractive option. He claims for it only that it remains undefeated by the sorts of considerations adduced so far.

No doubt there remains scope for discussion. But it is very difficult to see, it seems to me, how the inferential case is to be plausibly assimilated to the admittedly non-inferential warrant provided for the belief that the sky is blue by the observation of a blue sky under favorable circumstances.

Admittedly, we don't have very refined ways of deciding when a warrant for a particular belief is direct and when it is fundamentally inferential in nature. What we seem to operate with is a rough-and-ready criterion which says in effect, when the gap between the content of an apparent observation and the content of the belief that it is supposed to justify is too large, the justification must be inferential in nature, even if that may not be apparent from its presentation in everyday conversation.

So, for example, in response to the question 'How do you know it is going to rain?' I may simply point to the dark and threatening clouds. But as everyone would agree, the observation of the dark and threatening clouds doesn't justify the belief in rain all by itself, but only by way of an inference in which the content of that observation serves as a premise. The gap between the content of the observation and the content of the belief it is supposed to ground is simply too large.

Similarly, I say, in the case before us. The gap between the content of the apparent observation

If (1) and (2) are true, then (3) must be true

and the belief

    I am justified in believing (3)

is simply to large for the warrant to be direct, even if in most conversational contexts the inference could be left unsaid.[16]

To sum up, in order to ensure that a thinker's inference from particular MPP premises to a particular MPP conclusion not be blameworthy, the simple inferential internalist insisted that the inference's justifiedness be transparent to the thinker— the thinker has to be in a position reflectively to appreciate that her inferring this conclusion from these premises is justified. But this runs into two major problems. First, it requires us to take seriously a notion of rational insight, a notion that no one has been able to render respectable. Second, and even if we waived this first worry, the aimed-for transparency will still be unattainable, since the only way to attain it will require that the thinker use such knowledge as rational insight is able to afford her as the basis for an inference to the justifiedness of her conclusion. So no matter how concessive we are about rational insight and about the knowledge of logical implication that it is supposed to engender, there seems to be no way to satisfy the transparency insisted upon by Simple Inferential Internalism.

6. Blind Yet Blameless Inference: Deflationary Options

The question is where we go from here. Simple Inferential Externalism is false. Simple Inferential Internalism, construed as requiring some form of reflectively accessible warrant, is unsatisfiable. We know, furthermore, that we cannot say that deductive inferences do not transfer warrant; that would be not merely implausible but self-undermining. Hence, unless we are to admit that our epistemic system is subject to deep and crippling paradox, there had better be a stable and coherent account of what the conditions for warrant-transfer are.

In searching for a solution, we must respect the following facts. On the one hand, the failure of Simple Inferential Internalism teaches us that it must be possible for certain modes of reasoning to be entitling without our knowing, or being able to know, anything about them. I'll put this by saying that it must be possible for certain inferences to be *blind* but justifying.[17]

On the other hand, the counterexamples to Reliabilism teach us that the way *not* to accommodate this phenomenon is through Simple Inferential Externalism. So our question is, How should we construe warrant-transfer consistent both with Simple Internalism's and Simple Externalism's falsity?

If there is to be a way forward, the following had better be true: the anti-Reliabilist examples, properly understood, don't really motivate Access Internalism, even though they seem to do so. Rather, they motivate something weaker which *can* be reconciled both with the falsity of Reliabilism and with the falsity of Access Internalism. What could that intermediate position be?

The minimal lesson of the anti-Reliabilist examples, as we saw, is that being justified cannot coexist with being epistemically blameworthy. To get from here to Access Internalism you need to assume furthermore that what *makes* a belief epistemically blameworthy is the *absence* of a reflectively appreciable warrant for it.

And although all the known examples uniformly support this construal, it's not actually forced. For all that the examples show, in other words, it is possible that there should be some *other* way in which a belief might be held blamelessly other than by being supported by some reflectively appreciable warrant.

Some philosophers are inclined to think that there isn't much of a problem here because they think that it isn't all that hard to be epistemically blameless. Gilbert Harman, for example, thinks that just about any belief, or method for forming beliefs, that one cares to have is blameless, at least initially. He writes,

What I take to be the right theory of justification goes something like this (Goodman, 1995; Quine, 1960a; Quine and Ullian, 1978; Rawls, 1971). In deciding what to believe or what to do, you have to start where you are with your current beliefs and methods of reasoning. These beliefs and methods have a privileged status. You are justified in continuing to accept them in the absence of a serious specific challenge to them, where the challenge will typically involve some sort of conflict in your overall view. Conflict is to be resolved by making conservative modifications in your overall view that makes your view more coherent in certain ways. Your goal in resolving conflict is to reach what Rawls calls a 'reflective equilibrium', in which your various views are not in tension with each other...The crucial point is that, to a first approximation, continuing to accept what you accept does not require justification. What requires justification is making changes in your view.[18]

On this view, which Harman dubs 'General Conservatism', we have a quick and painless answer to our question. We are now justified in using MPP because MPP is one of the methods with which we 'start' and we have, so far, encountered no incoherence in our overall view to which the best response would have been to reject or modify it.

The principal thought behind general conservatism is an 'innocent until proven guilty' model of epistemic justification. It doesn't matter what beliefs or methods one starts with—they are all *prima facie* justified. What matters is how one changes one's view in response to a developing incoherence.

But this is all very misleading, for the notion of 'coherence' is empty unless it embeds a specific conception of logical consequence and logical consistency. (Actually, it would probably have to include not just that but conceptions of probabilistic consistency, and a great deal more, but I'll let that pass.[19]) That in effect implies, however, that talk about 'coherence' *presupposes* an answer to our question, rather than providing one. You need to have figured out which deductive rules are justifying in order to have a substantive coherence theory rather than the other way around.

This brings us to the second 'deflationary' answer to our question: a *list*. You want to know which inference patterns are permitted to be blind? These ones: Modus ponens, Non-Contradiction, and a few others. Don't ask *why* it is precisely these inference patterns that are sanctioned. There is no deep answer to that question; there is just the list.

What makes this brand of deflationary answer unsatisfactory is that it is hard to believe that the property of being warrant-transferring is simply a primitive property that an inference pattern either has or fails to have. Surely, if an inference pattern is warrant-transferring there must be some property by virtue of which it is warrant-transferring. And our question is, What, in the most basic cases, in which reflectively available support is not possible, could that property be?

7. Blind Yet Blameless Inference: Concept Constitution

An important question—which I don't wish to prejudge for present purposes—is whether the validity of the inference is a *necessary condition* on warrant-transfer. What I will be exclusively concerned with in the remainder of this paper is the question of blamelessness.

The 'inflationary' answer to that question that I want to explore may be roughly formulated as follows (we'll see how to refine it later):

A deductive pattern of inference P may be blamelessly employed, without any reflective appreciation of its epistemic status, just in case inferring according to P is a precondition for having one of the concepts ingredient in it.

Now, in some sense this is a very old answer to our question. It falls into what may broadly be called 'analytic' explanations of the a priori. Previous versions of such views, however, have suffered, I believe, in two respects.[20] First, they did not adequately distinguish between questions concerning our entitlement to certain logical beliefs, and questions concerning our entitlement to certain belief-forming methods of inference (like the one I have dubbed MPP). Second, they did not adequately explain what concept-constitution has to do with the epistemology of blind inference. In both of these respects, I hope here to do a little better.

Prima facie, there is a difficulty seeing how appeal to concept constitution can help with our question. What is the connection supposed to be?

The thought is this. Suppose it's true that my taking A to be a warrant for believing B is constitutive of my being able to have B-thoughts (or A-thoughts, or both, it doesn't matter) in the first place. Then doesn't it follow that I could not have been epistemically blameworthy in taking A to be a reason for believing B, even in the absence of any reason for taking A to be a reason for believing B? For how could I have had *antecedent* information to the effect that A is a good reason for believing B, if I could not so much have had a B-thought without taking A to be a reason for believing B in the first place? If inferring from A to B is required, if I am to be able to think the ingredient propositions, then it looks as though so inferring cannot be held against me, even if the inference is blind.

Applied to the case of deductive inference before us, then, the thought would be that we would have an explanation for the blameless blindness of MPP if it's constitutive of having the concept *conditional* that one take p and 'p→q' as a reason for believing q.

Now, of course, the idea that, in general, we come to grasp the logical constants by being disposed to engage in some inferences involving them and not in others, is an independently compelling idea. And the thought that, in particular, we grasp the conditional just in case we are disposed to infer according to MPP is an independently compelling thought. So, if the meaning–entitlement connection that I've gestured at is correct, it looks as though we are in a position to mount an explanation of the blameless blindness of MPP that that we were after.

8. Problems for the Meaning–Entitlement Connection

Unfortunately, matters are not quite so straightforward. If we spell out the principle underlying the meaning-based explanation of blameless blindness gestured at, it would be this:

(**Meaning–Entitlement Connection, or MEC**):   Any inferential transitions built into the possession conditions for a concept are *eo ipso* entitling.

And the trouble is that, at least as stated, there seem to be clear-cut counterexamples to the MEC: it doesn't in general seem true that if my taking A as a reason for believing B is constitutive of my believing B, that this *automatically* absolves me of any charge of epistemic blameworthiness. For there seem to be clear cases where the acceptance of some inference is written into the possession of a given concept but where it is also clear that the inference isn't one to which the thinker is entitled.

One famous illustrative case is Arthur Prior's connective 'tonk'.[21] To possess this concept, Prior stipulated, a thinker must be willing to infer according to the following introduction and elimination rules:

$$(\text{Tonk}) \quad \frac{A}{A \text{ tonk } B} \qquad \frac{A \text{ tonk } B}{B}$$

Obviously, no one could be entitled to infer any B from any A; but this entitlement appears to flow from the possession conditions for 'tonk' along with the MEC.

A similar conclusion can be drawn from the case of racist or abusive concepts, for example the concept *boche* discussed by Dummett.[22] Plausibly, a thinker possesses the concept *boche* just in case he is willing to infer according to the following rules:

$$(\text{Boche}) \quad \frac{x \text{ is German}}{x \text{ is boche}} \qquad \frac{x \text{ is boche}}{x \text{ is cruel}}$$

Yet no one is entitled—let alone simply as the result of the introduction of a concept into the language—to the view that all Germans are cruel. How should we think about such cases?

Robert Brandom has this to say about *boche*-like concepts:

The use of any concept or expression involves commitment to an inference from its grounds to its consequences of application. Critical thinkers, or merely fastidious ones, must examine their idioms to be sure that they are prepared to endorse and so defend the appropriateness of the material inferential commitments implicit in the concepts they employ ... The proper question to ask in evaluating the introduction and evolution of a concept is not whether the inference embodied is one that is already endorsed, so that no new content is really involved, but rather whether the inference is one that *ought* to be endorsed. The problem with 'boche' is not that once we explicitly confront the material inferential commitment that gives the term its content it turns out to be novel, but that it can then be seen to be indefensible and inappropriate—a commitment we cannot become entitled to.[23]

From the standpoint of a proponent of the MEC, there is nothing in this passage that helps protect it from the threatening examples. It's no answer to the challenge they pose to observe that whatever entitlement concept-possession gives rise to, it can be defeated by further considerations. No one should expect more than a defeasible entitlement, even from concept-possession; and what's implausible in the case of 'tonk' and 'boche' is that there is any entitlement there at all, defeasible or no.

If we are to save the MEC, it seems to me that we must do one or both of two things: either restrict it to certain concepts from which entitlement really does flow, or restrict what we count as a genuine concept. I will advocate doing the former.

The latter strategy is suggested by the work of Christopher Peacocke who has long urged that we should require that the meaning-constituting rules of a genuine concept be truth-preserving.[24]

If we adopt this requirement, we can say that what's wrong with both 'tonk' and 'boche' is precisely that there is no concept that those terms express, for there is no reference for 'tonk' and 'boche' that's capable of making all of their constitutive rules truth-preserving.

While this might seem to yield the right result for 'tonk' it doesn't yield the right result for 'boche': it's hard to believe that racists who employ *boche*-like concepts fail to express complete thoughts.

And even if we were to put this complaint to one side, it seems clear that truth-preservation alone will not suffice for dealing with our problem about the MEC.

Imagine someone theorizing about water and coming to believe, for whatever reason, that the way in which it is correct to say that water is composed of H_2O is that there is some *other* stuff that composes water and that *it* is composed of H_2O.[25] So he introduces a term—'aqua'—to name this stuff and he stipulates that it is to be governed by the following introduction and elimination rules:

$$(\text{Aqua}) \quad \frac{\text{x is water}}{\text{x is aqua}} \quad \frac{\text{x is aqua}}{\text{x is } H_2O}$$

Unlike the case of 'boche', we have no independent reason for thinking that these rules are not truth-preserving. But there is clearly something fishy about this concept. And however one feels about that, there is certainly a problem for the MEC, given only the resources that we've been accorded so far: for no one could think that the mere act of introducing the concept *aqua* into one's repertoire could give one a priori entitlement to the inference from x's being water to x's being H_2O.

Or consider the concept *flurg* individuated by the following introduction and elimination rules:

$$\frac{\text{x is an elliptical equation}}{\text{x is flurg}} \quad \frac{\text{x is flurg}}{\begin{array}{l}\text{x can be correlated with}\\ \text{a modular form}\end{array}}$$

It turns out to be a result that Wiles had to prove on the way to proving Fermat's Last Theorem that every elliptical equation can be correlated with a modular form (the Taniyama–Shimura conjecture). Once again, therefore, we have no independent reason to think that these introduction and elimination rules are not necessarily truth-preserving. But it's hard to see that one is a priori entitled, merely on the basis of introducing the term 'flurg' to the Taniyama–Shimura conjecture. So there is still a problem for the claim that entitlement flows from meaning-constitution, given only the requirement that a concept's introduction and elimination rules be truth-preserving.

9. Defective Concepts and Blameless Inference

I would like to propose a different diagnosis of what has gone wrong with concepts such as *aqua* and *flurg*, one that doesn't depend on denying that they constitute genuine thinkable contents.

That denial can be sustained, I believe, in the case of 'tonk', but that is a rather extreme case. No one can actually possess the concept allegedly expressed by 'tonk', because it isn't possible for someone to follow the rules that are constitutive of that connective. For to follow those rules one would have to be prepared to infer anything from everything, and that is no longer recognizable as belief or inference. But no such extreme claim can be made with respect to all the other examples that have been causing problems for the hypothesized connection between meaning and entitlement.

Start with the example of 'aqua'. The theorist who has conceived the need to introduce a term for the concept *aqua* has come to hold the following *theory*: 'There is some stuff, distinct from water, that composes water and that is itself composed of H_2O. Let me call it "aqua".' Such a theorist already believes in water and H_2O, we may suppose. He has come to hold an additional belief about the world, namely, that it contains another substance, one that is related to water and H_2O in the specified way.

Now, the way we have written down the inferential rules for 'aqua' essentially amounts to insisting that, in order to have the concept *aqua* you must be prepared to *believe* this little *aqua* theory. Given that you already believe in water and H_2O, the only way for you to acquire the concept *aqua*, on this account of its inferential rules, requires you to *believe* that there is such a thing as aqua. One cannot so much as have the concept of *aqua* without being prepared to believe that there is such a thing.

And although it seems to me that one *can* define and then think in terms of such a concept, it does seem like an epistemically questionable thing to do. Even if the aqua theorist were *certain* that there is such a thing as aqua, he should want the concept he expresses by that term to leave it open whether there is. He should allow for the conceptual possibility that he is mistaken; and he should certainly allow others intelligibly to disagree with him about aqua's existence. The concept itself should not be designed in such a way that, only those who believe a certain creed are allowed to possess it.

Ordinary scientific terms in good standing—'neutrino' for example—are held to have just this feature, of intelligibly allowing for disagreement about their extension. Thus, we don't think of the rules which correspond to our possession of the concept *neutrino* as consisting in the propositions that would actually be believed by a proponent of neutrino theory, but rather as corresponding only to what someone would be willing to believe who was *conditionalizing* on the truth of neutrino theory.

If we follow Russell, Ramsey, Carnap, and Lewis, and represent neutrino theory

T(neutrino)

as the conjunction of the two propositions

(S)   (∃x) Tx

and

(M)   (∃x) Tx → T(neutrino)

then the point is that we think of possession of the concept *neutrino* as requiring someone to affirm only M and not S as well.[26]

Now, someone could certainly introduce a concept that did not have the conditionalized structure that I've claimed is actually true of *neutrino*, but which consists rather in the inferences that are characteristic of neutrino theory unconditionalized. Call this *neutrino+*. Such a person would insist that it is a condition on having *her* concept of neutrino that one be willing to endorse the characteristic claims and inferences of neutrino theory, and not merely the conditionalized claim captured in (M). But, for the reasons previously articulated, there would be something epistemically *defective* about this concept, even if its constitutive rules turned out to be truth-preserving.

Flurg, aqua, and *neutrino+,* then, all suffer from the same problem: they are all unconditional versions of a concept, when only its conditionalized version would be epistemically acceptable. I don't think we should put this by saying that they are not real concepts. Concepts are relatively cheap. But they are *defective* concepts. They are structured in such a way that perfectly reasonable questions about their extensions are foreclosed.

Under what conditions is only a conditionalized version of a concept acceptable? Here I want to make two claims: one bold, one sober.

(Bold)   Whenever both a conditional and an unconditional version of a given concept are available, it is the conditional version that ought to be used. Given the availability of both versions, the unconditional version counts as epistemically defective.

(Sober)   In the case of some concepts, only the unconditionalized version will be available.

Start with Bold. Whenever a conditionalized version of a concept is available, that is the version that ought to be used. In those contexts, an unconditionalized version would be defective.

The argument for this is quite straightforward and recapitulates the considerations we have just been looking at. You don't ever want the *possession conditions* for a concept to foreclose on the possible falsity of some particular set of claims about the world, if you can possibly avoid it. You want the possessor of the concept to be able coherently to ask whether there is anything that falls under it, and you want people to be able to disagree about whether there is.

If in a certain range of cases, however, it is logically impossible to hold the governing theory at arm's length then, in those cases, obviously, it can hardly be a requirement that one do so. But in all those cases where that is possible, it ought to be done.

What about Sober? It should be clear, given the kind of conditionalization that is in view here, that not every meaningful term in a language can be thought of as expressing a concept that conditionalizes on the existence of an appropriate semantic value for it. Take the case of 'flurg'. The stipulation that would correspond to a conditional version for 'flurg' would amount roughly to this:

If there is a property which is such that, any elliptical equation has it, and if something has it, then it can be correlated with a modular form, then if x has that property, x is flurg.

The corresponding introduction and elimination rules could then be specified as follows:[†]

b is F   (∀x)[x is an elliptical equation → x is F]   (∀x)[x is F → x can be correlated with a modular form]   ¬(∀x)[x is F → x is an elliptical equation]
_____
b is flurg

_____
b is flurg

(∃F)[b is F & (∀x)[x is an elliptical equation → x is F] & (∀x)[x is F → x can be correlated with a modular form] & ¬(∀x)[x is F → x is an elliptical equation]]

As this makes clear, the only thinkers who could follow such rules—and, hence, the only thinkers who may be seen as implicitly conditionalizing on the existence of an appropriate semantic value for 'flurg'—are those who (a) possess a basic set of logical constants and (b) are able to refer to and quantify over properties in particular, and semantic values, more generally.

It follows, therefore, that conditional counterparts for one's primitive logical constants will not be available and hence that one could hardly be blamed for employing their unconditionalized versions. In particular, if the conditional is one of your primitive logical constants, you couldn't conditionalize on the existence of an appropriate truth function for it, for you would need it in order to conditionalize on anything. In such a case, there is no alternative but to accept 'conditional theory'—Modus ponens in effect—if you are so much as to have the conditional concept. It thus couldn't be epistemically irresponsible of you just to go ahead and infer according to Modus ponens without conditionalizing on the existence of an appropriate truth function for it—that is simply not a coherent option in this case.

What is the full range of those concepts for which conditional counterparts would not be available? To answer this question, one would need to have a clear view of what the minimal logical resources are that are needed to conditionalize in the envisaged answer on the truth of an arbitrary theory, and I don't have a systematic theory of that to present at the moment. What does seem clear, though, is that some set of basic logical constants would have to be presupposed and that is enough to get me the result that inference in accord with their constitutive rules can be entitling even though blind.

If we go back to the MEC, then, it seems clear what we should say: Any rules that are written into the possession conditions for a *non-defective* concept are a fortiori entitling.

With that in hand, we have the answer to our question, How could MPP premises warrant MPP conclusions while being blind? Answer: They do, because they are

† [This formulation of the rules replaces the incorrect one that was printed in the original paper and which, as Williamson correctly notes in his (2003) response, mistakenly suggests that 'flurg' has an explicit definition. (Thanks to Crispin Wright for helping set this straight.)]

written into the possession conditions for the conditional, and the conditional is a non-defective concept.

10. Conclusion

If we are to make sense of the justified employment of our basic logical methods of inference, we must make sense of what I have called *blind but blameless* reasoning—a way of moving between thoughts that is justified even in the absence of any reflectively appreciable support for it.

In this paper, I have attempted to sketch the outlines of an account of this phenomenon, one that avoids the pitfalls both of an overly austere Reliabilism and an overly intellectualized Internalism. The account seeks to revive and exploit two traditionally influential thoughts: first, that following certain inferential rules is constitutive of our grasp of the primitive logical constants; and, second, that if certain inferential rules are constitutive of our grasp of certain concepts, then we are *eo ipso* entitled to them, even in the absence of any reflectively appreciable support.[27]

Notes

1. Even with this restriction in place, the paper covers a lot of ground rather quickly. I am aware that many of its claims need more detailed support than is possible within present limits. My aim is to offer a broad view of the terrain with the hopes of distinguishing the dead ends from the promising pathways.
2. It's a tricky question how this 'taking' is to be understood, but I can't pause to consider the matter here. In this paper, I shall use the terms 'justification', 'warrant', and 'entitlement' interchangeably.
3. I shall soon be contrasting this externalist conception of inference with a diametrically opposed internalist conception. The idea of converging onto the (hopefully) correct view of inference by picking a course between these two traditionally opposed extremes was first suggested in my 'How are Objective Epistemic Reasons Possible?', reprinted in J. Bermudez and A Millar (eds.), *Reason and Nature* (Oxford: Oxford University Press, 2002), pp. 1–47; see pp. 35–9. In his commentary on that paper, 'Basic Logical Knowledge: Reflections on Paul Boghossian's "How are Objective Epistemic Reasons Possible?"', also reprinted in Bermudez and Millar, Crispin Wright suggested the labels 'simple internalism' and 'simple externalism' for the traditionally opposed extremes, labels which I am happy now to modify and adopt.

     I should emphasize that I am asking *by virtue of what facts* a deductive inference transfers warrant, and not just under what conditions it does so.
4. I shall come back to the question whether it is necessary.
5. I have often encountered this suggestion in conversation; I didn't manage to track down a published reference.
6. See L. Bonjour, *The Structure of Empirical Knowledge* (Cambridge, MA: Harvard University Press, 1985), p. 41.
7. In insisting on knowledge here, as opposed merely to justified belief, I follow standard presentations of Internalism, though my arguments will depend only on the weaker condition.

8. Note that what I am calling 'Access Internalism' is the weaker of the two possible versions of Internalism: it requires only that the epistemic fact be reflectively accessible, if the person is to be justified, not that the person actually have accessed it.

9. See my 'Knowledge of Logic', in P. Boghossian and C. Peacocke (eds.), *New Essays on the A Priori* (Oxford: Oxford University Press, 2000), and my 'How are Objective Epistemic Reasons Possible?'

10. See my 'How Are Objective Epistemic Reasons Possible?'

11. L. Bonjour, *In Defence of Pure Reason* (Cambridge: Cambridge University Press, 1998), pp. 106–7.

12. Lewis Carroll, 'What the Tortoise Said to Achilles', *Mind*, 4 (1895): 278–80.

13. This argument was originally presented in my lecture at the Pacific APA in Albuquerque in April 2001.

14. The idea that Internalism suffers from the difficulties outlined in the preceding two arguments was first presented in 'How are Objective Epistemic Reasons Possible?' In that paper, though, I followed Carroll in supposing that the inference to which the internalist is committed is an inference from knowledge of the validity of the MPP inference, along with its premises, P and 'If P, then Q', to the original target conclusion Q. In his commentary on my paper, Crispin Wright suggested that this second anti-internalist argument would be more effective if it claimed not that the internalist is committed to inferences to the target conclusion itself, but rather to the conclusion: the inference to Q is justified. I am not entirely persuaded that Wright's is a better way of running this second argument; but I am persuaded that it raises fewer distracting objections than my original presentation, and so I adopt it for the purposes of this paper.

15. Wright, 'Basic Logical Knowledge', p. 81.

16. What if we imagined that we are able to gain rational insight not only into the validity of specific inferences but directly into their justifiedness? Not only is this unimaginable but I believe that a Carroll-style problem will arise for it as well. I hope to elaborate on this elsewhere.

17. The allusion here is to Wittgenstein's remark at *Philosophical Investigations* 219:

    When I obey a rule, I do not choose.
    I obey the rule blindly.   (219)

    One of Wittgenstein's fundamental insights, it seems to me, was to realize that we must be capable of a form of blameless reasoning that did not depend on any other cognitive state of the thinker's and, in particular, not on anything analogous to sight. As he put the matter in *On Certainty*, 'Giving grounds, however, justifying the evidence, comes to an end—but the end is not certain propositions' striking us immediately as true, i.e., it is not a kind of seeing on our part; it is our acting, which lies at the bottom of the language game.'

18. G. Harman, 'The Future of the A Priori', *Journal of Philosophical Research*, 28 (2003): 25–6.

19. See, for example, Bonjour, *The Structure of Empirical Knowledge*, ch. 5, for a discussion of coherence conceptions of justification.

20. See, for example, Christopher Peacocke, 'How Are A Priori Truths Possible?', *European Journal of Philosophy*, 1 (1993): 2–175.

21. A. Prior, 'The Runabout Inference Ticket', *Analysis* 21 (1960): 38–9.

22. M. Dummett, *Frege's Philosophy of Language* (New York: Harper and Row, 1973), p. 454.

23. R. Brandom, *Articulating Reasons* (Cambridge, MA: Harvard University Press, 2000), pp. 70–2.

24. See Christopher Peacocke, 'Proof and Truth', in J. Haldane and C. Wright (eds.), *Reality, Representations and Projection* (New York: Oxford University Press, 1993). I myself took this line in 'How Are Objective Epistemic Reasons Possible?', so the present paper represents a change of heart.

25. For the purposes of this example, I am assuming that composition is not identity.

26. This paragraph follows Paul Horwich's discussion of the conditional nature of semantic stipulation in 'Stipulation, Meaning and Apriority', in Boghossian and Peacocke (eds.), *New Essays on the A Priori*. I ignore various complexities that a thorough discussion of the representation of scientific theories would require.

27. For valuable comments on previous drafts I am grateful to Gregory Epstein, Kit Fine, Paul Horwich, Stephen Schiffer, Joshua Schechter, and Crispin Wright; and to audiences at the Quine Conference in Berlin, the Summer School in Analytic Philosophy in Parma, the SOFIA Conference in Veracruz, and the colloquia series at Smith College and the University of Toronto.

3

Understanding and Inference[1]

Timothy Williamson

1. Introduction

In his paper 'Blind Reasoning' (Chapter 2), Paul Boghossian asks how deductive reasoning can transfer justification for belief from the premises of an argument to its conclusion. According to the view that he calls *Simple Inferential Externalism* the key to the answer is just the validity of the inference itself, provided that the justification for believing the premises does not inappropriately depend on the conclusion itself. Although a deductively valid inference is perfectly reliably truth-preserving, Boghossian rejects Simple Inferential Externalism as subject to counterexamples similar to those that undermine other forms of reliabilism: cases in which someone is epistemically blameworthy for using a reliable process because he is completely in the dark about its reliability (Bonjour 1985: 41). At the opposite extreme, *Simple Inferential Internalism* tries to solve the problem by requiring the thinker to be able to know that the inference is deductively good. Boghossian rejects this alternative because, he argues, it is forced to invoke a mystifying faculty of rational insight and in any case generates circular justifications. Thus the condition that the inference is valid is insufficient for the transfer of justification, even granted the background conditions on the standing of the premises and conclusion; the condition that the thinker is able to know that the inference is valid is unnecessary. In Boghossian's Wittgensteinian terminology, the elusive condition must permit the inference to be blind but entitling. After dismissing some deflationary accounts of blind entitlement, Boghossian devotes the rest of his paper to refining the proposal that 'a deductive pattern of inference P may be blamelessly employed, without any reflective appreciation of its epistemic status, just in case inferring according to P is a precondition for having one of the concepts ingredient in it'.[2] For example, if inferring according to modus ponens is a precondition for having the concept of the conditional, then modus ponens may be blamelessly employed without any reflective appreciation of its epistemic status. The thought is that inferring unreflectively according to P cannot be blameworthy per se, for one can properly reflect on P only after one has its ingredient concepts, therefore only after one is already inferring according to P.

This paper concentrates on the concept-constitution account of blameless blindness. It casts doubt on the existence of the requisite tight connections between what concepts one has and how one infers. At the metalinguistic level, the rules of

Debating the A Priori. Paul Boghossian and Timothy Williamson, Oxford University Press (2020).
© Paul Boghossian and Timothy Williamson.
DOI: 10.1093/oso/9780198851707.001.0001

inference for a connective are in a sense not analytic: accepting them is not a precondition for understanding it. Thus doubt falls on inferentialist accounts of concept possession and linguistic understanding.

2. Logical Unorthodoxy and Concept Possession

As concept possession is usually conceived, a paradigmatic way to have a concept C is to understand a word that means C. For example, one can have the concept of the conditional, the concept *if*, by understanding the English word 'if' or a synonym in another language. Although understanding a word that means *if* may not be necessary for having the concept *if*, it is sufficient.[3] For to understand the word is to know what it means; since 'if' means *if*, to understand 'if' is to know that 'if' means *if*; how could one know that without having the concept *if*? To know that 'if' means *if* is not merely to know that the sentence '"If" means *if*' expresses a truth, for a monolingual speaker of Chinese could know that '"If" means *if*' expresses a truth on the reliable testimony of a bilingual speaker of Chinese and English without understanding a single word of English, in particular, without knowing that 'if' means *if*.

Is making inferences by modus ponens of the form 'If A then B; A; therefore B' a precondition for having the concept *if*? Vann McGee, a distinguished logician, has published purported counterexamples to modus ponens.[4] Presumably, he refuses to make some inferences by modus ponens. Does McGee lack the concept *if*? Although I deny that his purported counterexamples to modus ponens are genuine, I admit that they have some initial plausibility on the ordinary understanding of 'if'. In conversation with McGee, he appears to understand the word 'if' quite well by ordinary standards. He certainly seems to know what we other English speakers mean when we use the word 'if'. Before he had theoretical doubts about modus ponens, he understood the word 'if' if anyone has ever understood it; surely his theoretical doubts did not make him cease to remember what it means. We may therefore assume that McGee has the concept *if*, just like everyone else.

Are only some inferences by modus ponens such that a willingness to make them is a precondition for having the concept *if*? Presumably, McGee will accept most inferences by modus ponens. However, any particular inference by modus ponens might be rejected by a student who, having just read McGee's article, was sufficiently impressed to try to put it into practice, sometimes unfortunately misapplying its doctrine through excess of zeal. Has the student ceased to understand the word 'if'? He may still use it competently in ordinary conversation; he may reject only very salient inferences by modus ponens, while making many others unawares. The student still has the concept *if*.

Is a willingness to make most inferences by modus ponens (no matter which ones) a precondition for having the concept *if*? Even this watered-down claim seems too weak for a concept-constitution account of blameless blindness. For suppose that we wish to explain why a given inference that you made by modus ponens was blameless. The proposed explanation is that making the inference is a precondition for having the concept *if*. But we have just seen that making *that* particular inference, the relevant instance of modus ponens is not a precondition for having the concept *if*, because the foolish student might have refused to make the same inference yet still had the concept *if*. Although the student might be willing to make lots of other inferences by modus ponens, how does that help to explain the blamelessness of the inference that you actually made? You could have refused to make it yet still retained the concept *if*. The inference is not unavoidable in the way assumed by the motivating thought behind the concept-constitution account of blameless blindness.

Could we invoke Putnam's division of linguistic labour, and say that making any given inference by modus ponens is a precondition only for *full* understanding of 'if', the kind of understanding characteristic of the expert rather than the layman?[5] The trouble is that McGee *is* an expert on conditionals. He publishes on them in the best journals. He does not defer in his use of 'if' to any higher authorities. Although the student is not an expert, any given inference by modus ponens might be rejected by some expert on conditionals, on the basis of a complex theoretical argument. The expert would be mistaken, but making a theoretical error about the logic of conditionals is quite compatible with fully possessing the concept *if*.

The problem is not specific to modus ponens, which is as good a candidate as any for an inferential precondition for concept possession. Consider any concept C, any word 'C' of a natural language that means C and any deductive pattern of inference P of which C is an ingredient. It is proposed that inferring according to P is a precondition for having C. Let Inst be any instance of P. An expert on C and P fully understands 'C'. She then becomes convinced by a complex theoretical argument that Inst is invalid, and therefore rejects Inst; her argument does not generalize in any obvious way to more than a small proportion of instances of P. By ordinary standards, the expert continues to understand 'C' fully. In conversation, she uses 'C' appropriately, and responds appropriately when others use it. She still has the concept C, despite her unorthodoxy over Inst. Thus willingness to make the inference Inst is not a precondition for having C, even if willingness to infer in most instances according to P is such a precondition. Consequently, we cannot explain why one is blameless in making the inference Inst by saying that willingness to make it is a precondition for having C.[6]

The argument is independent of the validity of the pattern of inference P, and of the validity of its instance Inst. If Inst is valid, then the expert is mistaken in ruling it invalid, but she is nevertheless still an expert; complex theoretical arguments sometimes seduce even experts into accepting wildly false conclusions. If Inst is invalid, then its rejection by the expert may just manifest her expertise.

Might the person who has the concept C while unwilling to make the inference Inst retain the defeasible *disposition* to make the inference, overridden by another disposition, the latter induced by theoretical reflection? For something can be disposed to X in certain circumstances yet be prevented from Xing in those very circumstances by some defeating condition.[7] Someone generally disposed to accept inferences of the form 'A, B; therefore A and B' may assent to the premise 'Ticket *i* will not win' for each ticket in a lottery, yet dissent from the conjunctive conclusion. Boghossian might prefer not to put much weight on such an appeal to dispositions, for he has argued vigorously elsewhere against dispositional accounts of concept possession (1989: 528–40), although in the present paper he does say 'We come to grasp the logical constants by being disposed to engage in some inferences.' It is certainly unclear how having a concept could *consist in* having a disposition that is overridden by one's conscious reflection. Most of us have dispositions to commit various logical fallacies which we control by conscious reflection; presumably, the latter dispositions play no decisive role in determining which concepts we possess. One is not following a rule when one consciously refuses to act in accordance with that rule.[8]

What has not been argued is that one could have the concept *if* without any disposition at all to infer by modus ponens. The disposition will be defeasible by theoretical reflection. It may even be defeated pretheoretically by features of some kinds of examples; perhaps McGee's are like that, since they have some initial plausibility.[9] However, the mere disposition is not enough for Boghossian's account of justification, even when the disposition is undefeated. Perhaps someone can happily make the inference although justification is not transferred from premises to conclusion because he was surrounded by fallacious yet plausible theoretical considerations to which he had no answer; they left him unmoved only as a result of his pigheadedly obstinate character; he *ought* to have been moved to doubt. However, the main issue is whether, when justification is transferred, Boghossian can explain why it is transferred. For his explanation depends on the idea that one is blameless because one has no option: one cannot so much as entertain the inference unless one is willing to make it. If one can entertain the inference while unwilling to make it, provided that one has a defeasible disposition to make it, no such account of blamelessness is forthcoming. Suppose that there is a kind of cruelty that one cannot so much as imagine unless one has a defeasible disposition to commit cruel acts of that kind: it does not follow that one is blameless in committing such acts. Even if one compulsively imagines them, one can still be blamed for not resisting the temptation to live out one's fantasies, for not defeating one's disposition.[10]

As will emerge in the next section, Boghossian restricts the simple form of his explanation to concepts that he classifies as non-defective: but even the qualified explanation does not work if concept possession is a matter of defeasible dispositions. For it does not answer the question about an inference involving a non-defective concept: if a defeasible disposition to make the inference is necessary for the ability to entertain that concept, how does that justify one in indulging the disposition?[11]

3. Pejoratives and Conventional Implicature

Boghossian first considers an unqualified form of the concept-constitution account, based on this principle about the meaning–entitlement connection:

(MEC) Any inferential transitions built into the possession conditions for a concept are *eo ipso* entitling.

He objects that there are clear counterexamples to (MEC).

Arthur Prior (1960) stipulated these disastrous rules for a connective 'tonk':

Tonk-Introduction	*Tonk-Elimination*
A	A tonk B
A tonk B	B

If inferring according to both Tonk-Introduction and Tonk-Elimination is a precondition for having the concept *tonk*, then by (MEC) such inferences are entitling, so anyone who has the concept can blamelessly infer anything from anything. However, Boghossian does not treat that as a clear counterexample to (MEC), because one might plausibly deny that 'tonk' expresses any concept whatsoever. It is certainly hard to see how anyone could seriously make unrestricted use of both Tonk-Introduction and Tonk-Elimination. But in other cases no such defence of (MEC) seems plausible.

Boghossian gives the example of pejorative terms such as 'Boche'. Following Dummett's treatment (1973: 397 and 454), he suggests that to have the concept *Boche* is to be willing to infer according to these introduction and elimination rules:

Boche-Introduction	*Boche-Elimination*
x is German	x is Boche
x is Boche	x is cruel

Thus, according to (MEC), inferences by Boche-Introduction and Boche-Elimination are entitling, so anyone who has the concept can *eo ipso* blamelessly infer that Germans are cruel.[12] As Boghossian points out, it would be highly implausible to deny that the word 'Boche' expresses a concept; surely xenophobes use sentences in which it occurs to express complete thoughts, however bad those thoughts are. Since, in having the concept, one is not *eo ipso* in a position blamelessly to infer that Germans are cruel, Boghossian concludes that (MEC) requires modification.

The 'Boche' objection to (MEC) rests on the premise that one has the concept *Boche* only if one is willing to infer according to both Boche-Introduction and Boche-Elimination. Is that premise plausible? I think that I am one counterexample, and that Boghossian is another. Unlike someone who thinks that the word 'Boche' means *master*, we both fully understand the word, for we understand the sentences in which it occurs that xenophobes utter; we know what 'Boche' means; we know that it means *Boche*. We find racist and xenophobic abuse offensive because we understand it, not because we fail to do so. Presumably, therefore, we have the concept *Boche*. Yet neither of us is willing to infer according to both Boche-Introduction and Boche-Elimination. Similarly, imagine a reformed xenophobe who once was willing to infer according to those rules but now has seen the error of his ways, while vividly recalling with shame what it was like to shout xenophobic abuse. He still remembers what 'Boche' meant. Since he knows that it meant *Boche*, he retains the concept *Boche*. But how can one have a concept while rejecting its constitutive rules?

Let us consider the example in more depth. On a widespread simple picture, the introduction and elimination rules for an atomic expression play a constitutive role in determining its reference. If exactly one assignment of reference makes the rules truth-preserving, then that assignment is correct (this is supposed to be the case for the connectives of standard first-order logic). If more than one assignment of reference makes the rules truth-preserving, then it is indeterminate which of those assignments is correct (a supervaluationist treatment is sometimes suggested). If no assignment of reference makes the rules truth-preserving, then every assignment is incorrect: the expression does not refer (although it may still have a sense, and express a concept). Since there are non-cruel Germans, no assignment of reference to 'Boche' makes both Boche-Introduction and Boche-Elimination truth-preserving. Therefore, on the picture just sketched, 'Boche' does not refer. We might therefore expect ascriptions of 'Boche' to lack a truth value. On this picture, Boche-Introduction and Boche-Elimination carry equal weight in determining reference, or the lack of it, for 'Boche'. Let us test this claim by considering two candidate assignments of reference to 'Boche'.

(A). Suppose that 'Boche' refers to the property of being German. Thus 'Lessing was Boche' is true, because Lessing was German, but 'Nero was Boche' is false, because Nero was not German.[13] Boche-Elimination is not truth-preserving: every non-cruel German yields a counterexample. But Boche-Introduction is truth-preserving; in fact, being German is the strongest property that makes Boche-Introduction truth-preserving (when assigned as referent to 'Boche', given the intended interpretation of the other words). Equivalently, the converse of Boche-Introduction is also truth-preserving:

*Boche-Elimination**

$$\frac{x \text{ is Boche}}{x \text{ is German}}$$

In Dummett's terms, the rules of Boche-Introduction and Boche-Elimination* are in harmony: Boche-Elimination* merely allows one to infer from 'x is Boche' what Boche-Introduction allows one to infer 'x is Boche' from, and Boche-Introduction merely allows one to infer 'x is Boche' from what Boche-Elimination* allows one to infer from 'x is Boche'. Consequently, if the two rules are added to a theory in a language without 'Boche', they yield a conservative extension: anything in the original language provable with them was already provable without them.[14] Boche-Elimination* is the elimination rule that naturally corresponds to Boche-Introduction. Together, Boche-Introduction and Boche-Elimination* would determine the property of being German as the referent of 'Boche'. This is the assignment of reference that naturally corresponds to Boche-Introduction.

(B). Suppose that 'Boche' refers to the property of being cruel. Thus 'Lessing was Boche' is false, because Lessing was not cruel, but 'Nero was Boche' is true, because Nero was cruel. Boche-Introduction is not truth-preserving: every non-cruel German yields a counterexample. But Boche-Elimination is truth-preserving; in fact, being cruel is the weakest property that makes Boche-Elimination truth-preserving. Equivalently, the converse of Boche-Elimination is also truth-preserving:

*Boche-Introduction**

$$\frac{x \text{ is cruel}}{x \text{ is Boche}}$$

The rules of Boche-Introduction* and Boche-Elimination are in harmony: Boche-Introduction* merely allows one to infer 'x is Boche' from what Boche-Elimination allows one to infer from 'x is Boche', and Boche-Elimination merely allows one to infer from 'x is Boche' what Boche-Introduction* allows one to infer 'x is Boche' from. Consequently, if the two rules are added to a theory in a language without 'Boche', they yield a conservative extension: anything in the original language provable with them was already provable without them. Boche-Introduction* is the introduction rule that naturally corresponds to Boche-Elimination. Together, Boche-Introduction* and Boche-Elimination would determine the property of being cruel as the referent of 'Boche'. This is the assignment of reference that naturally corresponds to Boche-Elimination.

On the picture of Boche-Introduction and Boche-Elimination as carrying equal weight in determining reference, or the lack of it, for 'Boche', cases (A) and (B) have exactly the same status; the advantages and disadvantages of the two putative assignments of reference are symmetrically related. But that result is wildly implausible. Intuitively, Boche-Elimination* is just as intimately linked to the meaning of 'Boche' as Boche-Introduction is. By contrast, Boche-Introduction* has no standing at all; even most xenophobes would reject it, for they think that Germans are not the only cruel foreigners.[15] Again, although both 'Lessing was Boche' and 'Nero was Boche' are regrettable utterances, the former seems to combine xenophobic abuse with literal truth while the latter combines it with literal falsity. The xenophobic abuse is preserved under negation, but 'Lessing was not Boche' seems to be literally false while 'Nero was not Boche' seems to be literally true. Thus Boche-Introduction trumps Boche-Elimination.

A further asymmetry between the two rules is observable in practice. Xenophobes typically treat Boche-Elimination as defeasible, because they allow that there are a few good Germans ('Some of my best friends are Boche'), whereas they treat both Boche-Introduction and Boche-Elimination* as indefeasible. Indeed, Boche-Elimination scarcely makes sense for many adjectival uses of 'Boche': xenophobes do not reason from 'He owns a Boche car' to 'He owns a cruel car.'

As a further check, we may briefly consider a third proposal about the reference of 'Boche'. It attempts a compromise between (A) and (B).

(C). Suppose that 'Boche' refers to the conjunctive property of being both cruel and German. Like (B), (C) makes Boche-Elimination truth-preserving and Boche-Introduction not truth-preserving; (C) has an advantage over (B) in making Boche-Elimination* truth-preserving and counting 'Nero was Boche' as literally false and 'Nero was not Boche' as literally true. But (C) is at a disadvantage with respect to (A), since it counts 'Lessing was Boche' as literally false and 'Lessing was not Boche' as literally true. The new proposal also licenses the silly inference from 'He owns a Boche car' to 'He owns a cruel car.' Indeed, its classification of Boche-Elimination as exceptionlessly truth-preserving is a demerit rather than a merit, for that rule, we have noted, is defeasible even from the perspective of those who use 'Boche'. By contrast, Boche-Introduction is supposed to be indefeasible, so (A) has the advantage over (C) in classifying Boche-Introduction as exceptionlessly truth-preserving.

The natural conclusion is that, far from suffering reference-failure or massive indeterminacy of reference, 'Boche' has the same reference as 'German'. That is certainly the dictionary view of the matter. Under 'Boche', the *Concise Oxford Dictionary* gives the definition '(Contempt[uous] for) German'. Thus Boche-Introduction and Boche-Elimination* are exceptionlessly truth-preserving, while Boche-Elimination is very far from truth-preserving. Accounts that make Boche-Introduction and Boche-Elimination the basic rules of use for 'Boche' are therefore highly implausible.

In Fregean terminology, we may say that 'Boche' has the same reference as 'German' but a different tone. Indeed, since the differences between 'Boche' and 'German' apparently play no role in determining reference, and so make no difference to the way in which the terms contribute to the truth-conditions of sentences in which they occur, a Fregean might even count 'Boche' and 'German' as having the same sense. Frege himself gives just such an account of another pejorative term (1979: 140): 'cur' has the same sense and reference as 'dog' but a different tone. According to Frege, 'This dog howled the whole night' and 'This cur howled the whole night' express the same thought (the same sense). They differ in that only the latter conveys an attitude of contempt for the dog on the part of the speaker. Frege denies that 'This cur howled the whole night' expresses the further thought that the speaker has such an attitude, because the absence of the attitude would not falsify the sentence.[16]

It might be objected to Frege's account that if the words 'dog' and 'cur' have the same sense, then, on Frege's own account of propositional attitude ascriptions, the sentences 'Mary believes that every dog is a dog' and 'Mary believes that every dog is a cur' must have the same truth value, however much Mary loves dogs. Mary, a fully competent speaker of English, assents to 'Every dog is a dog'; will she assent to 'Every dog is a cur'? If she agrees that 'Every dog is a cur' is true but misleading, we can surely agree that 'Mary believes that every dog is a cur' is also true but misleading. What if Mary, under the influence of too much inferentialist reading, claims that 'Every dog is a cur' lacks a truth value in virtue of its badly matched introduction and elimination rules? If she believes that every dog is a cur, why does she not assent to 'Every dog is a cur', for surely she knows that it expresses her belief that every dog is a cur? Such problems undermine Frege's simple account of propositional attitude ascriptions, not his claim that pairs like 'cur' and 'dog' have the same truth-conditional meaning. For similar problems arise even for pairs of synonyms with the same tone. Kripke (1979) gives the example of the synonymous natural kind terms 'furze' and 'gorse'. A speaker might learn the two words on different occasions, from ostension of examples, and acquire normal competence with both without being sure that they refer to exactly the same kind of plant. Thus 'He believes that all furze is furze' and 'He believes that all furze is gorse' appear to differ in truth value. It does not follow that 'furze' and 'gorse' are not synonyms after all. Such problems show nothing special about pejoratives. Whatever the right account of propositional attitude ascriptions, it is compatible with the Fregean view that 'cur' and 'dog' differ in tone but not sense (truth-conditional meaning).

Unfortunately, Frege's category of tone is too miscellaneous to take us very far in the analysis of the example. It includes stylistic differences, such as that between 'sweat' and 'perspire', which are significantly unlike the difference between 'Boche' and 'German'. Frege discusses his examples by speaking unhelpfully of the images and feelings that the words evoke in hearers. Nevertheless, the classification of the difference between 'Boche' and 'German' as truth-conditionally irrelevant is at least a useful start, for it respects intuitive distinctions over which the original inferentialist account rides roughshod.

What needs explaining is this. Competent English speakers know, or are in a position to know, that 'German' and 'Boche' have the same reference, and therefore that 'Lessing was German' and 'Lessing was Boche' have the same truth value. If educated, such speakers know, or are in a position to know, that both sentences are true. Nevertheless, although such speakers are willing to assert 'Lessing was German', they are not willing to assert 'Lessing was Boche', even on reflection, unless they are xenophobes. I know that 'Lessing was Boche' is true, but I refuse to assert 'Lessing was Boche.' Why?

The natural answer is that to assert 'Lessing was Boche' would be to *imply* that Germans are cruel, and I do not want to imply that, because the implication is both false and abusive. Since the false implication that Germans are cruel does not falsify 'Lessing was Boche', it is not a logical consequence of 'Lessing was Boche.' Rather, in Grice's terminology, 'Lessing was Boche' has the *conventional implicature* that Germans are cruel, in much the same way that 'Helen is polite but honest' has the conventional implicature that there is a contrast between Helen's being polite and her being honest.[17] Just as 'Lessing was Boche' and 'Lessing was German' differ in conventional implicatures while being truth-conditionally equivalent, so too 'Helen is polite but honest' and 'Helen is polite and honest' differ in conventional implicatures while being truth-conditionally equivalent. In Grice's terms, conventional implicatures are *detachable*, because they can differ between truth-conditionally equivalent sentences. But they are not easily *cancellable*, for someone who says 'Lessing was Boche, although I do not mean to imply that Germans are cruel' merely adds hypocrisy to xenophobia; equally deviant would be an utterance of 'Helen is polite but honest, although I do not mean to imply that there is any contrast between her being polite and her being honest.' By contrast, Gricean conversational implicatures are easily cancellable but not detachable. Whether one says 'She is either in Paris or Rome' or something truth-conditionally equivalent to it, the maxims of conversation generate the implicature that one does not know which city she is in; nevertheless, one can easily cancel it by adding 'I know which city she is in, but I am not going to tell you.' The implicature that 'Boche' carries must be conventional rather than purely conversational, for if there were not already a significant difference between the words 'Boche' and 'German', the norms of conversation could not generate any difference in implicature between 'Lessing was Boche' and 'Lessing was German.'

The conventional implicatures of 'Boche' and 'but' are preserved under embedding in more complex sentences. For example, 'If Lessing was Boche then he was European' still conventionally implicates that Germans are cruel, and 'If Helen is polite but honest then she is honest' still conventionally implicates that there is a contrast between her being polite and her being honest. The implicatures are present just as strongly in non-indicative sentences, such as 'Is he Boche?', 'Translate this into Boche!', 'Is she polite but honest?', and 'Be polite but honest!' In this respect, such conventional implicatures are like presuppositions rather than logical consequences. However, the relevant sense of 'presupposition' is closer to Stalnaker's than to Strawson's: although a presupposition modifies the context of utterance, its failure does not deprive the sentence of a truth value.[18] In the case of 'Boche', the very use of the word generates the xenophobic implicature, irrespective of its position in the sentence.[19]

The false implicature of 'Lessing was Boche' is not merely that Lessing was cruel. For otherwise the corresponding implicature of 'Hitler was Boche' would merely be that Hitler was cruel, which is commonly known to be true. Then I could decently assert 'Hitler was Boche': but I cannot. Thus even a singular ascription of 'Boche' carries the false general implicature that Germans are cruel. But since xenophobes treat Boche-Elimination as a defeasible rule, the implicature is not that all Germans without exception are cruel. The implicature is expressed by 'Germans are cruel' read as a generic sentence, meaning something like 'There is a tendency for Germans to be cruel.'

The implicature that 'Boche' carries is not merely about the speaker's psychological state. In particular, what is implicated is not merely that the speaker *believes* that Germans are cruel; such an implicature might well be true. When someone uses the word 'Boche' one can legitimately ask him to withdraw the anti-German implication; but if it is clear, as it may well be, that he does believe that Germans are cruel, then it is hardly legitimate to ask him to withdraw the implication that he has that belief. Although one might try to persuade him to abandon the belief, and even succeed, the view at issue makes the implicature of his original remark be that he had the belief at the time of utterance, not that he has it now, which leaves no false implicature to withdraw. The false implicature is that Germans are cruel, not that the speaker believes that they are cruel. Perhaps the use of 'Boche' does also carry the additional implicature that the speaker believes that Germans are cruel, since a linguistically competent speaker who uses 'Boche' without believing that Germans are cruel is being insincere; but such a belief condition would be a by-product of the simple implicature that Germans are cruel, combined with the conversational norm of sincerity; it is not the source of what is most objectionable in the use of 'Boche'.

One might argue that the use of 'Boche' implies more than that Germans are cruel, namely, that the speaker knows that Germans are cruel, or even that it is common knowledge that Germans are cruel. In asserting p, one implies in some sense that one knows p, although of course one does not thereby assert that one knows p, for one is in an epistemic position to assert p only if one knows p. Might implying p similarly generate the further implication that one is in an epistemic position to imply p? Such putative implications are not generated directly by the use of the pejorative word, but at best indirectly by the application of general principles of conversation to the direct implication; they will not be further discussed here.[20]

The conventional implicatures that words such as 'but' and 'Boche' generate are part of their meaning, in a broad sense of 'meaning'. If one is ignorant of them, one is at least partially ignorant of the meaning. An Englishman in Italy who thinks that 'ma' is synonymous with 'and' and 'e' with 'but' is mistaken, for 'e' is synonymous with 'and', not with 'but', and 'ma' is synonymous with 'but', not with 'and'. Fully to understand a word, one must have some awareness, however inexplicit, of the conventional implicatures that it generates. In the case of 'Boche', one might say, in Putnam's terminology, that cruelty is part of its associated *stereotype*; a stereotypical Boche is cruel. Putnam allows that stereotypes may be inaccurate; perhaps ferocity is part of the stereotype associated with the natural kind term 'gorilla', although really gorillas are gentle. On his view, the stereotype for a word plays no direct role in determining its reference, but to be competent with the word one must have the stereotype (1975; reprinted in 1975b: 247–52). Since a competent speaker may know that the stereotype is inaccurate, to have the stereotype is not to believe that it is accurate; what one must be aware of is that it is the stereotype. Someone who understands 'Boche' may know that cruelty is an inaccurate part of the associated stereotype. The exact relation between conventional implicatures and stereotypes deserves further investigation, but we have a clear enough view for present purposes. What is most crucial is the separation of those aspects of meaning that contribute to truth-conditions from those that do not.[21]

'Boche' and 'German' have the same reference, so 'The Boche are the Germans' is true, but in using 'Boche' one implies that Germans are cruel. One can fully understand the word 'Boche' and know all that without being committed to the claim that Germans are cruel, for one can refuse to use the word 'Boche'. One is not obliged to utter every sentence that one knows to be true. One can know that a rule of inference is truth-preserving without using it. The inferentialist accounts of pejoratives in Dummett, Brandom, and Boghossian misconstrue the linguistic data. They lump together a deductive inference (Boche-Introduction) and a mere conventional implicature (Boche-Elimination) as if they played equal roles in the use of the term; if they predict anything about the reference of pejoratives, they falsely predict reference failure; by making willingness to use the roles a precondition for understanding they falsely imply that only those with the relevant prejudices can understand pejoratives.

Could one base a better inferentialist account of 'Boche' on the truth-preserving rules Boche-Introduction and Boche-Elimination*? On such an account, inferring according to those rules would be a precondition for understanding 'Boche'. But that too is false, just as the previous section would lead us to expect. Non-xenophobic speakers of English may acknowledge that the rules are truth-preserving yet still refuse to infer according to them. For one must *use* 'Boche' to infer according to those rules, whereas to classify them as truth-preserving is only to *mention* the word. Again, a philosopher of language may understand the word 'Boche' as well as the rest of us do, but misconstrue the nature of pejoratives and reach the false conclusion that no instance of Boche-Introduction is truth-preserving, on the mistaken grounds that 'Boche' suffers reference failure. His false philosophical theory does not cause him to forget the meaning of the word 'Boche'.

A further problem for any inferentialist account of 'Boche' that relies on its inferential links with 'German' is that someone might understand 'Boche' without understanding 'German' or any other non-pejorative word with the same reference. One might grow up in a narrow-minded community with only pejorative words for some things. One would articulate the relevant conventional implicature by saying 'Boche people are cruel.'

Pejoratives pose a quite general problem for use-theories of understanding on which using a term in a given way is a precondition for understanding it. Unprejudiced speakers may understand a pejorative term but still refuse to use it in the specified way: in order to avoid commitment to a conventional implicature, they refuse to use it at all.[22]

In one respect the foregoing result may be good news for Boghossian, since it removes a class of putative counterexamples to the unqualified meaning–entitlement connection (MEC). The consequent danger for (MEC) is not that it is false but that it is vacuously true, and therefore cannot help to explain our inferential entitlements.[23]

Pejoratives raise a further question about the nature of concepts. A vital feature of a pejorative *word* is that it carries a conventional implicature, but how could a pejorative *concept* do so? Conventional implicatures seem to arise from the communicative use of language. Although synonymous words in different languages carry the same conventional implicatures, how could they share those implicatures with a non-verbal concept? In the study of pejoratives, it is dangerous to give thought methodological priority over language by treating concepts as intrinsically non-linguistic yet still capable of doubling as linguistic meanings. For that treatment is appropriate only if the false pejorative implicature is a feature of the concept *Boche*; but then it is unclear how one could have the concept other than by understanding a word synonymous with 'Boche'. On such a view, the notion of having a concept seems to be parasitic on the notion of understanding a word, and language takes methodological priority over thought. If, on the other hand, the false implicature is not a feature of the concept *Boche*, then presumably *Boche* is the same concept as *German*: since 'Boche' is not synonymous with 'German', the meaning of a word is therefore not exhausted by the concept that it means, and the study of meanings cannot be subsumed under the study of concepts.[24] An adequate theory of concepts must resolve such questions.[25]

4. Stipulated Possession Conditions

One might wonder why Boghossian could not respond to the argument of the previous section by simply considering an artificial concept *Quoche*, stipulated to satisfy his account of *Boche*: one has it if and only if one is willing to infer according to rules like Boche-Introduction and Boche-Elimination (with *Quoche* in place of *Boche*). Boghossian makes a similar move when he considers modifications of the meaning–entitlement connection (MEC) on which the inferential transitions built into concept possession are required to be truth-preserving, or even knowable a priori to be truth-preserving on some assignment of reference. If the original version of (MEC) is vacuously true, then so a fortiori are these restricted versions. But Boghossian constructs putative counterexamples to them involving artificial concepts with introduction and elimination rules that together generate consequences to which merely having the concepts does not *eo ipso* entitle one. In effect, he stipulates that inferring according to the rules is a precondition for having the concepts.

How far can one go in stipulating possession conditions for concepts? Perhaps not all the way, according to Boghossian, for he allows that 'tonk' may express no concept. Consider this stipulation for an artificial concept *mansquare*:

MANSQUARE   One has the concept *mansquare* if and only if one is male and has the concept *square*.

It seems clear that there is no such concept; MANSQUARE is as futile as the stipulation that one is immortal. Suppose that a man tries to introduce a word 'mansquare' to mean *mansquare*. He starts using 'mansquare' just as he uses 'square'. When the rest of us try to understand him, being a man gives one no special advantage, even if he insists that it does. Whatever is to be known about the meaning of 'mansquare', women can know it just as well as men.

Is the problem with MANSQUARE that being male is not an inferential condition? Consider this stipulation for an artificial concept *comsquare*:

COMSQUARE   One has the concept *comsquare* if and only if one can prove the completeness of the propositional calculus and has the concept *square*.

Although the new conjunct is inferential, that does not help. COMSQUARE seems as futile as MANSQUARE. For although I already meet the condition that I can prove the completeness of the propositional calculus and have the concept *square*, that seems to give me no extra concept *comsquare*.

One might think that such doubts about the power of stipulation are out of place when one considers the possession conditions that Boghossian proposes, which simply involve willingness to make various inferences with the putative concept itself. However, the underlying difficulty from Section 2 remains. Suppose, for *reductio*, that one has a concept C if and only if one is willing to infer according to a deductive pattern P in which C occurs, and that P leads to inferences to which one is not *eo ipso* entitled. The community uses a word 'C' to mean C. One member of the community understands 'C' in the usual way, but then comes to realize that P leads to inferences to which one is not *eo ipso* entitled. She is therefore no longer willing to infer according to P. Before the change, she knew that 'C' means C. Her warranted rejection of P does not cause her to lose the knowledge that 'C' means C. She still knows that 'C' means C, so she still has the concept C. Thus the original supposition that one has C if and only if one is willing to infer according to P is false; it led to absurdity, given that P really does lead to inferences to which one is not *eo ipso* entitled.

The trouble is that having the concept is necessary for understanding the word (with its actual meaning), understanding the word is necessary for knowing what it means, and willingness to reason according to an objectionable pattern is not necessary for knowing what the word means. Thus willingness to reason according to the pattern is not necessary for having the concept. For all that has been said, someone could have a concept and reason with it according to the rules that Boghossian specifies. The point is that, if so, then someone else could have the same concept and not reason with it according to those rules. From Section 2 we know that the problem generalizes even to cases in which the pattern of reasoning is not really objectionable but is taken to be so. At any rate, one cannot simply take an objectionable pattern of inference and define a concept as the one for having which it is necessary and sufficient to be willing to infer according to the pattern. There may be no such concept. That is why artificial stipulations are no substitute for accurate descriptions of concepts that we actually possess.

Could an inferentialist respond by pulling concept possession much further apart from linguistic understanding? The proposal might be that different thinkers can understand the same unambiguous word in virtue of using it to express different concepts, which are equated with different inferential roles. For example, neo-Fregeans such as Gareth Evans (1982: 40) sometimes claim that different speakers can achieve linguistic competence with the same proper name by associating it with different concepts (modes of presentation) of the same object. The distinctions between inferential roles would thus cut finer than the distinctions between linguistic meanings. On this view, when our unorthodox thinker refuses to infer any longer according to P, she associates the word 'C' with a new concept, because she changes the associated inferential role, while retaining the same meaning for the same word. Hence we cannot properly give the meaning of 'C' by saying that it is used to express the concept C, for the association with C is not essential to that meaning. Thus the word 'C' can hardly be said to *express* the concept C even in the mouth of a speaker who does in fact associate 'C' with C.

Large methodological questions arise for the view that concepts are individuated much more finely than linguistic meanings. For example: to which concept does the phrase 'the concept *square*' refer if the word 'square', with its usual meaning in English, is associated with different concepts in the minds of different speakers of English at one time, or in the mind of the same speaker at different times? Presumably, in writing 'the concept *square*' one intends to refer to the concept that one associates with the word 'square' at the time of writing, but what happens if the reader associates a different concept with the word? Without the use of phrases like 'the concept *square*', accounts of concept possession would lose most of their examples. Since much of the discussion is anchored to examples presented in just that way, their loss would cast it adrift. An account full of phrases like 'my present concept *square*' would be disappointingly autobiographical.

The inferentialist might reply that the problem will be manageable if most speakers do in fact reliably associate the same concept with a given word. Since there are likely to be at least minor differences between any two speakers in their willingness to accept inferences that involve the word, some principle is needed to distinguish those patterns of inference that are essential to the concept from those that are not. The meaning of the word supplies no such principle, on the envisaged view of concepts. It is deeply unclear whence the required principle is to come. Without such a principle, discussion of concepts becomes dangerously unconstrained.

This is no place to engage properly in the vast debate over the relative methodological priority of thought and language. Fortunately, Boghossian does not take refuge in the envisaged separation of the two sides. He assumes that words express concepts; his argument moves freely between concept possession and linguistic understanding. This paper will continue to follow that methodology.

5. Conditional and Unconditional Concepts

Boghossian classifies concepts like *Boche* as defective. He introduces his positive account of the difference between defective and non-defective concepts with the example of the concept *neutrino*, as expressed by the word 'neutrino'. Let 'T(Neutrino)' abbreviate neutrino theory. In the tradition of Ramsey (1929), Carnap (1966: 269–72), Lewis (1970), and, more immediately, Horwich (2000), Boghossian divides T(Neutrino) into two components:

(S) $\exists F\ T(F)$

(M) $\exists F\ T(F) \rightarrow T(\text{Neutrino})$

T(Neutrino) is logically equivalent to the conjunction of the Ramsey sentence (S) and the Carnap sentence (M). According to Boghossian, our concept *neutrino* is *conditionalized*, in the sense that to have it one must assent to (M) but need not assent to (S), the latter being no logical consequence of the former.[26] Thus one can have our concept *neutrino* while still denying neutrino theory, because one denies (S): one agrees that if any things play the role that neutrino theory specifies for neutrinos then neutrinos do, but holds that no things play that role. Consequently, our concept *neutrino* leaves room for substantive scientific debate on whether any things do play the neutrino role; it is an epistemically non-defective concept. Boghossian allows that there is a correspondingly defective concept *neutrino+* which prejudges the scientific issue; it is unconditionalized in the sense that to have it one must accept both (S) and (M). The concept *neutrino+* is supposed to be the approximate analogue for physics of the concept *Boche*.

Boghossian relates entitlement, defectiveness and conditionalization by means of several theses. We may slightly amplify his account thus:

(Bold)   If a conditionalized version of an unconditionalized concept is available, then the unconditionalized concept is defective.

(Sober)   For some concepts no conditionalized version is available.

(Bold-C)   If no conditionalized version of an unconditionalized concept is available, then the unconditionalized concept is non-defective.

(Cond)   Any conditionalized concept is non-defective.

(MEC*)   Any inferential transitions built into the possession conditions for a non-defective concept are *eo ipso* entitling.

Boghossian provides the obvious defence for (Bold): whenever possible, we should avoid prejudging factual questions; therefore, given the choice between an unconditionalized concept and a conditionalized version, we should use the latter. For (Sober), he argues that we cannot conditionalize away the very logical concepts (the conditional →, the quantifier ∃) that we must use in defining conditionalized concepts, otherwise, presumably, we should have nowhere to start. Boghossian states the principle here labelled '(MEC*)' as the natural modification of (MEC) within this framework to handle the objection from defective concepts. We should not expect the inferential transitions built into the possession conditions for a defective, unconditionalized concept to be *eo ipso* entitling, because they may prejudge issues that we do not have to prejudge. Boghossian does not explicitly state (Bold-C), which is in effect the converse of (Bold), but he seems to assume it when, having argued that no conditionalized version of the unconditionalized concept of the conditional is available, without further ado he applies (MEC*) to conclude that we are entitled to infer by modus ponens, which is built into the unconditionalized concept of the conditional. Thus he treats the move from the unavailability of a conditionalized version of the unconditionalized concept to the non-defectiveness of the unconditionalized concept as immediate; the principle on which he thereby seems to rely is explicit in (Bold-C). This is in effect to assume that the only relevant defect in a concept is unforced lack of conditionalization. Thus a conditionalized concept is never defective, so (Cond) also holds, although again Boghossian does not make it explicit.

Is Boghossian correct in claiming that willingness to affirm the Carnap sentence (M) is necessary for having the concept *neutrino*? Doubts arise when one asks how neutrino theory, T(Neutrino), is to be demarcated. Presumably, not every small change in what physicists believe about the referent of 'neutrino' counts as their adopting a new concept *neutrino*; the possession condition for the concept associated with 'neutrino' remains constant through at least some such changes. Thus T(Neutrino) consists of some but not all of physicists' beliefs about neutrinos. Which are the privileged beliefs? Whatever the answer, an expert physicist might reject it on subtly mistaken theoretical grounds. The physicist might reason thus: 'It is crucial to the role of neutrinos that our current theory T*(Neutrino) hold. But T(Neutrino) is too weak to entail T*(Neutrino). If T(F) is true but T*(F) false, then the Fs are not neutrinos. Perhaps T(F) is true for some Fs while T*(F) is false for all Fs; then there are no neutrinos, so ∃F T(F) → T(Neutrino) is false. Therefore, I had better not commit myself to that conditional.' Thus the physicist explicitly refuses to affirm the Carnap sentence (M). Although his reasoning is by hypothesis unsound, it does not seem to show that the physicist lacks the concept *neutrino*, contrary to Boghossian's account. The physicist may be an acknowledged world authority on neutrinos, having played a leading role in the development of current neutrino theory, while being less than fully convinced of its truth. All his colleagues regard it as obvious that he understands the word 'neutrino'. His mistake about the Carnap sentence does not impinge on his work in physics. Perhaps circumstances never arise in which physicists agree that ∃F T(F) is true and ∃F T*(F) false, so they never have to decide whether there are neutrinos in such circumstances. Even if those circumstances do arise, and he thinks that it has turned out that there are no neutrinos while other physicists do not, he may still decide to assent to the sentence 'There are neutrinos' for purposes of communication while insisting that he does so in a new sense of 'neutrino'. That still does not seem to show that he previously failed to understand the word 'neutrino'. His unorthodoxy at the metalinguistic level does not impair the fruitfulness of his interactions with other physicists. They may all regard the metalinguistic issue as a trivial matter of terminology. Thus considered refusal to affirm the Carnap sentence for neutrino theory seems to be quite compatible with full understanding of the word 'neutrino' as used by physicists, and with full possession of the concept *neutrino*.[27]

If one tries to avoid that problem by building more into the theory T(Neutrino) for the purposes of the Carnap sentence, new problems arise. For example, since the strengthened T(Neutrino) will be more controversial, some expert physicists may suspect that some neutrinos satisfy it in some states (making ∃F T(F) true) but not in others (making T(Neutrino) false); on those grounds, they refuse to affirm the Carnap sentence. As before, it does not seem to follow that those physicists lack the concept *neutrino* or fail to understand the word.

Such problems suggest that concept-constitution accounts of blameless inference rest on mistaken expectations of a theory of concept possession or linguistic understanding. They seek a conceptual shibboleth, an inference or principle acceptance of which is necessary and sufficient for knowing what a word means or possessing a given concept. Yet understanding words in a natural language has much to do with being able to use them in ways that facilitate smooth and fruitful interaction with other members of the community. That ability can be realized in indefinitely various forms. Speakers can compensate for their deviance on one point by their orthodoxy on others, their ability to predict the reactions of non-deviant speakers, their willingness in the long run to have their utterances evaluated by public standards. We have seen that such compensation is often possible when the deviance results from localized interference in the normal practice of using a word by high-level theoretical concerns. On that picture, there is no litmus test for understanding. Whatever local test is proposed, someone could fail it and still do well enough elsewhere with the word to be counted as knowing what it means. If linguistic understanding is linked to concept possession in the standard way, so that fully understanding the word 'neutrino' as used in English is sufficient for having the concept *neutrino*, then there is also no litmus test for concept possession. Variety in use amongst those who understand 'neutrino' is *ipso facto* variety in use amongst those who have the concept *neutrino*.

   Could an inferentialist reply that such objections trade on an everyday sense of 'understanding' that must be replaced by something more precise for theoretical purposes? It is far from clear that the inferentialist has a better alternative. The relevant features of the ordinary notion of understanding are not mere untheoretical sloppiness. Rather, they look like an appropriate response to an important constraint on a theory of concepts or linguistic meanings: that there is little point in talking about them unless they can be shared across differences in belief, between different individuals at the same time or the same individual at different times. They can survive factual learning and factual disagreement. Although inferentialist accounts respect the letter of that constraint, they violate its underlying spirit, by setting inflexible limits to the scope for genuine disagreement. The more holistic ordinary notion of understanding permits localized disagreement at virtually any point.

   The cases just discussed hint at ways in which the failure of individualist accounts of meaning may go deeper than the immediate lessons of the famous anti-individualist arguments of Putnam (1975b) and Burge (1979). Their cases are often analysed in terms of a distinction between experts with full understanding and laypeople with partial understanding who defer to the experts, in virtue of which one may correctly ascribe to them attitudes to the contents that the experts determine.[28] But we have seen that experts themselves may make deviant uses of words as a result of theoretical errors and still count as fully understanding their words. Although they defer to nobody on the matters at issue, they are more than adequately integrated members of the speech community with respect to those very words. Their assignments of meaning to those words are not parasitic on the assignments that more privileged individuals make. Rather, each individual uses words as words of a public language; their meanings are determined not individually but socially, in virtue of the spectrum of linguistic activity across the community as a whole. The social determination of meaning requires nothing like exact match in use between different individuals; it requires only enough connection in use between them to form a social practice. Full participation in that practice constitutes full understanding. Consequently, there is no litmus test for understanding. Although this does not exclude the possibility of concept possession by an isolated individual, the link from linguistic understanding to concept possession precludes a litmus test for concept possession too.[29]

It is useful to come at these matters from several angles. The next two sections assess Boghossian's positive account in more detail.

6. Unique Characterizations and Unique Realizations

When Belnap (1962) discussed the desiderata for good rules for a new concept, he did not merely require the rules to yield a conservative extension of the old theory. He also required them to characterize the new concept uniquely, in the sense that any two expressions subject to the rules are provably equivalent to each other. Inferentialists want the implicit definition to be satisfied by at least one concept; they also want it to be satisfied by at most one concept. Standard introduction and elimination rules for the usual logical connectives meet this unique characterization requirement (Harris (1982)). For example, if one introduces two connectives $\rightarrow_1$ and $\rightarrow_2$, both subject to conditional proof and modus ponens, one can easily use those rules to derive $p \rightarrow_1 q$ from $p \rightarrow_2 q$ and vice versa. If some pattern P of inferences does not provide unique characterization, then one can use both the expressions C_1 and C_2 according to P without being obliged to treat C_1 and C_2 as equivalent; thus P appears to single out no unique concept.[30]

For the defective, unconditionalized concept *neutrino+*, the governing rules are supposed to be tantamount to full neutrino theory, which is equivalent to the conjunction of (S) and (M). Thus the requirement of unique characterization is that when we introduce two predicates, 'Neutrino$_1$' and 'Neutrino$_2$', both subject to full neutrino theory, they should be provably equivalent. In other words, this argument should be valid:[31]

$(! + A)$ $T(\text{Neutrino}_1)$
          $T(\text{Neutrino}_2)$

$$\overline{\forall x(\text{Neutrino}_1(x) \leftrightarrow \text{Neutrino}_2(x))}$$

The relevant notion of validity is broadly logical and independent of neutrino theory, which has instead been packed into the premises. Since the only constraints on the new predicates 'Neutrino$_1$' and 'Neutrino$_2$' are the premises of $(!+A)$, it is valid if and only if this sentence is a truth of second-order logic:

$(!+)$ $\forall G \forall H((T(G) \& T(H)) \rightarrow \forall x(Gx \leftrightarrow Hx))$

Roughly, $(!+)$ says that at most one lot of things play the role specified for neutrinos: neutrino theory is uniquely realized. Let us provisionally assume that neutrino theory is indeed so strong that $(!+)$ is logically true.

For our non-defective, conditionalized concept *neutrino*, the governing rules are tantamount just to (M). Thus the requirement of unique characterization is that, when we introduce two new predicates, 'Neutrino$_1$' and 'Neutrino$_2$', this argument should be valid:

(!A) $\exists F\, T(F) \rightarrow T(Neutrino_1)$

$\qquad \exists F\, T(F) \rightarrow T(Neutrino_2)$

$\qquad \forall x\, (Neutrino_1(x) \leftrightarrow Neutrino_2(x))$

Just as (!+A) is valid if and only if (!+) is a truth of second-order logic, so (!A) is valid if and only if this sentence is a truth of second-order logic:

(!) $\forall G \forall H\, ((\exists F\, T(F) \rightarrow T(G))\, \&\, (\exists F\, T(F) \rightarrow T(H))) \rightarrow \forall x(Gx \leftrightarrow Hx))$

But we can easily show that (!) is logically true only if the Ramsey sentence (S) of neutrino theory is logically true, which it is not: for all logic says, no things behave as neutrino theory says the neutrinos behave (otherwise the conditionalized concept would collapse into the unconditionalized one).[32] Thus Boghossian's conditionalized rule for 'neutrino' fails Belnap's unique characterization requirement. The problem is simple: the supposed possession condition for the conditionalized concept *neutrino* involves only the Carnap sentence (M), which says nothing about which things are neutrinos if the Ramsey sentence is false. Each of the following is consistent with (M), and is therefore left open by Boghossian's possession condition for our concept *neutrino*: (S) is false and the neutrinos are the philosophers; (S) is false and the neutrinos are the non-philosophers; (S) is false and everything whatsoever is a neutrino. The problem obviously generalizes from 'neutrino' to other conditionalized terms: Boghossian's rules for them fail to achieve unique characterization.

David Lewis addresses related issues in his classic exposition (1970) of how to define theoretical terms using the Ramsey–Carnap method. Treating theoretical terms as names, he holds that they should name something only if the relevant theory has a realization. For present purposes, we can take that as the requirement that the predicate 'Neutrino' should be non-vacuous (apply to something) only if neutrino theory has a realization. Thus, if there are neutrinos, then some things behave as neutrino theory says the neutrinos behave:

(1) $\exists x\, Neutrino(x) \rightarrow \exists F\, T(F)$

Since the consequent of (1), the Ramsey sentence, is a logical consequence of T(Neutrino), so is (1) itself. If we make acceptance of (1) as well as Boghossian's (M) the possession condition for a modified conditionalized concept *neutrino–*, then unique characterization holds for the latter concept if and only if it holds for the unconditionalized concept, as it was assumed to do in the case of the concept *neutrino+*.[33] Together, (1) and (M) entail that if there are neutrinos, then they behave as neutrino theory says the neutrinos behave, so neutrino theory is true:

(2) $\exists x\, Neutrino(x) \rightarrow T(Neutrino)$

If neutrino theory entails that there are neutrinos, as it presumably does, then the conditional in (2) can be strengthened to a biconditional:

(3) $\exists x\, Neutrino(x) \leftrightarrow T(Neutrino)$

Neutrino theory is true if and only if there are neutrinos. The addition of (1) to (M) in the possession condition for our modified conditionalized concept *neutrino–* does not obviously violate the spirit of Boghossian's account. One might hope that the possession condition for a non-defective concept would uniquely determine its reference across all logically possible cases.

Further modifications of Boghossian's account are needed to align it fully with what Lewis says about theoretical terms. For Lewis also requires that there are neutrinos only if neutrino theory has at most one realization:

(4) $\exists x \, \text{Neutrino}(x) \to \forall G \forall H \, ((T(G)) \, \& \, T(H)) \to \forall x \, (Gx \leftrightarrow Hx))$

For if neutrino theory has several realizations, which of them determines the extension of 'Neutrino'? Without something like (4), the Ramsey–Lewis method does not enable one to *define* theoretical terms. By contrast, the Carnap sentence (M) requires that if neutrino theory has multiple realizations, and therefore at least one, then neutrino theory is true, and therefore by (3) that there are neutrinos. Earlier, we assumed that (!+) is logically true; on that assumption, neutrino theory is logically incapable of multiple realizations, so the further difference between Lewis and Boghossian does not arise. However, even if unique realization is plausible for neutrino theory, we can hardly expect it to hold in all cases; the relevant theory may simply be too weak. Applications of the Ramsey–Lewis method often fail to make unique realization plausible.[34] Since we are using 'neutrino' as a representative case, we had better drop the assumption that (!+) is logically true. Thus even the unconditionalized concept *neutrino+* may fail the unique characterization requirement. But then so too may the modified conditionalized concept *neutrino–*, for we noted above that the concept *neutrino–* satisfies unique characterization if and only if the concept *neutrino+* does. If we want a non-defective concept which satisfies unique characterization, we must in general modify the possession condition again. The natural move is to follow Lewis in weakening the Carnap sentence (M) to require only that neutrino theory is true if it has exactly one realization:

(M*) $(\exists F \, T(F) \, \& \, \forall G \forall H \, ((T(G) \, \& \, T(H)) \to \forall x (Gx \leftrightarrow Hx))) \to T(\text{Neutrino})$

The principles (M*), (1), and (4) correspond to what Lewis calls his three 'meaning postulates' for theoretical terms. The corresponding possession condition for our concept *neutrino* would require acceptance of (M*), (1), and (4). This possession condition too secures unique characterization.[35]

The analogues of (1) and (M*) for other concepts are always logical consequences of the relevant theory, the analogue of T(Neutrino), but the analogue of (4) is often not, for the relevant theory may not entail that it has a unique realization. Even if it does in fact have a unique realization, that may not be guaranteed by the form of the theory itself. Nevertheless, the use of the theory in fixing the reference of the term in question might still be held to involve an implicit commitment to the analogue of (4).

A further complication is that, when Boghossian states introduction and elimination rules for a conditionalized concept, they are equivalent neither to the original Carnap sentence (M) nor to the Lewis-like meaning postulates (1), (4), and (M*). Boghossian's rules have this form:[36]

Neutrino-Introduction	Neutrino-Elimination
$\dfrac{\exists F \, (T(F) \, \& \, Fx)}{\text{Neutrino}(x)}$	$\dfrac{\text{Neutrino}(x)}{\exists F \, (T(F) \, \& \, Fx)}$

Evidently, these rules are equivalent to an explicit definition of Neutrino(x) as $\exists F \, (T(F) \, \& \, Fx)$. Automatically, therefore, the extension is conservative and the characterization unique. In effect, 'Neutrino' is defined as the disjunction of the realizers of neutrino theory. But, in cases of multiple realization, the disjunction of the realizers of a theory need not itself be a realizer of that theory. Consequently, there is no general guarantee independent of the specific structure of neutrino theory that the Carnap sentence (M) is derivable from Neutrino-Introduction and Neutrino-Elimination.[37] For other theories T, when we implicitly define a conditionalized concept by means of rules analogous to Neutrino-Introduction and Neutrino-Elimination, the corresponding Carnap sentence is false. Without recourse to the structure of T, we can derive only the weakening (M*) of (M) from Neutrino-Introduction and Neutrino-Elimination (in classical second-order logic).[38] Although we can regain (M) from (M*) given the auxiliary assumption that T has at most one realization, that assumption is not generally true. Conversely, without recourse to the structure of T, we cannot derive either Neutrino-Introduction or Neutrino-Elimination from (M). For other theories T and terms C, the Carnap sentence $\exists F \, T(F) \rightarrow T(C)$ is true but the analogues of Neutrino-Introduction (from $\exists F \, (T(F) \, \& \, Fx)$ infer $C(x)$) and Neutrino-Elimination (from $C(x)$ infer $\exists F \, (T(F) \, \& \, Fx)$) are invalid.[39] The special auxiliary assumption that T has at most one realization would enable us to derive the introduction rule from the Carnap sentence; to derive the elimination rule from the Carnap sentence we need instead the Lewis postulate analogous to (1), that C applies to something only if it realizes T.

How are Boghossian's introduction and elimination rules related to the three Lewis meaning postulates (M*), (1), and (4)? As already noted, (M*) is always derivable from the introduction and elimination rules. Moreover, the elimination rule easily yields (1). However, the remaining postulate (4) cannot be derived from the introduction and elimination rules without recourse to the structure of the theory. For other theories T, when we implicitly define a conditionalized concept by means of rules analogous to Neutrino-Introduction and Neutrino-Elimination, the analogue of (4) is false.[40] In the converse direction, Boghossian's elimination rule is always derivable from the three Lewis postulates.[41] However, his introduction rule is not derivable from those postulates without recourse to the structure of the theory. For other theories T and terms C, the analogues of (M*), (1), and (4) are true but the analogue of Neutrino-Introduction is invalid.[42] These failures of equivalence are hardly surprising. The Lewis meaning postulates and Boghossian's introduction and elimination rules embody incompatible treatments of multiple realization, in case of which the former make the new concept apply nowhere while the latter make it apply wherever at least one of the realizations applies. The two approaches coincide given the special auxiliary assumption that the theory has at most one realization.

Despite their complicated differences, the various strategies considered in this section all remain within the general spirit of Boghossian's approach. Nevertheless, the complexity itself reinforces earlier doubts about that approach in at least two ways.

First, it is far from obvious that expert physicists who understand 'neutrino' as well as anyone does will know what to make of complex, highly abstract principles such as (1), (4), and (M*) or Neutrino-Introduction and Neutrino-Elimination. Probably some physicists will assent to them once the symbols are explained while others will not. The reason for the failure to assent will not be failure to grasp their own concept *neutrino* (perhaps it is simply that they lack training in philosophy). Although one might maintain that the physicists are implicitly committed by their practice to (1), (4), and (M*) or Neutrino-Introduction and Neutrino-Elimination, that would not vindicate Boghossian's account, which formulates possession conditions in terms of positive affirmation rather than mere commitment.

The second problem arises with respect to people who are experts on both neutrinos and concept possession. Consider such a prodigy who, understanding neutrino theory and the various meaning postulates and rules as well as anyone does, nevertheless makes a subtle mistake in the theory of concept possession and adopts an account with deviant consequences for the case of multiple realization. Consequently, our expert consciously rejects some meaning postulate or inference rule assent to which is a precondition, on some account, for understanding 'neutrino' as used in the rest of the scientific community. Nevertheless, when talking physics he continues to use the word in a way that other physicists regard as normal, because they never discuss the possibility of multiple realization. The claim that he does not fully understand the word 'neutrino' as used by others is implausible, and quite at variance with ordinary standards for linguistic competence. The natural description of our expert is that he fully understands the word 'neutrino' in the normal way while holding false theoretical beliefs about its meaning. Therefore the account of what it takes to understand 'neutrino' is false.

Could Boghossian fall back on a set of minimal inference rules or meaning postulates that are neutral with respect to the case of multiple realization, and perhaps even with respect to the case of no realization? Such weakenings of content often involve increases of complexity in formulation, in order to express the qualifications, as in the retreat from the comparatively simple Carnap sentence (M) to the more complex Lewis postulate (M*). Moreover, even if some principles are in fact neutral with respect to a certain case, that does not prevent someone from mistakenly believing them on theoretical grounds not to be neutral, and rejecting them as a result. Thus the envisaged fall-back position is still vulnerable to the problems raised in the two preceding paragraphs.

The complexities uncovered in this section have reinforced the conclusions of Section 5. There is no litmus test for understanding a word or having a concept. In particular, willingness to infer according to a specified pattern is not a necessary condition.

7. Logical Concepts

Boghossian suggests that our basic logical concepts are unconditionalized but non-defective, because no conditionalized version is available. For example, what understanding the conditional commits one to is that it obeys conditional proof and modus ponens, not just that it obeys them if anything does. The reason proposed for the unavailability of the conditionalized version is that the basic logical concepts already occur as auxiliaries in the rules for any conditionalized concept. More specifically, second-order quantification ($\exists F$) and the conditional ($\rightarrow$) occur in the Carnap sentence; second-order quantification and conjunction occur in rules such as Neutrino-Introduction and Neutrino-Elimination; the Lewis meaning postulates deploy still further conceptual resources.

Boghossian's reasoning is somewhat elliptical. If basic logical concepts occur in all rules for conditionalized concepts, it does not immediately follow that one must have those basic logical concepts *before* one can acquire any conditionalized concepts. It is not straightforward to say why the occurrence of a concept in the rules for con-ditionalized concepts should imply that it is not itself a conditionalized concept. However, before we address that question we should ask whether it has really been shown that basic logical concepts must occur in the rules for all conditionalized concepts.

Although $\exists$ and $\rightarrow$ occur in the Carnap sentence $\exists F\ T(F) \rightarrow T(\text{Neutrino})$, in place of that sentence Boghossian could have used the rule that allows one to infer T (Neutrino) directly from any premise of the form T(A). That rule is formulated without reference to any logical operators in the object-language, but is interderivable with the Carnap sentence once one has the standard rules for $\exists$ and $\rightarrow$. Similarly, one could replace Neutrino-Introduction by the rule that permits one to infer Neutrino(x) from premises of the form T(A) and A(x), and Neutrino-Elimination by the rule that permits one to infer a conclusion B(x) from Neutrino(x) and auxiliary premises, given a deduction of B(x) from those auxiliary premises and T(F) and Fx (where the second-order variable F does not occur free in B(x) or the auxiliary premises). These rules too do not involve any logical operators in the object-language but are interderivable with Neutrino-Introduction and Neutrino-Elimination once one has the standard rules for $\exists$ and &. The three Lewis meaning postulates (M*), (1), and (4) could in principle be replaced by more elaborate inference rules that also do not involve any logical operators in the object-language. Thus the occurrence of $\exists$, $\rightarrow$, and & in Boghossian's rules for conditionalized concepts is an inessential artefact of their formulations.

Logical operators may of course occur in the theory T itself, although Boghossian does not appeal to that point. In any case, it seems insufficiently general for his argument, since for some less highly theoretical concepts than *neutrino* the analogue of the theory T for conditionalization may consist of some simple sentences free of logical operators.

What would the rules for a conditionalized logical concept be like? For conjunction, the standard (unconditionalized) introduction rule permits the deduction of the single conclusion A & B from the separate premises A and B, and the standard (unconditio-nalized) elimination rule permits the deduction of the separate conclusions A and B from the single premise A & B. Thus corresponding conditionalized rules for & might take this form: given deductions of a single sentence C from the separate premises A and B, and of the separate conclusions A and B from the single premise C, deduce the single conclusion A & B from the separate premises A and B, and deduce the separate conclusions A and B from the single premise A & B. In other words, if anything behaves like the conjunction of A and B, A & B does. Such rules are indeed intelligible, but of what use would they be? If one already had another sentence C with the desired inferential powers, such as ¬(¬A ∨ ¬B), one could deduce that A & B also had the desired inferential powers, but from where is that other sentence C to come?

Suppose that one starts with a set of atomic sentences, each logically independent of all the others, and then adds to the language the operators &, ∨, →, ¬, each subject to conditionalized versions of its standard introduction and elimination rules. The original language has the feature that any conclusion derivable from a set of premises is interderivable with one of those premises. Since the expanded language inherits that feature, it yields nothing like the usual inferences. For example, where p and q are distinct atomic sentences, we cannot derive p & q from p and q (because p & q is derivable neither from p nor from q); we cannot derive $p \vee q$ from p or from q (because neither p nor q is derivable from $p \vee q$); we cannot derive q from $p \rightarrow q$ and p (because q is derivable neither from $p \rightarrow q$ nor p); we cannot derive q from p and $\neg p$ (because q is derivable neither from p nor $\neg p$). Thus the expanded language is deductively almost inert.[43]

Evidently, we need unconditionalized rules for at least some logical concepts. We may need them even for logical concepts that do not appear in Boghossian's conditionalized rules. For example, negation does not appear in those rules. If we start with just the standard introduction and elimination rules for &, ∨, →, ∃, and ∀, and conditionalize the rules for ¬ and everything else, then we cannot derive any classically valid inferences that are intuitionistically invalid. For the standard introduction and elimination rules for &, ∨, →, ∃, and ∀ in classical logic are intuitionistically valid, and the conditionalized rules for the other operators never take one outside the realm of intuitionistic validity.[44] The intuitionist agrees that if any sentence B behaves inferentially as the classical logician takes ¬A to behave, then ¬A behaves in that way; but the intuitionist does not concede that any sentence does behave in that way. For consider the sentence $(p \rightarrow q) \vee (q \rightarrow p)$, which is classically valid but intuitionistically invalid. It is therefore not provable from the standard introduction and elimination rules for → and ∨, since they are intuitionistically valid, but it can be proved from those rules and standard classical rules for ¬, by *reductio ad absurdum* of its negation. If the intuitionist conceded that any other sentences had the inferential powers attributed to sentences involving ¬ in the classical proof, then those other sentences could be used in an intuitionistically acceptable derivation of $(p \rightarrow q) \vee (q \rightarrow p)$, for ¬ does not occur in that conclusion itself; but the intuitionist denies that there is any such derivation.[45] Thus if one wants to recover the full power of classical logic, one had better have the unconditionalized classical rules for negation, even though it does not occur in Boghossian's rules for all conditionalized concepts.

The problematic weakness of conditionalized rules is not limited to logical concepts. Consider a standard version of Zermelo–Fraenkel set theory as a theory ZF(∈) of the set membership relation ∈. The corresponding Carnap sentence is ∃R ZF(R) → ZF(∈). Suppose that the precondition for having the concept of set membership is affirming the Carnap sentence. Of what use would it be in reasoning about sets? Mathematically, the Ramsey sentence ∃R ZF(R) is almost as strong a commitment as

ZF($\in$) itself, for the consistency of $\exists$R ZF(R) implies the consistency of ZF($\in$). What reason might one have for affirming $\exists$R ZF(R) other than ZF($\in$) itself? Our mere inductive failure so far to find an inconsistency in ZF provides weaker evidence for $\exists$R ZF(R) than we seem to have for ZF($\in$), and therefore for $\exists$R ZF(R). If we knew how to justify $\exists$R ZF(R), we should already have overcome the main obstacle to justifying set-theoretic reasoning. Although it might be claimed that not all the principles of Zermelo–Fraenkel set theory play a role in the constitution of the concept of set membership, so that ZF should be replaced by a weaker theory in the account of the conditionalized concept, it remains hard to see what the rules for that concept would contribute to set-theoretic reasoning.[46]

Conditionalized rules for logical and mathematical concepts are not unavailable: they are simply too weak to generate most of the interesting inferences. But that is not a justification of the unconditionalized rules of the kind for which Boghossian was looking. It is merely the crude pragmatic idea that we are justified in making inferences because we could not do without logic: an idea which does little to explain how any particular inference transmits justification from premises to conclusion.

8. Conclusion

In 'Blind Reasoning', Boghossian does not aim to defend an inferentialist account of concept possession. Rather, he takes such an account as a premise, and makes ingenious use of it in attempting to explain how deductive inference transmits justification. Fine-tuning apart, the present paper has not provided a better strategy for inferentialism to pursue. It has concentrated instead on questioning the inferentialist premise. In doing so, it has relied on this schema, which connects linguistic understanding to concept possession:

(Have)   If one understands the word 'C', one has the concept C.[47]

Unfortunately for inferentialism, the nature of language as a medium of communication between individuals who disagree with each other in indefinitely various ways undermines attempts to make accepting a given inference a necessary condition for understanding a word; therefore, by (Have), it undermines attempts to make accepting the inference a necessary condition for having the concept. The problem arose both for patterns of inference acceptance of which Boghossian regards as necessary for having defective concepts, such as pejoratives, and for patterns of acceptance which he regards as necessary for having non-defective concepts, such as conditionalized theoretical concepts and unconditionalized logical concepts. His attempt to find a special place for basic logical concepts as unconditionalized but non-defective led to problems of its own in the previous section.

One response to the failure of accepting given patterns of inference to be necessary for having a concept might be that the required conditions are normative rather than psychological. For instance, one understands $\rightarrow$ if one *ought* to use it in reasoning by conditional proof and modus ponens, whether or not one actually so reasons. Deviant logicians are not counterexamples to that proposal. Nevertheless, it is apt to seem unsatisfying: if one ought to reason in some way, should not something deeper explain why one ought to reason in that way? In any case, normative inferentialism does not fit Boghossian's project. For he is trying to explain how deductive inference can transfer justification from premises to conclusion. An account of concept possession that simply helps itself to the idea of an inference that one ought to make seems far too close to what he is trying to explain to promise much illumination. If having a concept is a matter of being obliged to reason according to given rules, one might equally ask for an explanation of how one can have the concept, that is, of how one can be obliged to reason according to those rules. That seems no less reasonable than Boghossian's request for an explanation of how reasoning according to those rules can transmit justification.

In very broad terms, the strategy of Boghossian's paper is to reduce a question in the theory of knowledge to questions in the theory of thought and meaning. If the attempt fails, as it apparently does, that is more evidence for the autonomy of the theory of knowledge with respect to the theory of content.[48]

Notes

1. [This chapter was first published as 'Understanding and Inference', *Aristotelian Society*, sup. 77 (2003): 249–93, as a response to Paul Boghossian's 'Blind Reasoning', now Chapter 2; both were presented at a symposium on 'Blind Reasoning' at the 2003 Joint Session of the Aristotelian Society and Mind Association at Queen's University Belfast.]

2. All quotations are from Boghossian (2003a) unless otherwise specified. The substitution of blamelessness for justification can be challenged; one may be blameless in making an excusable mistake in a complex and difficult inference without being justified (Plantinga (1993: 39); Pryor (2001: 114–18); Wedgwood (2002: 351–2)).

3. 'According to Chrysippus, who shows special interest in irrational animals, the dog even shares in the far-famed "Dialectic." This person, at any rate, declares that the dog makes use of the fifth complex indemonstrable syllogism when, on arriving at a spot where three ways meet, after smelling at the two roads by which the quarry did not pass, he rushes off at once by the third without stopping to smell. For, says the old writer, the dog implicitly reasons thus: "The creature went either by this road, or by that, or by the other: but it did not go by this road or by that: therefore it went by the other"'; Sextus Empiricus, *Outlines of Pyrrhonism*, i 69 (2000: 41–3). Does the dog have the concept *if*? Does he have a word in his language of thought that means *if*?

4. Here is one of McGee's cases; the others are similar:

   Opinion polls taken just before the 1980 election showed the Republican Ronald Reagan decisively ahead of the Democrat Jimmy Carter, with the other Republican in the race, John Anderson, a distant third. Those apprised of the poll results believed, with good reason:
   If a Republican wins the election, then if it's not Reagan who wins it will be Anderson.
   A Republican will win the race.
   Yet they did not have reason to believe
   If it's not Reagan who wins, it will be Anderson. (1985: 462)

   Some people claim that such examples involve equivocation, and that on the reading on which they are invalid they are not genuine instances of modus ponens. That would not undermine the points in the text, for even if they are correct the inference still has a reading on which it is an instance of modus ponens, and someone may reject it on that very reading by illicitly shifting away from the reading and back again in the course of theoretical reflection. Note that McGee's putative counterexamples are directed at modus ponens for the 'if' of English, not at the truth-functional conditional → of formal logic. Nevertheless, a similar problem about concept possession arises concerning modus ponens for →, which is equivalent to disjunctive syllogism (from p and $\neg p \lor q$ infer q), a rule that technically competent relevance logicians and dialetheists such as Graham Priest reject (Priest 1995: 5). According to Priest, the best account of paradoxes such as the Liar is that in special circumstances a sentence can be both true and false; when p is true and false while q is merely false, the premises of the disjunctive syllogism are true (for p is true; since p is also false, $\neg p$ is true, so $\neg p \lor q$ is true) but its conclusion is straightforwardly false. Whatever the errors underlying the rejection of modus ponens for →, they do not arise from a lack of ordinary linguistic understanding of → on the part of relevance logicians and dialetheists.

5. Putnam (1975b: 228): 'HYPOTHESIS OF THE UNIVERSALITY OF THE DIVISION OF LINGUISTIC LABOR: Every linguistic community ... possesses at least some terms whose associated "criteria" are known only to a subset of the speakers who acquire the terms, and whose use by the other speakers depends upon a structured cooperation between them and the speakers in the relevant subsets.'

6. For a related argument about the understanding of words such as 'sofa' and congenial discussion see Burge (1986). Goldberg (2002) replies on behalf of Burge to Bach (1988) and Elugardo (1993).

7. See Martin (1994), Lewis (1997), Martin and Heil (1998), and Bird (1998) for discussion. Harman (1999: 213) relies on defeasible dispositions to infer in his conceptual-role semantics.

8. Although there may be self-defeating rules such as 'Never follow a rule!', the rules associated with the usual logic constants are not of that kind.

9. Given that being disposed to use modus ponens for *if* is trivially sufficient for having the concept *if*, the disposition might be held to be both necessary and sufficient for having the concept. But *if* is not the only concept C such that being disposed to use modus ponens for C is necessary and sufficient for having C; the dispositionalist presumably thinks that the concepts of conjunction and of the biconditional satisfy that condition too. Modus ponens is an introduction rule; an elimination rule for *if* is also needed. The standard elimination rule for the conditional is conditional proof, although that would make *if* equivalent to the truth-functional →. It might be held that *if* is the only concept C such that being disposed to use both modus ponens and conditional proof for C is necessary and sufficient for having C. That does not entail that *if* is the only concept for which one may be disposed to use both modus ponens and conditional proof. Someone who understands 'if and only if' in the normal way and thereby has the biconditional concept but convinces himself through fallacious theoretical reflection that it validates conditional proof may thereby acquire a disposition to use both modus ponens and conditional proof for the biconditional concept too; that disposition defeats but does not destroy his original disposition to make the standard inferences with the biconditional. A variant of that example suggests that being disposed to use modus ponens and conditional proof for 'if' is insufficient for understanding the word. Imagine an Italian learning English as a second language told by an incompetent teacher that 'if' translates 'se e solo se' in Italian: the pupil falsely believes that 'if' in English means *if and only if*; he does not understand the word. Later, he convinces himself through fallacious theoretical reflection that the biconditional concept validates conditional proof; he acquires a new disposition to use both modus ponens and conditional proof for 'if', but he still does not understand the word, for he still falsely believes that it means *if and only if*. It is doubtful that requiring the inferences to be immediate or primitive would help, for many standard rules seem to lack that status for many speakers (compare Harman (1986b)). Peacocke (1998) treats related issues by means of his theory of implicit conceptions, although he does not apply the theory to examples like the present ones.

10. Harman (1986a: 29–42) defends a form of epistemological conservatism on which our beliefs are justified by default until some incoherence arises. Such a view might also be taken of our inferential dispositions. However, in 'Blind Reasoning', Boghossian rejects Harman's account of justification on the grounds that it depends on a notion of incoherence that is tantamount to what was to be explained.

11. [The argument of the foregoing section is developed in more detail in a more general setting in Williamson (2007a: 73–133).]

12. It is not clear that 'cruel' exactly captures the pejorative connotation of 'Boche', but it will do for the sake of argument. Dummett has 'barbarous and more prone to cruelty than other Europeans' (1973: 454).

13. The change from present to past tense is immaterial.

14. Belnap (1962) emphasizes the failure of the rules for 'tonk' to yield a conservative extension; Dummett (1973: 397 and 454) extends the point to 'Boche'. Dummett (1991: 246–51) makes the connection with harmony. As Boghossian notes, Robert Brandom accepts much of Dummett's account of pejoratives but rejects his constraints of harmony and conservative extension (2000: 69–76).

15. A xenophobe might apply the term 'Boche' to someone he knew to be Asian whom he regarded as displaying a distinctively German kind of cruelty, but that is a recognizably metaphorical use. The xenophobe would not apply 'Boche' even metaphorically to someone he knew to be Asian whom he regarded as displaying a distinctively Asian kind of cruelty.

16. The example involves complications about the proper treatment of indexicals and of descriptive elements in demonstratives, but Frege's general line is clear. Dummett (1973: 84–9) gives a nuanced account of Frege on tone.

17. See Grice (1989: 41) and (1961: section III). The example of the truth-conditionally irrelevant difference between 'and' and 'but' goes back to Frege (1879: section 7), but he misdescribes the difference by requiring the contrast to consist in the unexpectedness of what follows 'but' (Dummett (1973: 86). Frege (1979: 140) obscures the conventional nature of the implicature by giving this analogy for someone who uses the word 'cur' without feeling the contempt that it implies: 'If a commander conceals his weakness from the enemy by making his troops keep changing their uniforms, he is not telling a lie; for he is not expressing any thoughts, although his actions are calculated to induce thoughts in others.' A question by Owen Greenhall about the relation between the pairs 'Boche'/ 'German' and 'but'/'and' in a class at Edinburgh first interested me in the present line of thought about pejoratives.

18. Contrast Stalnaker (1999: 38–40 and 47–62) with Strawson (1952: 175–9). For a related view of conventional implicature see Karttunen and Peters (1979).

19. If the mere use of the pejorative word is what generates the implicature, then the compositional properties of this kind of conventional implicature may contrast with those of the usual paradigms of presupposition. For example, a conditional does not automatically inherit the presuppositions of its consequent: whereas 'He has stopped beating his wife' presupposes 'He once beat his wife', the conditional 'If he once beat his wife then he has stopped beating his wife' lacks that presupposition (for a related approach to compositional features of conventional implicature, see Karttunen and Peters (1979, 33–48)). It is less clear that 'If Germans are cruel then he is a Boche' fails to inherit the conventional implicature 'Germans are cruel' from 'He is a Boche.' These are matters for a more detailed account of pejoratives.

20. On assertion see Williamson (2000: 238–69). Evidently, an infinite regress looms if implying p involves implying that one knows p (in the same sense of 'imply'), for then one also implies that one knows that one knows p, and so ad infinitum. Arguably, all but

the first few of these implications are false, even if 'know' is weakened to 'is in a position to know' (2000: 114–30). But no such regress flows from the principle that when one conventionally implicates p, one conversationally implicates that one knows p.

21. The argument in the text does not require conventional implicatures to form a homogeneous category, and therefore withstands recent arguments that they do not (Bach (1999), criticized by Carston (2002: 174–7)). Much recent discussion of conventional implicatures focuses on their role in organizing discourse, as in the case of 'but'; pejoratives typically play no such role. See also n. 19 above.

22. [Williamson 2009 further develops the foregoing account of pejoratives.]

23. Vagueness is another case in which willingness to infer by rules that are not truth-preserving has been treated as a precondition for having some defective concepts. Thus Dummett (1975) argues that observational predicates in natural language are governed by rules that infect the language with inconsistency: for example, to understand 'looks red' one must be willing to apply a tolerance principle by which one can infer from 'x is visually indiscriminable from y' and 'x looks red' to 'y looks red', which generates sorites paradoxes because visual indiscriminability is non-transitive. More recently, Roy Sorensen (2001) has argued that linguistic competence with vague terms involves willingness to make inferences such as that from 'n seconds after noon is noonish' to '$n + 1$ seconds after noon is noonish', which commits us to inconsistent conclusions by sorites reasoning (given our other commitments, such as 'Noon is noonish' and 'Midnight is not noonish'); he combines that view with an epistemic account of vagueness on which vague expressions have non-trivial classical extensions. By the present arguments, such claims about linguistic competence and concept possession are mistaken. An ordinary speaker of English who understands 'looks red' and 'noonish' and has the concepts *looks red* and *noonish* in the normal way but then rejects the relevant tolerance principles in the light of the sorites paradoxes does not thereby cease to understand those expressions or to have those concepts (perhaps she treats the premises of the tolerance principles as providing excellent defeasible evidence for their conclusions, an attitude which is less than Dummett and Sorensen require for competence). Even if the whole linguistic community abandons its supposed commitment to the tolerance principles, without stipulating any cut-off points, that would not make 'looks red' or 'noonish' any more precise, so speakers' acceptance of tolerance principles is in any case quite inessential to vagueness.

24. If concepts are thought constituents, and *Boche* and *German* are the same concept, then in judging *Germans are German* one simultaneously judges *Germans are Boche*, however much one's reactions discriminate between the sentences 'Germans are German' and 'Germans are Boche.' Compare: if *furze* and *gorse* are the same concept, then in judging *furze is furze* one simultaneously judges *furze is gorse*, however much one's reactions discriminate between the sentences 'Furze is furze' and 'Furze is gorse.'

25. Despite the remarks in the text, I share Boghossian's scepticism about the capacity of Wittgensteinian appeals to the community to solve (or dissolve) fundamental problems of philosophy.

26. Proof: (S) is a logical consequence of (M) only if (S) is a logical truth. For (M) is a logical consequence of ¬(S), so (M) logically entails (S) only if ¬(S) logically entails (S), in which case (S) is logically true. But (S) is not logically true; logic does not guarantee that some things play the role that neutrinos play according to the theory.

27. Like Boghossian, I treat 'neutrino' as a schematic example, without reference to any specific features of its actual use in physics.

28. See for example Peacocke's (1992: 29–33) discussion of deference-dependent propositional attitude ascriptions. Burge extends his earlier arguments and argues for such a deeper lesson in his (1986).

29. For the relevance of the model of full understanding as full induction into a practice to the theory of vagueness see Williamson (1994: 211–12).

30. For more discussion of the unique characterization requirement see Williamson (1987/88), McGee (2000), and references therein.

31. For simplicity, the comparatively weak condition of the provability of coextensiveness from the two theories is used as the criterion of equivalence. Since the provability of coextensiveness does not guarantee the provability of necessary coextensiveness, this leaves it open that equivalent terms do not stand for the same property. A fuller discussion would address such modal matters; they will be ignored here, as not central to the present issues.

32. Proof: Since the main antecedent in (!) follows by propositional logic from $\neg \exists F\,T(F)$, (!) is logically true only if $\forall G \forall H\,(\neg \exists F\,T(F) \rightarrow \forall x(Gx \leftrightarrow Hx))$ is logically true; but it is logically equivalent to $\neg \exists F\,T(F) \rightarrow \forall G \forall H \forall x(Gx \leftrightarrow Hx)$ since the variables G and H do not occur in T(F); the consequent of that formula is logically false, since we may substitute $\neg G$ for H and assume that there is at least one individual; thus the formula as a whole is equivalent to $\exists F\,T(F)$. That argument treats $\rightarrow$ in (M) as the material conditional, contrary to the stipulation of Horwich (2000: 157). However, Horwich specifies no alternative reading of $\rightarrow$. Horwich's assumption that a theory is equivalent to the conjunction of its Ramsey sentence and its Carnap sentence also becomes questionable on a non-material reading of $\rightarrow$, for why should T(Neutrino) entail $\exists F\,T(F) \rightarrow T(\text{Neutrino})$? The present paper follows the standard practice in discussion of these issues by using a material conditional.

33. Proof: Unique characterization for the modified conditionalized concept is equivalent to the logical truth of this formula:

(‼) $\forall G \forall H\,(((\exists F\,T(F) \rightarrow T(G)) \,\&\, (\exists x Gx \rightarrow \exists F\,T(F)) \,\&\,$
$(\exists F\,T(F) \rightarrow T(H)) \,\&\, (\exists x Hx \rightarrow \exists F\,T(F)))$
$\rightarrow \forall x(Gx \leftrightarrow Hx))$

Now (‼) is easily seen to be logically equivalent to the following conjunction [where S is $\exists F\,T(F)$] : $(S \rightarrow !+) \,\&\, (\neg S \rightarrow \forall G \forall H\,(\neg \exists x Gx \,\&\, \neg \exists x\,Hx) \rightarrow \forall x\,(Gx \leftrightarrow Hx))$

The latter conjunct is logically true, so the whole formula is logically equivalent to $S \rightarrow !+$. But since $\neg S \rightarrow !+$ is a vacuous logical truth, $S \rightarrow !+$ is logically equivalent to $!+$ itself. Thus ‼ is logically equivalent to $!+$. Since the modified conditionalized concept satisfies unique characterization if and only if ‼ is logically true, and the unconditionalized concept satisfies unique characterization if and only if $!+$ is logically true, the modified conditionalized concept satisfies unique characterization if and only if the unconditionalized concept does.

34. For the problem of unique realization in the case of Frank Jackson's (1998) attempt to apply the Ramsey–Lewis method to ethical terms see Williamson (2001: 629–30).

35. Proof: We can abbreviate M*, (1), and (4) as $(S \,\&\, !+) \rightarrow T(\text{Neutrino})$, $\exists x\,\text{Neutrino}(x) \rightarrow S$, and $\exists x\,\text{Neutrino}(x) \rightarrow !+$, respectively. In this case, therefore, unique characterization is equivalent to the logical truth of this formula:

$\forall G \forall H\,((S \,\&\, !+) \rightarrow T(G)) \,\&\, (\exists x Gx \rightarrow (S \,\&\, !+)) \,\&\, (S \,\&\, !+) \rightarrow T(H)) \,\&\,$
$(\exists x\,Hx \rightarrow (S \,\&\, !+))) \rightarrow \forall x(Gx \leftrightarrow Hx)$

That formula is easily seen to be equivalent to this one:

$((S \,\&\, !+) \rightarrow \forall G \forall H\,((T(G)) \,\&\, T(H)) \rightarrow \forall x(Gx \leftrightarrow Hx))) \,\&\, (\neg(S \,\&\, !+) \rightarrow$
$\forall G \forall H\,((\neg \exists x Gx \,\&\, \neg \exists x Hx) \rightarrow \forall x(Gx \leftrightarrow Hx)))$

But the consequents of the two conjuncts are just $!+$ and a logical truth, respectively, so the whole formula is a logical truth.

36. Boghossian states his rules for the conditionalized version of one of his artificially stipulated concepts, but the form of his discussion is quite general. The rules are adapted to 'neutrino' here for ease of comparability with the other principles. [He amends the rules in an addition to the version reprinted here, p. 43, n. †]

37. Example: Let T(F) be $\forall x$ (Fx $\leftrightarrow$ Square(x)) $\lor$ $\forall x$ (Fx $\leftrightarrow$ ¬Square(x)), where Square applies to all and only square things. Thus T(Square) and T(¬Square) are both true, so the Ramsey sentence $\exists$F T(F) is also true. Define C(x) as $\exists$F (T(F) & Fx). Since everything is either square or not square, C applies to everything. So T(C) is false, since some things are squares and others are not. Thus the Carnap sentence $\exists$F T(F) $\to$ T(C), the analogue of (M), is false. Here as elsewhere, more realistic cases could be provided, but trivial examples are logically the most perspicuous.

38. Proof: From Neutrino-Elimination we derive

$$! + \to \forall F\,(T(F) \to \forall x\,(\text{Neutrino}(x)) \to Fx)).$$

Putting the two together yields

$$! + \to \forall F\,(T(F) \to \forall x\,(\text{Neutrino}(x)) \leftrightarrow Fx)).$$

We may assume that T is extensional in this sense:

$$\forall G \forall H\,(\forall x(Gx \leftrightarrow Hx) \to (T(G) \leftrightarrow T(H))).$$

Thus we have

$$! + \to \forall F\,(T(F) \to T\,(\text{Neutrino})), \text{ which is equivalent to } (M^*).$$

39. Examples: Let C apply to all and only squares. For the introduction rule, let T be tautologous; thus $\exists$F T(F) $\to$ T(C) is logically true (because its consequent is) and everything satisfies $\exists$F (T(F) & Fx) (because everything satisfies T(C) & C(x) or T(¬C) & ¬C(x)), so every non-square yields a counter-instance to the inference from it to C(x). For the elimination rule, let T be inconsistent; thus $\exists$F T(F) $\to$ T(C) is logically true (because its antecedent is logically false) and nothing satisfies $\exists$F (T(F) & Fx), so every square yields a counter-instance to the inference to it from C(x).

40. Example: As in note 37.

41. Proof: (1), (4), and (M*) yield $\exists x$ Neutrino(x) $\to$ T(Neutrino). Thus from Neutrino(x) we derive T(Neutrino) & Neutrino(x) and thence $\exists$F (T(F) & Fx).

42. Example: Let T be tautologous and C apply to nothing.

43. A few trivial inferences can still be made. For instance, p is interderivable with p & p, p $\lor$ (p & p), and so on.

44. The reason is that even the intuitionistic introduction and elimination rules are strong enough for the proof of unique characterization; the full power of classical logic is not needed. Thus the intuitionistic negation rules for an operator imply the conditionalized classical rules for that operator. See Williamson (1987/88: 110–14) for discussion.

45. The example shows that the standard classical rules for negation yield a non-conservative extension of the standard classical rules for the other connectives, a point crucial to Dummett's (1991) meaning-theoretic case against classical logic. For an alternative way of formulating classical logic in response to Dummett's critique see Rumfitt (2000).

46. We cannot expect set theory to characterize set membership uniquely, for if set theory has one realization, it has many. At most we can hope that our set theory will characterize set membership uniquely up to isomorphism; McGee (1997) provides a strengthening of Zermelo–Fraenkel set theory with individuals that does that. For set theory with individuals, we need a concept of set in addition to the concept of set membership, in order to distinguish the null set from the individuals; this is immaterial to the argument in the text. For simplicity, issues about unique characterization have been largely ignored in this section; they do not affect its main line of argument.

47. Understanding the word 'C' in (Have) must be read as understanding 'C' with its present meaning.

48. Thanks to Paul Boghossian and participants in classes at Oxford for discussion of some of the ideas in this paper, and to Nico Silins, Jason Stanley, and Ralph Wedgwood for written comments on an earlier version.

4

Williamson on the A Priori and the Analytic*

Paul Boghossian

In *The Philosophy of Philosophy*, Timothy Williamson provides us with a provocative, insightful, and richly argued account of philosophical inquiry. According to the picture he lays out, philosophy is often interested in claims about the metaphysically necessary and the metaphysically contingent. But such claims should not be understood as being *about* meanings or concepts; nor should our knowledge of them be explained exclusively in terms of our grasp of their ingredient meanings or concepts. Rather, our knowledge of metaphysical modalities derives from our general competence with assessing counterfactuals; and that competence is not usefully described as being either a priori or a posteriori. Hence, that venerable distinction should be demoted from its central place in the theory of knowledge and replaced by a distinction between armchair knowledge and non-armchair knowledge. Since, as Williamson conceives it, the natural sciences are also capable of armchair knowledge, the upshot is a Quinean blurring of the distinction between philosophy and mathematics, on the one hand, and the more empirical disciplines on the other.

There is an enormous amount that it would have been good to discuss: even those who end up disagreeing with Williamson on many of his central claims will have reason to admire his illuminating discussions of a host of fundamental topics. Owing to limitations of space, I will concentrate on those bits that most closely intersect with my own work—Williamson's discussions of the a priori and the analytic.

Williamson's view of the a priori is subtle. His is not the crude view that nothing is a priori knowable, that all knowledge is a posteriori. It is not even the more refined view that the distinction is somehow ill-defined. Rather, his view is that the distinction between the a priori and the a posteriori, while definable clearly enough, and while applying clearly enough in a wide range of cases, ultimately doesn't cut the epistemic facts at the joints. It obscures the epistemic patterns that matter most.

The point is not that we cannot draw a line somewhere with traditional paradigms of the *a priori* on one side and traditional paradigms of the *a posteriori* on the other. Surely we can; the

* [This paper was published as 'Williamson on the A Priori and the Analytic', *Philosophy and Phenomenological Research*, 82 (2011a): 488–97, as a contribution to a symposium on Timothy Williamson's book, *The Philosophy of Philosophy*.]

Debating the A Priori. Paul Boghossian and Timothy Williamson, Oxford University Press (2020).
DOI: 10.1093/oso/9780198851707.001.0001

point is that doing so yields little insight. The distinction is handy enough for a rough initial description of epistemic phenomena; it is out of place in a deeper theoretical analysis, because it obscures more significant epistemic patterns. We may acknowledge an extensive category of *armchair knowledge*, in the sense of knowledge in which experience plays no strictly evidential role, while remembering that such knowledge may not fit the stereotype of the *a priori*, because the contribution of experience was far more than enabling. For example, it should be no surprise if we turn out to have armchair knowledge of truths about the external environment.   (2007a: 169)

Williamson's argument for this begins with the observation that the distinction between the a priori and the a posteriori depends on the distinction between sense experience's playing an *evidential* role in justifying a belief and its playing a merely *enabling* role. Sense experience plays an evidential role in my knowledge that this shirt is green, but only an enabling role in my knowledge that all green things are colored: it was required only so that I may grasp the concepts *green* and *colored*.

However, Williamson claims, in a large number of central cases, sense experience is doing something *in between* these two things: while not playing a strictly evidential role, it is doing much more than merely enabling the thinker to have the relevant belief. We need to decide, therefore, whether to identify a priori knowledge with knowledge in which sense experience is playing a merely enabling role, or whether to identify it with knowledge in which sense experience is not playing a strictly evidential role, even if that role exceeds a merely enabling one. Unfortunately, no matter how we decide this question, we will get results that are intuitively incorrect: cases that intuitively belong together will be grouped separately and vice versa. Hence, the distinction between the a priori and the a posteriori should be discarded (and replaced by the distinction between armchair and non-armchair knowledge).

If we ask how we know that in a large class of central cases sense experience's contribution is neither strictly evidential nor merely enabling, the answer depends on two further big claims of Williamson's book: first, that knowledge of modal claims is knowledge of counterfactual conditionals; and, second, that the role played by sense experience in our knowledge of counterfactual conditionals is often neither strictly evidential nor merely enabling.

In defending the latter claim, Williamson appeals to the imagination-based account of knowledge of counterfactuals that he had outlined earlier in the book (chapter 5, sec. 3).[1] Roughly speaking, that account involves the idea that, in evaluating a counterfactual like

(6)   If the bush had not been there, the rock would have ended up in the lake

(asserted in a certain context about a given rock, bush and lake), 'one supposes the antecedent and develops the supposition, adding further judgments within the supposition by reasoning, offline predictive mechanisms and other offline judgments... To a first approximation, one asserts the counterfactual if and only if the development leads one to add the consequent' (2007a: 152–3).

Even if we were to accept Williamson's description of our actual procedures for evaluating counterfactuals as correct, we would still be owed an explanation of why those evaluations count as knowledge. Williamson is not explicit about this. His only remarks on this score seem to suggest that it is the *safety* of our imagination-based procedures—their reliability in actual and relevantly similar circumstances—that qualifies them to be sources of knowledge.

As Williamson himself remarks, his account is the 'merest sketch' (155) of an epistemology for counterfactuals. It's a very interesting sketch, but one that leaves many fundamental questions unanswered, including Goodman's famous problem of cotenability: in imagining the antecedent to be true, which bits of our background knowledge are we allowed to retain and which bits do we need to discard? Furthermore, it relies on several only dimly understood notions, such as that of the 'offline' application of a cognitive faculty. It is steeped in psychological speculation ('the default for the imagination may be to proceed as "realistically" as it can, subject to whatever deviations the thinker imposes by brute force' and 'an attractive sugges-tion is that some kind of simulation is involved'). And it seems to depend on a controversial (and to me, implausible) reliabilist criterion for knowledge.

If we grant Williamson his epistemology for counterfactuals, then his claim that, in our knowledge of counterfactuals, sense experience *may* play neither a strictly evidential role nor one that is merely enabling is plausible. For it is plausible that, on that account, even when sense experience does not survive as part of our total evidence, 'it can mold our habits of imagination and judgment in ways that go far beyond a purely enabling role' (2007a: 165). The insight that Williamson is giving voice to here is that if we think of the reliability of our cognitive mechanisms as epistemically relevant, then we will have to think that sense experience may play a more than enabling role in explaining a given judgment, a role that will be epistemically relevant (since it influences reliability) without being strictly evidential.

My own view, though, is that the proffered epistemology for counterfactuals is too speculative and controversial to support anything very consequential.

However, let's concede Williamson's account for the purposes of argument along with its attendant claim about the possible role of sense experience in our knowledge of counterfactuals. I would have thought that the natural solution to the challenge that that concession poses for the theory of the a priori is to say that knowledge is a priori provided that the role of sense experience in generating it was purely enabling, a posteriori otherwise.

Williamson thinks that can't be right because he thinks that it would lead one to classify as knowable only a posteriori many philosophically significant modal judg-ments that most philosophers would regard as paradigms of a priori knowledge. For he thinks that there is no question but that sense experience plays a more than enabling role in the following item of knowledge:

(27)   It is necessary that whoever knows something believes it.

How does Williamson know that sense experience has to be playing a more than enabling role in our knowledge of (27)?

He offers two considerations, one tied to this particular example and one more general. The example-specific consideration is that

Many philosophers, native speakers of English, have denied (27)...They are not usually or plausibly accused of failing to understand the words 'know' or 'believe'.   (2007a: 168)

Williamson's thought seems to be that it is only if assent to (27) is necessary for possession of the ingredient concepts, that we could say that whatever experience was required for assent to (27) was merely enabling. But assent to (27) is not necessary for possession of the ingredient concepts, as is shown by the number of competent philosophers who deny it. Hence, we can't say that the experience that was required for assent to (27) was merely enabling.

One problem with this argument is that it ignores the possibility that the difference between those who grasp (27) and assent to it and those who grasp (27) and don't assent to it is not sense experience per se but rather the exercise of a faculty of a priori insight. This idea may be fraught with difficulty, but it cannot just be ignored.

A second problem is that we are already aware, from reflection on the paradox of analysis, that analytic truths do not have to be transparent. If correct analyses can sometimes be informative, that must be because they don't always seem correct. So we can't conclude from the fact that a person competent with word w denies S(w) that S(w) is not analytic for that person.

Finally, showing that (27) would not come out a priori on the proposed definition doesn't show that there are lots of other similarly problematic cases.

It is at this point that Williamson can (and does—see 2007a: 166) appeal to his general discussion of epistemological conceptions of analyticity and its attendant denial that there are *any* constitutive understanding–assent links: no particular sentence (or inference) need by assented to (or performed) by a thinker as a condition of that thinker's understanding a given word. We need to turn, then, to look at Williamson's case for that general claim.

The idea that there are such links has, of course, traditionally exerted considerable influence within philosophy. Even Quine, who may be thought to be its most implacable enemy, came around to saying that the deviant logician merely changes the subject (see Quine 1970: 81). So Williamson's claim that there are *no* such links, three prima facie plausible examples of which are given below, is very interesting and very radical.

(A) Necessarily, whoever understands the sentence 'Every vixen is a female fox' assents to it.

(B) Necessarily, whoever understands the sentence 'All squares have four sides' assents to it.

(C) Necessarily, whoever understands 'and' is prepared to infer from any sentence of the form 'A and B' to 'A'.[2]

Why have philosophers been so tempted by such understanding-assent links?[3] There are two main arguments, one from below and one from above.

The argument from below stems from intuitions about meaning ascriptions: under sufficiently ideal conditions, no one who understands 'square', for example, could deny that squares are four-sided.

In the case of the logical constants, there is a further argument, one from above: it's hard to see what else could constitute meaning *conjunction* by 'and' except being prepared to use it according to some rules and not others (most plausibly, the standard introduction and elimination rules for 'and'). Accounts that might be thought to have a chance of success with other words—information-theoretic accounts, for example, or explicit definitions, or teleological accounts—don't seem to have any purchase in the case of the logical constants.

Now, Williamson thinks that there are *no* understanding–assent links—none. Why is he so confident that all such links fail? He can't have thought of each and every one of them and come up with a counterexample to each.

The answer is that he thinks he's got a general *recipe* for generating a counter-example to any putative link that might be proposed. Take any word w and any meaning *M*. Suppose it is maintained that T's assenting to the sentence S(w) is required for T to mean *M* by w. Then we can always describe a case of an expert on *M* who becomes convinced, however incorrectly, by a complex theoretical argument, that S is false and so refuses to assent to it but who, by any ordinary standards, still fully understands w. So there can be no S such that assenting to it is necessary for T to mean *M* by w. Ditto for any inference rule I(w), inference in accordance with which is said to be necessary for T to mean *M* by w.

In a previous exchange, I had suggested to Williamson that conjunction-elimination seemed as safe an example of a meaning-constituting rule as one could wish for and so that it would be an especially good test of the general effectiveness of his recipe.[4] In 2007a: chapter 4, Williamson aims to provide a counterexample to the analyticity of conjunction-elimination. He describes the case of Simon, an expert on the philosophy of language who has views on vagueness. Simon holds that borderline cases constitute truth-value gaps. He generalizes classical two-valued semantics by treating the gap as a third value and by conforming his practice to Kleene's weak three-valued tables. According to these tables, a conjunction is indefinite (neither true nor false) if at least one conjunct is, irrespective of the value of the other conjunct. Furthermore, Simon regards truth and indefiniteness as designated (acceptable) semantic values for an assertion: what matters to him is to avoid falsity. So he accepts sentences that are either true or indefinite.

It is easy to see that someone with Simon's semantic commitments would have reason to reject conjunction-elimination as a rule of inference, for there could be cases where 'A' is simply false while 'B' is indefinite. In such cases 'A and B' would be indefinite, but 'A' false. Thus, the corresponding instance of conjunction-elimination would have a designated premise and an undesignated conclusion, and so Simon would reject it. This, then, is the basis for Williamson's confidence that not even something as seemingly safe as conjunction-elimination is required for meaning *and* by 'and'.

I am not persuaded. I don't believe that Simon presents us with an intelligible counterexample to the analyticity of conjunction-elimination; and I don't believe that Williamson has provided us with a general recipe for dispatching any understanding–assent link that might be proposed.

To see why, imagine that Simon has come to the view that someone other than John Wilkes Booth shot Lincoln. According to him, Booth had a co-conspirator, Schmidt, who was actually responsible for pulling the trigger. Both men were there, in Lincoln's box at Ford's theater, but it was Schmidt that shot Lincoln, not Booth. So Simon asserts 'Schmidt, not Booth, shot Lincoln.'

However, Simon is very willing to assent to the sentence 'Booth saw the balding Lincoln and shot him', since he takes Booth to have been there and seen Lincoln, and, since he regards the first conjunct as indefinite, he regards the whole sentence as indefinite and so acceptable. So, he is willing to assert 'Booth saw the balding Lincoln and shot him' but not to assert 'Booth shot Lincoln.' In fact he rejects 'Booth shot Lincoln.'

It's not clear to me that we understand what it is that we are saying about Simon, for two reasons.

First, it's not clear that we understand the notion of assent or belief that is being invoked. It is certainly not clear that it is the same notion of assent (or belief) that is implicated in the understanding–assent links thesis, which is clearly the notion of assenting to something as (or believing it to be) true. This notion we understand well enough. But what is it to assent to something as indefinite or believe it indefinite? (This is not the question: What is it to believe that something is indefinite? That could be glossed as the question, What is it to believe true that something is indefinite?)

The problem is especially severe in Simon's case because he is said to classify any sentence as indefinite if it is borderline; and there are so many such sentences. Thus, he would be willing to assent to 'Lincoln was bald' but also to 'Lincoln was not bald' and even to 'Lincoln was both bald and not bald.' He would exhibit a similar pattern for any other borderline sentence. This stretches my grip on the notion of assent (or belief) to the breaking point.

Second, Williamson's assurances notwithstanding, I am not persuaded that Simon really does mean what we do by 'and' since he denies that it follows from 'Booth saw the balding Lincoln and shot him' that Booth shot Lincoln. Williamson is adamant that a refusal to see Simon as meaning the same as us would be misguided and unwarranted. After all, Simon insists that he is using the same meaning as we are, that we are simply mistaken to think that conjunction-elimination is constitutive of our shared meaning, and so on and so forth.

But such insistence is not sufficient to make it true. What matters is that, when we look at the example as described, we should find it intuitive that Simon means the same as we do by 'and' rather than some other, perhaps closely related, meaning. But, as I have just been saying, I don't find that intuitive.

So I'm not persuaded that we have been given a general recipe with which to dispatch any understanding–assent link that might be proposed.[5]

This brings us to the argument from above for the existence of understanding–assent links.

I am most tempted by this argument in the case of the logical constants, although the case of theoretical terms in science is compelling as well. In both of those cases, it is tempting to think, *faute de mieux*, that understanding the meaning of a word involves grasping its constitutive conceptual/inferential role. It goes without saying that there are many outstanding problems for such an account of meaning; but that could of course be said about any account of meaning.

Williamson is well aware that inferentialism will continue to look plausible for a certain range of words unless some alternative account is given of the difference between understanding and not understanding words in that range. In a section of his chapter 4 he attempts to sketch such an alternative. But what he is able to give, on such a complex matter, in the course of eight pages, raises more questions than it answers.

His picture claims that our meanings are determined socially. A solitary individual *is* capable of meaning—Williamson rejects those readings of Wittgenstein's private language argument that contend otherwise. But 'when an individual does use a shared language, as such, individual meaning is parasitic on social meaning' (2007a: 125).

How do societies determine these social meanings? The answer is that 'a complex web of interactions and dependences can hold a linguistic or conceptual practice together even in the absence of a common creed that all participants at all times are required to endorse' (2007a: 125). This repeats the rejection of inferentialism but without providing a substantive alternative.

Williamson rightly worries about how, on this picture, we might make sense of the synonymy of two expressions belonging to two distinct social languages. His answer is that two expressions are synonymous when they have exactly the same semantic properties; and that truth-conditional semantics provides us with a rich enough store of such properties: extension, intension, intensional isomorphism, character, conventional implicature. It is possible for two words belonging to two different social languages to have the same truth-conditional properties.

However, as Williamson is quick to recognize, we can easily think of pairs of expressions that are intuitively not synonymous but that share all their semantic properties as so identified. Consider 'phlogiston' (an example discussed by Williamson himself (2007a: 129)). This term is semantically atomic, has no conventional implicatures, fails to refer with respect to any circumstance of evaluation (since it designates rigidly, if at all), and fails to refer in any context of utterance (since it is non-indexical). Still, it is clearly not synonymous with 'aether', even though it shares all of its semantic properties as so identified. By contrast, the inferentialist would be able to provide a good explanation of why 'aether' is not synonymous with 'phlogiston'.

Furthermore, someone need not count as *understanding* 'phlogiston' just by knowing its semantic properties as so identified. Once again, the inferentialist would have a good explanation for this: since such a person need not have grasped the expression's constitutive inferential role, he need not count as understanding it.

Williamson tries to argue that this consideration does nothing to support an inferentialist account of understanding on the grounds that knowing the meaning of a term never qualifies one, all by itself, for 'full participation' in the practice of using that term (2007a: 129). He gives the examples of 'gob' and 'mouth', which, he says, mean the same, but are not appropriately used in all the same contexts. Someone may know that 'gob' means 'mouth' and yet not be fully competent to use it, by failing to grasp its slang coloring.

It seems to me, though, that a huge gulf separates the 'gob' and 'phlogiston' examples. Someone may be missing some subtle aspect of the tone of 'gob' if all he knows is that it means *mouth*; and so may not count as *fully* understanding it. But someone who knows about 'phlogiston' only that it's a non-referring theoretical term counts as not understanding it *at all*. Williamson says:

Although no particular piece of knowledge is necessary for participation, such abject ignorance is not sufficient. We should resist the temptation to build all qualifications for participation in the practice of using a term into its meaning, on pain of turning semantic theory into a ragbag of miscellaneous considerations... (2007a: 129)

Well, if we don't want to use 'understanding w' to mark the contrast between being competent to use w and not being competent to use w, then let's use some other expression to do so—for example, the expression 'competent to use w'. We will then need to decide what it takes for someone to be competent to use w and the most plausible answer is that a person would have to know some of the sentences or inferences in which w is correctly used. Of course, not any old correct sentences or inferences, but rather those that really are constitutive of competence. And now we are back at the same spot we thought we had abandoned—trying to figure out which bits of a word's role are constitutive of 'competence' with it and which aren't.

In conclusion, I am not persuaded that there are no assent conditions on understanding or meaning, and so not convinced that sense experience is guaranteed to play a more than enabling role in our knowledge of (27) and similar modal judgments. As a result, I am not yet convinced that we need to demote the distinction between the a priori and the a posteriori from its central place in the theory of knowledge.[6]

Notes

1. I am very doubtful that knowledge of modal claims can be reduced to knowledge of counterfactuals. It seems to me that, on any plausible account, knowledge of logical, mathematical, and constitutive truths will be presupposed in accounting for our knowledge of counterfactuals. But limitations of space prevent me from discussing this point.
2. Commitment to such links need involve no commitment to a use-dispositional *analysis* of meaning.
3. For convenience, I lump the case of inference under the 'understanding/assent' label. I also won't be fussy about the distinction between meanings and concepts since it won't matter for anything that follows.
4. At the Joint Session of the Mind Association and the Aristotelian Society held in Belfast in the summer of 2003.
5. Even if Williamson were right that there are no atomic understanding–assent links of the form—necessarily, one understands w only if one accepts S(w)—that wouldn't show that there aren't *clusters* of such links of the form: necessarily, anyone who understands w accepts S(w) or S'(w)....or S*(w). A friend of epistemological analyticities might well be satisfied with the existence of such clusters. Unfortunately, I can't pursue this thought here either.
6. For helpful comments I am grateful to Sinan Dogramaci, Anna-Sara Malmgren, Christopher Peacocke, Stephen Schiffer, Declan Smithies, and Crispin Wright.

5

Reply to Boghossian on the A Priori and the Analytic[1]

Timothy Williamson

In 'Williamson on the A Priori and the Analytic' (Chapter 4), Paul Boghossian defends a conception of a priori knowledge as knowledge in which sense experience plays a purely enabling role: we know a priori that all green things are coloured even though sense experience was crucial to our acquisition of the concept of green, for that is a purely enabling role. On Boghossian's conception, assent conditions on concept possession are central to at least some a priori knowledge, especially of logic. His defence of this view involves him in resisting the arguments of *The Philosophy of Philosophy* at several points. In particular, Boghossian maintains that the book's objections to understanding–assent links (assent conditions on concept possession) do not generalize as far as I claim; he rejects my alternative model of understanding, on which understanding–assent links are not required. I will explain why Boghossian's critique leaves me unmoved.

In previous work, Boghossian developed an epistemology of logic based on understanding–assent links corresponding to fundamental rules of logic. His paradigm was modus ponens: a necessary condition for understanding 'if' was supposed to be willingness to assent to inferences by modus ponens involving 'if'. The book presents a series of counterexamples, some actual, some possible, to such putative understanding–assent links, for both modus ponens and other equally fundamental rules (Williamson (2007a: 85–121)). The counterexamples concern native speakers of a natural language who come to understand the logical words at issue in the usual way but then go in for deviant logical theorizing without losing their linguistic competence; most philosophers know such people. In response, Boghossian picks what he regards as the clearest understanding–assent link, willingness to assent to 'and'-elimination (the inference from 'P and Q' to 'P' or to 'Q') as a condition for understanding 'and', and denies that the counterexamples I propose to it (95–6) make sense.[2]

Strategically, Boghossian's response is not very promising. If he can rely on understanding–assent links only for 'and'-elimination and a few other equally banal rules, but not for modus ponens or other fundamental principles, then he is in no position to base either a *general* epistemology of logic or a *general* account of the understanding of logical constants on understanding–assent links. It is a little

Debating the A Priori. Paul Boghossian and Timothy Williamson, Oxford University Press (2020).
© Paul Boghossian and Timothy Williamson.
DOI: 10.1093/oso/9780198851707.001.0001

lame for him to claim in effect that not *every* fundamental rule of logic is a counterexample to his original account. A bolder strategy for him would be to seek a way of defending the claim that *no* fundamental rule of logic is a counterexample to his original account, and in particular of defending his original test case, modus ponens, as a putative understanding–assent link for 'if' against my counterexamples. In keeping away from the bolder strategy, Boghossian concedes so much ground that it is quite unclear what his fall-back general epistemology of logic or his fall-back general account of the understanding of logical constants could be.

In any case, Boghossian's defence of 'and'-elimination as a putative understanding–assent link for 'and' is unconvincing. Boghossian notes that in some circumstances my proposed counterexample, Simon, will assent to (1) but not to (2):

(1)   Booth saw the balding Lincoln and shot him.
(2)   Booth shot Lincoln.

Obviously, if we have just met Simon, and know nothing about his background beliefs, we are likely to find his combined reactions to (1) and (2) utterly bewildering. We may reasonably wonder whether he knows what the word 'and' means. In practice, independently of his reaction to (1), since it is so well known that Booth shot Lincoln we may also find Simon's rejection of (2) initially puzzling, and wonder whether he is using the name 'Booth' to refer to the man we mean. Once we become aware of Simon's conspiracy theory of the assassination, we realize that there was no linguistic misunderstanding over (2); we simply disagree with him about the historical facts. Similarly, once we become aware of Simon's deviant theory of logic, an explanation of his unwillingness to deduce (2) from (1) in terms of linguistic incompetence looks much less attractive. On theoretical grounds, Simon holds that borderline cases for vague terms induce truth-value gaps, and that such gaps should be treated by Kleene's weak three-valued tables, which coincide with the classical two-valued tables when all the constituent sub-sentences are true or false but make the complex sentence gappy when at least one sub-sentence is gappy. Simon also thinks that it is legitimate to assent to gappy sentences as well as to true ones; what matters is to avoid falsity. Since he thinks that Booth saw Lincoln and regards Lincoln as a borderline case for the vague term 'bald', he thinks that 'Booth saw the balding Lincoln' is gappy, and that (1) inherits its gappiness. He concludes that it is legitimate to assent to (1). The gappiness does not infect (2). Simon rejects (2) as straightforwardly false.

Of course, Simon would be quick to point out that in conversational terms it would be highly misleading to assert (1) on grounds of its gappiness when one's audience had no reason to suspect that one was doing so. In the absence of special background assumptions, asserting 'A(P)' leaves it open whether 'A(P)' is true or gappy, on Simon's view. If one knows that 'A(P)' is gappy because it has the gappy constituent 'P', one can therefore make a simpler and more informative assertion by simply asserting that 'P' is gappy, omitting the other material in 'A(P)' as irrelevant. On Simon's view, one can gain the effect of asserting that 'P' is gappy without going metalinguistic by asserting 'P and not P'. Thus if Simon asserts (1), his audience is entitled for Gricean reasons to assume that he is not doing so merely on the grounds that 'Lincoln was bald' is gappy, since otherwise he is being conversationally uncooperative and should have said something like 'Was Lincoln bald? Well, he was and he wasn't' instead. The default conversational assumption is that one is not dealing with borderline cases; under that assumption one can defeasibly move from 'P and Q' to 'P' and to 'Q'. Nevertheless, according to Simon, the move is not deductively valid, and the case of (1) and (2) is a counterexample.

Once Simon has explained his view, it is much less plausible that his unwillingness to infer (2) from (1) manifests linguistic incompetence. It looks much more like a case of theoretical disagreement. Imagine a community in which no alternative to geocentrism has ever been contemplated. Now someone develops a heliocentric theory. This first emerges one morning when she dissents from the assertion 'The sun has risen.' She agrees that before the sun was in that direction (pointing down) and now it is in this direction (pointing up), but refuses to conclude 'It has risen.' Initially, other speakers are utterly bewildered, and wonder whether she understands the word 'risen'. However, once she has explained her view, they realize that it is a case of cosmological disagreement. Whether or not her geocentric theory is really correct, and whether or not it really entails the literal falsity of 'The sun has risen', her denial of that assertion does not constitute linguistic incompetence. Similarly, an unexplained refusal to conclude 'There are more natural numbers than even numbers' from the two premises 'Every even number is a natural number' and 'Not every natural number is an even number' causes utter bewilderment amongst those unacquainted with Cantorian reasoning, and doubts as to whether the speaker understands the word 'more', but filling in that reasoning makes it clear that no linguistic incompetence is involved. Unlike Copernicus and Cantor, Simon chose the wrong direction for theoretical unorthodoxy, but that does not make him linguistically incompetent.

Boghossian objects that Simon's tolerance of assent to gappy statements undermines the presumption that he is assenting to them as true. Quite what Boghossian means by 'assenting to something as true' is unclear. If it means assenting to the explicit claim that it is true, then it involves too much theorizing on the speaker's part to be pertinent here. For instance, some bad philosophers assent to 'The earth is not flat' but not to 'It is true that the earth is not flat', on the grounds that Nietzsche or Derrida has deconstructed the idea of truth. Presumably Boghossian does not want their deviant inferential role for 'true' to make their inferential roles for all other words automatically deviant too. Many bad philosophers have quite sensible views about non-philosophical matters. Moreover, unsophisticated thinkers such as children may genuinely assent to various claims about their external environment without having an explicit concept of truth at all.

In any case, Simon applies the same weak Kleene treatment to the sentential operator 'it is true that' as he does to other sentential operators. The classical two-valued truth-table for 'it is true that' maps true to true and false to false; thus the corresponding weak Kleene three-valued table for 'it is true that' maps true to true, gappy to gappy, and false to false. Thus 'It is true that A' always has the same status as 'A'. Consequently, Simon assents to 'It is true that A' when and only when he assents to 'A'. So far, his assenting to something looks like assenting to it as true.

Perhaps it is different when Simon goes metalinguistic. Let 'T' be the predicate in his metalanguage corresponding to the top line of his three-valued tables. If quoted occurrences of sentences do not count as constituents, then the object-language sentence 'A' is not a constituent of the metalanguage sentence T('A'), and we may suppose that T('A') is true when 'A' is on the top line but false when 'A' is on the second or third line. Thus when Simon regards 'A' as gappy, he will assent to 'A' but not to T('A'). Does that show that he is not really assenting to 'A' as true?

The easiest way to finesse that objection is by refining the example. Let Simon think of the weak Kleene tables as using a three-way classification into the definitely true, the indefinite, and the definitely false, and of being indefinite as a way of being true, indefinitely true. Thus, strictly speaking, 'T' does not mean true; it means definitely true. The failures of 'and'-elimination on this semantics have the same structure as before: 'A' is indefinite, so 'A and B' is also indefinite, even though 'B' is definitely false. When Simon regards 'A' as gappy, he will assent to both 'A' and True('A'), which on his view is true when 'A' is definitely true or indefinite, although he will not assent to T('A'). Like Graham Priest, Simon is a dialetheist, for when he regards something as gappy he assents to it, to its negation, and their conjunction. Nevertheless, his theoretical aberrations provide no sound basis for denying that his assent is genuine.

Simon's assent to both 'Lincoln was bald' and 'Lincoln was not bald' may be compared to our assent to both 'Every weapon of mass destruction in Iraq belonged to Al Qaeda' and 'No weapon of mass destruction in Iraq belonged to Al Qaeda': both are vacuously true, because there never were any weapons of mass destruction in Iraq. In both cases the assent is genuine, even though its unusual grounds defeat various expectations it might arouse in a hearer ignorant of those grounds. Simon regards both 'Lincoln was bald' and 'Lincoln was not bald' as something like vacuously true. Thus the main counterexample in the book to the understanding–assent link for 'and'-elimination goes through, despite Boghossian's protests.

The book briefly mentions two other types of counterexample to the understanding–assent link for 'and'-elimination, one concerning actual and robust experimental evidence of a human tendency in some circumstances to treat conjunctions as more probable than their conjuncts, the other concerning possible speakers who dissent from one conjunct in the absence of the others because they mistake a false conversational implicature for a false entailment (96). Since Boghossian offers no objection to either of these types of counterexample, they too stand.[3]

In addition to contesting my main counterexample to the understanding–assent link for 'and'-elimination, Boghossian asks what competence with a logical word could consist in, if not in assent of the kind understanding–assent links require. The book sketches an alternative answer, one consequence of which is that when the word belongs to a public language, competence with it constitutively involves causal relations with other speakers of the language, which do not supervene on patterns of assent and dissent. As an analogy, consider what competence in the casual game of beach soccer consists in. There is no rule R of beach soccer such that, necessarily, one is competent in beach soccer only if one assents to R. Someone who thinks that the slightly different rule R* is in force, rather than R, can still be competent in beach soccer. Oscar and Twin-Oscar may have the same intrinsic dispositions even though Oscar is competent (although not expert) in beach soccer while Twin-Oscar is not even competent in beach soccer, because the game played in Oscar's world is beach soccer while the game played in Twin-Oscar's world is beach twin-soccer, which differs from beach soccer in subtle respects of which neither Oscar nor Twin-Oscar is aware. Once one has joined a game of beach soccer, it takes rather extreme deviance to get slung out. The same applies to participation in a linguistic practice. The unorthodox theorists who counterexemplify understanding–assent links remain competent with the relevant words because they maintain an adequate level of participation in the social practice of using those words. Of course, such remarks are only a beginning. The discussion in the book goes further (2007a: 121–30), and far more remains to be done. Nevertheless, the analogy already shows the possibility of an account of linguistic competence that differs structurally from one based on understanding–assent links.

It is not clear that Boghossian has come to grips with the alternative model of linguistic competence. He asks how societies determine the social meanings that on my view a public language makes available to its speakers. He gives as my answer a sentence from the book: 'A complex web of interactions and dependences can hold a linguistic or conceptual practice together even in the absence of a common creed that all participants at all times are required to endorse' (2007a: 125). Boghossian comments, 'This repeats the rejection of inferentialism but without providing a substantive alternative.' But the quoted sentence was not intended to address the question of how societies determine social meanings. On my view of meaning, that would involve explaining how the referential properties of expressions of the language supervene on lower-level facts, for example about causal connections between uses of those expressions and objects in the environment. That is a huge task for the philosophy of language, whether the language is public or private. It was not the business of the book to attempt to carry out that task, although the comments in the final chapter on knowledge maximization as a principle of charity are at least relevant (2007a: 262–73). The quoted sentence addressed a different question: What unifies a linguistic or conceptual practice enough for it to be a locus for the assignment of meanings, by contrast with a mere collection of such loci corresponding to the more or less similar idiolects of different speakers? The partial answer is that the unification consists in causal interrelations of speakers, not merely in their shared monadic properties. Since competence with the public language depends on participation in such a unity, an inferentialist account of competence in terms of understanding–assent links cannot be right, because it has the wrong structure: the understanding–assent links do not capture the causal interrelations. Even someone who rejects that alternative to inferentialism should be able to see that it is substantive on the point at issue.

Boghossian suggests that the inferentialist is better placed than I am to handle empty terms such as 'phlogiston'. However, purported understanding–assent links for empty terms are subject to counterexamples of just the same sort as purported links for non-empty terms. What is unusual about empty atomic terms such as 'phlogiston' is that knowing their referential properties (that they do not refer) is typically of little help in attaining competence with them, whereas knowing the referential properties of non-empty terms (what they refer to) is typically of great help in attaining competence with the latter. That difference is hardly surprising. It does nothing to show that the standard for competence is inferentialist in nature. Even the practice of using 'phlogiston' was unified by a complex web of inter-actions and dependences; it did not require a universally shared creed to hold it together.

Given the failure of Boghossian's attempt to rehabilitate the appeal to understanding–assent links or epistemological analyticity, we may turn to his more general remarks about the a priori at the beginning of his piece. In the book, I argue that however the distinction between a priori and a posteriori knowledge is made precise, it does not cut very deep. Modal claims are used as a test case. The idea is that modal claims are logically equivalent to combinations of counterfactual conditionals, and that our cognitive capacity to handle the latter is what gives us the capacity to handle the former too. Our cognitive capacity to handle counterfactual conditionals involves the offline deployment of cognitive capacities originally developed online to handle the antecedents and consequents of those conditionals separately. Consider the example that Boghossian quotes:

(3)   It is necessary that whoever knows something believes it.

I argue that our knowledge of (3) does not involve an understanding–assent link; there is no 'epistemologically analytic' connection between 'knows' and 'believes'. Rather, in a nutshell, our knowledge of (3) involves the offline deployment of concepts of knowledge and belief, in a way not radically different from that which occurs in our assessment of a contingent counterfactual such as:

(4)   If Mary had known more about John, she would have believed that he was untrustworthy.

Whether we know (3) or (4) depends in part on our skill in applying the concepts of belief and knowledge. That skill was partly developed online, in the classification of cases encountered in sense experience as cases of knowledge or ignorance, belief or unbelief; those encounters are constitutively relevant to the epistemic status of our present applications of our concepts of knowledge and belief. Thus sense experience plays a more than purely enabling role in our knowledge of (3) as well as (4) (168). Yet our knowledge of (3) would usually be classified as a paradigm of a priori knowledge. But it would be no less crude to classify our knowledge of (3) as a posteriori, since sense experience does not play a strictly evidential role in that knowledge.

Boghossian complains that the argument ignores the possibility that the difference between those who grasp (3) and assent to it and those who grasp (3) and don't assent may concern 'the exercise of a faculty of a priori insight' (although that is not his own view). My argument is openly speculative. It attempts nothing like proof; that would be hopelessly premature for any account of the matter at this stage. Nevertheless, as the book emphasizes (2007a: 162), considerations of theoretical economy and psychological plausibility strongly favour explanations of armchair knowledge that invoke more general cognitive capacities for which there is inde-pendent evidence (such as our capacity to evaluate counterfactual conditionals) over accounts that postulate specialized faculties to do philosophically exciting things for which there is no independent evidence.

Boghossian briefly expresses scepticism as to whether 'knowledge of modal claims can be reduced to knowledge of counterfactuals', on the grounds that 'on any plausible account, knowledge of logical, mathematical and constitutive truths will be presupposed in accounting for our knowledge of counterfactuals' (p. oo). Those comments suggest a misunderstanding of what is at issue. *Pace* Boghossian, I did not claim that 'knowledge of modal claims is knowledge of counterfactual conditionals'. My point was rather that 'Despite the non-synonymy of the two sides, our cognitive capacity to evaluate the counterfactual conditionals gives us exactly what we need to evaluate the corresponding modal claims too' (2007a: 162). More important, *modal* truths must be distinguished from *necessary* truths. A theorem of first-order non-modal logic expresses a necessary truth; it does not express a modal truth, for it employs no modal terms. 'It is necessary that $2 + 2 = 4$ and John knows that $2 + 2 = 4$' does not entail 'John knows that it is necessary that $2 + 2 = 4$'. Logical, mathematical, and constitutive truths are typically necessary but not modal. Thus even when our prior knowledge of them plays a role in our knowledge of relevant counterfactual conditionals, that role does not imply any circularity in the account of our knowledge of modal truths. In particular, that role does not require us to have prior knowledge that the logical, mathematical, and constitutive truths are necessary; rather, that knowledge of modality is generated by the same means as the knowledge of counterfactuals. The book explains in more detail how the interplay of modal and counterfactual knowledge involves no circularity in its account (2007a: 169–71).

The attraction of epistemological analyticity was that it promised to demystify a priori knowledge. If there were no promising alternative means to do that, we might have some reason to think that there *must* be understanding–assent link links, despite all the evidence that there are not. Once we see that our ability to handle counterfactual conditionals provides independent evidence of cognitive capacities that are well placed to explain armchair knowledge, we have no need to hanker after epistemological analyticity.

Notes

1. [Originally published as 'Reply to Boghossian', *Philosophy and Phenomenological Research*, 82, 2 (2011): 498–506, as a reply to Boghossian 2011a (Chapter 4), in a book symposium on *The Philosophy of Philosophy* (Williamson 2007a).]
2. Parenthetical numbers are page references to *The Philosophy of Philosophy* [= Williamson 2007a], except where they obviously refer to displayed sentences or propositions.
3. In a footnote, Boghossian suggests that even if all understanding–assent links in the strict sense fail, 'A friend of epistemological analyticities might well be satisfied with the existence' of clusters of links of the form 'necessarily, anyone who understands w accepts S(w) or S'(w).... or S*(w).' To be a genuine alternative, the latter must mean a disjunction of acceptances, not acceptance of a disjunction. Such a disjunctive link will not confer a priori status on knowledge of any one of the disjuncts (or on knowledge of their disjunction). Since Boghossian does not explain how it would serve his overall argumentative purposes, I discuss it no further.

6

Inferentialism and the Epistemology of Logic
Reflections on Casalegno and Williamson*

Paul Boghossian

1

Paolo Casalegno's 'Logical Concepts and Logical Inferences' (Casalegno 2004) is a searching and insightful critique of my attempt to explain how someone could be entitled to infer according to a basic logical rule. I will say a bit about what I take the problem to be before considering his discussion in detail.

Let us agree that we reason according to logical rules. (There are various issues about this, most forcefully pressed by Gilbert Harman (see Harman 1986a), which I propose to set aside for present purposes.) One of the most central of the rules by which we may be said to reason is Modus Ponens, which I will take to say (again ignoring many complexities which are irrelevant for present purposes):

(MP) Whenever both p and 'if p, then q', infer q.

Those of us who have learned to formulate this rule recognize it as a rule that we operate with and, putting aside some deviant logicians, consider it valid.

However, there are many perfectly rational persons who are not aware that this is a rule that they operate with. Despite this, we think that when such people reason according to MP,

(Rain) It rained last night.
         If it rained last night, then the streets are wet.
         So,
         The streets are wet.

they are perfectly *entitled* to do so; and that the justification that they have for their premises transmits smoothly to their conclusion. In what does their entitlement to reason according to MP consist?

---

* [This paper was presented at a conference in honor of the late Paolo Casalegno in Milan in April 2011. It was subsequently published as 'Inferentialism and the Epistemology of Logic: Reflections on Casalegno and Williamson', *dialectica*, 66(2) (2012): 221–36.]

Debating the A Priori. Paul Boghossian and Timothy Williamson, Oxford University Press (2020).
DOI: 10.1093/oso/9780198851707.001.0001

Obviously it cannot consist in some *argument* that they have formulated for the belief that this form of inference is valid. By assumption, they do not have the belief in question so could hardly have seen the need to formulate an argument for it. But if their entitlement does not consist in an explicit justification for the validity of MP, what does it consist in?

What about us sophisticated philosophers who have arrived at the knowledge that we reason according to the rule MP? In what does our entitlement to use this rule consist?

Have not we formulated an explicit justification for operating according to this rule? And if we have not actually bothered doing so, is it not clear that we are at least in a position to do so, if asked and given enough time for reflection?

It might seem as if the answer to the latter question is 'Yes'. For could we not offer something like the following argument (I will not bother with the niceties of semantic ascent and descent)?

(i)   If 'p' is T and '$p \to q$' is T, then 'q' is T (by knowledge of the truth table)

(ii)   'p' is T and '$p \to q$' is T (by assumption)

Therefore,

(iii)   'q' is T (by MP)

Well, this particular argument obviously cannot do much for us by way of justifying our use of MP, since it relies on MP at its third step and I am assuming that we cannot explain in what our entitlement to reason with a certain rule, R, consists by showing that we have to hand an argument for R that employs R.

Of course, we might be able to offer other justifications for MP that rely not on MP itself but on certain other rules, say $R1$ and $R2$. But then the question will arise what entitles us to use $R1$ and $R2$?

We could now repeat the process of providing a justification for $R1$ and $R2$. Pretty soon, though, our justifications will end up appealing either to Modus Ponens, or to $R1$ or $R2$, or to some other rules for which we will owe a justification.

It seems obvious, then, that even the most sophisticated and powerful philosopher will face the following dilemma: With regard to her most basic logical rules, either she has *no entitlement* to them, or she has an entitlement that is *not* grounded in her ability to provide an explicit *argument* for them.

The skeptical alternative is dire. For if she has no entitlement to her most basic rules, then she has no entitlement to anything that is based upon them; and that means that she will have *no* entitlement to *any* of the rules of logic that she is inclined to use and therefore no entitlement to any of the beliefs that she will have based on them. This seems to me too fantastic to believe.

It also seems to me to tee up an extreme form of *relativism* about rationality, one that I find worrisome, both philosophically and socially. For if none of us is entitled to the particular set of logical rules that we operate with, then if others among us were to find it natural to operate with a *different* and incompatible set of logical rules, then they would have to be deemed as rational as we are, in so far as their use of logical rules is concerned. We could not say that such people were irrational, for they are surely no worse off in their entitlements to their logical rules than we are with respect to ours.

The skeptical alternative, then, is fraught with difficulty.

The non-skeptical alternative, however, requires us to explain how someone might be entitled to operate according to some basic logical rule, say MP, without his being able to provide anything like a cogent argument for MP. How could someone be so entitled? In particular, how could someone be so entitled in a way that did not imply an 'anything goes' conception of 'logical rationality?'

I hope it's obvious that this is a highly non-trivial task. Indeed, it remains unclear to me even now that there is a way of executing it that is even remotely satisfying.

Large as the task may be, though, it is not quite as large as the task of providing an *overall* epistemology of logic. As I am thinking about it, refuting the skeptical threat involves showing that it is possible to get our entitlement to *some* logical rules off the ground, even if the means by which that is accomplished may not generalize to all the logical rules to which we feel intuitively entitled. What is needed, in other words, is a plausible answer to a Kantian-style 'How possible?' question. We may worry about how to account for the rest of logic later. This relates to a point that shows up in an exchange that I have had with Timothy Williamson on these issues. Williamson says:

In previous work, Boghossian developed an epistemology of logic based on understanding–assent links corresponding to fundamental rules of logic. His paradigm was modus ponens: a necessary condition for understanding 'if' was supposed to be willingness to assent to inferences by modus ponens involving 'if'. The book presents a series of counterexamples, some actual, some possible, to such putative understanding–assent links, for both modus ponens and other equally fundamental rules (85–121). The counterexamples concern native speakers of a natural language who come to understand the logical words at issue in the usual way but then go in for deviant logical theorizing without losing their linguistic competence; most philosophers know such people. In response, Boghossian picks what he regards as the clearest understanding–assent link, willingness to assent to 'and'-elimination (the inference from 'P and Q' to 'P' or to 'Q') as a condition for understanding 'and', and denies that the counterexamples I propose to it (95–6) make sense.

Strategically, Boghossian's response is not very promising. If he can rely on understanding–assent links only for 'and'-elimination and a few other equally banal rules, but not for modus ponens or other fundamental principles, then he is in no position to base either a *general* epistemology of logic or a *general* account of the understanding of logical constants on understanding–assent links. It is a little lame for him to claim in effect that not *every* fundamental rule of logic is a counterexample to his original account. A bolder strategy for him would be to seek a way of defending the claim that *no* fundamental rule of logic is a counterexample to his original account, and in particular of defending his original test case, modus ponens, as a putative understanding–assent link for 'if' against my counterexamples. In keeping away from the bolder strategy, Boghossian concedes so much ground that it is quite unclear what his fallback general epistemology of logic or his fallback general account of the understanding of logical constants could be.   (Williamson 2011: 500)

Now, I do not, of course, deny the desirability of having a general epistemology of logic, but, as I have just been emphasizing, to my mind the fundamental difficulty in this area is to show that there might be even a *single* promising pathway for avoiding skepticism about our entitlement to the fundamental rules of logic. So, *pace* Williamson, I would be happy if, in the first instance, I could come up with a plausible account just for one or two of the most 'banal' rules of logic.

2

Well, what are the possible anti-skeptical alternatives? We have ruled out accounts that trace our entitlement to using a basic rule of logic in terms of our ability to provide any sort of argument. Could we plausibly say that it consists in some sort of non-inferential warrant?

A traditionally influential answer along these lines deploys the idea of an 'intuition'. A thinker is entitled to MP if he intuits its validity in some essentially non-discursive and non-inferential way.

I find this answer very problematic, for reasons that I have developed elsewhere (see Boghossian 2003a), although I am now inclined to be more sympathetic to the notion of an intuition than I used to be.

If we put aside explanations in terms of intuition, then the anti-skeptical task before us becomes one of explaining how a thinker might be differentially entitled to MP *blindly*, without being in a position to point to *any* sort of justification for his use of MP, whether this be of an inferential or non-inferential variety.

How could we be blindly entitled to operate according to MP? There look to be two main options.

The first would consist in embracing a crudely reliabilist conception of inferential justification, according to which a thinker is entitled to the use of a rule if that rule is reliably truth-preserving, then we would have an easy answer to our problem. Any thinker would be blindly entitled to MP, since (let us assume) MP is necessarily truth-preserving.

However, such a crude reliabilism is clearly false. There are lots of logically valid inferences, for example, from the Peano axioms to any instance of the inequality of Fermat's Last Theorem, which no one would be entitled to perform merely as a result of their reliability.

The second avenue for explaining blind justification involves deploying the classical notion of *analyticity*. For one important strand in that notion is the *epistemic* idea that *understanding* alone can sometimes suffice for entitlement: it is plausible, for example, that the mere understanding of the word 'bachelor' suffices for our knowing that all bachelors are male. If, on analogy with this, our understanding of 'if' could be shown to suffice for our being entitled to use MP, we would have the answer to our skeptic.

Taking such a notion of epistemic analyticity seriously, though, required showing that it could be detached from the much more dubious doctrine of metaphysical analyticity—of truth (or validity) in virtue of meaning—with which it had always been associated, but this seemed doable (see Boghossian 1996).

The problem then became one of explaining concretely how our understanding of 'if' might suffice for our entitlement to use MP.

An obvious starting point was a theory of our understanding of the logical constants that had always found favor among philosophers, quite independently of epistemological issues, according to which to grasp a logical constant necessarily involves being prepared to use it according to some inference rules and not others.

In its strongest form, such a theory is called an Inferential Role Semantics and says that it is *in virtue* of our using a constant, say 'if', according to some basic rule involving it, say MP, that 'if' means *if* in our idiolect.[1]

A weaker doctrine, which is all I will assume here, would simply have it that meaning *if* by 'if' *requires* inferring according to MP, without necessarily being sufficient for it.

As I say, many philosophers, among whom we may number Michael Dummett, Robert Brandom, Paul Horwich, Ned Block, Stephen Schiffer, and Christopher Peacocke, have been partial to some version or other of an inferential-role semantics. Even one of the harshest critics of this style of meaning theory, Jerry Fodor, has always maintained that when it came to the case of the logical constants, no other style of theory seemed to be in the running—certainly not causal or teleological or definitional theories.

Accordingly, I got interested in the question: Suppose we assume that

(A)   Inferring according to MP is necessary for someone to mean *if* by 'if'.

could we make it plausible that

(B)   We are *blindly entitled* to infer according to MP.

I did not take it upon myself to argue for (A). I followed in the footsteps of the philosophers listed above and simply assumed (A). My main task was to try to show that if (A) is true (B) is true. In a series of papers, I experimented with a number of different ways of arguing for this conditional, none of which I am fully satisfied with.

3

My critics, however, Casalegno and Williamson included, have largely concentrated not on the arguments I provided for the conditional 'if (A), then (B)', but rather on the inferentialist assumption (A) itself.

This has thrust me into the role of defender of an inferential-role account of the meaning of the logical constants, although, as I say, my main focus was elsewhere. Nevertheless, the inferential-role theory is assumed by my account and my critics have brought up many interesting points. I am therefore happy to discuss them.

Now, the first two-thirds of Casalegno's paper consists in some very interesting observations about why we should not take inference according to some rule to be *sufficient* for possessing a particular logical constant. I find some of that discussion to be very interesting, but, as Casalegno realizes, it is not relevant to the sort of account that I was exploring, which depends only on the necessity claim.

Casalegno does eventually turn his attention to the necessity claim, and to the account of entitlement that is built upon it, and he has a number of telling objections to make against them both.

4

One objection that Casalegno makes is that my story about entitlement is bound to be incomplete. Casalegno claims that we are blindly entitled to many more inferences than could plausibly be said to be necessary for concept possession. When should we say that those non-concept-constituting inferences are also blameless? (When I say 'concept-constituting' in this paper, I shall just mean 'is necessary for possession of the concept in question'.)

To provide an answer to this question, the analysis should be substantially supplemented. On the other hand, once we have found a satisfactory account of blamelessness for blind inferences which are not instances of rules belonging to the possession conditions for the logical constants, why shouldn't we apply this account also to the blind inferences which are instances of those rules, so making the initial analysis superfluous? Unless, of course, what Boghossian intends to suggest is that only inferences which are instances of rules belonging to the possession conditions for logical constants can be at the same time blind and blameless. But this would be hard to maintain. Take Ramanujan, the great Indian mathematician. We are told that he had an astonishing capacity to draw immediately very remote and complex consequences from given premises. He was often unable to justify those conclusions by means of what most mathematicians would have regarded as an acceptable proof; in fact, we are told that he had only a very vague notion of what a proof is. Well, I think it would be wrong to deny that Ramanujan's blind inferences were (at least in many cases) blameless, i.e. that they transferred knowledge. At the same time, it would make no sense to say that being able to perform inferences like those of Ramanujan is part of the possession conditions for logical constants, i.e. that it is necessary in order to know what they mean.   (2004: 406)

What I would say in response is that, in the sense I have in mind, it is plausible that Ramanujan *was* in a position to offer some justification for his feats of inference, even if he was not in a position to provide a rigorous proof of them. The kind of circumstance for which I coined the notion of 'blind entitlement' was for the case of a logical rule so basic that no person, no matter how well informed and how good at rigorous proof, *could* provide any sort of justification for the use of the rule, because of the inevitable circularity that such a justification would entrain.

So, I do not see that we have in Casalegno's description a clear example of a rule for which we are in principle not in a position to supply a justification, yet to which we are clearly entitled, and which could not plausibly be claimed to be concept-constituting.

5

Casalegno's next point, however, is more worrisome. He maintains that there is a general *recipe* for generating a counterexample to any claim of the form: Reasoning according to rule R is required in order to have logical constant C.

The idea that there is such a recipe strikingly anticipates an argumentative strategy developed by Timothy Williamson in his recent book (Williamson 2007a), although the recipes that Casalegno and Williamson have in mind are different from one another (and were no doubt developed independently of one another).

Before looking at these recipes in greater detail, let me comment on the importance of the claim that there is a *recipe* of this kind, a general method for generating a counterexample to any particular concept constitution claim.

The point is that there is, even among the friends of inferentialism, considerable uncertainty about exactly *which* rules are meaning-constituting for *which* constant.

Of course, this is not meant to be a virtue and is raised by Casalegno, as we shall see below, as a point of criticism of inferential theories. This uncertainty, though, can serve as a natural defense against proffered counterexamples. Faced with a counter-example to a particular concept-constitution claim, the inferential theorist can always distance himself from that particular claim, while clinging to the claim that some rule or other will be constitutive.

Vann McGee, for example, has developed what he takes to be a set of counter-examples to Modus Ponens (see McGee 1985). These examples all involve cases in which a conditional is embedded in another conditional. Does this show that MP is not necessary for possession of *if*? It may be hard to answer this question precisely because we may not be sure if assent to *all* instances of MP is necessary for possession of *if*. Perhaps it is enough that a thinker assents to all instances of MP that do not involve conditionals embedded in bigger conditionals. Perhaps MP is not involved in the possession of *if* at all. When the focus is, as mine was, on the conditional,

If *R* is concept constituting, then we are blindly entitled to *R*,

it can seem a matter of indifference that someone has come up with a counterexam-ple to any particular concept-constitution claim.

However, if someone can show that there is a general *recipe* for generating a counterexample to *any* pair of *C* and *R* such that reasoning with *R* is held to be necessary for *C*, then clearly that goes to the heart of inferentialism and of any epistemology that might be built upon it.

Here, then is Casalegno's recipe for generating such counterexamples:

Apart from this difficulty, the idea that, given a logical constant *C*, there is a well-defined set *R* of rules of inference such that a subject cannot be regarded as knowing the meaning of *C* unless she accepts the rules in *R* is intrinsically problematic. No matter how a rule of inference is chosen, it seems to me that we can imagine situations in which we would be disposed to say that a subject knows the meaning of *C* although the subject does not accept the rule in question. Suppose Mary suffers from a cognitive disability which makes her completely incapable of performing anything which could be counted as an inference. Nevertheless, she is able to use logically complex sentences to describe visually presented scenes. (I do not know whether this kind of cognitive disability has ever been observed; but it is no doubt conceivable.) For example, we can imagine that Mary, although unable to perform conjunction-introductions and conjunction-eliminations, would be able to assert, in appropriate circumstances, 'The box is red *and* the book is blue', or things like that. It seems to me that it would then be possible to say that, in spite of her disability, Mary knows the meaning of the word 'and'. At least: my intuition is that we would spontaneously adopt a homophonic translation for sentences such as 'The box is red and the book is blue' uttered by Mary; and wouldn't that be a way of acknowledging that, in Mary's mouth, the word 'and' has the same meaning it is has for us? (2004: 407)

So, the way Casalegno's recipe is supposed to work is that, for any rule, *R*, and constant, *C*, we can cook up a counterexample to the claim that inferring according to *R* is required for possession of *C*, by imagining someone who lacks the ability to infer with *R* but who, we might make plausible, possesses *C* because she uses it competently in sentences held true.

I am not convinced that there is a good recipe here for generating counterexamples to inferentialism. There are two ways in which we can develop the Mary example between which Casalegno's description does not distinguish and, however we develop the example, I do not see that we get a convincing counterexample to the necessity of either conjunction-elimination or conjunction-introduction for possession of *and*.

On the first way of developing the example, we may claim that Mary can think each of the atomic sentences 'The box is red' and 'The book is blue' separately, reliably asserting the first in the presence of a red box and the second in the presence of a blue book. Furthermore, we may claim that she can also think the compound sentence 'The box is red and the book is blue', reliably asserting it in the presence of a state of affairs that contains both a red box and a blue book. What, then, is she lacking?

What we are told is that she cannot *infer* from the atomic sentences taken together to the compound sentence, or from the compound sentence to either of the atomics.

Confronted with a red box and blue book she is prepared to assert 'The box is red and the book is blue', but if you ask her right after she has asserted that conjunction (perhaps this has to take place in a different room), 'So, is the box red?' she might say 'No'. Similarly, for a question about the book.

Having shown Mary a red box and gotten her to assert 'The box is red', and having shown her a blue book in a different room and gotten her to assert 'The book is blue', she then refuses to assent to 'The box is red and the book is blue', although, by hypothesis she is willing to assent to the compound sentence when she is shown the box and book together.

I find all this mystifying and certainly do not feel inclined to say, Clearly, Mary retains the ordinary concept of conjunction that ordinary people have, even as she fails to make various inferences that ordinary people would make.

We can also flesh out Casalegno's example by stipulating that Mary can think only the compound sentence and cannot think the atomic ones separately. This, I think, would make it even less plausible that Mary means *and* by 'and'.

6

Williamson's recipe for generating a counterexample to understanding–assent links is interestingly different from Casalegno's. Casalegno's example turns on a *disability*. Williamson goes in the other direction. His counterexamples consist of *experts* on logic and language who have allowed their linguistic behavior to be influenced by the somewhat kooky theories of logic and language that they have developed as adults. In some ways, this can seem a more promising strategy. It can seem easier to make it plausible that someone has retained a concept C by making him an expert on C than by giving him a disability with respect to C.

Here is how the recipe is supposed to work. Take any constant C and any rule R. Suppose it is maintained that T's inferring according to the rule R is required for T to have C. Then we can always describe a case of an expert on C who becomes convinced, however incorrectly, by a complex theoretical argument, that R is invalid and so refuses to infer according to it but who, by any ordinary standards, still fully understands C. So there can be no R such that inferring according to it is necessary for T to have C.

Williamson, too, uses his recipe to generate a putative counterexample to conjunction-elimination. He describes the case of Simon, an expert on the philosophy of language who has views on vagueness. Simon holds that borderline cases constitute truth-value gaps. He generalizes classical two-valued semantics by treating the gap as a third value and by conforming his practice to Kleene's weak three-valued tables. According to these tables, a conjunction is indefinite (neither true nor false) if at least one conjunct is, irrespective of the value of the other conjunct. Furthermore, Simon regards truth and indefiniteness as designated (acceptable) semantic values for an assertion: what matters to him is to avoid falsity. So he accepts sentences that are either true or indefinite.

It is easy to see that someone with Simon's semantic commitments would have reason to reject conjunction-elimination as a rule of inference, for there could be cases where 'A' is simply false while 'B' is indefinite. In such cases 'A and B' would be indefinite, but 'A' false. Thus, the corresponding instance of conjunction-elimination would have a designated premise and an undesignated conclusion, and so Simon would reject it. This, then, is the basis for Williamson's confidence that not even something as seemingly safe as conjunction-elimination is required for meaning *and* by 'and'.

Now, I find Williamson's examples as hard to understand as Casalegno's, although they raise different issues. I do not believe that Simon presents us with an intelligible counterexample to the analyticity of conjunction-elimination; and I do not believe that Williamson has provided us with a general recipe for dispatching any understanding–assent link that might be proposed.

To get a sense of how puzzling Williamson's Simon would be, imagine that Simon has come to the view that someone other than John Wilkes Booth shot Lincoln. According to him, Booth had a co-conspirator, Schmidt, who was actually responsible for pulling the trigger. Both men were there, in Lincoln's box at Ford's theater, but it was Schmidt that shot Lincoln, not Booth. So Simon assents to:

(0)   Schmidt, not Booth, shot Lincoln.

However, Simon is very willing to assent to the sentence

(1)   Booth saw the balding Lincoln and shot him.

since he takes Booth to have been there and seen Lincoln, and, since he regards the first conjunct as indefinite, he regards the whole sentence as indefinite and so acceptable.

He is not willing to assent to:

(2)   Booth shot Lincoln.

In fact he rejects (2). If we continue to spin the case out, we would have to say that Simon is also willing to assent to:

(3)   Booth didn't see the balding Lincoln and shot him.

He would also assent to:

(4)   Booth saw the balding Lincoln and didn't shoot him.

Also to:

(5)   Booth didn't see the balding Lincoln and didn't shoot him.

As well as to:

(6)   Lincoln is both bald and not bald.

When I look at the description of this case, I find myself with no clear intuitions about what Simon is saying or thinking. I certainly do not think: 'Oh, he clearly means conjunction by "and".'

Williamson has replied to this by saying:

Obviously, if we have just met Simon, and know nothing about his background beliefs, we are likely to find his combined reactions to (1) and (2) utterly bewildering. We may reasonably wonder whether he knows what the word 'and' means. In practice, independently of his reaction to (1), since it is so well known that Booth shot Lincoln we may also find Simon's rejection of (2) initially puzzling, and wonder whether he is using the name 'Booth' to refer to the man we mean. Once we become aware of Simon's conspiracy theory of the assassination, we realize that there was no linguistic misunderstanding over (2); we simply disagree with him about the historical facts. Similarly, once we become aware of Simon's deviant theory of logic, an explanation of his unwillingness to deduce (2) from (1) in terms of linguistic incompetence looks much less attractive. On theoretical grounds, Simon holds that borderline cases for vague terms induce truth-value gaps, and that such gaps should be treated by Kleene's weak three-valued tables, which coincide with the classical two-valued tables when all the constituent sub-sentences are true or false but make the complex sentence gappy when at least one sub-sentence is gappy. Simon also thinks that it is legitimate to assent to gappy sentences as well as to true ones; what matters is to avoid falsity. Since he thinks that Booth saw Lincoln and regards Lincoln as a borderline case for the vague term 'bald', he thinks that 'Booth saw the balding Lincoln' is gappy, and that (1) inherits its gappiness. He concludes that it is legitimate to assent to (1). The gappiness does not infect (2). Simon rejects (2) as straightforwardly false.

Of course, Simon would be quick to point out that in conversational terms it would be highly misleading to assert (1) on grounds of its gappiness when one's audience had no reason to suspect that one was doing so. In the absence of special background assumptions, asserting 'A(P)' leaves it open whether 'A(P)' is true or gappy, on Simon's view. If one knows that 'A(P)' is gappy because it has the gappy constituent 'P', one can therefore make a simpler and more informative assertion by simply asserting that 'P' is gappy, omitting the other material in 'A(P)' as irrelevant. On Simon's view, one can gain the effect of asserting that 'P' is gappy without going meta-linguistic by asserting 'P and not P'. Thus if Simon asserts (1), his audience is entitled for Gricean reasons to assume that he is not doing so merely on the grounds that 'Lincoln was bald' is gappy, since otherwise he is being conversationally uncooperative and should have said something like 'Was Lincoln bald? Well, he was and he wasn't' instead. The default conversational assumption is that one is not dealing with borderline cases; under that assumption one can defeasibly move from 'P and Q' to 'P' and to 'Q'. Nevertheless, according to Simon, the move is not deductively valid, and the case of (1) and (2) is a counterexample.

Once Simon has explained his view, it is much less plausible that his unwillingness to infer (2) from (1) manifests linguistic incompetence. It looks much more like a case of theoretical disagreement.   (Williamson 2011: 502)

Williamson raises many interesting points and there is a huge amount to be said in reply. Here I have space only to make a start.

First, a small terminological point. To call someone who is as sophisticated about logic and language as Simon is, 'linguistically incompetent', would be obviously misleading, just as it would be to so label Vann McGee for doubting Modus Ponens. All that the inferential-role theorist is committed to saying is that, if Simon succeeds in altering his behavior with 'and' and flouts a meaning-constituting rule for ordinary conjunction, then he necessarily means something different by 'and' than ordinary conjunction. It is better to call this 'meaning change' rather than incompetence.

Second, it might not be such a big meaning change (assuming we know how to measure such things). The new concept might play many of the same roles we associate with ordinary conjunction. It just would not be ordinary conjunction.

(Can we always rely on there being a sharp fact of the matter whether there has or there has not been meaning change? It would be surprising if meaning-facts were more determinate than facts in other domains, so a certain amount of indeterminacy about meaning change would have to be allowed for as well.)

Third, Williamson says that once we know about Simon's deviant theory of logic, the explanation in terms of change of meaning 'looks much less attractive'. I disagree with this assessment. There are two large reasons. First, in deciding whether Simon is best described as expressing one meaning versus another by 'and', we cannot rely on the fact that he has arrived at his inferential role for 'and' on the basis of theorizing. Second, I believe that explanations in terms of meaning change, rather than theory change, can sometimes be the most attractive. I will develop each point in turn.

When you look at formulations of inferential-role semantics, you find that theorists want to identify the concept-constituting inferences with those that are 'primitively compelling' (Peacocke) or that incorporate 'underived conceptual roles' (Schiffer). The inferences that are said to be concept-constituting for a thinker are those that the thinker finds compelling, is willing to engage in, without the benefit of any prior theory. As Peacocke puts it in connection with possession of the concept of conjunction: 'On any theory, this possession-condition will entail that thinkers must find the transition from A and B to A compelling, and must do so without relying on any background information' (Peacocke 2004: 172; quoted in Williamson 2007a: 125).

This is obviously a very important feature of inferential-role theories. It would make no sense to identify a meaning-constituting inferential rule for a constant with a *derived* rule for that constant, arrived at on the basis of rationally optional theorizing involving inferences with that very constant. Such a procedure can lead you to all sorts of mistaken views about what the meaning-constituting inferences for that constant are.

Simon's deviant inferences, however, are obviously highly derived. He does not find them primitively compelling, but compelling only on the basis of lots of (bad) theorizing. No inferential-role theorist would look to those derived inferences to say what concept Simon expresses by 'and'. They would look, rather, to the rules that Simon found primitively compelling, before engaging in all of that bad theorizing. By assumption, those rules are just the standard ones. So far, then, we have not yet got a counterexample to the necessity of conjunction-elimination for possession of conjunction.

To get one, we would have to argue that even a non-theoretically minded analogue of Simon's, who did not have fancy views about vagueness and gappiness, but who exhibited the same pattern of behavior with 'and' as has been stipulated for Simon, would clearly be credited with possession of ordinary conjunction.

I do not believe that many would be sympathetic to such a verdict.[2]

7

Does not the mere fact that it is possible for Simon to intelligibly question whether conjunction-elimination is valid, however, show that conjunction-elimination is not meaning-constituting? This brings me to the second large point I signaled above. I believe that the inferential-role theorist can explain what Simon is up to in a way that is consistent with the theorist's commitments.

Consider a different case. I think it is very plausible that our pre-Einsteinian ancestors worked with a notion of simultaneity of which it was analytic that it denoted a two-place relation. They would not have understood how simultaneity— or time order more generally—could be relative to an observer's frame of reference, and so a three-place relation.

Einstein, however, came along and claimed just that. Here we can mimic something that Williamson might want to say: Surely, Einstein was not just committing some linguistic mistake. Surely, once we know about his Special Theory of Relativity, an explanation of his unwillingness to deduce 'x stands in a two-place relation to y' from 'x is simultaneous with y' in terms of a change in the meaning of 'simultaneous' becomes much less attractive.

I do not agree that an explanation that invokes a change of meaning is far less attractive. At any rate, I think that there is a perfectly good story in terms of change of meaning that can preserve many of the features of the case that seem worth preserving. (Grice and Strawson made this point some time ago.)

On the story I have in mind, Einstein is proposing that we get a better theory of motion if we work with three-place simultaneity relations rather than with two-place ones—that is, if the explanatory role for which we need a notion of simultaneity is filled by a particular kind of three-place relation, rather than the classical two-place one. This accommodates the Einsteinian achievement without having to deny that two-placedness was constitutive of the classical notion. Similarly, we do not have to deny that the Parallels Postulate is constitutive of Euclidean space just because we recognize that the best theory of physical space may involve spaces that are non-Euclidean.

Hence, I do not think it is true that once we become aware of someone's substantive reasons for preferring one theory of 'X' over another, that we can no longer think of the disagreement as involving a change in the meaning of 'X'.

It might be thought that in helping ourselves to the notion of meaning change, as opposed to mere change in belief, we are begging the question against Quine. Two points: first, the Quinean claim that there are no determinate facts about meaning change has yet to be earned; second, Casalegno and Williamson do not express the same general skepticism about determinate meaning-facts as Quine does. Williamson, in particular, is quite clear that he believes that there are determinate facts about meaning. It is just that he does not think they are constituted by facts about inference rules.

At this point, we come face to face with another question: Perhaps we do not *have* to think that there has been no change in meaning. How do we know whether there has been one? How do we know which inference rule is, and which inference rule is not, constitutive of someone's having concept *C*?

8

Casalegno presses this question, too:

Should we say that the acceptance of a logical rule is part of the possession condition for some logical constant if we find its instances easy and natural, if we apply it as a matter of course and irreflectively, and if we expect that anybody else would do the same? Unfortunately, a criterion of this kind is unlikely to work. What inferences different people find easy and natural varies greatly. Presumably, what was easy and natural for Gödel in the early thirties was not what is easy and natural for me now. One might try to overcome this problem by saying that the logical rules to be taken into account are the rules that are found easy and natural by everybody, or almost everybody. But this too would give rise to obvious difficulties. First: being easy and natural is a matter of degree. How easy and how natural should a rule be to be taken into account? At least at first sight, there is no principled way to draw the line. For example: for most people, Modus Tollens is slightly less easy and less natural than Modus Ponens. But only slightly. Does this slight difference matter? Is acceptance of Modus Tollens necessary to have the concepts of conditional and negation? Second: not only do different people find different inferences easy and natural, but the same person may apply a certain rule with great ease when she is reasoning on a certain topic (holidays, for example) and have a lot of trouble with it when she is reasoning on some other topic (abstract algebra, say). Being easy and natural are topic-dependent. What topics are to be regarded as relevant? Again, no principled answer seems possible. Third: let us imagine we have settled in some way the previous two problems. We might discover that the inferences which we have decided to count as easy and natural for everybody do not suffice to determine uniquely the denotation of logical constants. For example, they might be insufficient to establish whether 'or' stands for inclusive or exclusive disjunction, or which truth-value should be assigned to 'Every *P* is *Q*' when there are no *P*. For Peacocke and Boghossian this would be a problem for the reason explained at the outset.   (2004: 408)

Casalegno insists that the question here is *not* epistemic.

Note that the problem is *not* that of actually deciding whether this or that specific rule is or is not constitutive of some logical concept. The problem with the syllogism in Barbara and

Modus Ponens is *not* that we do not have all the data required to establish whether they are or are not constitutive of the logical concepts they involve. The problem is that we have not been told what sort of data would be relevant to establish this. Notice also that the problem is not one of vagueness. The case of Modus Tollens is not like the case of a man who is neither clearly bald nor clearly not bald. To establish whether a man is bald or not, I know that I must apply a certain criterion: then it may happen that, in a particular case, the criterion does not give a clear verdict and I remain uncertain. In the case of Modus Tollens, I have simply no idea of what the relevant criterion might be like.   (2004: 409)

What I want to say in reply is that, in an important sense, the only legitimate residual question in this vicinity *is* epistemic.

We have already been told *what* we are looking for. We are looking for those conditions that are necessary for having concept C. If we are working within an inferential framework, we are asking which inference rules are necessary for possessing concept C.

Casalegno says: 'we have not been told what sort of data would be relevant to establish this'. We have 'no idea what the relevant criterion might be like'.

Why, in addition to being told that we are looking to find out which inference rules are necessary for possession of C, must there be criteria by which this matter is to be decided?

It is, indeed, very common in discussions of this topic to think that there have to be behavioral markers by which concept-constituting inferences are to be recognized. I think it is a mistake to look for such markers.

The idea that there have to be such behavioral markers is encouraged by reflection on the case where a word is introduced via *explicit stipulation*. Suppose I introduce the word 'flurg' as follows:

(7)   By 'flurg' I shall mean: 'Any murder committed on a Tuesday.'

If I am rational, then, as a mere result of this stipulation, I will exhibit a certain kind of assent behavior. For example, I will assent to

(8)   A flurg always occurs on a Tuesday.

and I will do so without the benefit of any empirical evidence. I will not regard any empirical evidence as bearing upon its acceptability in any direct way, and so forth. Such assent behavior can be regarded as 'criterial' for (7)'s having a meaning-constituting status for me.

Now, of course, in the case of the basic logical constants, there is no question of having introduced them via explicit stipulation (one would need some constants in order to make any stipulations). When we think of an inference rule as having concept-constituting status for a particular constant, there is a natural tendency to think of it as a sort of *tacit* analogue of an explicit stipulation. Then it becomes natural to ask how to identify the *tacit analogues* of the assent behavior that's criterial in the explicit case.

There is a mistake here. The reason that we may expect my characteristic assent behavior in the explicit case depends on the fact that, in such a case, I *know* my definition and *know* that it has definitional status for me. In the explicit case, all such facts are open to view.

However, matters are different in the tacit case. A rule R can be concept-constituting for C in S's idiolect without S knowing that it is. As a result, S can come rationally to question R on the sorts of highly theoretical grounds that Williamson describes.

Such questioning by S need not mean that R is not concept-constituting for S's having C, but it does mean that ordinary speakers, who are not trained to think about such matters, can change their concepts without knowing that they have.

How can we tell whether that has happened? In the usual way, clearly being used both by Casalegno and Williamson—via intuitive judgments about possible cases.[†]

Notes

1. Such theories are best run over a mental language rather than a public language. I will not worry about this distinction in the present paper.
2. This is especially true if one finds it natural, as I do, to operate with an idiolectic rather than a social conception of meaning, although I do not think that the force of my point rests exclusively on that important divide.

† I am grateful to Elisa Paganini and the other members of the University of Milan Philosophy Department for this opportunity to pay tribute to a brilliant philosopher. I am also grateful to Timothy Williamson, my commentator on the occasion, and to other participants, for valuable comments.

7

Boghossian and Casalegno on Understanding and Inference[1]

Timothy Williamson

1. Introduction

What does it take to understand a logical constant, such as 'if' or 'and'? The most popular answer is inferentialist in spirit: to understand a logical constant is to be disposed to reason with it according to certain basic principles of logic. In a series of much-discussed papers, Paul Boghossian (1997, 2000, 2003a [= Chapter 2]) has used that answer in an attempt to explain our entitlement to reason according to such principles despite our inability to justify them in any non-circular way. Both Paolo Casalegno (2004) and I (2003 [= Chapter 3], 2006, 2007a) have criticized the inferentialist account of understanding on which he relies. That led to a further round of discussion (Boghossian 2011a [= Chapter 4], Williamson 2011 [= Chapter 5]) and now to Boghossian's response (2012 [= Chapter 6, p. 00]) to us both. In this reply, I defend both Casalegno's objections and my own to inferentialism. Although I cannot put words in his mouth, our agreement on so many points gives me hope that my arguments will not be alien to those he might have produced.

2. Using Logically Complex Sentences to Describe Visually Presented Scenes

To illustrate his account, Boghossian originally took the rule of Modus Ponens (MP) as his example of a basic principle of logic. In trying to explain our entitlement to reason according to MP, Boghossian relied on the inferentialist assumption that one understands the conditional 'if' only if one is disposed to reason with it according to MP. Both Casalegno and I offer counterexamples to that assumption. Indeed, as Boghossian emphasizes, we each give a general recipe for constructing a similar counterexample to any inferentialist assumption of the relevant form, that one understands the logical constant *C* only if one is disposed to reason with it according to the rule *R*. Thus we each provide a general strategy for arguing against any attempt along such lines to explain our entitlement to reason according to a basic logical principle *R*, no matter what *R* is.

Debating the A Priori. Paul Boghossian and Timothy Williamson, Oxford University Press (2020).
© Paul Boghossian and Timothy Williamson.
DOI: 10.1093/oso/9780198851707.001.0001

Boghossian highlights a difference between the two recipes. Casalegno's starts thus:

Suppose Mary suffers from a cognitive disability which makes her completely incapable of performing anything which could be counted as an inference. Nevertheless, she is able to use logically complex sentences to describe visually presented scenes.   (Casalegno 2004: 407)

Casalegno argues on general grounds that Mary can understand C, even though she is not disposed to reason with it according to R. By contrast, my recipe involves someone who, far from being cognitively disabled, is an acknowledged expert on the logic of C, but rejects R on the basis of high-level, subtly mistaken theorizing. A fluent native speaker of the language, he understands C, but again is not disposed to reason with it according to R.

Despite the obvious difference, the two recipes have much in common. To substantiate our claim that the agent understands C, both Casalegno and I point to hermeneutically relevant capacities of the agent that do not entail a disposition to reason according to R. Casalegno focuses on the ability 'to use logically complex sentences to describe visually presented scenes', while I emphasize the ability to engage smoothly in a wide variety of normal conversational interactions with other speakers. These two abilities clearly do not exclude each other, for ordinary speakers have both. Even together, they do not entail a disposition to reason according to R. The observation that the unorthodox logicians in my counterexamples can still use logically complex sentences to describe visually presented scenes significantly strengthens the case for ascribing understanding of C to them.

It is worth reflecting on the contribution of logical constants to the visual-descriptive process in more detail. As a first approximation, we may regard vision at a given time as presenting the subject with a small finite model, in the sense of first-order model theory. The domain contains all and only the visually noticed objects. The model also specifies the extensions over the domain of the visually noticed properties and relations. The truth-value of any atomic sentence of a standard first-order language in the model can be visually determined, when the atomic predicates are interpreted as standing for visually noticed properties or relations, the names as denoting visually noticed objects, and so on. We may assume that the visual system assigns each visually noticed object a temporary name, so that a universal generalization is equivalent in the circumstances to a finite conjunction of its instances and an existential generalization to a finite disjunction of its instances. Thus every sentence of the language is equivalent in the circumstances to a truth-function of atomic sentences, so its truth-value can be mechanically determined from theirs.

Someone might object that so evaluating a sentence is an inferential process, of which Mary is by hypothesis incapable, but the objection involves at least two mistakes.

First, even if we characterize the process in terms of inference rules for the object-language, they would not include the particular rules that have been treated as paradigmatic in the debate. For example, evaluating a conjunction by evaluating its conjuncts corresponds to these four derivation rules in the object-language, reflecting the four lines of the truth-table for &:

$$A, B \qquad \vdash A \,\&\, B \tag{1}$$

$$A, \neg B \qquad \vdash \neg (A \,\&\, B) \tag{2}$$

$$\neg A, B \qquad \vdash \neg (A \,\&\, B) \tag{3}$$

$$\neg A, \neg B \qquad \vdash \neg (A \,\&\, B) \tag{4}$$

Of these, (1) is the standard introduction rule for &, but none corresponds to the standard bipartite elimination rule for & ($A \,\&\, B \vdash A$ and $A \,\&\, B \vdash B$).[2] The latter is the rule at stake in what is now Boghossian's preferred example of the inferentialist account. In the case of the material conditional, none of the four analogous rules corresponds to either the standard introduction rule (conditional proof) or the standard elimination rule (MP). The closest of them to MP is the rule $A, \neg B \vdash \neg(A \rightarrow B)$, but it yields MP only when combined with a non-trivial rule of contraposition.

Second, the objection unwarrantedly assumes that the process of evaluating complex sentences is at the personal level, the level at which Boghossian's normative question about the agent's entitlement to make basic inferences seems to arise, but the evaluation of a logically complex sentence on the basis of visual input can occur at the sub-personal level, hidden from the agent's introspective gaze.[3] We may assume that Casalegno had such sub-personal processes in mind when positing Mary's ability to use logically complex sentences to describe visually presented scenes.

In the light of these considerations, the evaluation process is better formalized in terms of moves from perceptually based evaluations of simpler sentences to perceptually based evaluations of more complex ones, rather than inferences directly from the former sentences to the latter. Thus (1)–(4) become (1#)–(4#), where '# $\triangleright A$' means that the sentence A is verified on the basis of input information #, '# $\triangleleft A$' means that A is falsified on the basis of #, and $\Rightarrow$ is a causal connection:

$$\# \triangleright A, \# \triangleright B \Rightarrow \# \triangleright A \,\&\, B \tag{1\#}$$

$$\# \triangleright A, \# \triangleleft B \Rightarrow \# \triangleleft A \,\&\, B \tag{2\#}$$

$$\# \triangleleft A, \# \triangleright B \Rightarrow \# \triangleleft A \,\&\, B \tag{3\#}$$

$$\# \triangleleft A, \# \triangleleft B \Rightarrow \# \triangleleft A \,\&\, B \tag{4\#}$$

The rules for the other logical constants can be modified likewise.

Of course, to make the model more realistic we must allow for uncertainty in the evaluation of simple sentences and its ramifications upwards for more complex ones. We must also allow for the painstaking step-by-step evaluation of complex sentences to be increasingly pre-empted by faster processes of pattern recognition calibrated by past experience. Pattern recognition may take over even where stepwise evaluation is blocked by uncertainty over simpler sentences. For example, as Casalegno (2002) convincingly objected to verificationist theories of meaning, one may be in a position to verify a disjunction without being in a position to verify any disjunct. One can sometimes see that a thing is red or orange while unable to see whether it is red and unable to see whether it is orange. One may be able to see that there are five, six, or seven people over there while unable to see exactly how many people are over there. The capacity for pattern recognition is also needed to evaluate quantified sentences when the visually presented scene is hard to articulate into discrete objects. One can see that there is no elephant in the room even though one is uncertain how to list the things in the room individually.

If we elaborate the case of Casalegno's Mary along such lines, we can respond to the mystification Boghossian expresses about it. He writes,

Confronted with a red box and blue book she is prepared to assert 'The box is red and the book is blue', but if you ask her right after she has asserted that conjunction (perhaps this has to take place in a different room), 'So, is the box red?' she might say 'No.' Similarly, for a question about the book.   (2012 [= Chapter 6, p. 101])

Mary's disability was not supposed to include a bad memory. She can see that the box is red, and later remember that it is red, so she will answer 'Yes' to the question 'Is the box red?', but she is not deducing the answer from the conjunction 'The box is red and the book is blue.'

Boghossian continues:

Having shown Mary a red box and gotten her to assert 'The box is red', and having shown her a blue book in a different room and gotten her to assert 'The book is blue', she then refuses to assent to 'The box is red and the book is blue', although, by hypothesis she is willing to assent to the compound sentence when she is shown the box and the book together.

(2012 [= Chapter 6, p. 101])

Mary's disability was not supposed to include a feeble imagination. Since she remembers the red box and the blue book, when queried on the conjunction she can visually imagine the two relevant objects together and apply her capacity to use logically complex sentences to describe visually presented scenes offline in the imagination to deliver the correct answer.[4] None of this requires her to use the rule of conjunction-introduction. The closest she may come is the causal connection (1#), but unlike the rule (1) of conjunction-introduction it permits no direct transition from conjuncts to conjunction. Mary's transition is mediated by visual input (#), perceived or imagined, and cannot take place without it. If you merely ask her to suppose one conjunct and then to suppose the other too, without showing her anything, at best she may visually imagine them holding in separate scenes, then imaginatively combine the scenes and assent to the conjunction on the assumption of the conjuncts, but that is a derived inference. In his paper, Boghossian stresses that the relevant inferences are underived. Moreover, Mary may fail in the task when the subject-matter of the sentences is more abstract and harder to imagine perceptually, so she is not responding primarily to the logical form of conjunction-introduction, which is the same irrespective of subject-matter. By normal standards of understanding, Mary's competence with 'and' in the description of visually presented scenes far outweighs her shakier performance in logic tests.[5]

Similar points apply to my example of Simon, who accepts a conjunction while rejecting a conjunct, when he finds the latter false but another conjunct borderline. His descriptions of visually perceived, remembered, or imagined scenes are normal when none of the relevant atomic sentences looks borderline. His deviant patterns of response in the presence of borderline cases reflect a deviant attitude to vagueness, not a deviant understanding of 'and'.

Boghossian makes much of the origin of Simon's responses to borderline cases in his deviant theorizing about vagueness, as I characterized him. Boghossian counts theoretically mediated inferences as derived, and insists that an inferentialist account of understanding should be given at the level of underived inferences. He writes, 'Simon's deviant inferences, however, are obviously highly derived', and that the inferentialist 'would look, rather, to the rules that Simon found primitively compelling, before engaging in all of that bad theorizing' (2012 [= Chapter 6, p. 104]). Presumably, however, what really matters is not whether Simon once found conjunction-elimination primitively compelling, but whether he still does. Boghossian and I agree in not wanting to exclude by mere fiat the possibility that Simon no longer means what he once did by 'and'. If Simon still finds conjunction-elimination primitively compelling, his disposition to apply the rule remains, even if its manifestations are inhibited by more reflective dispositions that result from his bad theorizing.

But why suppose that Simon still finds conjunction-elimination primitively compelling? Indeed, why suppose that he ever did? Boghossian has not shown that most or all normal speakers of a natural language find conjunction-elimination primitively compelling. Perhaps we start more like Casalegno's Mary and our more purely logical inferential abilities develop later, mediated by education and theory. In the psychology of reasoning, that is not a far-fetched hypothesis. Boghossian quotes Christopher Peacocke's comment on the possession-condition for the concept of conjunction, and endorses it as a gloss on an inferential-role theory:

On any theory, this possession-condition will entail that thinkers must find the transition from A and B to A compelling, and must do so without relying on any background information.

(Peacocke 2004: 172)

A pervasive effect in the psychology of reasoning is that logically unsophisticated subjects tend to do far better on problems whose subject-matter is familiar and interesting to them than on problems whose subject-matter is unfamiliar and uninteresting, even though the underlying logical structure is exactly the same. It is not obvious that such thinkers make the transition from conjunction to conjunct 'without relying on any background information', however redundant that information in principle. Of course, the background information might serve to motivate the thinker to try harder to solve the problem, rather than providing extra premises for their solution, but how is such an intellectual struggle needed for us to understand elementary sentences of our native language?

Inferentialists often seem unaware of how far their theory is hostage to developments in the psychology of reasoning. In particular, there is evidence for a distinction between two modes of reasoning in humans, known as system 1 and system 2. System 1 is primitive, unreflective, fast, largely independent in effectiveness of individual differences in working memory and general intelligence, comparatively unresponsive to formal education, sensitive to associations with the immediate pragmatic context, and comparatively insensitive to abstract structure. System 2 is more sophisticated, reflective, slow, correlated in effectiveness with individual differences in working memory and general intelligence, comparatively responsive to formal education, sensitive to abstract structure, and comparatively insensitive to associations with the immediate pragmatic context.[6] Within this typology, competence with one's native language belongs mainly to system 1, whereas competence with abstract rules of deductive logic belongs mainly to system 2. That gives reason to doubt inferentialist accounts, which ground competence with one's native language in competence with abstract rules of deductive logic. Even principles such as (1#)–(4#) may well overstate the formal nature of the process of describing a visually presented scene.

Boghossian anyway slightly misrepresents the relevance of Simon to an inferentialist account of linguistic competence with conjunction, by focusing on 'Simon's deviant inferences'. What is really at issue is Simon's *unwillingness* to make *non-deviant* inferences, instances of conjunction-elimination. When Boghossian requires non-derivativeness of the disposition to perform conjunction-elimination as necessary for understanding 'and', he merely helps my counterexample by making it harder, not easier, for Simon to satisfy the condition.

Suppose that, despite Boghossian's doubts, Simon is indeed linguistically competent with 'and', as manifested by his ability to use it in both smooth conversational interactions and correct descriptions of visually presented scenes. What Boghossian then needs to argue is that Simon must still have the relevant disposition to accept instances of conjunction-elimination, masked by his theoretical dispositions to the contrary. Of course, Simon accepts some such instances, for example, when he regards the conjuncts as non-borderline. We may suppose that such 'background information' plays a positive role in his underlying reasoning, rather than merely its absence constituting an external higher-level defeater. Before proceeding to evaluate a complex sentence classically, the system requires an 'all clear' on its atomic sentential constituents. Once we fully appreciate what is going on in the example, we have no need to postulate a masked disposition to apply conjunction-elimination even in borderline cases in order to see Simon as linguistically competent with 'and' on its usual meaning. Thus the counterexample stands.

3. Is Conjunction-Elimination Enough?

Some remarks are needed on Boghossian's choice of conjunction-elimination for the rule at issue in his preferred example of the inferentialist account. In earlier work (up to Boghossian 2003a [= Chapter 2]) he used MP, but then retreated to conjunction-elimination when the inferentialist account for MP came under pressure. I objected (2011 [= Chapter 5]) that if the inferentialist story is defensible only for conjunction-elimination and perhaps a few other rules, from which most of the standard rules of first-order logic cannot be recovered, then it is too restricted to be of much use in explaining our entitlement to reason according to basic principles of logic. Boghossian replies:

As I am thinking about it, refuting the sceptical threat involves showing that it is possible to get our entitlement to *some* logical rules off the ground, even if the means by which that is accomplished may not generalize to all the logical rules to which we feel intuitively entitled.

(2012 [= Chapter 6, p. 96])

Presenting a story that does not generalize beyond one or two rules may indeed help us locate an unwarranted premise or step of reasoning in a particular sceptical argument. Moreover, if the nature of our entitlement to reason according to basic rules of logic varies radically from one rule to another, then such rule-specific stories are all that we can get.

On present evidence, however, the epistemology of logic is unlikely to be so radically heterogeneous. For example, the correct account (whatever it is) of what it takes to understand conjunction and to be entitled to use its introduction and elimination rules probably resembles the correct account (whatever it is) of what it takes to understand disjunction and to be entitled to use its introduction and elimination rules. Call a rule R for a logical constant C *inferentialist* just if a disposition to reason according to R is necessary for understanding C. If we have examples to show that most of the basic rules of logic are non-inferentialist, then the presumption is that the remaining few rules are non-inferentialist too, even if less obviously so, and moreover that some other theory explains how we are entitled to reason according to the former rules and the explanation generalizes to the latter rules too. Thus, even if we were to bracket the direct counterexamples to Boghossian's explanation of our entitlement to conjunction-elimination, its failure to generalize to other basic rules would be evidence that it is false even of conjunction-elimination.

Boghossian's considerations do not defeat the presumption in favour of a comparatively homogeneous epistemology of logic. His perplexity at the examples of Mary and Simon depends on no special feature of conjunction-elimination except its extreme obviousness. Many other basic rules, including MP, are almost equally obvious. Unfortunately, the long history of human error shows denying the obvious to be not just possible but common, without semantic change. For example, Simon is less irrational than many Holocaust deniers.

4. Semantic Integration

Boghossian treats Mary as not meaning by 'and' what we mean. He does not say whether she means something else by 'and'—if so, what is that other meaning?—or whether she means nothing at all by it. He treats Simon as meaning something different by 'and' from what we mean, but again does not say what that other meaning is. Of course, Simon believes a theory on which 'and' has a certain Kleene-inspired three-valued truth-table, but we cannot take that deviant theory even as a correct account of what *he* means by 'and' unless we accept the non-classical semantic framework within which it is articulated. Not every false theory of actual meanings is a true theory of possible meanings.

Boghossian does not characterize differences in meaning in terms of the reasonably clear standards of differences in reference, or intension, or character. Instead, he characterizes them as differences in which *concept* is expressed. He treats that as a relevantly clear standard, for to Casalegno's complaint that he has 'simply no idea of what the relevant criterion might be like' for whether a rule is constitutive of a logical concept (2004: 409), Boghossian responds:

We've already been told *what* we are looking for. We are looking for those conditions that are necessary for having concept C. If we are working within an inferential framework, we are asking which inference rules are necessary for possessing concept C.

(2012 [= Chapter 6, p. 107])

That answer is unsatisfying, for inferentialists use the word 'concept' as an inadequately constrained technical term. Until inferentialists tell us what criterion they intend for whether a rule is constitutive of a 'concept', it is hard for us to know what they mean by 'concept'. Boghossian seems to think that we already know what is meant, for in his concluding sentence he says that one can tell whether there has been a change of concept in 'the usual way, clearly in use both by Casalegno and by Williamson—via intuitive judgments about possible cases' (2012 [= Chapter 6, p. 107]), but the judgments that Casalegno and I made about the cases of Mary and Simon respectively concerned primarily sameness of meaning (by normal standards) rather than sameness of 'concept'. Of course, if the inferentialist stipulatively ties sameness of 'concept' to sameness of meaning (by normal standards), at least for verbally expressed 'concepts', then we are in no position to complain. However, when it is objected that characters like Mary and Simon are not normally treated as meaning something different by the word 'and', Boghossian and other defenders of an inferentialist account of 'and' typically take their stand on the claim that such characters have a different *concept* of conjunction.[7] They seem unwilling for their claims to be judged by the standard of sameness of linguistic meaning. Far from clarifying the issue, this switch to a more theoretical vocabulary obscures it.

The problem is particularly acute for Boghossian, because he does not commit himself to inferentialism in general. Rather, he assumes only an inferentialist account of what it takes to understand the logical constants, in order to meet a specific difficulty in the epistemology of reasoning, but logical constants do not seem anomalous when compared with other words with respect to the standards for meaning change. If the standard for meaning change in most non-logical words is non-inferentialist, is it not ad hoc to invoke an inferentialist standard when it comes to logical words?

The compositionality of meaning exerts strong pressure towards a homogeneous account of meaning, and therefore of meaning change. In general, if we characterize the meaning of an expression E_1 in one semantic framework, and the meaning of another expression E_2 in a different framework, within what framework are we to explain how those meanings combine in the meaning of a sentence that puts E_1 and E_2 together? For example, suppose that we treat the meaning of a sentence as a truth-condition, but the meaning of the logical constant 'and' as a norm of inference. Since the result of conjoining a pair of sentences with 'and' is another sentence, that norm of inference must somehow map pairs of truth-conditions to truth-conditions, but a norm of inference is the wrong sort of thing to operate like that on truth-conditions. Whatever its advantages elsewhere, a pick'n mix strategy is not obviously coherent in semantics, where a bit of inferentialism here and a bit of some other theory there may not gel. We should therefore expect a rather homogeneous standard for meaning change, applicable to logical and non-logical expressions alike.

Speakers are often wildly idiosyncratic in what they accept and reject while still using their words with their usual public senses. They refuse to comply with philosophers' expectations of them. Why should Casalegno's Mary and my Simon be any different?[8]

Notes

1. [This chapter was originally published as 'Boghossian and Casalegno on Understanding and Inference', *dialectica*, 66, 2 (2012): 237–47, as a reply to the previous chapter, in a special issue of the journal dedicated to the memory of the Milan philosopher Paolo Casalegno, entitled 'Paolo Casalegno's Good Points', edited by Elisa Paganini. Casalegno (1952–2009) taught at the University of Milan and was one of the leading Italian analytic philosophers of his generation.]

2. In systems of natural deduction, the conjunction-introduction rule often takes the form: for any sets Γ and Δ of formulas, if $\Gamma \vdash A$ and $\Delta \vdash B$ then $\Gamma \cup \Delta \vdash A \& B$; similarly for the other rules. This does not affect the argument in the text.

3. The evaluation process cannot be confined to a purely visual module, since it is sensitive to background information from non-visual sources.

4. The epistemological significance of our capacity to transfer cognitive skills honed online in perception to offline applications in the imagination is discussed extensively in Williamson (2007a: 134–207).

5. See Kroedel (2012) for more discussion of the descriptive, non-inferential use of logical constants.

6. See Evans and Over (2004: 7–10) for remarks on the distinction between system 1 and system 2.

7. In Williamson (2007a) and elsewhere I emphasize the relevance here of the social determination of meaning. Boghossian (2012 [=Chapter 6]) says that he prefers an idiolectic conception of meaning, but does not try to argue for one.

8. It is sometimes said that the greatest tribute one philosopher can pay another is disagreement, often in practice by rejecting their premises as false and their arguments as invalid. Here I pay Paolo Casalegno only the more banal tribute of agreement. I always learnt from talking with him (for instance, Williamson 2007a: 107–9 responds to a question he once asked me). His sober, self-critical acumen is sorely missed. I also thank Paul Boghossian and members of the audience at the 2011 Milan workshop in memory of Paolo for valuable discussion.

8

How Deep is the Distinction between A Priori and A Posteriori Knowledge?[1]

Timothy Williamson

1

The distinction between a priori and a posteriori knowledge can be introduced the bottom-up way, by examples. I know a posteriori whether it is sunny. I know a priori that if it is sunny then it is sunny. Such examples are projectible. We learn from them how to go on in the same way, achieving fair levels of agreement in classifying new cases without collusion. Of course, as well as clear cases on each side there are unclear cases, which elicit uncertainty or disagreement when we try to classify them as a priori or as a posteriori. But virtually all useful distinctions are like that. If we want to be more precise, we can stipulate a sharper boundary with the clear cases of the a priori on one side and the clear cases of the a posteriori on the other. How could such a distinction be problematic? If some philosopher's theory puts a clear case on the wrong side of the line, surely that is a problem for the theory, not for the distinction.

The risk for the bottom-up method of introduction is that it may make a distinction of no special significance. On that scenario, our classifications follow similarities and differences that, although genuine, are largely superficial, like a taxonomy of plants and animals based only on colour. If so, epistemologists would do better to avoid the distinction between the a priori and the a posteriori in their theorizing, because it distracts them from deeper similarities and differences.

The alternative method of introduction is top-down, by a direct statement of the difference between the a priori and the a posteriori in epistemologically significant theoretical terms. For instance: a priori knowledge is independent of experience; a posteriori knowledge depends on experience. The risk for the top-down method is that it may turn out that everything is on the same side of the theoretically drawn line. If Quine (1951) is right, all knowledge depends at least indirectly on experience. As with the risk for the bottom-up method, that would make the distinction epistemologically useless, but for a different reason.

Friends of the distinction typically assume that the bottom-up and top-down methods yield equivalent results and so are mutually supporting, each averting the

Debating the A Priori. Paul Boghossian and Timothy Williamson, Oxford University Press (2020).
© Paul Boghossian and Timothy Williamson.
DOI: 10.1093/oso/9780198851707.001.0001

risk to the other. Of course, the risk here is that the two methods may have incompatible results. If so, assuming otherwise leads us into epistemological error.

But are any of the risks realized? In this chapter I will suggest two ways in which reliance on a distinction between the a priori and the a posteriori does more harm than good in epistemology. Neither of them is exactly Quine's. As a framework for discussion, I first sketch the top-down distinction as contemporary philosophers tend to conceive it.

2

The distinction between the a priori and the a posteriori is primarily a classification of specific ways of knowing.[2] A way of knowing is a priori if and only if it is independent of experience. It is a posteriori if and only if it depends on experience. The relevant senses of 'independent' and 'experience' are discussed later. Every specific way of knowing is either a priori or a posteriori, and not both. One knows p a priori if and only if one knows p in an a priori way. One knows p a posteriori if and only if one knows p in an a posteriori way. Thus if one knows p, one knows it either a priori or a posteriori.

One may know p both a priori and a posteriori, if one knows it in several ways, some a priori, some a posteriori. Tradition excluded that case on the grounds that only necessities (truths that could not have been otherwise) are known a priori whereas only contingencies (truths that could have been otherwise) are known a posteriori. But that was a mistake. Here is a simple counterexample. Suppose that Mary is good at mathematics but bad at geography, while John is bad at mathematics but good at geography. Both of them can perform elementary deductions. Mary knows a priori by the usual standards that $289 + 365 = 654$ and does not know at all that there are cable cars in Switzerland. John knows a posteriori by the usual standards that there are cable cars in Switzerland but does not know at all that $289 + 365 = 654$. From the premise that $289 + 365 = 654$, Mary competently deduces the disjunctive conclusion that either $289 + 365 = 654$ or there are cable cars in Switzerland (since a disjunction follows from either disjunct), and thereby comes to know the disjunction a priori by the usual standards, since the logical deduction introduces no dependence on experience. Meanwhile, from the premise that there are cable cars in Switzerland, John competently deduces the same disjunctive conclusion, and thereby comes to know it a posteriori by the usual standards, for although the deduction itself is a priori, his knowledge of the conclusion inherits the dependence on experience of his knowledge of the premise. Thus John and Mary know the same disjunctive truth, but Mary knows it a priori while John knows it a posteriori. Since the disjunction that either $289 + 365 = 654$ or there are cable cars in Switzerland inherits necessity from its first disjunct, John knows a necessary truth a posteriori.

The primary distinction between ways of knowing can be used to effect a secondary classification of things known. A truth p is a priori if and only if p can be known a priori. If we stipulate analogously that p is a posteriori if and only if p can be known a posteriori, then a truth may be both a priori and a posteriori, as with the disjunction that either $289 + 365 = 654$ or there are cable cars in Switzerland.

Alternatively, if we stipulate that a truth is a posteriori if and only if it is not a priori, then a truth that cannot be known a posteriori counts as a posteriori if it also cannot be known a priori. There is no presumption that a truth can be known at all. Perhaps the best fit to current practice with the term is to stipulate that a truth is a posteriori if and only if it can be known a posteriori but cannot be known a priori. Even this way of drawing the distinction is subject to Kripke's forceful case (1980) that there are both contingent a priori truths and necessary a posteriori ones. Although some philosophers reject Kripke's arguments, even they now usually accept the burden of proof to show why the epistemological distinction between the a priori and the a posteriori should coincide with the metaphysical distinction between the necessary and the contingent.

To go further, we must clarify the terms 'independent' and 'experience'. One issue is that even paradigms of a priori knowledge depend in a sense on experience. For example, we supposedly know a priori that if it is sunny then it is sunny. But if our community had no direct or indirect experience of the sun or sunny weather, how could we understand what it is to be sunny, as we must if we are so much as to entertain the thought that it is sunny, let alone know that it is so?

The standard response is to distinguish between two roles that experience plays in cognition, one *evidential*, the other *enabling*. Experience is held to play an evidential role in our perceptual knowledge that it is sunny, but a merely enabling role in our knowledge that if it is sunny then it is sunny: we needed it only to acquire the concept *sunny* in the first place, not once we had done so to determine whether it currently applies. Experience provides our evidence that it is sunny, but not our evidence that if it is sunny then it is sunny; it merely enables us to raise the question. The idea is that an a priori way of knowing may depend on experience in its enabling role but must not depend on experience in its evidential role.

Another issue is how widely to apply the term 'experience'. It is mainly associated with 'outer' experience, involving perception by the usual five senses, but why should it exclude 'inner' experience, involving introspection or reflection? After all, one's knowledge that one is in pain is presumably a posteriori, even though the experience on which it depends is inner. Excluding inner experience by mere stipulation, without reference to any deeper epistemological difference, is liable to make the distinction between a priori and a posteriori knowledge epistemologically superficial. Inner and outer experience will therefore provisionally be treated on an equal footing.

One might worry that if inner experience is included, our experience of reflecting on the proposition that if it is sunny then it is sunny will play an evidential role in our knowledge that if it is sunny then it is sunny, and that Mary's experience of calculating that 289 + 365 = 654, on paper or in her head, will play an evidential role in her knowledge that 289 + 365 = 654. Presumably, the response is that the role is purely enabling. The relevant evidence is not the psychological process of reflecting or calculating, but rather in some sense the non-psychological logical or mathematical facts to which that process enables one to have access.

On further thought, however, that response causes more problems than it solves. For what prevents it from generalizing to outer experience? For example, part of the evidence that a massive comet or asteroid collided with the Earth about 250 million years ago is said to be that certain sediment samples from China and Japan contain

certain clusters of carbon atoms. That those samples contained those clusters of atoms is a non-psychological fact. Of course, in some sense scientists' outer experience played a role in their access to the fact. But, by analogy with the logical and mathematical cases, the relevant evidence is not the psychological process of undergoing those outer experiences, but rather the non-psychological physical facts to which that process enables us to have access. The role of the outer experience is purely enabling, not evidential. If so, what would usually be regarded as paradigm cases of a posteriori knowledge risk reclassification as a priori.

The threat is not confined to theoretical knowledge in the natural sciences. Even for everyday observational knowledge, it is a highly controversial move to put the psychological process of undergoing the outer experience into the content of the perceptual evidence we thereby gain. What we observe is typically a non-psychological fact about our external environment, not a psychological fact about ourselves.

One obstacle to resolving the problem is the unclarity of the terms 'experience' and 'evidence' as many philosophers use them. The top-down way of introducing the distinction between the a priori and the a posteriori promises to put it on a firm theoretical footing, but in practice relies on other terms (such as 'experience' and 'evidence') understood at least partly bottom-up, through examples and prototypes. Although bottom-up understanding often serves us well enough, in the present case it leaves us puzzled all too soon.

Of course, many attempts have been made to explicate the a priori–a posteriori distinction by introducing new theoretical apparatus. My aim here is not to discuss those attempts separately. Instead, I will address the distinctions more directly, by comparing what would usually be regarded as a clear case of a priori knowledge with what would usually be regarded as a clear case of a posteriori knowledge. I will argue that the epistemological differences between the two cases are more superficial than they first appear. The conclusion is not that the cases are borderline. I do not deny that they really are clear cases of a priori and a posteriori knowledge, respectively, at least by bottom-up standards. In any case, showing that a distinction has borderline cases does not show that it is unhelpful for theoretical purposes. Rather, the appropriate conclusion is that the a priori–a posteriori distinction does not cut at the epistemological joints.

An analogy may be helpful with an argument of the same kind about a political distinction. If one aims to criticize the distinction between liberal and non-liberal policies, one achieves little by producing examples of policies that are neither clearly liberal nor clearly non-liberal. Every useful political distinction has borderline cases. But if one can produce an example of a clearly liberal policy that is politically only superficially different from a clearly non-liberal policy, then one has gone some way towards showing that the liberal–non-liberal distinction does not cut at the political joints.[3]

3

Here are two truths:

(1)   All crimson things are red.
(2)   All recent volumes of *Who's Who* are red.

On the standard view, normal cases of knowledge of (1) are clearly a priori, because by definition crimson is just a specific type of red, whereas normal cases of knowledge of (2) are clearly a posteriori, because it takes direct or indirect experience of recent volumes of the British work of reference *Who's Who* to determine their colour (that is, the predominant colour of their official cover). But let us describe two cases in more detail.

Suppose that Norman acquires the words 'crimson' and 'red' independently of each other, by ostensive means. He learns 'crimson' by being shown samples to which it applies and samples to which it does not apply, and told which are which. He learns 'red' in a parallel but causally independent way. He is not taught any rule like (1), connecting 'crimson' and 'red'. Through practice and feedback, he becomes very skilful in judging by eye whether something is crimson, and whether something is red. Now Norman is asked whether (1) holds. He has not previously considered any such question. Nevertheless, he can quite easily come to know (1), without looking at any crimson things to check whether they are red, or even remembering any crimson things to check whether they were red, or making any other new exercise of perception or memory of particular coloured things. Rather, he assents to (1) after brief reflection on the colours crimson and red, along something like the following lines. First, Norman uses his skill in making visual judgments with 'crimson' to visually imagine a sample of crimson. Then he uses his skill in making visual judgments with 'red' to judge, within the imaginative supposition, 'It is red.' This involves a general human capacity to transpose 'online' cognitive skills originally developed in perception into corresponding 'offline' cognitive skills subsequently applied in imagination. That capacity is essential to much of our thinking, for instance when we reflectively assess conditionals in making contingency plans.[4] No episodic memories of prior experiences, for example of crimson things, play any role. As a result of the process, Norman accepts (1). Since his performance was sufficiently skilful, background conditions were normal, and so on, he thereby comes to know (1).

Naturally, that broad-brush description neglects many issues. For instance, what prevents Norman from imagining a peripheral shade of crimson? If one shade of crimson is red, it does not follow that all are. The relevant cognitive skills must be taken to include sensitivity to such matters. If normal speakers associate colour terms with central prototypes, as many psychologists believe, their use in the imaginative exercise may enhance its reliability. The proximity in colour space of prototypical crimson to prototypical red is one indicator, but does not suffice by itself, since it does not discriminate between 'All crimson things are red' (true) and 'All red things are crimson' (false). Various cognitive mechanisms can be postulated to do the job. We need not fill in the details, since for present purposes what matters is the overall picture. So far, we may accept it as a sketch of the cognitive processes underlying Norman's a priori knowledge of (1).

Now compare the case of (2). Norman is as already described. He learns the complex phrase 'recent volumes of *Who's Who*' by learning 'recent', 'volume', '*Who's Who*', and so on. He is not taught any rule like (2), connecting 'recent volume of *Who's Who*' and 'red'. Through practice and feedback, he becomes very skilful in judging by eye whether something is a recent volume of *Who's Who* (by reading the title), and whether something is red. Now Norman is asked whether (2) holds. He has not previously considered any such question. Nevertheless, he can quite easily come to know (2), without looking at any recent volumes of *Who's Who* to check whether they are red, or even remembering any recent volumes of *Who's Who* to check whether they were red, or any other new exercise of perception or memory. Rather, he assents to (2) after brief reflection along something like the following lines. First, Norman uses his skill in making visual judgments with a 'recent volume of *Who's Who*' to visually imagine a recent volume of *Who's Who*. Then he uses his skill in making visual judgments with 'red' to judge, within the imaginative supposition, 'It is red.' This involves the same general human capacity as before to transpose 'online' cognitive skills originally developed in perception into corresponding 'offline' cognitive skills subsequently applied in imagination. No episodic memories of prior experiences, for example of recent volumes of *Who's Who*, play any role. As a result of the process, Norman accepts (2). Since his performance was sufficiently skilful, background conditions were normal, and so on, he thereby comes to know (2).

As before, the broad-brush description neglects many issues. For instance, what prevents Norman from imagining an untypical recent volume of *Who's Who*? If one recent volume of *Who's Who* is red, it does not follow that all are. The relevant cognitive skills must be taken to include sensitivity to such matters. As before, Norman must use his visual recognitional capacities offline in ways that respect untypical as well as typical cases. We may accept that as a sketch of the cognitive processes underlying Norman's a posteriori knowledge of (2).

The problem is obvious. As characterized earlier, the cognitive processes underlying Norman's clearly a priori knowledge of (1) and his clearly a posteriori knowledge of (2) are almost exactly similar. If so, how can there be a deep epistemological difference between them? But if there is none, then the a priori–a posteriori distinction is epistemologically shallow.

One response is to argue that at least one of the cases has been mislocated in relation to the a priori–a posteriori boundary. Perhaps Norman's knowledge of (1) is really a posteriori, or his knowledge of (2) is really a priori (although presumably we did not make both mistakes). The risks of such a strategy are also obvious. If we reclassify Norman as knowing (1) a posteriori, we may have to do the same for all or most supposed cases of a priori knowledge, perhaps even of basic principles in logic and mathematics (such as standard axioms of set theory). For Norman's knowledge of (1) did not initially seem atypical as a supposed case of a priori knowledge. On the other hand, if we reclassify Norman as knowing (2) a priori, we may still lose the distinction between a priori disciplines such as logic and mathematics and a posteriori disciplines such as physics and geography. Either way, we end up with an a priori–a posteriori distinction that cannot do much theoretical work.

Another response to the descriptions of how Norman knows (1) and (2) is more sceptical: it may be suggested that if the cognitive processes are really as described, then they are too unreliable to constitute genuine knowledge at all. However, this option is also unpromising for friends of the a priori–a posteriori distinction, for at least two reasons. First, it imposes an idealized epistemological standard for knowledge that human cognition cannot be expected to meet. None of our cognitive faculties is even close to being globally infallible. More local forms of reliability may suffice for knowledge; sceptics have not shown otherwise. Second, even if we are sceptical about knowledge in such cases, we should still assign belief in (1) and (2) some other sort of positive epistemic status, such as reasonableness, to which the a priori–a posteriori distinction should still apply in some form. Norman's a priori reasonable belief in (1) and his a posteriori reasonable belief in (2) could still be used in a similar way to argue against the depth of the new distinction. For purposes of argument, we may as well accept that Norman knows (1) and (2).

In the terms used in Section 2, the question is whether Norman's experience plays an evidential or a merely enabling role in his knowledge of (1) and (2). Even in the case of (1), the role seems more than purely enabling. Consider Norbert, an otherwise competent native speaker of English who acquired the words 'crimson' and 'red' as colour terms in a fairly ordinary way, but has not had very much practice with feedback at classifying visually presented samples as 'crimson' or 'not crimson'. He usually makes the right calls when applying 'crimson' as well as 'red' online. By normal standards he is linguistically competent with both words. He grasps proposition (1). However, his inexperience with 'crimson' makes him less skilful than Norman in imagining a crimson sample. As a result, Norbert's reflection on whether crimson things are red comes to no definite conclusion, and he fails to know (1). Thus Norman's past experience did more than enable him to grasp proposition (1). It honed and calibrated his skills in applying the terms 'crimson' and 'red' to the point where he could carry out the imaginative exercise successfully. If Norman's knowledge of (1), a fortiori it also plays a more than purely enabling role in his knowledge of (2).[5]

If the role of Norman's experience in his knowledge of (1) is more than purely enabling, is it strictly evidential? One interpretation of the example is that, although Norman's knowledge of (1) does not depend on episodic memory, and he may even lack all episodic memory of any relevant particular colour experiences, he nevertheless retains from such experiences generic factual memories of what crimson things look like and of what red things look like, on which his knowledge of (1) depends. By contrast, Norbert fails to know (1) because his generic memories of what crimson things look like and of what red things look like are insufficiently clear. On this interpretation, Norman's colour experience plays an evidential role in his knowledge of (1), thereby making that knowledge a posteriori. But we have already seen that such reclassification is a risky strategy for defenders of the a priori–a posteriori distinction. Instead, it may be proposed, although colour experience can play an evidential role in a posteriori knowledge of what crimson things look like, and so indirectly in a posteriori knowledge of (1), we need not develop the example that way. The only residue of Norman's colour experience active in his knowledge of (1) may be his skill in recognizing and imagining colours.[6] Such a role for experience, it may be held, is less than strictly evidential. Let us provisionally interpret the example the latter way. In Section 5 we will reconsider, but reject, the idea that even supposed paradigms of a priori knowledge are really a posteriori.

Norman's knowledge of (2) can be envisaged in parallel to his knowledge of (1) as just envisaged. Although experience of recent volumes of *Who's Who* can play an evidential role in a posteriori knowledge of what such volumes look like, and so indirectly in a posteriori knowledge of (2), that is not what goes on with Norman.

The only residue of his experience of recent volumes of *Who's Who* active in his knowledge of (2) is his skill in recognizing and imagining such volumes. That role for experience is less than strictly evidential. Nor does Norman's present experience play any more of an evidential role in his knowledge of (2) than it does in his knowledge of (1).

On this showing, the role of experience in both cases is more than purely enabling but less than strictly evidential. This reinforces a suspicion raised in Section 2, that talk of 'experience' and 'evidence' does little to help us apply the a priori–a posteriori distinction top-down. Appeals to 'observation' as the hallmark of a posteriori knowledge hardly do better, for they leave us with the question: in what way does Norman's knowledge of (2) involve observation while his knowledge of (1) does not?

The most salient difference between Norman's knowledge of (2) and his knowledge of (1) is that (2) is contingent while (1) is necessary. That difference may be what inspires the idea that there must be a deep difference in his knowledge of them. But Kripke taught us not to read the epistemology of a truth off its metaphysical status. Of course, these two propositions do differ epistemologically:

(N1)   It is necessary that crimson things are red.
(N2)   It is necessary that recent volumes of *Who's Who* are red.

For (N1) is a known truth, while (N2) is false, so not known, indeed presumably impossible, so unknowable. But an epistemological difference between (N1) and (N2) does not imply any epistemological difference between (1) and (2). In general, knowing a necessary truth does not imply knowing that it is necessary. For example, John in Section 2 knew that either $289 + 365 = 654$ or there are cable cars in Switzerland by knowing that there are cable cars in Switzerland, without knowing that $289 + 365 = 654$; he did not know that it is necessary that either $289 + 365 = 654$ or there are cable cars in Switzerland, even though it is indeed necessary. Likewise, Norman may know (1) without knowing (N1). He may be a sceptic about necessity, or never even entertain modal questions. In particular, Norman can know (1) without knowing (N1) and deducing (1) from it. Indeed, the idea that a precondition of knowing a necessary truth is knowing that it is necessary generates an infinite regress. For since (N1) is itself necessary, a precondition of knowing (N1) would be knowing (NN1), and so on ad infinitum:

(NN1)   It is necessary that it is necessary that crimson things are red.

A subtler attempt to extract epistemological significance from the difference in modal status between (1) and (2) might exploit the modal nature of some proposed constraints on knowledge, such as various versions of reliability, sensitivity, and safety, many of which imply that one knows p only if falsely believing p is in some sense not too live a possibility.[7] For since (1) is necessary, false belief in (1) is impossible, whereas false belief in (2) is possible, although not actual. Of course, since Norman is granted to know both (1) and (2), he satisfies any modal necessary condition for knowledge with respect to both truths. However, he might still be *more* reliable, or sensitive, or safe, with respect to (1) than to (2). But how could any such contrast make the difference between a priori and a posteriori knowledge? No constraint that all necessary truths trivially satisfy explains why some of them are known a priori, others only a posteriori.

To consider the point more fully, imagine Gull, who believes whatever his guru tells him. The guru tosses a coin to decide whether to assert to Gull Fermat's Last Theorem (FLT), if it comes up heads, or its negation ($\neg$FLT), if it comes up tails. The coin comes up heads, and on the guru's testimony Gull obediently believes FLT, a necessary truth. It would generally be agreed that Gull does not know FLT. Indeed, in the nontechnical senses of the terms, Gull's belief in FLT does not look particularly reliable, or safe, or sensitive to the facts. If the coin had come up tails, Gull would have wound up believing the necessary falsehood $\neg$FLT instead, in a parallel way. Any version of a reliability, sensitivity, or safety condition on knowledge non-trivially applicable to knowledge of a necessary truth p will concern possibilities of false belief in other propositions suitably related to p, not just of false belief in p itself. On such a dimension, we have no reason to expect Norman's knowledge of (1) to do better than his knowledge of (2). He may be just as prone to error in his judgments of colour inclusion as in his judgments of the colours of types of book; the distribution of errors in modal space may be much the same in the two cases. Once again, the difference in modal status between (1) and (2) is not what matters epistemologically.

The main effect of the modal difference between (1) and (2) may be to distract us from the epistemological similarity. The necessity of (1) prompts us to assimilate Norman's knowledge of (1) to stereotypes of a priori knowledge, which we can vaguely do because the role of experience is not strictly evidential. The contingency of (2) prompts us to assimilate his knowledge of (2) to stereotypes of a posteriori knowledge, which we can vaguely do because the role of experience is not purely enabling. Even having accepted Kripke's examples of the contingent a priori and the necessary a posteriori, we may still operate on the default assumptions that knowledge of necessary truths is a priori and that knowledge of contingent ones is a posteriori. Unlike Kripke's, cases such as Norman's may trigger nothing to overturn either default, especially when they are considered separately, so by default we confidently classify knowledge of the necessary truth as a priori and knowledge of the contingent one as a posteriori, without noticing that there is no significant *epistemological* difference between them. We can use the qualifiers 'a priori' and 'a posteriori' that way if we like, but then we should not expect them to do much work in epistemology.

4

How widespread is the problem? It might be argued that although the a priori–a posteriori distinction does not mark any deep difference between Norman's knowledge of (1) and his knowledge of (2), the example is a special case, and that the distinction marks a deep difference in a wide range of other cases. A priori knowledge of logic and mathematics may be contrasted with Norman's knowledge of (1), and a posteriori knowledge by direct observation, preserved by memory, transmitted by testimony and extended by deductive, inductive, and abductive reasoning may be contrasted with his knowledge of (2). Thus, it might be claimed, the a priori–a posteriori distinction can still do plenty of useful work in epistemology after all.

I will argue that such an attitude is much too complacent. Many cases of a priori knowledge are relevantly similar to Norman's knowledge of (1), and many cases of a posteriori knowledge are relevantly similar to his knowledge of (2). Moreover, although epistemologists have become accustomed to treating the category of a priori knowledge as problematic, we still tend to treat the category of a posteriori knowledge as epistemologically explanatory. This attitude is particularly prevalent amongst those who deny that there is a priori knowledge. They think that it is clear enough how a posteriori knowledge works, but hopelessly obscure how a priori knowledge could work.[8] Once we appreciate how problematic the distinction itself is, we may rid ourselves of the illusion that we can understand what is going on in a case of knowledge by classifying it as a posteriori. The usual stereotype of a posteriori knowledge is just as epistemologically useless as the usual stereotype of a priori knowledge.

I will not discuss in detail how wide a range of other a posteriori knowledge resembles Norman's knowledge of (2). Since there is nothing very special about (2), it is fairly clear that if cognitive skills learnt online but applied offline can generate a posteriori knowledge of (2), without experience playing a strictly evidential role, then they can do likewise for many other truths. Examples include some knowledge of physical and practical possibility and of counterfactual conditionals.

In the case of (2), colour inclusions may look special. How much other putatively a priori knowledge resembles Norman's knowledge of (1)? He uses nothing like the formal proofs we associate with mathematical knowledge. A closer comparison is with knowledge of mathematical axioms, in particular with standard axioms of set theory (such as those of Zermelo–Fraenkel set theory).[9]

We may take as a typical example the Power Set Axiom, which says that every set has a power set, the set of all its subsets:

$$\text{PSA} \qquad \forall x \, \exists y \, \forall z \, (z \in y \leftrightarrow z \subseteq x)$$

Here $z \subseteq x$ abbreviates the formula $\text{Set}(z)$ & $\text{Set}(x)$ & $\forall u \, (u \in z \rightarrow u \in x)$ ($\text{Set}(z)$ means: z is a set).[10] Proofs of theorems throughout mathematics routinely and tacitly rely on PSA. But how do mathematicians know that PSA is true? The problem here is not how mathematicians know that there are any sets at all, for if there are no sets then PSA is vacuously true (since both $z \in y$ and $z \subseteq x$ are always false). Rather, the problem is how mathematicians know that if there is a set, it has a power set.

Some textbooks motivate PSA in effect by telling readers that, unless they accept it, they will be unable to do set theory. They do not claim that accepting the axiom is necessary for understanding the language of set theory, in particular 'Set' and '$\in$'. They introduced those symbols at an earlier stage of the exposition. Once the axiom has been stated, readers are treated as grasping its content but potentially still wondering why to accept it; that is the point of the pragmatic motivation. It might be interpreted as an appeal to authority: take the author's word for it, once you start working with this axiom you will see why it is needed in mathematics.

Other expositions of set theory attempt more intrinsic justifications of PSA. For instance:

If I have a set, then I can think of all possible subsets of this set. It is probably going to be a larger collection, but not so terribly much larger. It is reasonable to think of this as giving us back a set.[11]

This is an implicit appeal to the principle of limitation of size, that things form a set if and only if there are not too many of them (fewer than absolutely all the things there are). Sometimes the appeal is backed up by the calculation that a finite set with just n members has just 2^n subsets. But of course PSA is intended to apply to infinite sets too.[12]

An alternative to limitation of size is the picture of sets as built up by an iterative process; at each stage one forms all possible sets of things already built up or given. This picture too is sometimes used to justify PSA:

[S]uppose x is formed at [stage] S. Since every member of x is formed before S, every subset of x is formed at S. Thus the set of all subsets of x can be formed at any stage after S.[13]

Of course, the apparently causal and temporal talk of forming sets at earlier or later stages is intended metaphorically, without commitment to any genuinely constructivist conception of sets. Nevertheless, the point of the metaphor is to appeal to the imagination, enabling us to think about the question in a more vivid, concrete, and perspicuous way, and in particular to convince us that there will be a stage after S, without which the power set never gets formed.[14] The metaphor prompts us to undertake an imaginative exercise that makes offline use of our online skill in observing and engaging in processes of physical creation, a skill honed by past experience. This is not so distant from the imaginative exercise through which Norman came to know (1).

Something similar goes on in the justification from limitation of size. It starts with the supposition that 'I have a set', which already suggests a picture of the set as available to hand. On that supposition, 'I can think of all possible subsets of this set.' Of course, none of that is intended to suggest any idealist metaphysics of sets, on which it is essential to them to be thought by a subject. Rather, the aim is again to make us engage imaginatively with the question. The point of calling the subsets 'possible' is not to emphasize that they could exist, for it is not in question that they actually do exist; it is to suggest that I could select them. Imagine that I have to hand three objects, a, b, and c. They form a set from which I can make eight selections:

$$\{a, b, c\} \qquad \{a, b\} \qquad \{a, c\} \qquad \{b, c\}$$
$$\{\} \qquad \{c\} \qquad \{b\} \qquad \{a\}$$

Those eight sets are the members of the power set of the set of the original three objects. My online experience of making different selections from amongst perceptually presented objects facilitates my offline imagined survey of all possible selections, and enables me to make the judgment in the quotation, 'It is probably going to be a larger collection, but not so terribly much larger.' The cognitive tractability of the power set in such simple cases helps us accept PSA. Again, Norman's knowledge of (1) is not so far away.

If standard axioms of set theory are justified by general conceptions of the sets, such as limitation of size or iterativeness, we may wonder how those general conceptions are in turn to be justified. Although the answer is hardly clear, all experience in the philosophy of set theory suggests that the attempt to make such a general conception of sets intuitively compelling must rest at least as heavily on appeals to the imagination with metaphors and pictures as do attempts to make intuitively compelling one of the standard set-theoretic axioms.

An alternative view is that such intrinsic justifications of set-theoretic axioms are secondary to extrinsic ones from their fruitfulness, their explanatory and unifying power. This need not involve Quine's idea that mathematics is justified by its applications in natural science. Corresponding to the textbook's implied injunction above to the mathematical novice, 'wait and see', applications in mathematics itself may be more relevant.[15] Thus the strategy does not immediately commit one to an account of mathematical knowledge as a posteriori, even though the envisaged abductive methodology is strongly reminiscent of the natural sciences.

Bertrand Russell describes a similar order of proceeding:

[I]nstead of asking what can be defined and deduced from what is assumed to begin with, we ask instead what more general ideas and principles can be found, in terms of which what was our starting-point can be defined or deduced.[16]

He observes:

The most obvious and easy things in mathematics are not those that come logically at the beginning; they are things that, from the point of view of logical deduction, come somewhere in the middle.[17]

This suggests knowledge of the 'most obvious and easy things in mathematics' as a better candidate than knowledge of the axioms of set theory to fit the stereotype of a priori knowledge. An example is knowledge that $2 + 2 = 4$, an arduously derived theorem of Russell and Whitehead's system in *Principia Mathematica*. But if ordinary knowledge of elementary arithmetic is not by derivation from logically more basic principles, then presumably it is by something more like offline pattern recognition, and we still have not moved far from Norman's knowledge of (1). Only the very lazy-minded could be content with the explanation that we know that $2 + 2 = 4$ 'by intuition'. Even if it is true that we do so in some sense of 'intuition', how does saying that constitute a genuine alternative to a view that assimilates our knowledge to Norman's?

Even if experience plays no strictly evidential role in core mathematical practice, the suspicion remains that its role is more than purely enabling. Although we can insist that mathematical knowledge is a priori, it is unclear how it differs epistemologically from some examples of the a posteriori, such as Norman's knowledge of (2).

Rather than pursuing the epistemology of mathematics further, let us see whether the stereotype of a priori knowledge fares any better in the epistemology of logic. For a simple example, consider the reflexivity of identity, the principle that everything is self-identical:

$$\text{RI} \qquad \forall x \; x = x$$

We are not asking about a priori knowledge that RI is a logical truth. We are just asking about a priori knowledge of RI itself, knowledge that everything is self-identical.

A tempting reaction is that anyone who doubts RI thereby just shows that they do not understand it. In the jargon, RI may be claimed to be *epistemologically analytic*.

We need not discuss whether epistemological analyticity entails a priority, for it is false that basic logical truths are epistemologically analytic in the relevant sense. I know educated native speakers of English who deny that everything is self-identical, on the grounds that material substances that change their properties over time are not self-identical. I regard those speakers as confused, but the understanding they lack is primarily logical rather than semantic. Although they are mistaken about the logical consequences of identity, by normal standards they are not linguistically incompetent with the English expressions 'everything', 'is', 'self-', and 'identical', and the way they are put together, nor with their counterparts in a formal first-order language with '='. A language school is not the place for them to learn better. We might stipulate a sense of the tricky word 'concept' in which anyone who doubts RI counts as associating a different 'concept' with '=' from any logically standard one, but recycling a theoretical disagreement as a difference in 'concepts' hardly clarifies the position.[18]

Although RI is not epistemologically analytic, it of course does not follow that it is not known a priori. One competent speaker may know a priori what another denies. But how is RI known? The universal generalization is unlikely to be an axiom of a formal system that develops innately in the human head. In a standard natural deduction system, RI is derived by the introduction rule $\forall$I for the universal quantifier from a formula of the form $a = a$, which is itself a theorem (indeed, an axiom) by the introduction rule =I for the identity sign.[19] That is the formal analogue of imagining an object, within the scope of the imaginative supposition judging 'it' to be self-identical, and concluding that everything is self-identical. The $\forall$I rule is subject to the restriction that the term a on which one universally generalizes must not occur (free) in any assumption from which the premise of the application of $\forall$I was derived, otherwise one could derive $\forall x\, Fx$ from Fa. In this case the restriction is vacuously met; $a = a$ is a theorem and has no assumptions. Our informal thinking lacks a comparably clear way of keeping track of its assumptions. We make a judgment, perhaps within the scope of an imaginative supposition, but we may be unaware of its assumptions or sources. Thus it is often not transparent to us how far we can generalize. We may be imagining the case in a way that is less generic or typical than we think. For example, those who deny (however mistakenly) that a changing thing is self-identical may charge that if we imagine an unchanging thing in evaluating RI we thereby beg the question in its favour.

Such reflections should not drive us into a general scepticism about our putative knowledge of universal generalizations. That would be an overgeneralization of just the kind against which the reflections warn. They should not even drive us into a particular scepticism about our putative knowledge of RI. Knowing p does not require separately assessing in advance all possible fallacious objections to p. To require us to check that the imagined instance is typical of all members of a domain D before we universally generalize over D is to impose an infinite regress, for 'The imagined instance is typical of all members of D' is itself a universal generalization over D. What matters for knowledge may be that we do safely imagine the instance in a relevantly generic way, even though the process is opaque to us. Surely we can quite easily know RI. Whether or not something changes is not really relevant to whether it is self-identical, so it does not matter whether we imagine a changing object or an unchanging one.

A resemblance between our knowledge of RI and Norman's knowledge of (1) is starting to emerge. Of course, an important aspect of Norman's knowledge of (1) is his offline imaginative use of capacities to apply colour terms calibrated perceptually online. Is there anything similar in our knowledge of RI? Experience involves a process of continually judging numerical identity or distinctness among objects perceived or remembered in a wide variety of guises. This cognitive capacity for judging identity and distinctness in experience is non-logical, for pure logic gives us only the barest formal constraints. If we have a non-logical capacity to make such identity judgments, we need no additional logical capacity corresponding to the rule =I to make identity judgments of the special syntactic form $a = a$. After all, we could use the non-logical capacity to judge $a = b$ and $b = a$ (for some suitable term b syntactically distinct from a) and then apply the transitivity of identity to deduce $a = a$. The transitivity of identity does not depend on its reflexivity.[20] A simpler and more plausible way of using a non-logical capacity to make judgments of identity and distinctness to judge $a = a$ would be directly to feed in the term twice over as both inputs to some device for comparison, which would trivially return a positive result. That can be done online or offline.

Even the trivial comparison in $a = a$ can be mishandled. If the name a denotes an enduring, changing substance, but one associates the first token of a with the properties the object had at a time t (attributed in the present tense, not relativized to t) and the second token of a with the properties the object had at another time t^* (also attributed in the present tense, not relativized to t^*, and incompatible with the former properties), then the output from the identity test is a false negative. Through experience of material things undergoing slow large changes, one becomes less prone to such mistakes, although some adult metaphysicians still manage to make them, and so deny RI.

The foregoing remarks are not intended to suggest that knowledge of RI is a posteriori. Classify it as a priori by all means, but do not let that blind you to how much it has in common with a posteriori knowledge of identity and distinctness, just as Norman's a priori knowledge of (1) has so much in common with his a posteriori knowledge of (2).

The salient difference between (1) and (2) is modal rather than epistemological: (1) is metaphysically necessary, (2) metaphysically contingent. By contrast, $a = a$ and $a = b$ do not differ in modal status if both are true and the terms a and b are proper names or other rigid designators, for an identity claim with such terms is metaphysically necessary if true at all.[21] But in that case the salient difference between the formulas $a = a$ and $a = b$ is logical rather than epistemological. For $a = a$ but not $a = b$ is a logical truth. The property of logical truth is not demarcated epistemologically but by more formal criteria.[22] Just as the modal difference between (1) and (2) makes us overestimate the strictly epistemological difference between Norman's knowledge of (1) and his knowledge of (2), so the logical difference between $a = a$ and $a = b$ makes us overestimate the strictly epistemological difference between our knowledge of $a = a$ and our knowledge of $a = b$.

Naturally, far more work would have to be done to confirm the foregoing hints about logical and mathematical knowledge. Nevertheless, the indications so far suggest that what are often counted as the clearest cases of a priori knowledge are much less different epistemologically than they are usually depicted as being from cases of a posteriori knowledge. The epistemological similarity of Norman's a priori knowledge of (1) to his a posteriori knowledge of (2) is no isolated case. The usual stereotype of a priori knowledge is seriously misleading, because it omits a pervasive role of experience that is more than purely enabling, although less than strictly evidential.

5

The inadequacy of the usual stereotype of a priori knowledge may seem to support the idea that we can make progress by following some Quineans, if not Quine himself, in positively classifying all knowledge as a posteriori.[23] Doing so would at least have the negative advantage of not putting a distinction where there is no deep difference. But does it also yield some positive understanding of the general nature of knowledge?

On Quine's picture, a theory faces the tribunal of experience collectively, not sentence by sentence. Taken at face value, the image implies that two consequences of a theory cannot differ in epistemic status. But that is absurd. For Quine, the totality of a person's beliefs constitute a theory (perhaps an inconsistent one), their total theory of the world, but who thinks that two of a person's beliefs cannot differ in epistemic status? If some of my beliefs constitute knowledge, it does not follow that all of them do; it does not even follow that all of them are true. One's beliefs about science and mathematics may be on average epistemically better off than one's beliefs about religion and politics, or vice versa. Indeed, experience favours the belief that experience favours some beliefs more than others. Quine later restricted his holism to a moderate version that permits some discrimination amongst our beliefs.[24] Nevertheless, at least this mild form of global holism is surely right: no two of our beliefs are in principle epistemically insulated from each other.

To make progress, we need a more developed model, on which an individual belief has its own epistemic status, but that status depends in principle on the epistemic status of each other's belief. Holism is far more plausible as a claim about the pervasive interdependence of epistemic status than as the claim that only whole theories have epistemic status. The obvious and best-developed candidate for such a model is some form of Bayesian epistemology. It assigns evidential probabilities to individual propositions, subject to standard axioms of probability theory, which constrain the overall distribution of probabilities to all propositions.[25] The paradigmatic way of updating evidential probabilities is by conditionalization on new evidence, encapsulated in a proposition e. The new evidential probability $\text{Prob}_{\text{new}}(p)$ of any proposition p is the old conditional evidential probability $\text{Prob}_{\text{old}}(p|e)$ of p on e, which is equal to the ratio $\text{Prob}_{\text{old}}(p \ \& \ e)/\text{Prob}_{\text{old}}(e)$ whenever $\text{Prob}_{\text{old}}(e) > 0$. Conditionalization is a global process; one overall probability distribution, Prob_{new}, replaces another, Prob_{old}.

However, Bayesian epistemology does not vindicate a Quinean rejection of the a priori. For standard axioms of probability theory constrain every probability distribution to assign probability 1 to any theorem of classical propositional logic, and probability 0 to its negation. Probabilistic updating on new evidence cannot raise or lower the probability of theorems or anti-theorems. That is not just an optional convention. Loosening it deprives probability theory of the mathematical structure on which its utility depends. Although minor concessions to specific non-classical logics may not destroy that utility entirely, any version of probability theory worth having will give such a privileged status to some core of logic.

In Bayesian epistemology, logical truths are not the only propositions to enjoy a good epistemic status that they do not owe to the evidence. Let e conjoin all the relevant evidence, and Prob_{new} be the result of conditionalizing Prob_{old} on e as above. We may assume that the evidence was not certain in advance; $\text{Prob}_{old}(e) < 1$. Suppose that a hypothesis h is well supported by e, so $\text{Prob}_{new}(h)$ is high. Consider the material conditional $e \rightarrow h$. Since it is a logical consequence of h, $\text{Prob}_{new}(e \rightarrow h)$ is at least as high as $\text{Prob}_{new}(h)$. But we can prove that either $\text{Prob}_{new}(e \rightarrow h) = \text{Prob}_{old}(e \rightarrow h) = 1$ or $\text{Prob}_{new}(e \rightarrow h) < \text{Prob}_{old}(e \rightarrow h)$.[26] In other words, either $e \rightarrow h$ was already certain prior to the evidence, which did not confirm $e \rightarrow h$, or the evidence disconfirmed $e \rightarrow h$. Thus $e \rightarrow h$ enjoys a good epistemic status, because $\text{Prob}_{new}(e \rightarrow h)$ is high, but it does so despite the evidence or independently of it.

When holistic epistemology is made rigorous, the results do not support the idea that the only way of enjoying high epistemic status is by confirmation through experience; they do the opposite. That is not to deny the strong similarities between the epistemology of logic and the epistemology of other sciences evident in debates over proposals to revise or extend classical logic. For we cannot assume that those similarities are properly articulated on the model of confirmation or disconfirmation through experience.

Rather than appealing to formal models, those who claim that all knowledge is empirical or a posteriori may suggest that we understand the paradigm of such knowledge, simple cases of observational knowledge, well enough for the informal proposal to assimilate all knowledge to the paradigm to be illuminating and non-trivial. Although there are manifest differences between the paradigm and cases of highly theoretical knowledge, the idea is that on sufficiently deep analysis they will turn out to be differences in complexity, not in fundamental nature.

How well do we understand the paradigm, simple cases of observational knowledge? Presumably, the picture is that in such cases sense perception is a channel for a causal connection between the truth of a proposition p and the agent a's belief in p, creating a strongly positive local correlation between truth and belief. We may symbolize the correlation as $p \Leftrightarrow B_a p$. The proposition p should paradigmatically concern the state of the environment, not the state of the agent, for otherwise the case is too special to be a suitable model for knowledge in general.

A first step in making the model less simplistic is to note that the correlation depends on the receptivity of the agent. If a is too far from the relevant events or shuts her eyes or has bad eyesight, the preconditions for the correlation may not be met. We can symbolize this one-way correlation between receptivity and the previous two-way correlation as $R_a p \Rightarrow (p \Leftrightarrow B_a p)$.[27] Even at this utterly elementary level, it is clear that a causal connection between truth and belief is not the only way to achieve such a set-up. For suppose that p is a necessary truth (as it were, $\Rightarrow p$), and that the receptivity of the agent by itself causes the belief ($R_a p \Rightarrow B_a p$). Then we have $R_a p \Rightarrow (p \Leftrightarrow B_a p)$, even though there is no causal connection between p and $B_a p$.

The receptivity condition $R_a p$ here should not be envisaged as some mystical state of opening one's soul to Platonic heaven; it may be a mundane psychological process, for example of calculation. Thus the $R_a p \Rightarrow (p \Leftrightarrow B_a p)$ model carries no commitment to conceiving the modelled epistemic states as all a posteriori. For all it implies, some of them are a priori. Perhaps surprisingly, treating simple observation as the paradigm to which all knowledge must be assimilated does not in principle commit one to a uniformly a posteriori epistemology.

As an alternative paradigm of knowledge, many self-described naturalists prefer the experimentally based findings of the natural sciences. A conception of all knowledge as a posteriori or empirical may be an attempt to assimilate it all to natural science. Of course, one of the most salient obstacles to any such attempt is mathematics. Obviously, theorems of mathematics do not normally have direct experimental support. For Quine, they have indirect experimental support because mathematics is part of our total scientific theory, which is confirmed as a whole (if at all) by experimental tests. But we have already seen that theories are not the only bearers of epistemic status. The practice of the natural sciences themselves requires evaluating the epistemic status of much smaller units: for example, should we believe a report of a given astronomical observation or experimental result? Once we ask more discriminating questions about the epistemic status of individual axioms and theorems of mathematics, it becomes much harder to tell a plausible story on which they owe that status primarily to experimental support. Although some axioms and theorems are in a better epistemic position than others, that has far more to do with considerations internal to mathematics than with experimental support.[28] The same holds even more obviously for axioms and theorems of logic.

On present evidence, the slogan 'All knowledge is a posteriori' or 'All knowledge is empirical' is defensible only if the term 'a posteriori' or 'empirical' is emptied of all serious content. Unfortunately, that does not deprive the underlying prejudice of influence. Like other prejudices, it acts selectively, for instance by imposing more severe demands for external justification on armchair methods in philosophy than on other methods of inquiry.

6

We should not react to the inadequacy of the usual stereotype of a priori knowledge by declaring all knowledge a posteriori. Conversely, of course, we should not react to the inadequacy of the usual stereotype of a posteriori knowledge by declaring all knowledge a priori. Since the terms 'a priori' and 'a posteriori' are not meaningless by normal standards, some difference between a priori and a posteriori knowledge remains. But that does not rehabilitate the distinction as of great theoretical value for epistemology. After all, there is a difference between plants that are bushes and plants that are not bushes, but it does not follow that that distinction is of great theoretical value for botany.[29] When we start investigating some phenomena, we have little choice but to classify them according to manifest similarities and differences. As our understanding deepens, we may recognize the need to reclassify the phenomena on less obvious dimensions of greater explanatory significance.

Distinctions that aided progress in the early stages may hinder it later on. The a priori–a posteriori distinction is a case in point.

Cognitive psychology will have much to offer the epistemologist's attempt to overcome philosophical prejudices and classify according to deeper and less obvious similarities and differences. But that does not mean a reduction of epistemology to cognitive psychology. Epistemological questions are typically at a higher level of generality than those of cognitive psychology: for example, they may concern all knowledge, all epistemic probability, or all rationality. Epistemology also engages more fully with evaluative questions about how knowledge is better than mere true belief, or rationality than irrationality, or whether we ought to proportion our beliefs to the evidence. Of course, some 'naturalized' epistemologists abjure such evaluative questions as 'unscientific'. In doing so, they seem more under the influence of logical positivism, or the prejudice discussed in Section 5, than of actual scientific practice. In particular, cognitive psychologists do not abjure all evaluative judgments about what is rational or irrational, in their experimental studies of irrationality. Moreover, pursuing any scientific inquiry involves making numerous judgments that are evaluative in the way characteristic of epistemology. Are these data trustworthy? Is that argument valid? Which of these theories is better supported by the evidence? Even if those questions play a merely instrumental role in the natural sciences, there is no warrant for the idea that scientific practice somehow discredits the attempt to inquire more generally into the nature of phenomena like trustworthiness, validity, and evidential support. Indeed, it seems contrary to the scientific spirit to disapprove of systematic general inquiry into such matters while nevertheless continually relying on judgments about them.

Beyond the potential contribution of cognitive psychology, we need to develop a more detailed, precise, and specifically epistemological vocabulary for describing the fine structure of examples such as those in Sections 3 and 4, involving the offline application in the imagination of cognitive skills originally developed in perception, especially when they involve generic imaginary instances used to reach general non-imaginary conclusions.[30] That is likely to prove a far more fruitful project for epistemology than yet another attempt to reconstruct the tired-out distinction between the a priori and the a posteriori or to stretch the latter thin enough to cover all knowledge.

Notes

1. [This paper was first published in Albert Casullo and Joshua Thurow (eds.), *The A Priori in Philosophy* (Oxford: Oxford University Press, 2013), pp. 291–312, with the same title as here.] This paper develops the brief critique of the distinction between a priori and a posteriori knowledge in Williamson 2007a: 165–9. Earlier versions of the material were discussed at King's College London, the University of Santiago de Compostela, Moscow State University, St Petersburg State University, the University of Hertfordshire, a course on Mind, World, and Action at the Inter-University Centre in Dubrovnik, a 'master-class' for the British Postgraduate Philosophy Association in London where Giacomo Melis and Asger Steffensen commented on it, and a seminar at the University of Lisbon. I am grateful to them, to audiences on those occasions, to Anna-Sara Malmgren, and to an anonymous referee for Oxford University Press for comments, questions, and discussion.

2. Many contemporary epistemologists, especially those of an internalist bent, treat the distinction as primarily a classification of forms of justification rather than of knowledge. For reasons explained in Williamson 2000, I treat the classification of forms of knowledge as primary. Friends of justification should not find much difficulty in reworking the arguments of this chapter in their terms.

3. I am not actually endorsing the conclusion that the liberal–non-liberal distinction does not cut at the political joints, because I have not actually given an example of a clearly liberal policy that is politically only superficially different from a clearly non-liberal policy.

4. See Williamson 2007a: 137–78. [For more discussion of the cognitive role of the imagination, see Chapter 10.]

5. It is even more implausible that experience plays a purely enabling role in the more complex examples in Williamson 2007a: 166–7; (1) is used here for its simplicity.

6. Compare the huge debate on Mary's (a posteriori?) knowledge of what red things look like (Jackson 1982).

7. For some discussion see Williamson 2000: 123–30 and 147–63.

8. For an example of this attitude see Devitt 2005.

9. The axioms of group theory are simply clauses in the mathematical definition of 'group' and so raise no distinctive epistemological problem; likewise for the axioms for other kinds of algebraic or geometrical structure. The primary role of the axioms of set theory in mathematics is quite different. Proofs in all branches of mathematics rely on their truth. They are not clauses in the mathematical definition of 'set' (there is no such definition analogous to the mathematical definition of 'group'). Although they can be adapted to serve as such clauses in a mathematical definition of 'cumulative hierarchy' or the like, that is a secondary use; even proofs about all cumulative hierarchies rely on the axioms of set theory in their primary role. Some globally structuralist philosophers of mathematics may urge a different attitude, but mathematicians have not yet seen fit to indulge them, nor is it clear how they could coherently adopt a globally structuralist attitude.

10. The quantifiers in PSA are not restricted to sets. In applying mathematics, we may need the power set of a set of concrete objects. If x is a non-set, it has no subsets, so y can be {} (if we want a set) or x itself (if we want a non-set). If x is a set, then {} $\subseteq x$, so y must be a set since {} $\in y$ and only sets have members. If we did not impose Set(z) as a condition on $z \subseteq x$, every non-set would vacuously count as a subset of any set x and so have to belong to the power set of x.

11. Crossley, Ash, Brickhill, Stillwell, and Williams 1972: 61.

12. An infinite set with κ members also has 2^κ subsets, but in the infinite case the definition of 2^κ depends on PSA rather than offering it independent support. For the history of the limitation of size principle and scepticism about its capacity to motivate PSA, see Hallett 1984.

13. Shoenfield 1977: 326. For a more philosophical account of the iterative conception of set, see Boolos 1971.

14. The appeal to the imagination is explicit at 323–4 of Shoenfield 1977, in his general account of the process of set formation. Note that he is writing as a mathematician for mathematicians and others, not as a philosopher.

15. See Maddy 2011.

16. Russell 1919: 1. According to Russell, the latter order 'characterises mathematical philosophy as opposed to ordinary mathematics'. If Maddy is right, it also characterizes set theory as a branch of ordinary mathematics.

17. Russell 1919: 2.

18. See Williamson 2007a: 73–133, for a more detailed critique of epistemological analyticity.

19. Matters are more complicated in free logic, where the term a is not guaranteed to denote anything in the domain of quantification.

20. The standard proof of transitivity uses the elimination rule =E, the indiscernibility of identicals, but not the introduction rule =I.

21. The classic defence of the necessity of identity is, of course, Kripke 1980. On some metaphysical views, what is necessary in the case of both identities is only that if the objects exist then they are identical.

22. For present purposes logical truths are treated as formulas rather than propositions. The truth of $a = b$ does not make it the same logical truth as $a = a$.

23. 'It is overwhelmingly plausible that *some* knowledge is empirical, "justified by experience." The attractive thesis of naturalism is that *all* knowledge is; there is only one way of knowing' (Devitt 2005: 105).

24. See Quine 1981: 71.

25. More accurately, the constraints are on a distribution of probabilities to all propositions in the σ-field of propositions that receive probabilities at all.

26. $\text{Prob}_{old}(e \ \& \ \neg h) = \text{Prob}_{old}(e \ \& \ \neg h | e)\text{Prob}_{old}(e) + \text{Prob}_{old}(e \ \& \ \neg h | \neg e)\text{Prob}_{old}(\neg e)$. But $\text{Prob}_{old}(e \ \& \ \neg h | \neg e) = 0$ and $\text{Prob}_{old}(e \ \& \ \neg h | e) = \text{Prob}_{new}(e \ \& \ \neg h)$, so $\text{Prob}_{old}(e \ \& \ \neg h) = \text{Prob}_{new}(e \ \& \ \neg h)\text{Prob}_{old}(e)$. Since $\text{Prob}_{old}(e) < 1$, $\text{Prob}_{old}(e \ \& \ \neg h) < \text{Prob}_{new}(e \ \& \ \neg h)$ unless $\text{Prob}_{new}(e \ \& \ \neg h) = 0$. In the former case, $\text{Prob}_{new}(e \to h) = 1 - \text{Prob}_{new}(e \ \& \ \neg h) < 1 - \text{Prob}_{old}(e \ \& \ \neg h) = \text{Prob}_{old}(e \ \& \ \neg h)$. In the latter case, $\text{Prob}_{old}(e \to h) = 0$ too, so $\text{Prob}_{old}(e \to h) = 1$.

27. The correlation between receptivity and the former two-way correlation may itself be two-way ($R_a p \Leftrightarrow (p \Leftrightarrow B_a p)$), if receptivity is the only way of setting up the first correlation, but the other direction does not matter for present purposes.

28. For example, in the set theory ZFC, the Axiom of Replacement is usually considered to be better established than the Axiom of Choice, but not because it has more experimental support. For other objections to a purely holistic account of the confirmation of mathematics as part of total science see Maddy 2007: 314–17.

29. We are not concerned with more radical redefinitions of the words in the sentence.

30. For an introduction to psychological work on the cognitive value of the imagination, the case specifically relevant to the examples in Section 3, see Harris 2000.

9

Do We Have Reason to Doubt the Importance of the Distinction between A Priori and A Posteriori Knowledge?

A Reply to Williamson[1]

Paul Boghossian

1

The resilience of the a priori

The category of a priori justification has proven remarkably resilient.[2] Despite persistent and powerful attacks on its possibility, reality, and even its very coherence, it has remained part of the basic conceptual framework of philosophy. What explains this remarkable staying power?[3]

One of the reasons why the category of a priori justification has proven so resilient derives from the pull of certain intuitive *examples*: when we contemplate the pair of propositions

(i) It's sunny

and

(ii) If it's sunny, then it's sunny,

we can't help but be struck by the thought that experience plays a very different role in the way we typically know these two propositions. Roughly speaking, in the case of the first, we need to open our eyes to see whether it is sunny; in the case of the second, we don't.[4]

Furthermore, these examples are projectible: on their basis, we know how to classify *further* cases as a priori or a posteriori, and we achieve a high level of non-collusive convergence on those further classifications. For example, we are fairly confident that

(iii) All squares have four sides.

Debating the A Priori. Paul Boghossian and Timothy Williamson, Oxford University Press (2020).
© Paul Boghossian and Timothy Williamson.
DOI: 10.1093/oso/9780198851707.001.0001

(iv)   Nothing can be red and green all over at the same time.

(v)   In a Trolley Scenario, it is morally wrong to throw the heavy man off the bridge in order to save the five innocents trapped below.

(vi)   Two circles of different radii can at most intersect at two points.

(vii)   It is necessary that whoever knows p believes p.

all fall on the a priori side, while

(viii)   All wooden tables are squares.

(ix)   This volume of *Who's Who* is red.

(x)   In all societies, it is considered morally wrong to throw the heavy man off the bridge in a Trolley Scenario.

(xi)   There are two intersecting circles on this page.

(xii)   Whoever knows p enjoys knowing p.

fall on the a posteriori side.

While we have a fairly good handle on *how* we know propositions in an a posteriori way, we are not entirely sure how we know propositions a priori: How, for example, do we know (ii) without experience? Do we examine our concept of 'if'? Do we have an intuition that all instances of the sentence 'If p, then p' are necessarily true? Or is the story something else altogether?

To concede this is to say that we are not sure how to *explain* our capacity for experience-independent justified belief. But the datum itself, that there are such beliefs, seems firm enough.

All of this gives us a very strong basis on which to be confident that, through these examples, we have got hold of a genuine distinction, with the only question being, How exactly should that distinction be theoretically formulated and how should its various instances be explained?

And that is why, despite all the impressive and by no means fully answered challenges to the notion of the a priori, it continues to have a strong grip on us.

A new style of skepticism

Timothy Williamson has developed a novel form of skepticism about the a priori, one that sees no need to deny any of the observations made above—indeed, he makes most of them himself.

According to Williamson, although the robustness and projectibility of the examples warrant our confidence that we have got hold of a genuine distinction, they do not warrant our believing that the distinction is a significant one, of any great importance to epistemology.

Indeed, Williamson claims to be in possession of an argument that shows that *whatever* distinction we have got hold of through our examples it must be a *shallow* one, one that serves to obscure important epistemological generalizations, rather than illuminate them.

This is a genuinely novel form of skepticism about the a priori–a posteriori distinction: it accommodates our strong conviction that we have got hold of a real distinction, even while it purports to undermine our sense of the importance of that distinction.

In this paper, my main concern will be to show that Williamson's central argument for his novel form of skepticism about the a priori doesn't succeed.

However, en route to presenting his central argument, Williamson develops an interesting objection of another, more old-fashioned type, one that is directed against the very possibility of formulating a satisfactory theoretical (top-down) distinction between the a priori and the a posteriori. (As we shall see in a moment, this more traditional argument turns on the classic difficulty in saying what notion of experience is involved in the core apriorist notion of 'a justification that is independent of experience.')

Since this argument of Williamson's is of strong independent interest, and since it will enable us to introduce some basic concepts that will be important later on, I will begin by looking at it, before turning to his central argument.

2

A problem for characterizing 'experience'

The fundamental notion of a priori justification is one that applies to a *way of knowing* or *justifiably believing* a proposition. According to the traditional explication,

> S's belief that p is justified a priori if and only if S's belief that p is *justified in a way* that is *independent* of *experience.*

Derivatively, this notion of apriority can be applied to a *proposition*:

> The proposition that p is a priori if and only if p *can* be justifiably believed, by creatures like us, in an a priori way.

As is well known, even this rudimentary characterization immediately faces a glaring issue. According to our intuitive examples, typical ways of justifiably believing that if it's sunny then it's sunny are a priori. But my justifiably believing this proposition will certainly depend on experience in *some* sense: after all, my very ability to *entertain* the proposition that if it's sunny then it's sunny (plausibly) depends on my having had some experience with the sun.

The standard way of dealing with this issue is to say that my knowledge that if it's sunny then it's sunny can still count as a priori, even if experience is playing some role in my arriving at it, provided that it is playing at most an *enabling* role, but not a *justificatory or epistemic role.*[5]

What does it mean for experience to play a merely enabling role? Here there are two options that are sometimes conflated.

On the one hand, we might have a purely *negative* characterization of 'enabling' in mind, one that applies to *any* role that experience may play in generating belief apart from providing a justification for the belief in question.

On the other hand, we might have in mind a characterization that is in part *positive*, for example, having to do with the role that experience plays in enabling one to grasp and therefore entertain certain propositions.

On the negative view, *any* role that's non-epistemic is enabling. On the positive view, by contrast, it would be an open question whether experience occasionally plays a role that is neither epistemic nor enabling.

Williamson assumes that the friend of the a priori is committed to a *positive* characterization of 'enabling': one of his big themes, as we shall see, is that experience often plays a role that is *intermediate* between an enabling role and an epistemic role, a possibility that couldn't arise on the negative characterization.

However, Williamson doesn't explain why the friend of the a priori couldn't be content with simply insisting that experience *not* play an *epistemic role*, without also giving a positive characterization of all the roles that are thereby left over. Of course, Williamson's opponent would owe us an account of what it is for experience to have an 'epistemic role', but that is a perfectly general burden that any epistemologist must bear.

If we ask which positive characterization of 'enabling' Williamson assumes the friend of the a priori must have, the answer seems to be (although he doesn't quite spell it out) that it is a broad notion of *access* to a proposition.

Since it won't matter for present purposes, let us grant Williamson this positive, access-involving notion of an enabling role for experience. Let us turn instead to asking what the word 'experience' should be taken to cover in the expression 'experience that does not play an epistemic role'. Williamson says the following (it will be useful to quote him in full):

Another issue is how widely to apply the term 'experience'. It is mainly associated with 'outer' experience, involving perception by the usual five senses, but why should it exclude 'inner' experience, involving introspection and reflection? After all, one's knowledge that one is in pain is presumably a posteriori, even though the experience on which it depends is inner. Excluding inner experience by stipulation, without reference to any deeper epistemological difference, is liable to make the distinction between a priori and the a posteriori knowledge epistemologically superficial. Inner and outer experience will therefore provisionally be treated on an equal footing.

One might worry that if inner experience is included, our experience of reflecting on the proposition that if it is sunny then it is sunny will play an evidential role in our knowledge that if it is sunny then it is sunny, and that Mary's experience of calculating that $289 + 365 = 654$, on paper or in her head, will play an evidential role in her knowledge that $289 + 365 = 654$. Presumably, the response is that the role is purely enabling. The relevant evidence is not the psychological process of reflecting or calculating, but rather in some sense the non-psychological logical or mathematical facts to which that process enables one to have access.

On further thought, however, that response causes more problems than it solves. For what prevents it from generalizing to outer experience? For example, part of the evidence that a massive comet or asteroid collided with the Earth about 250 million years ago is said to be that certain sediment samples from China and Japan contain certain clusters of carbon atoms. That those samples contained those clusters of atoms is a non-psychological fact. Of course, in some sense scientists' outer experience played a role in their access to the fact. But, by analogy with the logical and mathematical cases, the relevant evidence is not the psychological process of undergoing those outer experiences, but rather the non-psychological physical facts to which that process enables us to have access. The role of the outer experience is purely enabling, not evidential. If so, what would usually be regarded as paradigm cases of a posteriori knowledge risk reclassification as a priori.

The threat is not confined to theoretical knowledge in the natural sciences. Even for everyday observational knowledge, it is a highly controversial move to put the psychological process of undergoing the outer experience into the content of the perceptual evidence we thereby gain. What we observe is typically a non-psychological fact about our external environment, not a psychological fact about ourselves.[6]

Williamson's argument may be rendered as follows:

1. In the locution 'justification that is epistemically independent of experience', 'experience' might apply just to 'outer experience', or it might apply both to 'outer experience' and to 'inner experience.'

2. If it applies only to 'outer experience'—thereby including perception by the usual five senses, but excluding introspection, reflection, and mental calculation—then the distinction between the a priori and the a posteriori will be superficial, since we will have to classify both our knowledge of mathematics and our knowledge that we are in pain (when we are) as a priori.

3. If it applies both to 'outer' and to 'inner' experience, then we will have to say that the role of the mental process of mathematical *calculation* is merely enabling, giving us access to the relevant mathematical facts in a computation, rather than playing a role in the justification of the result that we arrive at.

4. However, if we take that line about mental calculation, we will have to generalize it to the case of outer experience as well, with the result being that what were supposed to be paradigm cases of a posteriori knowledge (for example, that an asteroid collided with the Earth 250 million years ago) end up being reclassified as a priori.

Williamson's argument poses a dilemma for any theoretical, top-down characterization of the notion of 'justification that is epistemically independent of experience'. The dilemma turns on whether 'experience', in this phrase, is to be construed so as to include or exclude 'inner' experience. Either way, the thought is, it appears impossible to get a characterization of the distinction that lines up with the distinction indicated bottom-up by our intuitive examples.

Discussion of Williamson's problem for characterizing 'experience'

A central difficulty with this argument is that it seems to assume that there is some natural, joint-carving, distinction between 'inner' and 'outer' experience, one which forces us to choose, en bloc, whether to include or exclude 'inner' experience. But there is no such distinction.

In fairness to Williamson, it should be admitted that the existence of such a distinction has often been presupposed by writers in the philosophy of mind (including the present author). On reflection, though, it is hard to see what it could consist in.

For what exactly is the distinction between 'inner' and 'outer' experience supposed to track? Williamson doesn't say, but the only candidate would appear to be the status of the *intentional objects* of the relevant types of experience. Thus, visual perception would count as 'outer' because its intentional objects are outside the head, whereas introspection would count as 'inner' because its intentional objects, such as pains, are inside the head.

But the distinction, as so characterized, is not well defined, and doesn't correspond well to the use that Williamson makes of it. Numbers, for example, on most views, including Williamson's own, are outside the head—but he regards mental calculation, whose intentional objects are numbers, as 'inner'.

And where should we say that memory falls on this way of drawing the distinction between inner and outer? Some of the intentional objects of memory are 'outer', when they concern worldly events, and some are 'inner', when they concern past mental states. So, memory could not be classified neatly as either inner or outer.

However, if the distinction between inner and outer experiences is not based upon the status of their characteristic intentional objects, then I don't see what the distinction could be based upon. In the only other sense that's available, all experiences are inner, in that they are inner states of the mind of the subject.

Williamson might object that it is not *he* who is endorsing the 'inner'–'outer' distinction, but rather the theorist of the a priori; and he could point to his use of shudder quotes around 'inner' and 'outer' to support his claim. But this response requires him to explain why he thinks *anyone* is committed to the distinction, and in particular why he thinks the friend of the a priori is.

Another possible response on Williamson's behalf would have it that the distinction between inner and outer is given not by a principle, but by a list: sense experience is outer and all the rest—including introspection, memory, intuition, imagination, and calculation—are inner.

I am not averse to specifying distinctions via lists, as I will explain further below. But if we did so in this case, it would be open to the friend of the a priori to insist that while 'experience' will cover at least some 'inner' experiences, as given by the list, it won't cover them all. So, while it will include substantive uses of memory and introspection, it *won't* include intuition, most uses of the imagination, and most uses of the capacity for mental calculation: those faculties, it is natural to think, provide a priori warrants for belief, when they provide any warrant at all.

Wouldn't such a response count as hopelessly gerrymandered?

Well, it would count as a gerrymandered response if the stipulated distinction between inner and outer experience had been a natural one, one that carved experience at its natural seams. But, as we have seen, it is no such thing.

There remains a good question, of course, whether we can articulate a *principle* that will capture the distinction between those types of experience that are included in 'epistemically independent of experience', or whether we have to rest content with specifying the distinction via a list.

While there have been some promising attempts, it would be fair to say that, as of yet, no one has formulated a principle that captures the intuitive distinction between a priori and a posteriori sources of warrant correctly.[7] But that is a weak reason to think it can't be done, or that the distinction at issue is not a good one. And it is worth bearing in mind that, as Allan Gibbard has wisely reminded me, there isn't in the end such a large difference between a principle and a list, since a principle is just a list of one.[8]

Justifiers as propositions

Now, while I believe that this particular argument of Williamson's can be answered, it is worth pausing for a moment on an important lesson that is implicit in it.

Williamson's argument identifies a crucial danger for the friend of the a priori, one that perhaps has not been previously sufficiently emphasized. It arises at the point at which the friend seems driven to say that, in the case of a mental calculation, the *justifier* for the belief that the sum of 289 and 365 is 684 is not the *mental process* of calculating those numbers, but rather just the relevant arithmetical propositions to which the calculation provides access.

And the important lesson is that once we begin to think of the justifiers of our beliefs as propositions rather than as mental states, the threat of overgeneralizing a priori belief becomes hard to avert.

For, as we saw above, if the justifier for my 'empirical' belief that an asteroid collided with Earth is just the proposition that samples of sediment contain certain clusters of carbon atoms, rather than any visual observations that justified the premise belief in the first place, then we would have to say that, even in 'empirical' knowledge, sensory experience itself plays at most an enabling 'access' role, and we would thereby have lost any interesting contrast between a priori justification and a posteriori justification.

A priori belief is belief that is held with a priori justification. The relevant notion of justification here can't be merely that of a proposition, but must include reference to the mental states that have those propositions as intentional objects. If we were restricted to making reference only to propositions, the natural thought would be that an a priori justified belief would be a belief that is justified solely by an a priori justified proposition. But which propositions would those be? The resultant view would be hopelessly impredicative.

This is an interesting result, one that, so far as I know, neither friend nor foe of the a priori has sufficiently emphasized. The friend of the a priori cannot afford to adopt the view that justifiers are propositions, rather than mental states, for that commitment is incompatible with an interesting distinction between a priori and a posteriori justification.

In the argument as Williamson presents it, he suggests that the case of mathematical calculation will drive the friend of the a priori to think of justifiers as propositions. As we have seen, his argument for this is based on the optional demand that the friend make up her mind on whether all 'inner' experience is included in the term 'experience', and so we were able to skirt around it.

These days, though, the view that justifiers are propositions, rather than mental states, is a view that has very broad appeal to epistemologists for reasons having nothing to do with the debate about the a priori.[9]

I myself do not see that appeal, and not merely because of my views on the a priori. To me it seems obvious that my justification for believing that, for example, there is a red wall in front of me, is irreducibly dependent on my having a *visual impression* of there being a red wall in front of me.

However, there is a case that has sometimes seemed, even to friends of the a priori, to provide strong motivation for the justifiers as propositions view. The case is still based on the example of mathematics, but stems not from reflecting on the distinction between inner and outer experience, but by looking at the role of memory and perception in proof.

In the remainder of this section, I will lay out this motivating argument and suggest a way of blocking its conclusion.

Proof and memory

In the case of some lengthy proofs, it is not possible for creatures like us to carry the whole thing out in our minds. Unable to keep all the steps of the proof in mind, we need to write them down and look them over. In such cases, memory of the earlier steps in the proof, and perceptual experience of what has been written down, enter into the full explanation of how we arrive at our belief in the conclusion of the proof.

And these facts raise a puzzle that has long worried theorists of the a priori: How could belief arrived at on the basis of this sort of lengthy proof be a priori warranted? Won't the essential role of memory and perceptual experience in the process of carrying out the proof undermine the conclusion's alleged a priori status?[10]

To acquiesce in a positive answer to this question would be counterintuitive. By bottom-up standards, lengthy proof can deliver an a priori warrant for its conclusion just as well as a short proof can. The theoretical puzzle is to explain how it can do so given the psychologically necessary role of perceptual and memory experiences in the process of proof.

One natural way of responding to this puzzle has been developed by Tyler Burge (1993) (Burge focuses on memory, but much the same could be said for perception):

Memory does not supply for the demonstration propositions about memory, the reasoner or past events. It supplies the propositions that serve as links in the demonstration itself. Or rather, it *preserves* them, together with their judgmental force, and makes them available for use at later times. Normally, the content of the knowledge of longer demonstration is not more about memory, the reasoner, or contingent events than that of a shorter demonstration. One does not justify the demonstration by appeals to memory. One justifies it by appeals to the steps and the inferential transitions of the demonstration...In a deduction, reasoning processes' working properly depends on memory's preserving the results of previous reasoning. But memory's preserving such results does not add to the justificational force of the reasoning. It is rather a background condition for the reasoning's success.[11]

What exactly is the distinction between preservative memory and substantive memory that Burge is invoking here? As he notes, it is reminiscent of the distinction, familiar from psychology textbooks, between episodic memory and semantic memory. We distinguish between remembering *being told* that the Battle of Hastings was in 1066, and remembering that the Battle of Hastings was in 1066. The former is substantive memory, which can import the event of being told about the battle into reasoning and can justify believing that it happened. The latter is just (preservative) memory of the proposition itself. It only serves to preserve the proposition itself (along with its 'judgmental force') and does not contribute any new justification.[12]

Given this distinction, we can say that the reason why a long proof is able to provide a priori justification for its conclusion is that the only use of memory that is essential in a long proof is preservative memory, rather than substantive memory. If substantive memory of the act of writing down a proposition were required to arrive at justified belief in the conclusion of the proof, that might compromise the conclusion's a priori status.

However, once we lean on the notion of preservative memory in this way, we might be tempted to think, as Burge clearly does, that the justifiers in a proof must be just the mathematical propositions themselves, rather than any sort of accompanying mental state.

For while we think we understand how a *proposition* might be the object of a merely preservative memory, we might find ourselves mystified by how a *mental state* or *event* could be the object of such a memory. It looks as though remembering a mental state or event will involve a substantive use of memory, rather than just a preservative one.

If you are impressed with this line of thought, you might find yourself driven to think that, in the case of a mathematical proof, the justifiers must consist in propositions, rather than in any mental states, like those of intuition or mental calculation, which might have those propositions as their intentional objects.

And, as I emphasized earlier, once you have arrived at this point, it is bound to look as though Williamson's difficulty simply reasserts itself. For, if the correct view of justifiers in the mathematical case is that they are propositions, that would presumably also be the correct view in the empirical case. However, if one adopts such a view in the empirical case, the role of perceptual experience, just like that of preservative memory, would have to be thought of as simply *providing access* to the relevant justifiers (the propositions themselves), rather than playing any essential role in justifying them. And at that point we would be landed back again with the difficulty of dramatically over-generating the beliefs that would have to count as a priori justified.

Resolving the puzzle

The correct reply to this argument is to reject its assumption that the only things that preservative memory is capable of preserving are propositions (along with, at most, their judgmental force).

Rather, there is no reason why we should not regard preservative memory as being able to preserve a proposition not only with its judgmental force but *also* along with its *epistemic status*. Doing so will allow us to say that justifiers are mental states, but that no substantive memory of those states is required in order for the proposition that is justified by them to be later used in warrant-transmitting reasoning. Once the proposition is justified by the relevant mental states, it, along with its judgmental force and epistemic status, is preserved in memory for use in later reason-generating inference.

This way of construing matters is reinforced by the consideration that even at the point of *onset* of belief in the proposition, the justification of the proposition by the relevant mental state doesn't depend on a second-order *awareness* of that mental state, but only on the existence of the first-order mental state itself.

To illustrate the claims I am making here, consider an empirical case involving justification by visual perception. Suppose you believe, as I do, that my justification for believing that these sediment samples' containing certain clusters of carbon atoms can be irreducibly dependent on my having a certain sort of visual experience of them (I will assume for the purposes of argument that this proposition is purely observational). When I later come to use this proposition in an inference to the best explanation, to conclude that the Earth collided with an asteroid 250 million years ago, it would be counterintuitive to say that substantive memory of my having had the earlier visual experiences enters into the justification for my conclusion. Rather, the original experiences serve to justify the observational premise, and then that positive epistemic status gets simply preserved in mounting the inference on its basis. My justification for believing the conclusion rests on the justification that I have for the premises, which in turn depends on my prior visual experiences; the justification doesn't rest on my remembering those experiences or, at the point of origin, on my being aware of having those experiences (even if it may not be possible to have an experience without having some awareness of it).

So, even in a humdrum empirical case, it is natural to think that preservative memory can preserve propositions not merely with their judgmental force but also with their epistemic status intact.[13]

And, of course, what goes for empirical inference also goes for mathematical proof. Just because a mental state was involved in the justification of an earlier step in the proof doesn't mean that one needs to have a substantive memory of that mental state in order to justifiably infer from that premise to a later step in the proof. It is sufficient that the premise was justified, and that its justificational status was preserved by preservative memory.[14]

Although I have rejected Williamson's argument against the possibility of formulating a cogent theoretical distinction between the a priori and the a posteriori, it has provided us with an opportunity to learn an important lesson: Taking the distinction between the a priori and the a posteriori seriously is not compatible with an increasingly influential conception of justifiers as propositions. Rather, taking the distinction seriously depends on a traditional view of justification as stemming from mental states and events, some types of which are taken to be sources of a posteriori warrant, while others of a priori warrant.

The discussion itself illustrates a more general phenomenon to which we will have occasion to return: that the distinction between the a priori and the a posteriori interacts very closely with issues in other areas of epistemology, and in philosophy more generally. Commitments arrived at elsewhere, on grounds having nothing to do with the a priori, may put pressure on one's ability to make sense of the notion. Once the dependence is made clear, a useful discussion about the trade-offs involved can ensue.[15]

3

Williamson's central argument

Having attempted to show that no top-down characterization of the a priori–a posteriori distinction can hope to succeed in lining up with the paradigm intuitive examples, Williamson changes tack. He next attempts to argue that whatever distinction is marked by the paradigm examples, it cannot be of epistemological significance. How does Williamson propose to support this strong and surprising conclusion?

Williamson's argumentative strategy is striking: it is to describe a pair of examples with the following features:

(A) One of them is a clear case of someone's justifiably believing a proposition in an a priori way;
(B) The other is a clear case of someone's justifiably believing another proposition in an a posteriori way;
(C) The ways of justifiably believing involved in the examples are *broadly representative* of the ways in which propositions are justifiably believed a priori and a posteriori, respectively; and, finally,
(D) There is no epistemologically interesting difference between the two ways of believing specified.

I am prepared to concede that, if we really did have a pair of examples with all these features, we would have to admit that the distinction between a priori and a posteriori ways of knowing is not epistemologically interesting.

I will argue, however, that Williamson's pair of examples lack *any* of these features. Williamson's examples involve the following two truths:

(1) All crimson things are red.
(2) All recent volumes of *Who's Who* are red.

He describes the case of Norman who is said to come to know (1) in the following distinctive way: Having acquired competence with the concepts involved in (1) independently of one another, he comes to know (1) by using his imagination in the following way: he imagines a crimson thing, notes that it is red, under the imaginative supposition, and so concludes that (1) is true.

Williamson is aware that a reader will worry that Norman may have imagined a peripheral shade of crimson. If one shade of crimson is red, it does not follow that all are. In reply, he says,

The relevant cognitive skills must be taken to include sensitivity to such matters.

Williamson then wants to give a very similar story for Norman's knowledge of (2).

Norman is as already described. He learns the complex phrase 'recent volumes of *Who's Who*' by learning 'recent', 'volume', '*Who's Who*' and so on. He is not taught any rule like (2), connecting 'recent volume of *Who's Who*' and 'red'. Through practice and feedback, he becomes very skilful in judging by eye whether something is a recent volume of *Who's Who* (by reading the title), and whether something is red. Now Norman is asked whether (2) holds. He has not previously considered any such question. Nevertheless, he can quite easily come to know (2), without looking at any recent volumes of *Who's Who* to check whether they are red, or even remembering any recent volumes of *Who's Who* to check whether they were red, or any other new exercise of perception or memory. Rather, he assents to (2) after brief reflection along something like the following lines. First, Norman uses his skill in making visual judgments with 'recent volume of *Who's Who*' to visually imagine a recent volume of *Who's Who*. Then he uses his skill in making visual judgments with 'red' to judge, within the imaginative supposition, 'It is red'. This involves the same general human capacity as before to transpose 'online' cognitive skills originally developed in perception into corresponding 'offline' cognitive skills subsequently applied in imagination. No episodic memories of prior experiences, for example of recent volumes of *Who's Who*, play any role. As a result of the process, Norman accepts (2). Since his performance was sufficiently skilful, background conditions were normal, and so on, he thereby comes to know (2). (2013: 296)

And so Williamson concludes:

The problem is obvious. As characterized above, the cognitive processes underlying Norman's clearly a priori knowledge of (1) and his clearly a posteriori knowledge of (2) are almost exactly similar. If so, how can there be a deep epistemological difference between them? But if there is none, then the a priori–a posteriori distinction is epistemologically shallow.   (2013: 296–7)

Williamson goes on to give a theoretical *diagnosis* of what makes these two cases of putative knowledge similar and of why they pose a problem for the traditional distinction between the a priori and the a posteriori. He contends that it is because, in both of them, experience plays a role that is *intermediate* between a purely enabling role and an epistemic one. I will come back to this diagnosis.

Discussion of Williamson's central argument

Williamson's argument is interesting in a number of ways, especially in its focus on the imagination as a source of a posteriori justification. While the imagination has always been regarded as a potential source of a priori justification, much less thought has been given to the way in which it can sometimes serve as a source of a posteriori justification.

While I agree with Williamson that the imagination can serve as a source of a posteriori justification, I don't believe that its use is anywhere near as ubiquitous as his argument requires.

Nor do I believe that, when it does serve as a source of such justification, it functions in the basically externalist, Reliabilist way in which Williamson's stories about Norman presuppose.

I will start by looking critically at (B) and move on to show that none of propositions (A) through (D) is satisfied.

In my experience, many philosophers have greeted with raised eyebrows Williamson's claim that Norman could come to justifiably believe (2) in the way described. That is my own reaction as well.

Norman is said to *imagine* a single instance of a volume of *Who's Who*, note that, within the imaginative supposition, its color is red, and conclude on this basis that *all* recent volumes of *Who's Who* are red. And his belief is supposed to be justified, indeed, justified with a strength sufficient for knowledge.

That should certainly seem prima facie puzzling. We wouldn't credit Norman with justified belief that *all* recent volumes of *Who's Who* are red on the basis of his vivid and accurate *perception* of a *single* red volume. Why would we be so much more epistemically generous with regard to his act of *imagining* a single such volume? Isn't imagining even less constrained by actual truth than perception?

In fairness to Williamson, we should emphasize that there is supposed to be more to Norman's method of forming a belief in (2) than a single act of imagination. On those bare bones, Williamson sprinkles a heap of reliability-securing counterfactuals. He is not explicit about what they are, but perhaps something along these lines: If all the recent volumes of *Who's Who* had not been red, but had rather been green, Norman would not have imagined a red volume of *Who's Who*, but rather a green one; and if they not been of any uniform color, then Norman would have drawn a blank while trying to imagine one. And so on.

According to Williamson, then, while Norman's single act of imagining may not, by itself, be enough for Norman to justifiably believe (2), Norman's act of imagining, along with the truth of these counterfactuals, *is*.

To my mind, and as I will explain in much greater detail below, this verdict looks less like the deliverance of intuition than the deliverance of a prior allegiance to the dubious doctrine of Epistemic Reliabilism—roughly, the view that the reliability of a belief-forming method, regardless of whether the agent is aware of its reliability, is *sufficient* for a belief based upon that method to be epistemically justified.

Since I take there to be clear-cut and decisive counterexamples to Reliabilism—for example, Keith Lehrer's Mr. TrueTemp—I am not moved by Williamson's claims about Norman's reasonable belief in (2).[16]

Williamson's choice of name for his fictional subject is risky, since it can't help but bring to mind one of the most well-known and persuasive counterexamples to Reliabilism, namely, Lawrence Bonjour's clairvoyant Norman.[17] No doubt meant as an act of defiance, it nonetheless vividly reminds us of all the reasons we have for rejecting the epistemic upshot that Williamson claims for his examples.

I take the existence of such counterexamples to Reliabilism to derive from the fact that epistemic justification is a normative notion, one that is internally tied to notions of praise and blame. So, I don't agree with Williamson that Norman ends up reasonably believing (2).[18]

From this perspective, Williamson's sprinkling of Reliabilist counterfactuals onto Norman's single act of imagining does very little to render plausible the claim that Norman's belief in (2) is justified.

On the contrary, since Reliabilism predicts that Norman *is* justified in believing (2), whereas he intuitively is not, all that Williamson's example accomplishes is to add to the already rich trove of *other* Normans who serve as powerful counterexamples to Reliabilist views of justification.[19]

In other words, Williamson's Norman teaches us more of an old lesson about the tenability of Reliabilist views of justification than a new lesson about the shallowness of the a priori–a posteriori distinction.

I will now proceed to arguing in detail that Norman could not have come to know (2) in the way that Williamson's argument claims.

Using the imagination to justify belief in (2)

Suppose Norman (who has seen nothing but red volumes of *Who's Who*) sets himself the task of imagining an instance of such a volume and comes up with an image of one that is white and decorated with a smattering of small green and yellow polka dots.

There is a perfectly good sense in which his imagination did not misfire and his performance cannot be called unskilled. In this sense, Norman is free to imagine whatever he can. We may call this sense *fanciful* imagining.

We often want imagining to be fanciful, especially when we are exploring not how things *are* but how they *might possibly have been* in the most unrestricted sense of term—metaphysically possible, as we have come to say.

How can it be that one case of imagining a false scenario is faultless, while another case of imagining a false scenario is said to be mistaken precisely because it is false? The obvious answer is that there are two different types of imaginative task here, subject to different norms. We may call this second type of imagining, *realistic* imagining as opposed to *fanciful* imagining.

Fanciful imagining is not answerable to what reality is actually like, and may not even be answerable to what reality is possibly like: Escher's drawings of geometrically impossible configurations are not faulty. Realistic imagining, on the other hand, is answerable to what reality is actually like, or to what it would be like, were certain non-actual conditions to obtain (for example, when the imagination is used to assess counterfactuals).

The kind of imagining that Norman has to engage in has to be, of course, a species of *realistic* imagining, since he is trying to use it to figure something out about the actual world.

How would Norman get himself to perform the one sort of imagining as opposed to the other? Presumably, the answer is to be found in his *intentions*. If he imagines with the intention of figuring out what is merely possible, or without any purpose at all, he imagines fancifully. If he imagines with the intention of figuring out how things are actually, or how they would have been if certain conditions had obtained, he imagines realistically.

What would it be to imagine something with the intention of using that imagining as a way of finding out about the actual world? Presumably, it would be to imagine in such a way that what one allows oneself to imagine is constrained by what one knows about the actual world. One brings to bear what one already knows, or justifiably believes, about the actual world to rule out certain imagined scenarios. When Williamson says, 'The relevant cognitive skills must be taken to include sensitivity to such matters', he is assuming that Norman is engaging in realistic imagining and constraining his imagination by his perceptually acquired background knowledge of what volumes of *Who's Who* are like.

The question is how this process is best described, and, in particular, whether it can be correctly characterized by the sort of resolutely externalist, Reliabilist picture sketched by Williamson.

In answering this, we must bear in mind that Norman is not merely using his imagination to figure out what a *particular event* was like—for example, what it was like to be at Barack Obama's first inaugural; rather, he is trying to use his imagination to figure out what property *all* the members of a given set have, on the basis of imagining a single member of that set. That is a significantly more ambitious cognitive task and carries specific epistemic burdens.

To get a better sense of what these burdens are, let's switch examples. Suppose Norman sets out to realistically imagine a VW Beetle and he imagines one accurately enough, as it happens a red one. We can't accuse Norman of imagining inaccurately, for there have been red Beetles.

But he certainly wouldn't be justified, on this basis alone, in concluding that all Beetles are red. And Norman himself, being a competent thinker, would know that. He wouldn't be tempted to conclude anything about the color of all Beetles because (we may suppose) it would be part of his background knowledge that there is no dominant color that all Beetles have.

To reasonably conclude something about the color of all Beetles from a single imagined instance, Norman would at least have to *fail* to believe that they have no dominant color. But is that enough?

Suppose Norman has no views whatsoever about whether all Beetles have the same color. He imagines a red Beetle and concludes that they all are red. I think it is clear that he would not be justified, even if in fact they were all red.

So, it looks as though, for Norman to be justified in using his single act of imagining to conclude something about the color of all the members of the set to which the imagined item belongs, he must antecedently be justified in believing that there is a single color possessed by all the members of the set, the only question being which one.

But is even this background belief sufficient to yield reasonable belief? Suppose Norman recalls a trip he took to London some years ago. He remembers being struck by the taxis there and by their distinctive dark color. But as he casts his mind back, he finds he can't recall what that color was. He remembers that all the taxis he saw had the same dark color, but for the life of him, he can't recall what that color was. Were they navy blue, or brown, or black?

I don't see Norman settling this question by thinking to himself, Let me go ahead and imagine one; surely, they are all likely to be of the color that I imagine this one to have. If Norman can't recall what color the taxis have, I don't see how his imagining one at will is going to be a good basis on which he can settle this factual question. I am not aware of any result that says that, if a subject can't recall what color F's mostly have, they are most likely to have the color that he imagines them to have, even if he's trying to imagine realistically.

Well, under what conditions *would* Norman be able to use his imagining of a single taxi to generate a justified belief about the color that all London taxis have?

It is entirely unclear to me that there are *any* conditions under which Norman would be able to do this. At a minimum, it seems to me, he must have reason to believe (a) that the taxis have a dominant color, and (b) that the taxi he imagines is appropriately representative of that dominant color.

But how could Norman possibly satisfy these two conditions without being able to *recall* what the dominant color of London taxis is? How could he know that there *is* a single color that London taxis tend to have and that *this* color is appropriately representative of what that color is, without actually being able to recall that color?

Williamson seems to think that it is enough to scotch the suggestion that Norman is *recalling*, as opposed to imagining, to stipulate that no feats of recalling particular experiences or events is involved in his description of Norman's way of coming to know (2).

But not all acts of recall need involve the recall of a particular experience or event. To advert to our earlier discussion of preservative memory, just as we may recall propositions without remembering specific events in which we learned those propositions, so we may recall generic facts about how an F looks, without recalling the look of any particular encountered F.

Having seen many London taxis, Norman may be able to recall what a London taxi looks like, without recalling any particular London taxi. He calls up a stored generic image. Having seen many frogs, Norman may be able to recall what a frog looks like, without recalling any particular frog that he has encountered. He calls up a stored generic image.

And the point is that, unless that is what is in fact going on in Norman's 'imagining' of a recent volume of *Who's Who*—unless what he's actually doing is recalling a stored generic image of a recent volume of *Who's Who*, under roughly that description—he cannot have arrived at a justified belief about all recent volumes of *Who's Who*.

I conclude that Williamson's argument's reliance on (B) leaves it open to serious doubt: Norman could not have come to know (2) in the way that it claims.

Using the imagination to justify belief in (1)

What, though, about Williamson's story about how Norman comes to know (1), his claim (A)?

Williamson's account here is not easy to wrap one's mind around, because it is hard to see how someone might have learned 'crimson' and 'red' completely independently of one another.

I certainly agree that one can acquire the concepts of the primary colors independently of one another; indeed, I believe it's an important point in the theory of the a priori (to be discussed in a later piece in this volume) that one can acquire the concept *red* independently of acquiring the concept *green*. It's harder for me to see how one could acquire *red* and *crimson* without realizing that crimson is a shade of red. Borderline cases aside, having the concept *red*, one might think, is in part to have a recognitional capacity to recognize shades of red on the basis of their looks.

But let's put this worry to one side. Let's play along with the idea that Norman comes to know (1) by imagining something colored a particular shade of crimson and noting, within the imaginative supposition, that it is red, and concluding on that basis, that all crimson things are red.

Well, we saw in our discussion of (2) that if Norman is to be able to justifiably generalize on the basis of isolated acts of imagining, that he needs to satisfy certain background conditions. He needs already to know (or reasonably believe):

(2a)   That the volumes of *Who's Who* have a typical color,
and
(2b)   That the imagined instance is appropriately representative of that typical color.

Similarly, in the case of (1) he will need to know (or reasonably believe):

(1a)   that there is a dominant color determinable to which all shades of crimson belong,
and
(1b)   that the shade that he has imagined is properly representative in that respect of all shades of crimson.

Now, by bottom-up standards these two sets of beliefs are very different from one another: the first set could only have been justified a posteriori, while the second set would typically have been justified a priori.

Hence, under the only conditions under which Norman's beliefs could have resulted in knowledge, we see that there is a glaring difference between the two cases that Williamson insists are epistemologically identical. Once the cases are redescribed, so that they do in fact yield knowledge on Norman's part of the relevant propositions, (D) comes out false.

Perhaps Williamson will respond that he can concede that knowledge of (1) involves a priori background beliefs, while knowledge of (2) involves a posteriori background beliefs, while insisting that the differences between them are bound to be epistemologically shallow.

In the present context, however, that answer would be question-begging. We are owed an argument that the distinction is shallow. And, so far, the only argument we have been given for that rests on claims (A), (B), (C), and (D), all of which, I have argued, are false.[20]

4

The epistemic–enabling distinction redux

At the beginning of this paper, I rejected one attempt by Williamson to raise a theoretical difficulty for satisfactory top-down formulations of the a priori–a posteriori distinction. That difficulty turned on the claim that it is impossible to specify the notion of 'experience', in the phrase 'epistemically independent of experience', in a way that coheres with the classifications that we are prepared to make bottom-up.

My reply stated, in effect, that we could specify the notion well enough with a *list*: a justification for a belief is epistemically independent of experience provided that it does not epistemically depend on sensory experience, introspection, or substantive uses of memory. Intuition, certain uses of the imagination, and reflection could, consistently with the justification's being a priori, play an epistemic role.

Williamson has a further difficulty for putative top-down formulations that needs to be addressed, even if my reply to his challenge about the characterization of 'experience' were to be accepted.

This further difficulty, according to Williamson, is that, however exactly 'experience' is characterized, in most of its uses it will be neither purely epistemic nor purely enabling, but will somehow fall between those two poles.

Indeed, Williamson believes that that is precisely what his Norman examples illustrate. When Norman comes to 'know' that all recent volumes of *Who's Who* are red, through the use of his imagination, sense experience is not playing an evidential role—he's said not to be relying on actually perceiving such volumes or on recalling seeing such volumes. On the other hand, it's also not the case that sense experience is playing a merely enabling role, since it is doing much more than merely enabling Norman to 'access' the relevant thoughts.

Since we have rejected the claim that Norman could come to know (1) and (2) in the way claimed, we don't have much reason to worry about this particular argument.

We should point out, though, that the issue engaged here is another good example of how our topic interacts with other central issues in epistemology. For Williamson is surely right that if we were Reliabilists about justification, if we were to think of the *reliability* of our cognitive mechanisms as epistemically sufficient for the justification of the beliefs formed using them, then we would have to maintain that sense experience may often play a role intermediate between enabling and evidential. For it will often play a role in honing the reliability of our cognitive abilities, thereby going beyond a merely enabling role, but yet fall short of playing an evidential role.

My rejection of Williamson's Norman examples is of a piece with my rejection of Reliabilist conceptions of justification: their failings, in my view, stem from the same source.

Having said that, we can hardly fault Williamson for following through on his foundational ideological commitments in epistemology and for ingeniously tracing out their consequences for the a priori–a posteriori distinction.

As a good rhetorician, Williamson tries to make us believe that the reasons he provides for his novel style of skepticism about the a priori–a posteriori distinction are independent of the ideology of Reliabilism, or the conception of justifiers as propositions. But if my counterarguments are correct, he has not succeeded in providing such ideology-independent reasons.

5

Conclusion

What have we learned?

Our non-collusive agreement about a wide range of examples shows that the a priori–a posteriori distinction is a genuine one. And we have yet to be given a good reason for doubting that this distinction has the importance for philosophy that it appears to have.

Of course, the distinction between a priori and a posteriori, like all complicated notions in philosophy, interacts with a number of other issues—most notably, those concerning the nature of experience, independence, justification, and understanding. If you adopt certain (in my view, radical and implausible) views about these related issues, you may well end up not being able to make sense of the distinction or to find much importance in it.

But this may well show us more about your take on the related issues than about the a priori.

I do not want to minimize the challenges that remain for the distinction between the a priori and the a posteriori. For the moment, however, I want to emphasize that we have yet to be given a good reason for not giving the distinction the centrality in philosophy that it seems to deserve.[21]

Notes

1. This paper originates as a reply to Timothy Williamson's Chapter 8, an early version of which was given at the NYIP's conference on the a priori held at NYU's Villa La Pietra in June of 2013. It has not previously been published.

2. I will focus on justification rather than knowledge, since I continue to regard justification as the more fundamental notion. Even in the context of this debate with Williamson, this is non-prejudicial, since Williamson is explicit that his style of skepticism about the a priori is not supposed to depend on his well-known 'knowledge first' conception of epistemology (see Williamson 2000).

3. For some influential criticisms of the notion of a priori justification see Quine 1951; Kitcher 1983, 2000.

4. I use the same examples that Williamson uses to illustrate a 'bottom-up' approach to the a priori–a posteriori distinction.

5. Williamson tends to say 'evidential' rather than 'epistemic'. Since evidentialism, the view that experience can only justify by providing evidence, is controversial, it is more neutral to frame the issue in the way that I have.

6. Williamson 2013: 293–4.

7. For a useful discussion of various attempts, see Casullo (2003).

8. Gibbard, private correspondence.

9. For obvious reasons, it's especially popular for those working within Bayesian frameworks.

10. See, for example, Chisholm 1977.

11. Burge 1993: 462–3.

12. Burge 1993: 465. A few paragraphs earlier, Burge allows that even substantive memories might sometimes play a non-epistemic role:

> Substantive memories of specific events, objects, experiences . . . may play a role in deductive reasoning. They may aid reasoning without being elements in the justification they aid. So, for example, we may draw pictures in a proof, or make use of mnemonic devices to aid understanding and facilitate reasoning, without relying on them to enhance the mathematical justification. (Burge 1993: 464)

> On this view, even *substantive* memories of past events, e.g., what one drew on a diagram, can play a merely enabling role, rather than an epistemic one. Sometimes Burge talks about experience 'triggering' something that makes a warrant available. I think this view is probably right, but I won't dwell on it now.

13. See Burge 1993: 462–3.

14. The thesis concerning justificational status urged in the preceding paragraphs is also supported by reflection on the well-known case of 'forgotten evidence', though I won't be able to pause to discuss it here.

15. This point is also emphasized in Casullo (2012), although we don't necessarily have the same interactions in mind.

16. See Lehrer 1990: 163–4.

17. See ch. 3 of Bonjour (1985).

18. Notice that Williamson's claim that reliability is *sufficient* for justified belief goes well beyond a claim to which some may be sympathetic, namely, that reliability is necessary for justification. I also believe, but won't argue for it here, that cases of surreptitious envatment show the necessity claim is also false.

19. See Bonjour (1985). For further critical discussion of Reliabilism see Cohen (1984) and Foley (1985).

20. Although I did not discuss (C) explicitly, its falsity follows directly from the falsity of (A) and (B).

21. This paper was initially drafted in 2012 for a session on Timothy Williamson's paper at a New York Institute of Philosophy meeting slated for November of that year. That meeting had to be postponed because of Hurricane Sandy. It was subsequently rescheduled for the summer of 2013 at NYU's Villa La Pietra, in Florence. I benefited from the comments of the audience there, and from those at the University of North Carolina at Chapel Hill, the University of Texas at Austin, and the Philosophical Society at Oxford University. I have also benefited from comments by Crispin Wright, Paul Horwich, Susanna Siegel, Antonella Mallozzi, and Jim Pryor.

10

Reply to Boghossian on the Distinction between the A Priori and the A Posteriori[1]

Timothy Williamson

In 'How Deep is the Distinction between A Priori and A Posteriori knowledge?' (Chapter 8, originally Williamson 2013), I argue that, although a distinction can be drawn between a priori and a posteriori knowledge, it marks no deep epistemological difference (the argument was adumbrated in *The Philosophy of Philosophy* (2007a: 165–9)). Naturally, I did not expect defenders of the depth (or importance) of the distinction to give it up without a fight. A challenge like mine is best evaluated in light of the unfolding history of attempts to answer it. Boghossian responds in 'Do We Have Reason to Doubt the Importance of the Distinction between A Priori and A Posteriori Knowledge? A Reply to Williamson' (Chapter 9). A thoughtful and sophisticated reply such as his provides a welcome test of my arguments. In this chapter, I will use his objections to demonstrate the robustness of my original considerations.[2]

1. Preliminaries

Boghossian raises some preliminary concerns about my way of setting up the dialectic. I will get them out of the way before moving on to the main issues.

Unlike me, Boghossian regards justification as a more fundamental matter than knowledge, and so formulates his critique in terms of the former rather than the latter. I will speak of both. For present purposes, I will not assume the priority of knowledge.

In Chapter 8, I made the standard assumption that for a priori knowledge or justification, experience can play an *enabling* role, but cannot play an *evidential* one. Boghossian prefers the terms 'epistemic' and 'justificatory' to 'evidential', on the grounds that 'Since evidentialism, the view that experience can only justify by providing evidence, is controversial, it is more neutral to frame the issue' his way (Chapter 9, n. 4). I will use his word 'epistemic' here to emphasize that my argument does not depend on a contentious choice of terminology.

Debating the A Priori. Paul Boghossian and Timothy Williamson, Oxford University Press (2020).
© Paul Boghossian and Timothy Williamson.
DOI: 10.1093/oso/9780198851707.001.0001

Boghossian also objects to the assumption that the alternative to an epistemic role must be positively characterized as 'enabling', since that opens up the possibility of a role intermediate between the epistemic and the enabling, which he takes my argument to exploit. As he points out, the friend of the a priori might simply forbid experience to play an epistemic role in a priori knowledge or justification, without positively characterizing its permitted roles. That negative approach has a cost, however, for if one refuses to specify an appropriate contrast for 'epistemic', the latter term loses clarity. A good explanation of a term typically gives paradigms of cases where it does *not* apply, as well as paradigms of cases where it *does* apply. But that reservation is not urgent, for Boghossian is mistaken in thinking that my critique relied on the claim that some roles for experience in knowledge or justification are neither epistemic nor enabling. When I used formulations such as 'sense experience can play a role that is neither strictly evidential nor purely enabling' (2007a: 165) and 'the role of experience in [some] cases is more than purely enabling but less than strictly evidential' (Chapter 8, p. 125), the words 'strictly' and 'purely' were there for a purpose. Just as a long rambling speech in a debate on some question may be neither strictly relevant nor purely irrelevant, without being neither relevant nor irrelevant, so a role for experience can be neither strictly epistemic nor purely non-epistemic, without being neither epistemic nor non-epistemic. I was not denying that all the roles at issue are either epistemic or enabling; I was pointing out that some of those roles differ crucially from both the paradigms of the epistemic and the paradigms of the enabling, in ways that make trouble for the picture of a deep divide between the a priori and the a posteriori.

In brief, I was not insinuating any intermediate space between 'evidential' and 'enabling' roles for experience in which to do any of the alleged dirty work.

Boghossian also has concerns about my use of the distinction between 'inner' and 'outer' experience. It figures only briefly in my argument (Chapter 8, pp. 120–1), when I ask whether the term 'experience' in the definition of 'a priori' and 'a posteriori' should be understood as restricted to 'outer' experience (experience by the usual five senses), or as applying to 'inner' experience too (experience not by the usual five senses). I point out that excluding 'inner' experience would have intro-spective knowledge of one's inner states count as a priori, an unwanted result. I therefore assumed that no such restriction was to be read into 'experience' in defining 'a priori' and 'a posteriori', and went on to raise a difficulty for the resulting definitions by comparing the role of experience (usually classified as 'outer') in observation-based knowledge of nature and the role of experience (usually classified as 'inner') in proof-based knowledge of mathematics. Boghossian makes two com-plaints. First, he finds the distinction between 'inner' and 'outer' experience unclear. Second, he accuses me of using it to smuggle in the unwarranted assumption that all 'inner' experience must be treated uniformly in defining 'a priori' and 'a posteriori'. By contrast, he suggests, one might treat introspective experience very differently from some imaginative experience, even if both count as 'inner'.

I agree with Boghossian that the distinction between 'inner' and 'outer' experience is not wholly clear: for instance, imagining how the landscape ahead would look if the weather were different has both 'inner' and 'outer' elements. But since I only needed to apply the distinction to clear cases, and was anyway doing so in order to argue that one should *not* rely on the distinction in defining 'a priori' and 'a posteriori', its residual unclarity was harmless for my purposes. As for Boghossian's concern that I was sneaking in a requirement to treat all 'inner' experience uniformly, closer reading of my challenge at issue shows it to depend only on a comparison of two more specific kinds of experience, in observation-based knowledge of nature and proof-based knowledge of mathematics, respectively (Chapter 8, pp. 120–1). It did not depend on classifying the former as 'inner' and the latter as 'outer', nor on generalizing over all 'inner' experience. As I originally formulated the relevant challenge, it was this: if my experience of going through the proof merely gives me access to the mathematical support for its conclusion, despite being essential to my knowledge of the conclusion, why suppose that my experience of observing facts about the external environment does *more* than merely give me access to the physical support for a natural scientific conclusion, again despite being essential to my knowledge of that conclusion? In the next section, I will develop a more detailed version of the challenge in terms more like Boghossian's, without ever using the terminology of 'inner' and 'outer'.

In his own remarks towards distinguishing the a priori from the a posteriori, Boghossian largely (but not entirely) avoids the term 'experience'. Instead, he speaks of 'mental states'. I find that an improvement, for 'experience' has become problematic jargon in philosophy, often invoking a background theory on which experience is made up of qualia, entities explained only by the utterance of the magic words 'what it is like'. Of course, the word also has an everyday use, as in 'He has never had the experience of being a government minister, but he knows what it is like, because his sister is one', but that is not what such philosophers have in mind: knowing what it is like to be a government minister is presumably not a matter of knowing what qualia a government minister typically has (see also Snowdon 2010). Not using the word 'experience' as a load-bearing term is a step towards avoiding unwarranted assumptions in the philosophy of mind. I used it in expounding the traditional distinction between the a priori and the a posteriori just because it is traditional to use the word in that context. But I do not suggest that friends of the distinction *must* use the word (or a synonym) in explaining the distinction: Boghossian is a counterexample. In fairness, I will therefore avoid the word 'experience' at key points in what follows.

2. The Initial Challenge

Boghossian expresses a tentative preference for an account of a priori and a posteriori justification along the following lines: a justification for a belief is a priori if and only if 'it does not epistemically depend on sensory experience, introspection, or substantive uses of memory', even if it epistemically depends on '[i]ntuition, certain uses of the imagination, [or] reflection' (Chapter 9, p. 154). The justification is a posteriori if and only if it epistemically depends on sensory experience, introspection, or substantive uses of memory. He says little to explain the difference between epistemic and non-epistemic dependence, but explicitly disavows the idea that epistemic dependence must be evidential dependence.

Boghossian speaks of mental states as *justifiers*; he may be equating epistemic dependence on a mental state with the latter's doing the justifying itself, as opposed to merely being a precondition for something else to do the justifying. However, in practice that form of words does not get one very far when applying the distinction. For it is unclear which of the conditions for being justified in believing something count as doing the justifying and which do not, especially if the justification is not by evidence.

In the case of perceptual justification, Boghossian writes, 'To me it seems obvious that my justification for believing that, for example, there is a red wall in front of me, is irreducibly dependent on my having a *visual impression* as of there being a red wall in front of me' (Chapter 9, p. 144; his italics). But what is supposed to determine whether this irreducible dependence is *epistemic*?

Rather than attempt to resolve these issues on Boghossian's behalf, we can see how they play out in a comparison between perceptual justification of beliefs about the environment and proof-based justification of beliefs about mathematics.

Consider first a mixed case: someone reading a correct proof of a new mathematical theorem. To avoid complications with testimonial knowledge, assume that he does not defer to the proof's author; indeed, he initially distrusts her. However, he goes through the proof, understands it, and is convinced. By a normal mathematical process, he acquires both knowledge and justified belief that the theorem holds. Are his knowledge and justification a priori? Consider the point in reading the proof when he comes to a step of modus ponens, from '*A*' and 'If *A*, *B*' to '*B*'. He already has knowledge and justified belief that *A* and that if *A*, *B*. He visually recognizes what he sees written in front of him as an instance of modus ponens, and—being a competent logician—consequently acquires knowledge and justified belief that *B*. He has a visual impression as of there being a written instance of modus ponens in front of him. If he lacked that impression, he would not be justified in believing that *B*. Of course, a brilliant mathematician could start ignoring their visual impressions and just work out the proof for themselves, but that is not what our uncreative mathematician is doing. He is just following the proof in front of him; it was not salient to him before being pointed out in the proof that the premises for a step of modus ponens were available. *His* justification in Boghossian's sense for believing that *B* is irreducibly dependent on his having a visual impression as of there being an instance of modus ponens in front of him. Moreover, the dependence seems to be epistemic by Boghossian's standards, for if visual impressions are justifiers in the way he suggests, the mathematician's visual impression is part of what justifies his belief that *B*, rather than a mere precondition of what justifies, since it is integral to his recognition of the step's validity.

A natural objection at this point is that what justifies is the mathematical proof itself, and that the very same proof can be both imagined and seen written down. But that objection is not open to Boghossian. For he is at pains to argue that justifiers are *mental states*, not propositions or the like. A mathematical proof is not a mental state. Moreover, given his account of the distinction between a priori and a posteriori justification, he must treat contemplating a proof in sense experience and contemplating it in imagination as *different* mental states for these purposes, since he lists epistemic dependence on sense experience on the a posteriori side of his line and epistemic dependence on 'certain uses of the imagination' on the a priori side. Indeed, Boghossian insists that his justification for believing that there is a red wall in front of him is irreducibly dependent on his having a *visual impression* as of there being a red wall in front of him; he does not treat a more generic mental state such as having prima facie evidence of there being a red wall in front of him as a suitable candidate. Presumably, having such a generic attitude to the instance of modus ponens would be equally unsuitable for his purposes.

Thus our plodding mathematician's justification for his belief that the theorem holds seems to depend epistemically on sensory experience, so Boghossian's criterion counts it as a posteriori. That is not a happy result, for the case is typical of much proof-based justification for mathematical beliefs, the supposed paradigm of non-trivial a priori justification. Furthermore, natural attempts to reinterpret the criterion in order to extract the opposite verdict risk making a standard justification for the belief that there is a red wall in front of one too generic to depend epistemically on sensory experience, and so perhaps to come out a priori by the criterion—an even more unhappy result.

Could Boghossian bite the bullet and say that, strictly speaking, only going through a proof in the imagination (or internally) rather than on paper provides a priori justification? That would add support to my charge that the distinction between a priori and a posteriori knowledge or justification is shallow. In mathematical practice, the difference between going through a proof in the imagination and going through it on paper is insignificant. If a mathematician presents a complex alleged proof in conversation, and a colleague says that she would need to see it written down before she could decide whether it was valid, there is no sense that she is resorting to importantly different standards of justification, or no longer working in a properly mathematical way.

Thus, given my challenge to undermine in a principled way the unexpected analogy between observation-based and proof-based knowledge or justification, Boghossian's response makes things worse for the distinction he aims to defend. In particular, his shift to mental states as justifiers makes it harder to dismiss the role of sense perception in understanding mathematical proofs as merely 'enabling'. Of course, his account of a priori and a posteriori justification is not fully worked out, and in improving it he can choose from a wide range of devices. The dialectic will not achieve closure any time soon. But the effect of his initial response is to provide evidence that my initial challenge is robust.

Boghossian characterizes me as '[h]aving attempted to show [with the initial challenge] that no top-down characterization of the a priori–a posteriori distinction can hope to succeed in lining up with the paradigm examples' (Chapter 9, p. 147), but my aim with the initial challenge was more modest. It was to note an overlooked and rather general problem for top-down accounts of the distinction, and challenge their proponents to solve the problem. As I hinted in the original paper, we cannot circumscribe in advance what kinds of 'new theoretical apparatus' friends of the distinction may introduce in hopes of constructing a top-down characterization (Chapter 8, p. 121). The realistic attitude for the rest of us is patience: wait for them to offer their best solution to the problem, then see whether it succeeds. As far as I can see, Boghossian's proposed solution does not.

3. The Central Argument

I now turn to the central argument of my paper. It was a bottom-up objection to the supposed depth of the distinction between a priori and a posteriori knowledge. My strategy was to describe two hypothetical examples, by bottom-up standards one a clear case of a priori knowledge, the other a clear case of a posteriori knowledge, and to argue that the differences between the two cases are epistemologically shallow. If the argument works, so should a corresponding argument with knowledge replaced by justified belief; in this respect, Boghossian's substitution of the former by the latter is harmless.

Boghossian's response to my argument is sceptical. He claims that the cases as I described them exemplify neither knowledge nor justified belief; a fortiori, they exemplify neither a priori nor a posteriori knowledge or justified belief. He interprets my argument as depending on a brutely reliabilist conception of knowledge and justification, and takes my cases to manifest the implausibility of such an approach. Actually, my argument did not invoke reliabilism as a premise, although I did specify that the thinker's skill at the relevant cognitive tasks made their judgments reliable; it would be strange to treat such reliability as simply *irrelevant* to knowledge. But Boghossian holds that my cases look like examples of knowledge or justified belief only to someone already under the influence of doctrinaire reliabilism.

A problem for Boghossian's sceptical response to the argument is that my proposed clear case of a priori knowledge or justification came from a domain from which friends of the distinction regularly draw their paradigm cases of a priori knowledge (or justified belief): knowledge of colour relations. Specifically, it was a proposed clear case of a priori knowledge of (1):

(1)   All crimson things are red.

The contrast was with a proposed clear case of a posteriori knowledge of (2):

(2)   All recent volumes of *Who's Who* are red.

On my description of the example, Norman comes to know (1) a priori by a simple imaginative exercise, and to know (2) by a similar imaginative exercise.

Since Boghossian denies that one can acquire a priori knowledge in the way I describe, he needs to describe an alternative way of acquiring a priori knowledge (or justified belief) about colour relations, on pain of having to abandon what are meant to be some of the best cases of a priori knowledge (or justified belief).

In attempting to describe an alternative route, Boghossian follows the usual tactic of internalist epistemology, by postulating a hidden inference. He claims that to acquire a priori knowledge of (1), or a priori justification for believing (1), from imagining a shade of crimson that is also a shade of red, one 'will need to know (or reasonably believe)' both (1a) and (1b):

(1a)   There is a dominant colour determinable to which all shades of crimson belong.

(1b)   The shade that one has imagined is properly representative in that respect of all shades of crimson.

Boghossian then says that (1a) and (1b) 'would typically have been justified a priori', whereas (2a) and (2b), the corresponding premises for (2), 'could only have been justified a posteriori', marking an epistemological difference between the two examples:

(2a) The volumes of *Who's Who* have a typical colour.

(2b) The imagined instance is appropriately representative of that typical colour.

As Boghossian points out, for me to dismiss the difference between a priori justification of (1a) and (1b) and a posteriori justification of (2a) and (2b) as shallow would make my argument circular, since the shallowness of the distinction is exactly what it was meant to show.

It may not be immediately obvious how (1a) and (1b) are meant to combine to deliver (1). However, with a bit of work we can reconstruct a valid argument. For convenience, we may follow Boghossian in generalizing over shades rather than things of those shades. Thus (1) becomes (1*):

(1*) All shades of crimson are shades of red.

That is near enough (1) for present purposes. Assuming for simplicity that red, yellow, and blue are the only dominant colours, we can regiment (1a) as (1a*):

(1a*) Either all shades of crimson are shades of red, or all shades of crimson are shades of yellow, or all shades of crimson are shades of blue.

All we need to get from (1a*) to (1*) is a descriptive premise about the currently imagined shade, which we refer to as 'this':

(1c*) This is a shade of crimson and neither a shade of yellow nor a shade of blue.

We could add to (1c*) the conjunct 'this is a shade of red', but there is no need, for the argument from (1a*) and (1c*) to (1*) is already deductively valid, by disjunctive syllogism. In effect, Boghossian's (1b) is redundant given his (1a) and colour facts about the currently imagined shade.

A different argumentative route to the conclusion (1*) works with (1b) instead of (1a). We can regiment (1b) as (1b*):

(1b*) If this is a shade of red, then all shades of crimson are shades of red.

We could add to (1b*) analogous conjuncts for 'yellow' and 'blue' (and we could strengthen the conditionals to biconditionals), but there is no need. To get from (1b*) to (1*), we just need a descriptive premise about the currently imagined shade:

(1d*) This is a shade of red.

There is also no need to add to (1d*) the descriptive material in (1c*) (or vice versa). The argument from (1b*) and (1d*) to (1*) is already deductively valid, by modus ponens. In effect, Boghossian's (1a) is redundant given his (1b) and colour facts about the currently imagined shade.

In assenting to (1) or (1*), one may not have been aware of making an inference with premises like (1a*) and (1c*) or (1b*) and (1d*), but never mind.

A descriptive premise on the lines of (1c*) or (1d*) is indispensable. Without one, there is no non-circular route to (1) from (1a) and (1b) alone, or to (1*) from (1a*) and (1b*) alone, because the premises are logically consistent with the currently imagined shade's not being red. But is our knowledge of (1c*) or (1d*), or our justified belief in them, a priori? That is not obvious. On Boghossian's view, if our justification for believing (1c*) or (1d*) epistemically depends on introspection of the current imaginative state, then it is a posteriori. On the other hand, if it epistemically depends only on 'certain uses of the imagination' (he does not specify which), then it is a priori. It matters, for if the justification for an essential premise is a posteriori, then Boghossian has not provided a way of getting a priori knowledge or justification of (1) or (1*) that works on his own assumptions. A defence of the traditional distinction between a priori and a posteriori justification should not undermine traditional paradigms of a priori justification.

Even if we grant that the minor premises (1c*) and (1d*) are somehow justified a priori, what about Boghossian's major premises (1a*) and (1b*) (or (1a) and (1b))? How might they be justified a priori?

Let us start with (1a*). It does look like the sort of thing that, on the traditional view, 'would typically have been justified a priori', in Boghossian's words. The trouble is that the disjunction (1a*) is more naturally derived from (1*) itself (by disjunction introduction) than the other way round. If one does not already know that all shades of crimson are shades of red, why should one expect there to be a dominant colour determinable to which all shades of crimson belong? Some regions of the colour sphere overlap a dominant colour determinable without being fully included in any. Why should one rule out in advance the possibility that crimson corresponds to one of those regions? There is no natural way of justifying (1a*) a priori without appealing to (1*), thereby making the supposed a priori justification of (1*) via (1a*) circular.

Let us try (1b*) instead. Like (1c*) and (1d*), it characterizes the currently imagined shade, so one may wonder whether its justification epistemically depends on introspection, and so counts as a posteriori by Boghossian's standards. Indeed, the occurrence of the definite description 'the shade that one has imagined' in his (1b) makes it look like an introspective report on one's imaginative processes. However, for the sake of argument, I assume that he intends the description to be somehow read *de re*, as captured by the use of the demonstrative 'this' in (1b*). But even so, if one does not already know that all shades of crimson are shades of red, why should one expect *this* shade of crimson to be 'properly representative' of all shades of crimson with respect to red? Why should one rule out in advance the possibility that this shade of crimson is a shade of red while some other shades of crimson are not? There is no natural way of justifying (1b*) a priori without appealing to (1*), thereby making the supposed a priori justification of (1*) via (1b*) circular.

Clearly, given Boghossian's anti-reliabilism, it is not open to him to give a reliabilist account of a non-inferential a priori justification for (1a*) or (1b*) (or (1a) or (1b)).

The difficulty into which Boghossian has got himself is rather typical of internalist epistemology, and all the more notable because he is one of the most skilled and subtle practitioners of that approach. In trying to avoid a brutely reliabilist account of our justification for a given belief, the internalist posits an inferential justification reliant on premises and rules of inference themselves just as much in need of justification as the original belief. There is an obvious danger of an infinite regress, though if each stage requires its own published exchange then at least the regress can be slowed down. Even the infinite chain of justifications as a whole is just much in need of justification as the original belief. In the present case, the justifications are supposed to be a priori. Strikingly, the new premises on offer are not merely no closer than the original belief to the sort of a priori self-evidence with which the internalist might hope to end the regress, they are further way: (1a*) and (1b*) (and (1a) and (1b)) are *less* obvious than (1*) (and (1)). Going down the regress is a process of epistemic decline, not progress.

Would Boghossian have done better to propose an account of a priori justification for believing (1) more different from mine, perhaps not involving the imagination at all?

One proposal is that understanding the words 'crimson' and 'red', or possessing the concepts *crimson* and *red*, requires awareness of a connection like (1). That would be a kind of epistemological analyticity, a supposed phenomenon against which I argue elsewhere in this volume. In my original description of Norman's a priori knowledge of (1), I stipulated that he learned the words 'crimson' and 'red' independently of each other. Although Boghossian agrees that one can learn words for primary colours such as 'green' and 'red' independently of each other, he is more sceptical about the present case. He writes,

It's harder for me to see how one could acquire *red* and *crimson* without realizing that crimson is a shade of red. Borderline cases aside, having the concept *red*, one might think, is in part to have a recognitional capacity to recognize shades of red on the basis of their looks.

(Chapter 9, p. 153)

It was indeed part of my original description of Norman that he has independent recognitional capacities for each of 'crimson' and 'red'. However, not all recognitional capacities are active all the time. For instance, someone who knows many languages which divide up the colour sphere differently from each other may have recognitional capacities for the various colour terms of each language, but that does not mean that whenever she observes the colour of an object she mentally classifies it according to the colour vocabulary of every language she knows. Only colour words salient in the given context may be activated. Perhaps 'crimson' and 'red' have never been simultaneously salient for Norman. To elaborate the story: first he learned 'crimson' by examples in the country, and it is salient for him only in the country or when it has recently been uttered; then he learned 'red' by examples in the city, and it is salient for him only in the city or when it has recently been uttered; he has never previously heard 'crimson' uttered in the city or 'red' in the country. Thus the stipulated kind of independent learning of 'crimson' and 'red' is not problematic in principle. In any case, given Boghossian's concession that one can learn primary colour words independently of each other, it is not a point on which he can resist all similar examples concerning knowledge of colour relations—for instance, knowledge that no shade of red is a shade of green. Let us therefore follow him in putting his worry about independent learning of 'crimson' and 'red' to one side. Someone can learn them independently and come to know (1) a priori without relying on analytic or conceptual connections.

Could Boghossian say that one can know (1) a priori, or have a priori justification for it, by *intuition*? Given the vagueness of the term 'intuition', just saying so does not provide an alternative account to mine. 'Intuition' might even be a label, however misleading, for the very cognitive process I describe in more detail. Some philosophers would add that one can know (1) a priori on the basis of a non-perceptual seeming, but that too explains very little. In my view, the resort to appearances as standard bases for knowledge or justified belief involves an ill-motivated psychologization of evidence which has taken much epistemology down a blind alley. But there is no immediate need to insist on that concern, for to postulate that one can know (1) or be justified in believing it on the basis of a non-perceptual seeming does nothing to meet the central challenge of my original paper, to differentiate epistemologically between (1) and (2) in cases like those I describe. For *if* Norman can know (1) or be justified in believing it on the basis of a non-perceptual seeming, why can't he know (2) or be justified in believing it on the basis of a non-perceptual seeming too?

Could it be replied that the relevant non-perceptual seemings attribute *necessity* to (1) but not to (2)? In the original paper, I considered just such a move of modalizing the content of the knowledge or justified belief, and argued that it does no strictly epistemological work (Chapter 8, pp. 125–6). We do not normally know necessary truths by knowing them to be necessary; the main effect of the modal difference between (1) and (2) is to distract us from the epistemological similarities. Since Boghossian does not contest that part of the original paper in his reply, I will not repeat those arguments here. More generally, since his paper does not invoke intuition in its attempt to differentiate epistemologically between (1) and (2), I will not labour the reasons why doing so would be unlikely to help.

In brief, Boghossian provides no plausible alternative account of a priori knowledge or justification of (1) to meet the central epistemological challenge.

Why is Boghossian so reluctant to give the key role in a priori knowledge or justified belief to the imagination? A clue lies in his account of the distinction between *realistic* and *fanciful* imagining. As he notes, if any kind of imagining can play the key role, it is realistic imagining. Indeed, on my own account, the imagination is reality-oriented by default, because its primary function is as a means to knowledge, though that function also requires the possibility of inhibiting the default in order to impose deviations from reality on the imaginative process, to explore their consequences (Chapter 12). However, Boghossian assumes that what makes realistic imagining realistic is that it is 'constrained by what one knows about the actual world. One brings to bear what one already knows, or justifiably believes, about the actual world to rule out certain imagined scenarios' (Chapter 9, p. 151). But then this input of background knowledge or justified belief to the imagining will take over much of the epistemic role from the imagining itself, and if it is a posteriori, so will be any output knowledge or justified belief.

Boghossian is surely right that any relevant background knowledge one has should constrain one's realistic imaginings. But that does not entail that such constraints *exhaust* the reality-orientation of realistic imagining, as though they left nothing for the imagination to do but draw their consequences. For the default reality-orientation of imagining is also a matter of one's dispositions to imagine given scenarios one way rather than another. Such dispositions can get calibrated to reality by experience (in the non-philosopher's sense), without ever being encapsulated into known propositions. Just that had happened to Norman's dispositions to imagine, as described in my paper. Such cases involve no epistemic role for background knowledge or justified belief, to be classified as a priori or a posteriori. Thus concerns about the epistemic role of background knowledge and justified belief do not affect Norman's knowledge of (1) and (2) as I described it.

So far, I have said very little specifically in response to Boghossian's scepticism about Norman's putative knowledge of (2). His argument depends on the assumed epistemic role for background knowledge or justified belief in Norman's realistic imagining, which I have just rejected. But there is a further issue about the structure of the dialectic. In the article, I described Norman's a priori knowledge of (1) before describing his a posteriori knowledge of (2). The point of taking the cases in that order was to start with a paradigm case of a priori knowledge, which friends of the epistemological distinction reject only on pain of endangering the distinction itself. Since Norman can in principle be as well off epistemologically in respect of (2) as he is in respect of (1), in the ways I describe, it is unprincipled for friends of the distinction to concede his knowledge of (1) but deny his knowledge of (2). Boghossian misses that aspect of the dialectic by starting with Norman's putative knowledge of (2). That may have contributed to his misapprehension that I must have been appealing to a reliabilist premise. Of course, he also denies that Norman could know (1) in the way I describe. But his brief argument for that conclusion is by analogy with the case of (2) (Chapter 9, pp. 153–4). He takes himself to have shown that Norman could know (2) by imagination only if he already knows, or has justification for, something like (2a) and (2b) (contrary to my description). Relying on the structural analogy, he concludes that Norman could know (1) by imagination only if he already knows, or has justification for, something like (1a) and (1b) (contrary to my description). But, as already seen, that view of the epistemology of (1) is implausible, and leads to a scepticism about a priori knowledge of (1), and a priori justification for (1), that a friend of the a priori can ill afford. Consequently, the structural analogy in reverse undermines Boghossian's claim that Norman could know (2) by imagination only if he already knows, or has justification for, something like (2a) and (2b). More positively, my account of knowing by imagining provides an alternative route not reliant on such background knowledge or justified belief.

Could Boghossian simply deny the possibility of a priori knowledge of, and a priori justification for, (1), and fall back on other paradigms of a priori knowledge? He does not pursue that strategy. In the original paper, I explicitly addressed it, and argued that paradigms of a priori knowledge and a priori justification in mathematics and logic are more similar to the case of (1) than one might suppose; in his reply, Boghossian does not take issue with that argument.

Boghossian has not identified a viable alternative for a non-sceptical friend of the distinction to admitting that Norman can know (1) a priori in something like the imaginative way I described. Nor has he identified a viable alternative for someone who makes that admission to also admitting that Norman can know (2) a posteriori in a similar imaginative way. By that test, my case for the shallowness of the distinction between a priori and a posteriori knowledge is robust. The unintended effect of Boghossian's critique is to cast doubt on the epistemological internalism that drove him to demand prior background knowledge in a way whose only beneficiary is the old-fashioned sceptic.

Notes

1. This paper is published here for the first time.
2. For my replies to two other critiques of Williamson 2013 (Chapter 8), Casullo forthcoming, and Melis and Wright forthcoming, see Williamson forthcoming a and forthcoming b. For critical discussion in a spirit sympathetic to my view of the a priori–a posteriori distinction of two more critiques of it, Casullo 2013 and Jenkins, Kasaki, and Masahi 2015, see Sgaravatti 2018.

11

Williamson on the Distinction between the A Priori and the A Posteriori Once Again[1]

Paul Boghossian

1. The Initial Challenge

In his 'How Deep is the Distinction between A Priori and A Posteriori Knowledge?'
(2013; reprinted as Chapter 8 of this volume), and en route to his central argument,
Williamson develops a challenge for any top-down characterization of the distinction
between a priori and a posteriori justification. The challenge turns on a dilemma
about how to characterize the notion of 'experience' as it figures in the phrase
'justification that is independent of experience'. According to Williamson's original
argument, one could opt either to construe 'experience' as 'outer experience' or as
'inner experience', with an alleged problem emerging either way.

In my reply (Chapter 9 of this volume), I criticized Williamson's argument on the
grounds that the distinction between 'inner' and 'outer' experience is not well-
defined and so cannot do the work he was putting it to. Williamson seems to accept
this criticism, but claims that an argument to the same effect can be reformulated
without it.

Naturally, I agree, since I offered such a reformulation myself. On my reformulation, the problem turns on how we construe the *justifiers* of our beliefs. In particular,
it turns on whether we construe those justifiers as consisting in *propositions*, on the
one hand, or in *mental states* that have those propositions as their contents, on
the other.

I argued that the friend of the a priori cannot accept the view, increasingly
influential within epistemology, that the justifiers of our beliefs are propositions.
For if the justifiers are propositions, then perceptual experiences can at most have an
enabling role in empirical belief, giving us *access* to the propositions that do the
justifying, rather than occasionally serving as the justifiers themselves. However, in
order to have a viable distinction between a priori and a posteriori justification, we
need a robust distinction between experience having a merely *enabling* role and its
having an *epistemic* role. Thus, we see that a proponent of the distinction cannot
endorse the justifiers as propositions view.[2]

Debating the A Priori. Paul Boghossian and Timothy Williamson, Oxford University Press (2020).
© Paul Boghossian and Timothy Williamson.
DOI: 10.1093/oso/9780198851707.001.0001

The picture that I end up tentatively endorsing, then, is this: Justifiers are mental states. A belief is a posteriori justified when it is justified by sensory experience, introspection, or a substantive use of memory; it is a priori justified when it is justified by intuition, the understanding, empirically unconstrained uses of the imagination, or reflection. When a belief is justified by a particular mental state, I also say that it is its epistemic basis, and that it 'epistemically depends' on that state.

In the piece to which this is a reply (Chapter 10 of this volume), Williamson attempts a reformulation of his argument against the feasibility of a top-down characterization of the a priori–a posteriori distinction.

At the heart of his new argument is an example. We are to imagine Mathematician examining the proof of a new mathematical theorem authored by someone else, Author. Mathematician goes through the proof, understands it, and is convinced by it. In this way, he comes to have seemingly a priori justified belief in the theorem that it proves. Williamson's aim is to show that, in this case, sense perception plays an irreducibly epistemic role for Mathematician's knowledge, thus jeopardizing the intuitive a priori status of the knowledge that he arrives at. Thus, my characterization of the distinction between the a priori and the a posteriori is shown not to line up with the bottom-up examples, just as Williamson had originally claimed.

Two stipulations are essential to the functioning of the example. First, Mathematician is not 'working out the proof for himself', he is just 'lazily' following the proof as it is written. This stipulation is essential to making it seem plausible that Mathematician's knowledge of the theorem epistemically depends on his visual perception of the written lines of the proof. Second, he doesn't simply accept the proof because he *defers* to the author; indeed, initially, he distrusts her. This stipulation is essential if we are to dispel the idea that all that's going on here is *testimonial* knowledge, which would naturally be classified as a posteriori knowledge.

The crucial step in the example comes in the following passage:

Consider the point in reading the proof when he comes to a step of modus ponens, from 'A' and 'If A, B' to 'B'. He already has knowledge and justified belief that A and that if A, B. He visually recognizes what he sees written in front of him as an instance of modus ponens, and— being a competent logician—consequently acquires knowledge and justified belief that B. He has a visual impression as of there being a written instance of modus ponens in front of him. If he lacked that impression, he would not be justified in believing that B. Of course, a brilliant mathematician could start ignoring their visual impressions and just work out the proof for themselves, but that is not what our uncreative mathematician is doing. He is just following the proof in front of him; it was not salient to him before being pointed out in the proof that the premises for a step of modus ponens were available. *His* justification in Boghossian's sense for believing that B is irreducibly dependent on his having a visual impression as of there being an instance of modus ponens in front of him. Moreover, the dependence seems to be epistemic by Boghossian's standards, for if visual impressions are justifiers in the way he suggests, the mathematician's visual impression is part of what justifies his belief that B, rather than a mere precondition of what justifies, since it is integral to his recognition of the step's validity.

(Chapter 10, p. 159)

I have to confess to not really getting how this is supposed to work. If I read a proof by an author I distrust, I would check the steps to make sure that they are sound; otherwise, I would just read the proof deferentially, trusting it to be sound. Even in the latter case, a certain amount of thinking the proof through for oneself is presumably required to read the proof with 'understanding'.

Now, if I am justified in believing 'A' and 'If A, B', and I am a competent logician, I recognize immediately that I am justified in believing 'B'; I don't need to see that Author has written 'B' in the next line of the proof. Even if I don't deduce it myself, and read on to the next line and see it to be a 'B', I would check briefly to see that it does indeed follow from what came before, even if I am reading in a 'lazy', but non-deferential way (as I remarked above).

So, I simply don't see why Williamson says, "[Mathematician's] justification... for believing that B is irreducibly dependent on his having a visual impression as of there being an instance of modus ponens in front of him." I'm not seeing why Williamson thinks his argument has any prospect of succeeding.

Let us step back a bit and ask, When you get knowledge, or justified belief, on the basis of a proof, how many epistemically important possibilities are there?

One possibility, of course, is that you accept the proof *on authority*. You cannot yourself properly assess either whether each and every one of the premises is a good starting point, or whether each and every one of the steps of the proof is valid; at some point in reading through the proof, you will need to accept *something* on authority. On this scenario, at the end of reading through the proof, you would know the theorem partly by testimony, and so you would know it a posteriori (*pace* Burge (1993) and in agreement with Malmgren (2006)).

Another possibility is that you work out the proof for yourself, in more or less detail, seeing both how each one of the premises is true, and how each one of the steps is valid. This needn't involve replicating the proof in gory detail, but just in having a rough sense of how the steps could be validated if necessary. In such a case, barring a skepticism about the very possibility of a priori knowledge, you would know the theorem a priori.

What Williamson is after is some case intermediate between these two possibilities, in which you don't accept *any* element of the proof on authority, but nor do you work it out for yourself. And in this sort of case, he thinks, you will get a disconnect between the natural classification of the case as a priori and the irreducible epistemic role for sensory experience.

Unfortunately, he hasn't shown us that there is such an intermediate case and so, not shown that there is a recipe here for generating a problem for top-down characterizations of the enabling–justifying distinction.

2. The Central Argument

Let me turn now to a discussion of Williamson's reply to my critique of his central argument. Williamson's reply to me is vitiated by some fairly serious misunderstanding of what I said.

Williamson's central argument, in his original paper, was designed to show that the distinction between a priori and a posteriori justification is a shallow one, of no clear interest in epistemology. As I explained in my critique, he proposes to demonstrate his conclusion by presenting a pair of examples with the following features:

(A)   One of them is a clear case of someone's justifiably believing a proposition in
an a priori way, namely:
(1)   All crimson things are red
(B)   The other is a clear case of someone's justifiably believing another proposition in an a posteriori way, namely:
(2)   All recent volumes of *Who's Who* are red;
(C)   The ways of justifiably believing involved in the examples are *broadly
representative* of the ways in which propositions are justifiably believed a
priori and a posteriori, respectively; and, finally,
(D)   There is no epistemologically interesting difference between the two ways of
believing specified; they are both known on the basis of similar exercises of
the imagination.

I admitted that, had Williamson succeeded in presenting a pair of examples with all
these features, he would have succeeded in his ambitious aim. I argued, however, that
(A), (B), and (C) are, in fact, all false.

Williamson doesn't come close to countering my claim that (C) is false (although
that he doesn't come close to doing so may not have been apparent to him; see below).
However, (C) is central to his case: if the way of knowing (1) or (2) that he describes is
unusual, we could bracket it off as a borderline case that poses no interesting problem
for a clear-enough distinction between the a priori and the a posteriori.

Williamson argues at some length that there is no alternative to his imagination-
based account of (1); and he then has this to say about our knowledge of (2):

> The point of taking the cases in that order was to start with a paradigm case of a priori
> knowledge, which friends of the epistemological distinction reject only on pain of endangering
> the distinction itself. Since Norman can in principle be as well off epistemologically in respect
> of (2) as he is in respect of (1), in the ways I describe, it is unprincipled for friends of the
> distinction to concede his knowledge of (1) but deny his knowledge of (2).
>
> (Chapter 10, p. 166)

Even if I were to concede Williamson's imagination-based account of our knowledge of (1); and concede that it is a representative way in which knowledge of a priori
knowable propositions is often achieved; and also concede that this implied that
anyone coming to believe (2) in structurally analogous ways would come to know (2);
it would *still* not follow that this imagination-based account of knowing (2) was a way
in which empirical, a posteriori propositions are *typically* known. For all that would
have been conceded, acts of imagination could be, and indeed look to be, very
unusual ways in which anyone would try to come to know empirical propositions
like (2). So, Williamson has done nothing to counter the obvious falsity of (C).

Let us turn to (B). Much of my critique of Williamson's original paper centered on
disputing (B)—that is, on arguing that his imagination-based account of (2) could
not result in knowledge or justified belief in (2). I subsequently used that argument to
argue, by structural analogy, that his imagination-based account could also not
account for our knowledge of (1).

Williamson claims that I loaded the decks against him by reversing the order of
exposition. He thinks it's important to start with (1). The reasoning seems to be this:
There is no real alternative to his imagination-based account of (1). He then says:

Consequently, the structural analogy in reverse undermines Boghossian's claim that Norman could know (2) by imagination only if he already knows, or has justification for, something like (2a) and (2b). (Chapter 10, p. 166)

((2a) and (2b) are background knowledge conditions that would spoil Williamson's argument.)

Several points need to be made.

First, it really can't matter in which order one considers the examples. If the proffered accounts work for both (1) and (2), they should work separately and individually, in whatever order they are discussed.

Second, I spent most of my time looking at Williamson's discussion of (2) because his claim that someone could come to know an empirical proposition such as (2) through the exercise of a single act of the imagination is the most striking claim of his paper; and it deserved a thorough examination. That examination reveals a quite general structural problem with his account, one that arises whenever a single act of the imagination is claimed to ground our knowledge of a universal generalization. The structural flaw is that, *if the imagination is to succeed in delivering knowledge of the generalization at all*, it needs to be backed up by background knowledge of propositions such as (2a) and (2b). Call this the Background-Backed Knowledge by Imagination (BBKI) account.

Third, Williamson spends much of his paper criticizing the BBKI account of (1) and, as he takes it, by analogy, of (2). He does this because he assumes two things: first, that I have to provide *some account or other* of how we know propositions like (1), and second, that the BBKI account is my best shot at providing such an account. In both of these assumptions, Williamson is very much mistaken.

To begin with the second, I believe I made it amply clear that I was not for a second endorsing the BBKI. Recall: I was looking at Williamson's knowledge by imagination account in the context of our knowledge of (2), an empirical proposition that we have zero prospect of knowing by an act of the imagination, let alone a single such act. The point of the exercise was not to *improve* on Williamson's account, but rather to show that his account was hopeless; that if it were to have any prospect of succeeding it would have to be modified in the ways I indicated; and that, when this was done, (i) it would show that it was not imagination, but rather *recollection*, that was doing the epistemic work; and, hence, (ii) that his central argument against the depth of the a priori–a posteriori distinction fails completely. I believe all of this is made perfectly clear in the following passage from my paper:

Well, under what conditions *would* Norman be able to use his imagining of a single taxi to generate a justified belief about the color that all London taxis have?

It is entirely unclear to me that there are *any* conditions under which Norman would be able to do this. At a minimum, it seems to me, he must have reason to believe (a) that the taxis have a dominant color, and (b) that the taxi he imagines is appropriately representative of that dominant color.

But how could Norman possibly satisfy these two conditions without being able to *recall* what the dominant color of London taxis is? How could he know that there *is* a single color that London taxis tend to have and that *this* color is appropriately representative of what that color is, without actually being able to recall that color?

Williamson seems to think that it is enough to scotch the suggestion that Norman is *recalling*, as opposed to imagining, to stipulate that no feats of recalling particular experiences or events is involved in his description of Norman's way of coming to know (2).

But not all acts of recall need involve the recall of a particular experience or event. To advert to our earlier discussion of preservative memory, just as we may recall propositions without remembering specific events in which we learned those propositions, so we may recall generic facts about how an F looks, without recalling the look of any particular encountered F.

Having seen many London taxis, Norman may be able to recall what a London taxi looks like, without recalling any particular London taxi. He calls up a stored generic image. Having seen many frogs, Norman may be able to recall what a frog looks like, without recalling any particular frog that he has encountered. He calls up a stored generic image.

And the point is that, unless that is what is in fact going on in Norman's 'imagining' of a recent volume of *Who's Who*—unless what he's actually doing is recalling a stored generic image of a recent volume of *Who's Who*, under roughly that description—he cannot have arrived at a justified belief about all recent volumes of *Who's Who*.

I conclude that Williamson's argument's reliance on (B) leaves it open to serious doubt: Norman could not have come to know (2) in the way that it claims.

(Chapter 9, pp. 151–2)

Mutatis mutandis for (1).

I conjecture that part of what made Williamson overlook these emphatically clear passages is his first assumption, that I *must* be offering *some* account or other of how we typically know (1). Since the BBKI seemed to be the only account on the table, he assumed that it must be the one. As he puts it,

> Since Boghossian denies that one can acquire a priori knowledge in the way I describe, he needs to describe an alternative way of acquiring a priori knowledge (or justified belief) about colour relations, on pain of having to abandon what are meant to be some of the best cases of a priori knowledge (or justified belief).   (Chapter 10, p. 161)

However, I was not at all trying to offer any positive account of how we know (1) a priori. All I was trying to do was show that Williamson had not succeeded in casting doubt on the depth of the distinction between the a priori and the a posteriori, and so had not succeeded in establishing the main claim of his paper.

And, of course, it's not true that unless I describe some alternative way of acquiring a priori justified belief about color relations, I would have to abandon what are meant to be some of the best cases of a priori knowledge. If I had been trying to describe an alternative route to our knowledge of (1), it would surely have been perverse of me to spend all my time on our knowledge of (2), with barely a word about our knowledge of (1). Indeed, I said right at the start of the paper that, although we have every right to be confident that the a priori–a posteriori distinction is real, we are still very much in the dark about how feats of a priori knowledge are accomplished.

There is an interesting meta-philosophical issue behind this particular dustup. Williamson seems to think that, for the friend of the a priori, it's time to put up or shut up. Either say how we manage to know things a priori, or admit that there may not be much at all that's distinctive about the notion.

My reaction to this is to ask, Why this impatience? Why now?

I conjecture that the real culprit in Williamson's eyes is not the a priori per se, but, rather, as we have often had occasion to see in these exchanges, an internalist conception of justification.

Williamson's opposition to internalism is well known and one of his insights is that it will be hard to make much of the a priori–a posteriori distinction on externalist, especially Reliabilist, views of justification. Thus, if epistemology is to be made safe for externalism, it would be useful to show that, independently of externalist/Reliabilist assumptions, there isn't much to the a priori–a posteriori distinction to begin with.

Unfortunately for Williamson's campaign, his argument doesn't work—certainly not without a doctrinaire Reliabilism about justification being presupposed; and, arguably, not even with it.[3]

Notes

1. This reply is published for the first time here.
2. This is a bit quick in the retelling. For further details, see the original presentation of the argument in Chapter 9.
3. For helpful comments on an earlier version I am grateful to Crispin Wright and Christopher Peacocke.

12

Knowing by Imagining[1]

Timothy Williamson

1

Imagining is often contrasted with knowing. When you know nothing about something, you have to imagine it instead. Knowledge deals in facts, imagination in fictions. This chapter sketches a way of thinking about the imagination on which that stereotypical contrast is utterly misleading. Far from being the opposite of knowing, imagining has the basic function of providing a means to knowledge—and not primarily to knowledge of the deep, elusive sort that we may hope to gain from great works of fiction, but knowledge of far more mundane, widespread matters of immediate practical relevance.

The assimilation of imagining and knowing is a card that can be played for either realist or idealist ends. The idealist wants to shift our conception of knowing towards our conception of imagining: somehow even knowing deals in fictions. By contrast, the realist wants to shift our conception of imagining towards our conception of knowing: somehow even imagining deals in facts. The spirit of this chapter is firmly realist. It aims more to rethink imagination than to rethink knowledge. Consequently, it is *not* appropriate to start by defining 'imagination'. Any such definition would be premature in advance of inquiry. Without one, we can still make progress with that inquiry on the basis of our capacity to recognize clear cases of imagination. What unifies them (if anything), and therefore which less clear cases should be grouped with them, are to be identified in the course of inquiry, not prejudged from the beginning.

A more useful starting point is to ask oneself why the elaborate capacity for imagining that normal humans possess should have arisen in our evolutionary history. Although this chapter will not attempt any detailed evolutionary considerations, one feature of the view to be proposed is that it makes the evolutionary advantage of having a good imagination obvious. That contributes to the view's explanatory power, and so to its abductive confirmation.

The reference to humans' evolutionary history does not imply that the imagination is an exclusively human capacity. It is quite plausible that some non-human animals engage in at least primitive imaginative exercises, and thereby gain a similar advantage. In this chapter, however, the examples will largely concern the human imagination, since we know so much more about it.

Debating the A Priori. Paul Boghossian and Timothy Williamson, Oxford University Press (2020).
© Paul Boghossian and Timothy Williamson.
DOI: 10.1093/oso/9780198851707.001.0001

Of course, that we possess an imagination does not prove that it confers or once conferred some evolutionary advantage on either the individual or the species. In principle, the imagination might have arisen as an accidental by-product of something else that did confer an evolutionary advantage at one or other level. Sometimes, for structural reasons, the easiest way for evolution to develop the capacity to do something useful involves developing the capacity to do something useless too. This chapter does not take for granted that the imagination confers an evolutionary advantage on either the individual or the species. Rather, it proposes a speculative view of the imagination on which it *does* confer an evolutionary advantage on both the individual and the species, and that aspect of the view's explanatory power contributes to its confirmation.

There are many kinds of evolutionary advantage. Presumably, peacocks have unwieldly magnificent tails because peahens prefer peacocks so endowed. One could develop a similar hypothesis about the imagination. Other things being equal, the more imaginative you are, the better your seduction technique: if you dance, talk, and do other things more imaginatively, you are more exciting to be with. In *One Thousand and One Arabian Nights*, Scheherazade's skill at telling stories keeps her alive and eventually enables her to pass on her genes. On the view to be proposed here, however, a good imagination also confers much more straightforward and direct advantages which do not depend on whether other members of the species are attracted by works of your imagination.

2

Consider a small group of our distant human ancestors, travelling across a difficult landscape previously unknown to them. How might they find an imagination useful?

One obvious answer is that an imagination will alert them to various potential dangers and opportunities. They are about to enter a forest. They imagine wolves in the forest; warned of the danger, they keep a sharper look-out for signs of wolves. They imagine edible berries in the forest; alerted to the potential opportunity, they look about for bushes of the right kind. In both cases, their imagination enables them to prepare for practically relevant possibilities, helping them avoid dangers and take advantage of opportunities.

To serve that purpose well, the imagination must be both selective and reality-oriented. They could imagine the wolves bringing them food to eat, but doing so would be a waste of time, and a distraction from more practically relevant possibilities. An imagination that clutters up the mind with a bewildering plethora of wildly unlikely scenarios is almost as bad as no imagination at all. It is better to have an imagination that concentrates on fewer and more likely scenarios. One's imagination should not be completely independent of one's knowledge of what the world is like.

Such examples suggest a distinction between two modes in which the imagination can operate: voluntary and involuntary. When you encounter a problem to which there is no obvious solution, you can turn your imagination to thinking up ways of solving it and to thinking through their consequences. Our little group may do that when they come to a deep river that they must cross. Such uses of the imagination are often voluntary. But sometimes we need our imaginations to work involuntarily too.

If the group is absorbed in joking together as it enters the forest, it may be saved by an imagination that breaks into the stream of consciousness with reminders of dangers and opportunities.

Imagination resembles *attention* in having both voluntary and involuntary modes of operation, and for similar reasons. We need to be able to focus our attention voluntarily on something: for example, to set ourselves to watch a hole in case an animal comes out. But we also need our attention to be capable of involuntary switches: for example, to be drawn by a slight movement at the periphery of vision, perhaps a predator or prey, despite our previous intention of watching something else. At least metaphorically, one might regard imagination as a form of attention to possibilities.

Since members of the group have imaginations, they can be expected to use them, voluntarily or even involuntarily, in ways that serve no immediate practical purpose too, for instance by inventing and telling stories. In the long run, of course, such uses of the imagination may help the group bond. Moreover, even the most playful uses of the imagination may also help to exercise the capacity and keep it in good trim, ready for more practical applications, just as a cat practices its hunting skills by playing with a mouse once caught, letting it go and recapturing it.

3

So far, the imagination has been described primarily as *raising possibilities*, rather than assessing the truth-values of propositions. One might therefore be tempted to suppose that the proper role of the imagination belongs, in Hans Reichenbach's terminology, to the *context of discovery*, rather than the *context of justification*. On a simpleminded version of the distinction, one dreams up scientific theories in the context of discovery, but assesses them as true or false, or as probable or improbable on the evidence, in the context of justification. Rationality is essential in the context of justification, but not in the context of discovery. If you came up with the theory in the first place under the influence of drink or drugs, never mind, but you must sober up or come down from your high before you reach a conclusion as to its status on the evidence. Similarly, someone might think, the imagination has done its work once it has delivered enough propositions to consciousness, to be entertained there. On this view, the imagination plays no further role in the assessment of those propositions as true or false, or as probable or improbable on the evidence.

The considerations of the previous section already include signs that such a view is inadequate. The need for the imagination to be selective and reality-oriented in bringing material to consciousness suggests that it must be capable of some sort of rational responsiveness to evidence. But in many examples we can see the imagination playing a far more direct role in the assessment of truth-value.

Think of a hunter who finds his way obstructed by a mountain stream rushing between the rocks. He reaches the only place in the vicinity where jumping the stream might be feasible. The best scenario for him is to jump and succeed in getting across the stream. Then he can continue on his way with little loss of time or energy. The worst scenario for him is to jump and fail to get across the stream, for then he will probably be drowned or smashed on the rocks. If he does not jump, and goes another way instead, he suffers a great loss of time and energy, but does not incur imminent death or injury; that is the intermediate scenario. Thus it is vitally important for the hunter to know whether he can jump the stream, whether he would succeed if he did try to jump it, before he decides whether to attempt the jump. Since the method of trial and error is too risky a way of finding out whether he can jump the stream, he needs a way of finding out whether he can do it in advance of trying. He can remember some of his past jumps, but he cannot remember failing with a jump that was clearly easier than this one, or succeeding with a jump that was clearly harder. He has to consider not only the width of the stream, but also the awkwardness of the place from which he would have to launch himself, the slipperiness of the rocks on which he would have to land, how tired he is, and so on. How should he try to determine whether he would succeed?

There is a natural human method of gauging one's capacities in such situations. One *imagines* oneself trying. If one then imagines oneself succeeding, one judges that if one tried, one would succeed. If instead one imagines oneself failing, one judges that if one tried, one would fail. If one is still uncertain, one repeats the thought experiment, perhaps many times. If our hunter cannot resolve the uncertainty, he will presumably take the long way round—unless he is being chased by a sabre-toothed tiger, in which case he may jump anyway.

A traditional stereotype of the imagination can make reliance on such an imaginative exercise look like a mad way of making up one's mind. For however difficult the jump, one can *imagine* succeeding with it, and however easy the jump, one can *imagine* failing with it. How can one learn anything relevant from what one chooses to imagine? Such incomprehension indicates neglect of the distinction in Section 2 between voluntary and involuntary exercises of the imagination. When the hunter makes himself imagine trying to jump the stream, his imagination operates in voluntary mode. But he neither makes himself imagine succeeding nor makes himself imagine failing. Rather, having forced the initial conditions, he lets the rest of the imaginative exercise unfold without further interference. For that remainder, his imagination operates in involuntary mode. He imagines the antecedent of the conditional voluntarily, the consequent involuntarily. Left to itself, the imagination develops the scenario in a reality-oriented way, by default.

Obviously, nothing has been said to guarantee that the imagination will reach a true answer. In some cases, it reaches a false one. The imagination, like perception, memory, and every other generic human cognitive capacity, is fallible. In other cases, when too much uncertainty is registered, the imagination reaches no answer at all. Nevertheless, under suitable conditions, the method constitutes a reliable way of forming a true belief as to what would happen in hypothetical circumstances. I have used it myself in situations like that described, and lived to tell the tale, as have other people I know. Indeed, there is no good reason to deny that, under suitable conditions, the method enables one to *know* what would happen in the hypothetical circumstances, because the conditional connection is *safe* from failure. Of course, hardly anything has been said so far to *explain* the method's reliability, except for the hint in Section 1 of evolutionary pressures. Later sections will suggest some links between the method and other normal human cognitive processes. First, however, it will be useful to have some more examples, to illustrate the range of cases over which the method is applicable.

The method can be applied with complex iterations. Suppose that now the hunter's way to the next valley is blocked by broken cliffs. Can he climb through or up them? The price of trying and failing is again high: perhaps becoming exhausted, perhaps getting stuck halfway up. The hunter stares at the rock face, trying to trace a route all the way to the top in his imagination, testing each step for feasibility by imagining what it would involve. No more rational method of answering the question is available to him.

Even in the modern world, important decision-making often relies on knowledge or beliefs acquired through the imagination. For example, you are looking round a house, wondering whether to buy it. You want to know whether, if you lived in it, you would like doing so. You voluntarily imagine the antecedent of the conditional; your final decision may depend on what consequent you involuntarily imagine.

Not all the knowledge gained from such imaginative exercises concerns the capacities and dispositions of agents. For example, if you look at a piece of furniture and then at a doorway, you can sometimes come to know whether the former would go through the latter, without measuring either, by imagining trying to get the former through the latter. You gain knowledge of spatial relations between the doorway and the furniture.

The examples so far may appear to involve an essential role for mental imagery, in some sense. But even if that appearance is veridical, we should not overgeneralize to the conclusion that all imagining involves imagery. For example, you are very busy, and wonder whether to postpone a lunch appointment with a friend. You want to know whether, if you did postpone the appointment, she would be upset. You voluntarily imagine the antecedent of the conditional. You *might* then involuntarily form a visual image of your friend with a composed or disappointed face. But no such imagery is *necessary* for imagining her reacting with composure or disappointment. Again, suppose that a politician is trying to work out what his core supporters would do at the next election if he voted for gun control. He imagines their reactions, but doing so need not involve mental imagery.

Given this heterogeneity of knowledge-yielding imaginative exercises, we need a more abstract characterization of what is going on.

4

As Frank Ramsey observed, how we evaluate conditionals is closely tied to how we update our beliefs on new information. For example, suppose that someone tells a shepherd 'The sheep have broken out of the pen and disappeared', and the shepherd concludes 'The sheep have gone down to the river.' Then presumably, even if the shepherd had not been given the testimony, he could still have reached the indicative conditional conclusion 'If the sheep have broken out of the pen and disappeared, they have gone down to the river' (or the subjunctive conditional conclusion 'If the sheep had broken out of the pen and disappeared, they would have gone down to the river', depending on subtle differences in the cognitive process). The testimony in the first case is the same as the antecedent of the conditional in the second case, and the unconditional conclusion in the first case is the same as the consequent of the conditional in the second case. If we regard the shepherd's updating of his beliefs in the first case as an online process, then we can regard his evaluation of the conditional in the second case as the corresponding offline process. If he accepted the conditional on the basis of an imaginative exercise similar to those in Section 3, as we may assume, then that imaginative exercise is the offline analogue of online updating. Very roughly, the online and offline processes take the same input—'The sheep have broken out of the pen and disappeared'—and deliver the same output—'The sheep have gone down to the river'—by the same means. One process is online and the other offline in virtue of the different sources of the input. If we apply the term 'imagine' on the basis of the source of the input, we shall classify only the offline process as an imaginative exercise. If we apply the term 'imagine' on the basis of the processing between input and output, we shall classify the online process as an imaginative exercise too. It is more important to see the underlying cognitive similarity than to decide exactly how to use the word 'imagine'.

In many of the examples in Section 3, the cognitive process took a mix of online and offline input. When the hunter imagines himself trying to jump the stream, he also has to look carefully at its banks in front of him, to tailor his imaginative exercise as exactly as he can to their actual contours. Voluntarily in imagination, he somehow adds his jumping to the perceived scene. But that element of offline input is enough to make it a clear case of imagination.

Typically, there are further differences between the online and offline processes. When the new information to be updated on derives from sensory perception, we are hard put to articulate it verbally in its full specificity, to be the antecedent of a conditional. Moreover, when we learn something by perception or testimony, we usually learn other things too. When you learn by sight that the sheep have gone, you usually also learn that *you can see that* the sheep have gone. When you learn by testimony that the sheep have gone, you usually also learn that *you have been told that* the sheep have gone. But often we do not build that extra information into the antecedent of the corresponding conditional. For conditionals such as 'If the sheep have gone, I can see that the sheep have gone' and 'If the sheep have gone, I have been told that the sheep have gone' are far from trivial. Nevertheless, these differences of detail do not undermine the strong cognitive analogy between the online and offline processes.

One consequence of the analogy is that any scepticism about the offline processes is liable to generalize to the online processes too. For example, someone who doubts that in suitable conditions the shepherd's imaginative exercise enables him to know that if the sheep have broken out of the pen and disappeared, they have gone down to the river should also doubt that in suitable conditions, on being told that the sheep have broken out of the pen and disappeared, the shepherd can know that they have gone down to the river. That looks like the thin end of the wedge for a far more general scepticism.

Much of our knowledge of the future depends on cognitive processes relevantly similar to imaginative exercises. For consider some cognitive process by which we form expectations about the future based on our knowledge of the present. Although we know far less about the future than we do about the recent past, we are not entirely ignorant of the future. The process may be more or less hardwired into our brains, such as one for forming expectations about where a moving object in our visual field will be in a fraction of a second's time. Alternatively, the process may involve complex conscious reasoning, such as one for forming expectations about the political situation a year from now. Our imagination enables us to apply such a cognitive process offline, to imagined input about a time t, to reach a conditional conclusion of the form 'If X were to obtain at t, then Y would obtain at $t+1$.' Similarly, we can reach a conditional conclusion of the form 'If Y were to obtain at $t+1$, then Z would obtain at $t+2$.' Under conditions that make it legitimate to assume transitivity for the conditionals at issue, we can derive the further conclusion 'If X were to obtain at t, then Z would obtain at $t+2$', and so on.[2] If these offline imaginative exercises are unreliable, the likeliest explanation is that the corresponding online processes for forming expectations about the future are also unreliable.

An analogous point applies to large tracts of our knowledge of the past. Consider cases where we use inference to the best explanation to solve a crime or to interpret an archaeological site. For such abductive reasoning, we need auxiliary conditional premises of the form 'If the explanans had obtained in the past, then the explanandum would obtain now.' We may have to obtain those conditionals in the same way as before, by an imaginative exercise. Unless one has general sceptical inclinations, it is unwise to deny that, in suitable conditions, imaginative exercises are a source of knowledge.

Could someone argue that what have here been called 'imaginative exercises' are really just inductive inferences? Most of them depend somehow on past experience, and go beyond it non-deductively. If that suffices for a cognitive process to be an inductive inference, then they are inductive inferences. But they do not depend on the subject's *remembering* the relevant past experiences. What matters is whether they have made the subject skilful enough in performing the imaginative exercise itself. It is irrelevant to the process whether the subject can assemble the particular premises of the supposed inductive inference. Nor is it remotely clear in the given cases how to fill in 'F' and 'G' in the conclusion of the supposed inductive inference, 'All Fs are Gs' (or 'Most Fs are Gs', for that matter). Thus it is also irrelevant to the process whether the subject can formulate the general conclusion of the supposed inductive inference. The imaginative exercises are inductive inferences only in a sense so loose as to be entirely unhelpful.

5

We can test the cognitive view of the imagination by confronting a genuine structural difference between imagination and perception, one sometimes used to contrast perception as reality-directed with imagination as supposedly not so. The structured difference is this. If you perceive an F, then there is an F that you perceive. Macbeth literally saw a dagger only if there was a dagger that he saw; otherwise he only seemed to himself to be seeing a dagger. By contrast, you may literally *imagine* an F even if there is no F that you imagine. I am imagining a golden mountain in Austria. Since there is no golden mountain at all in Austria, a fortiori there is no golden mountain in Austria that I am imagining. What should we make of this difference? I will argue that it is predicted by the cognitive account of the imagination sketched above, and so confirms rather than disconfirms that account.

First, consider the involuntary imaginative exercise of developing an initial hypothetical supposition, in effect answering a 'What if?' question. On the cognitive account, various offline cognitive procedures add further conclusions to a pool that starts with the initial supposition. The process can be iterated indefinitely. Although most of the procedures are non-deductive, reasoning by deductive logic is an especially good procedure from a cognitive point of view, since it guarantees truth-preservation. The deductive aspect of the whole process will look something like the method of tableaux in first-order logic, by which the consequences of the initial premises are teased out—although in our imaginative exercises the aim is not usually to reach a contradiction. For each logical constant, there is a rule for extending a branch of a tableau which contains a formula whose main connective is that constant. For present purposes, the rule that matters is the one for the quantifier $\exists$ ('something'). It says that if a branch contains a formula of the form $\exists x\ \Phi(x)$, then one may add to it the formula $\Phi(a)$, where a is an individual constant that has not previously appeared on that branch. One can then apply the rule for the main connective in $\Phi(a)$ (if it has one), and so on. Informally, we can regard a as an 'arbitrary name' for a satisfier of the formula $\Phi(x)$ as a value of the variable x—if there are several satisfiers, it does not matter which one. The point of the ban on previous occurrences of a in the branch is to avoid prejudging anything else about the satisfier. If an interpretation I verifies every formula on the branch before $\Phi(a)$, then it verifies $\exists x\ \Phi(x)$, so some interpretation differing from I at most in making an object o the value of x verifies $\Phi(x)$, so modifying I to make o the denotation of a yields an interpretation that verifies every formula on the branch up to and including $\Phi(a)$. The formula $\Phi(a)$ has the form of a formula expressing a singular proposition about a particular object, even if the individual constant a does not really denote anything: after all, $\exists x\ \Phi(x)$ may be false on its intended interpretation.

Now read $\Phi(x)$ as 'x is a golden mountain in Austria'. Thus $\exists x\ \Phi(x)$ expresses the proposition that there is a golden mountain in Austria. If an imaginative exercise starts from that false hypothesis, the cognitive account of the imagination (defeasibly) predicts that developing it properly will involve applying some informal analogue of the tableau rule for $\exists$, and thereby adding some informal analogue of $\Phi(a)$ to the development. That is, one will do something formally similar to thinking of some particular object that it is a golden mountain in Austria, even though really there is no particular object of which one is thinking that it is a golden mountain in Austria. But that is a good description of a case in which one imagines a golden mountain in Austria, even though there is no golden mountain in Austria that one imagines. Of course, the description does not entail that one forms a mental image of a golden mountain in Austria, but we saw in Section 3 that forming mental imagery is not necessary for imagining. Although one may imagine a golden mountain in Austria by forming a mental image of one, the informal analogue of $\Phi(a)$ may be a mental image. Thus the very feature that was supposed to differentiate imagining from reality-directed attitudes is predicted by the account of imagining *as* a reality-directed attitude.

In more general terms, the felt tendency of the imagination to be specific, to fill in details, is partly explained by the hypothesis that it uses something like the tableau rule for the quantifier ∃ in developing an initial supposition. The explanation can be strengthened with the additional hypothesis that the imagination also uses something like the tableau rule for disjunction, ∨, in developing the initial supposition. The rule says that if a branch contains a formula of the form Φ ∨ Ψ, then one may divide it into two sub-branches, one containing all formulas already on the branch and Φ, the other containing all formulas already on the branch and Ψ. Informally, the idea is to explore the two (not mutually exclusive) ways in which the disjunction may hold separately. This corresponds to the dissatisfaction one tends to feel about, for instance, just imagining that the keys are in either the kitchen or the bedroom while neither imagining that they are in the kitchen nor imagining that they are in the bedroom.

It is almost trivial that the imagination uses something like the other standard tableau rules in developing an initial supposition. For example, the rule for conjunction, &, says that if a branch contains a formula of the form Φ & Ψ, then one may add to it both the formula Φ and the formula Ψ. Similarly, it would be hard to imagine that Mary is tall and thin without also imagining that she is tall and imagining that she is thin. On the cognitive view of the imagination, one would expect it to use something like the tableau rules in developing an initial supposition. The imagination conforms to that prediction.

6

The cognitive view of the imagination does *not* predict that it will be cognitively reliable only for tasks just like those it evolved to serve. Its tendency to use something like rules of deductive logic is an example to the contrary, since they are quite generally truth-preserving. The simplest forms of reasoning to implement that are truth-preserving for practical matters are truth-preserving for all matters.

Once we appreciate the role of the imagination as a standard means for evaluating conditionals and modal claims, we should be much less inclined to regard the use of thought experiments in philosophy (or natural science) as constituting any highly distinctive method. Still less should we be tempted to characterize such a method in terms of cooked-up categories such as 'philosophical intuition', which serve mainly to obscure the similarities between thought experiments and more routine exercises of the imagination in virtually every branch of human inquiry. We simply reserve the term 'thought experiment' for the more elaborate and eye-catching members of the kind.

One might suppose that, as science progresses, the role of the imagination will increasingly be confined to the context of discovery, and that in the context of justification it will gradually be replaced by more rigorous methods. But there is evidence to the contrary. For rigorous science relies on mathematics, and so indirectly on the axioms or first principles of mathematics. But when one examines the justifications mathematicians give of their first principles, such as axioms of set theory, one finds unashamed appeals to the imagination. Things are complicated, because the justification is abductive: it involves the derivability of standard 'working' mathematics from the candidate first principles—and, one hopes, the non-derivability of contradictions. But it also involves the way in which the candidate first principles fit together as parts of an intrinsically simple, elegant, and unified picture of mathematical reality. Those theoretical virtues are needed to trump rival gruesomely gerrymandered pictures, for example, one on which the hierarchy of sets is truncated at an arbitrarily chosen large cardinal, in the usual manner characteristic of abductive theory comparison. Moreover, since by Gödel's second incompleteness theorem the axioms can be proved jointly consistent only on the basis of even stronger axioms that are inconsistent if the former are, much of mathematicians' confidence in the consistency of their axioms comes from the way in which they form such a coherent picture. Of course, they also have inductive evidence of their consistency, because no one has ever yet derived a contradiction from them, but mathematicians put comparatively little weight on such inductive evidence. They have much less confidence in the consistency of alternative axiom sets from which no one has ever yet derived a contradiction, but which do not seem to form a coherent picture. Without an imagination, one would be in no position to judge whether some candidate first principles form a coherent picture of mathematical reality. For the foreseeable future at the very least, imagination will play a crucial role in the context of scientific justification, not only in the context of scientific discovery.

Whatever the function or evolutionary origin of our capacities, we are not forbidden to use them for other ends, including playful ones. Imagination has enabled humans to produce works of art, great and awful. Indeed, the combination of voluntary hypothetical suppositions and involuntary developments of those suppositions is reminiscent of the way some novelists describe novel-writing. An imagination is cognitively powerful only if it is capable of producing and developing fictions. But if we try to understand the imagination while taking for granted that fiction is its central or typical business, we go as badly wrong as we would if we tried to understand arms and legs while taking for granted that dancing is their central or typical business.

Notes

1. [This chapter was first published as Williamson 2016, under the same title as here.] This chapter is based on my talk to the 2012 Claremont conference on Knowledge through Imagination. Other versions of the material were presented at a workshop at the Inter-University Centre in Dubrovnik and at the following universities: Belgrade, Bergen, Birmingham, Boğaziçi (Istanbul), Cambridge, Edinburgh, Gothenburg, Liverpool, London (King's College), Manchester, Oxford, Warwick (apologies to any I have forgotten). I am grateful to the audiences at all these events for stimulating discussion. The piece takes further ideas from my books *The Philosophy of Philosophy* (2007a) and, to a slight extent, *Knowledge and its Limits* (2000). Its development was so loosely related to the literature that I decided, contrary to the unanimous advice of editors and referees, not to add footnotes. Interested readers may find points of similarity with other chapters in this book.

2. [We can dispense with the qualification about transitivity by making the transition from 'If X were to obtain at t, then Y would obtain at $t + 1$' and 'If X were to obtain at t and Y at $t + 1$, then Z would obtain at $t + 2$' to 'If X were to obtain at t, then Z would obtain at $t + 2$', since

even logics for counterfactual conditionals such as those of Lewis (1973) and Stalnaker (1968), which invalidate transitivity, validate the quasi-transitivity principle that $p \; \Box \rightarrow q$ and $(p \; \& \; q) \; \Box \rightarrow r$ entail $p \; \Box \rightarrow r$. On such semantics, if there are no p-worlds then the conclusion is vacuously true, while if there are p-worlds then there are $(p \; \& \; q)$-worlds by the first premise, so, non-vacuously, the closest p-worlds are q-worlds and, non-vacuously, the closest $(p \; \& \; q)$-worlds are r-worlds; hence, non-vacuously, the closest p-worlds are r-worlds. Thus, by accumulating the results of the imaginative exercise as one goes along, one can iterate indefinitely. In the online case, this corresponds to using memories of the past as well as knowledge of the present in making predictions.]

13

Intuition, Understanding, and the A Priori[1]

Paul Boghossian

Introduction

Over the past several years, I have explored a particular version of the classical idea that we can explain the a priori justification that we have for certain of our beliefs by appealing solely to the *understanding* that we have of their ingredient concepts (see Boghossian 1996, 2003b, 2012). To use some terminology that has become standard, I have tried to show that some propositions are *epistemically analytic*, justifiably believable merely on the basis of being understood (see Boghossian 1996, Williamson 2007a).[2]

This proposal, I have argued, should be sharply distinguished from the idea that some propositions are *metaphysically analytic*, that is, true by virtue of their identity alone and without any contribution from the 'worldly facts'. The latter idea has been justly discredited: even paradigm examples of 'analytic' propositions, such as *All squares are four-sided*, are about squares and sides and not about the word 'square' or the concept *square*.[3] And when such an analytic proposition is true it is made true by the relevant worldly facts, in this case by facts about squares.

There are many reasons for taking an account of a priori justification in terms of epistemic analyticity seriously, not least among them being that, at least in certain cases, such an account seems true: for example, it is plausible that my justification for believing that all squares have four sides rests exclusively on my understanding of the ingredient concepts. Another consideration in favor of such an account is its promise to explain a priori justification without invoking the potentially obscure and problematic notion of *intuition*.

In what represents a substantial change of mind on my part, however, I have come to believe that this latter motivation—this fear of intuitions—is, ultimately, both futile and misguided.

It is futile in that one cannot escape appealing to intuitions in the theory of the a priori. And it is misguided in that intuitions are not as problematic or as obscure as I had previously thought. In this essay, I will make a start (but only a start) at explaining and defending these claims: an adequate treatment would have to be much longer than is possible in this volume.

Debating the A Priori. Paul Boghossian and Timothy Williamson, Oxford University Press (2020).
© Paul Boghossian and Timothy Williamson.
DOI: 10.1093/oso/9780198851707.001.0001

I should clarify at the outset that I am not abandoning understanding-based accounts of the a priori altogether. I continue to believe that such accounts are correct for a certain range of cases. However, to this ongoing commitment, I would now add the following three observations.

First, that understanding-based accounts won't cover the entire range of propositions that are known a priori, and that, as a consequence, intuitions are needed if we are to give a complete picture of this type of knowledge. As Kant would have put it, there are *synthetic* propositions known a priori, not just (epistemically) analytic ones.

Second, in certain cases, the deployment of an understanding-based account *itself* relies on appeal to the notion of an intuition.[4]

Finally, intuitions are not quite as problematic or obscure as I had previously assumed.

Two Types of Understanding-Based Account: Constitutive vs Basis

A priori justified beliefs that are good candidates to be explained by an understanding-based account include the following:

(1) All quadrilaterals have four interior angles.
(2) If Mary ate the apple and the pear, then Mary ate the apple.
(3) It is necessary that whoever knows p believes p.
(4) In the Gettier scenario, Mr. Smith has a justified true belief but does not know.
(5) In the standard Twin Earth scenario, Oscar's word 'water' has H_2O in its extension but not XYZ, while Toscar's word 'water' has XYZ in its extension but not H_2O.[5]

What has not been widely understood, however, is that there are *two* distinct, indeed, mutually incompatible, ways in which the understanding might be a source of a priori justification.[6]

On one type of account, S's understanding of p justifies S's assent to p in virtue of the fact that S's understanding of p is *constituted* in part by S's disposition to assent to p.

(Constitutive) S's assent to p is justified by S's understanding of p in virtue of the fact that S's understanding of p is partly constituted by S's disposition to assent to p.

On the other type of account, S's understanding of p justifies S's assent to p in virtue of the fact that S's understanding of p serves as a good *epistemic basis* for S's assent to p.

(Basis) S's understanding of p justifies S's assent to p in virtue of the fact that S's understanding of p serves as a good *epistemic basis* for S's assent to p.

Examples of both types of account may be found in the literature. Although they are very different, indeed, mutually exclusive, types of explanation, they are routinely conflated.[7]

The idea behind a Constitutive account is the thought that, under certain conditions, an assent that is constitutive of a thinker's understanding of a given proposition (or of one of its ingredient concepts), will be, eo ipso, an assent to which she is entitled.

To illustrate, suppose you are sympathetic, as many are, to a conceptual-role semantics for the logical constants. If so, you'll think that a disposition to assent to certain basic logical truths involving those constants (or to inferences involving them) is constitutive of your understanding them. For example, you may think that to possess the concept *and* you need to be disposed to assent to (at least some) instances of propositions of the form *If A and B, then A.*[8]

Of course, even if this were granted, there would still be a question about your justification for assenting to these propositions. Why should the metasemantic fact that your assenting to Conjunction Elimination (CE) is constitutive of your possessing *and* translate into the epistemic fact that you are *justified* in assenting to CE?

Clearly, the answer here can't be that your understanding of *and* provides an *epistemic basis* for your assenting to CE, since your disposition to assent to p is not in general a good basis for your assenting to p.

In the case of such understanding-constituting dispositions, explaining a priori justification in terms of the understanding will need to rely on the existence of true bridge principles of the form:

(Concept–Justification Connection):   For certain propositions p, if a disposition to assent to p is constitutive of understanding p, then a thinker who understands p is eo ipso entitled to assent to p.[9]

It's a non-trivial question in the theory of the a priori whether there are such bridge principles. (For more details on this see my 2003b and 2012.)

However, even if their existence were considered unproblematic, our job would hardly be done, since it is clear that there are many understanding-based a priori propositions that could not be accounted for in this way.

The key reason is that there are many understanding-based a priori propositions assent to which is not understanding-constituting.

For example, my knowledge of (1), that all quadrilaterals have four interior angles, is understanding-based; but the usual understanding of *quadrilateral* will advert only to its being a closed figure consisting of four line segments linked end to end. And yet, although the definition of *quadrilateral* makes no mention of interior angles, my grasp of that definition can serve as the epistemic basis for my knowledge that all quadrilaterals have four interior angles.

For these sorts of non-constitutive understanding-based assents, a thinker's understanding of the concepts ingredient in p serves as the *epistemic basis* for her assent to p. The assent is not constitutively built into the understanding, as on a Constitutive account, but is prompted by that understanding. And when it is prompted by it in the right way, the understanding is sufficient for justifying it.[10]

Both Basis and Constitutive models are important, then, in that neither model, by itself, can account for the entire range of cases of understanding-based a priori justification.

Competent Dissent

Understanding-based accounts face many difficult challenges; of these, one has become very influential. It has been pressed with great force and detail by

Williamson (2007a). Although I've discussed it in other writings, it will be useful to consider it again, against the backdrop of the distinction between Constitutive and Basis accounts.

Williamson draws our attention to the following fact: not *everyone* who understands (3) assents to it.

Many philosophers, native speakers of English, have denied [(3)] ... They are not usually or plausibly accused of failing to understand the words 'know' or 'believe.'   (2007a: 168)

Some epistemologists, and hence, presumably, *experts* on the concepts of knowledge and belief, have officially rejected (3). This fact appears to pose a prima facie problem for understanding-based accounts of (3), a problem that we can formulate in a first pass as follows: If understanding (3) were sufficient for assenting to (3) with justification, how is it that these experts, who ex hypothesi understand (3) perfectly well, insist on rejecting (3)?

Of course, if (3) were just a special case, we could quarantine it. But Williamson's idea is that there is nothing special about (3). For *any* proposition p that we might think of as epistemically analytic, we can imagine an 'expert' on p who, having developed sophisticated theoretical misgivings about p, rejects p with full understanding.[11]

On the basis of such examples, Williamson puts forward a thesis that I shall label:

(Generalized Competent Dissent, GCD)   For any proposition p, it is possible for someone to dissent from p while retaining full competence with p (full understanding of p).

Thus, Williamson (2011) has maintained that not even assenting to instances of CE could be considered constitutive of possession of *and* since, even in that seemingly ironclad case, we could *imagine* someone developing sophisticated reasons for doubting CE, and so ending up refusing to assent to

(2)   If Mary ate the apple and the pear, then Mary ate the apple.

Williamson takes the phenomenon of competent, indeed expert, dissent, to refute understanding-based accounts of the a priori. But, how, exactly, does it do so?

The challenge assumes a different form depending on the type of understanding-based account at which it is directed. In both cases, though, the challenge proves to be answerable.

Competent Dissent and Constitutive Accounts

Let us start with a Constitutive account. With such an account, the threat from GCD looks quite direct, since a Constitutive account needs to rely on some constitutive understanding–assent links, the existence of which GCD denies.

To sharpen our focus, let us look at a classic formulation of a proposed understanding–assent link, Christopher Peacocke's account of the possession conditions for *and*:

(CPC) Conjunction is that concept *C* to possess which a thinker must find transitions that are instances of the following forms *primitively* compelling, and must do so because they are of these forms:

$$\frac{\begin{array}{c}p\\q\end{array}}{p\,C\,q} \qquad \frac{p\,C\,q}{p} \qquad \frac{p\,C\,q}{q}$$

To say that the thinker finds such transitions primitively compelling is to say this: (1) he finds them compelling; (2) he does not find them compelling because he has inferred them from other premises and/or principles; and (3) for possession of the concept C in question (here conjunction) he does not need to take the correctness of the transitions as answerable to anything else.   (1992: 6; emphasis added)[12]

According to Peacocke, in order to understand the concept *conjunction* you need to find CE inferences primitively compelling: that is, compelling when considered on their own and independently of any other considerations.[13]

Why this play with the notion of the 'primitively compelling'? The answer should be obvious: If you're thinking of understanding a concept in terms of assent, either to propositions or to inferences involving that concept, you want to include only those assents that are *necessary* for understanding. A logician may know all sorts of interesting truths about Conjunction; but most of those would be extraneous to what is required for understanding it. A physicist may know all manner of empirical truths involving the concept Conjunction, but these, too, would be extraneous to what is required for understanding it.

Now, this observation poses a problem for Williamson's recipe for generating expert-based counterexamples to any proposed understanding–assent link, since it is obviously consistent with your refusing, on the basis of sophisticated theoretical considerations, to assent to a given inference form, that you continue to find that inference form *primitively* compelling, that is, when it is considered on its own and independently of these sophisticated considerations. Indeed, a natural description of Williamson's expert, who develops theoretical misgivings about CE, is that she retains the *disposition* to assent to CE but refuses to act on that disposition as a result of the theoretical misgivings.[14] As we may put it, she may continue to find CE *primitively* compelling, even as she now finds it *derivatively* uncompelling.

Williamson's expert, then, is not yet a counterexample to the claim that CE is constitutive of understanding Conjunction.

Williamson's unerring sense of dialectic leads him to take the further required step. He invites us to imagine the following possible future for our expert: at first, she continues to find CE primitively compelling, even as she stops finding it compelling all things considered. After a while, though, she stops finding it even primitively compelling. It becomes second nature to her to refuse to assent to CE. When she now looks at CE, she no longer finds it tempting. She even forgets the theoretical reasons that first inclined her to give up CE. If you ask her why she doesn't follow virtually every other person in endorsing CE, she says she just doesn't see its plausibility. She may even say that it's obvious to her that CE is fallacious, but offer nothing further. As so developed, Williamson claims, the imagined expert constitutes a decisive counterexample to the claim that assent to CE is constitutive of understanding Conjunction.

Unfortunately, the argument doesn't work. The problem is that the more unself-conscious we make our expert's refusal to assent to CE, the more implausible it becomes that she really does continue to possess *and* (as opposed to possessing some closely related concept).

If our expert dissenter really did succeed in relinquishing any disposition to assent to CE, and *presented no particular reason for her refusal*, insisting, for example, that it was simply *obvious* that *She ate the apple* does not follow from *She ate the apple and the pear*, it would cease to be plausible that she is disagreeing with us about *and*.[15]

Let me put this point another way. If the expert's offering sophisticated reasons for refusing to assent to CE were playing *no role* in securing the verdict that she continues to possess *and*, then it ought to be possible to describe an entirely unsophisticated person, a child, for example, who has mastered Conjunction but who also refuses to assent to CE without offering any particular reason for that refusal.

But it is clearly not possible to do any such thing.

Recall here Wittgenstein's discussion in the *Philosophical Investigations* of the conditions under which we would be willing to say that a child has grasped the concept of expanding the series +2 (1953: §185). As Wittgenstein points out, one of the conditions we insist on is that the child be able to expand the series correctly in a range of simple cases. Unless and until the child has been able to do this reliably enough, we are unwilling to attribute mastery of the concept to him. Deviation from these conditions would require special explanation, if it is to be compatible with mastery of the concept.

Williamson's strategy of using experts on a concept C to secure counterexamples to any proposed understanding–assent link p(C) is flawed. The fact that the person is an expert on C serves to make it plausible that the person possesses the concept C. But the fact that she arrives at her refusal to assent to p(C) via sophisticated theoretical reasons means that she can at most claim to find p derivatively uncom-pelling, not primitively uncompelling. To the extent to which we develop the example so as to make it seem that the expert now finds CE *primitively* uncompelling, to that extent the example loses its force.

So much, then, for trying to use expert-based competent dissent against the existence of constitutive understanding–assent links.

Competent Dissent and Basis Accounts

Let us turn to asking how the phenomenon of competent dissent might be used against a Basis account.

On such an account, S's a priori justification for assenting to (1),

(1)   All quadrilaterals have four interior angle

is said to be given by her understanding of the concept *quadrilateral* (and the other ingredient concepts). She is justified in assenting to (1) *not* because assenting to it is *constitutive* of understanding (1), but because her understanding is, somehow or other, a sufficient epistemic basis for assenting to (1), and she bases her assent on that understanding.[16]

But, now, if GCD is true, a problem seems to arise for a Basis account of (1): For how could the justification provided by the understanding of (1) be sufficient for assenting to (1), when some people with understanding assent to it precisely because they understand it, while others refuse to assent to it, despite understanding it just as well as those who do? How could the justification provided by the understanding be visible to some and yet hidden from others?

Although this can look like an impressive objection, and some important philosophers have endorsed it (e.g., Sosa, 2007), it is answerable.

We are familiar from other epistemic contexts with the phenomenon of a perfectly good justification for believing p being occluded from a thinker by his believing some misleading considerations that seem to support not-p. Take a perceptual case. I may have perfectly good visual evidence that there is a fox in front of me. But I ignore this good visual evidence because of my strongly held background belief that there are no foxes in New York, and that the creatures that look like foxes in New York actually belong to a species of locally bred dog. In such a case, the occlusion of a pre-existing justification by what is taken to be, rightly or wrongly, a trumping consideration is not hard to understand.

And there is no reason that I know of why this type of occlusion should not also occur in cases where it is the understanding, rather than perception, that is providing the relevant justification. That takes care of any potential threat that the phenomenon of expert competent dissent may be thought to pose for a Basis account.

Two Ways of Believing a Basis-Explicable A Priori Proposition

Consider again the examples of a priori beliefs that are plausibly explained by a Basis account.

(1)   All quadrilaterals have four interior angles.
(4)   In the Gettier scenario, Mr. Smith has a justified true belief but does not know.[17]
(5)   In the standard Twin Earth scenario, Oscar's word 'water' has H_2O in its extension but not XYZ, while Toscar's word 'water' has XYZ in its extension but not H_2O.

When we look at these examples of Basis Account-friendly propositions, we are liable to be struck by the fact that there seem to be two importantly distinct types.

In the case of an example like (1), it is plausible that you come to believe (1) because you *work out* that it is true. Indeed, it is plausible that you work it out by inferring it from the definition of *quadrilateral* that you have previously grasped.

Another case where you come to work out that a proposition is true on the basis of your understanding, but which is interestingly different from (1), is given by Elijah Chudnoff. Chudnoff (2013) considers a thinker who works out that

(6)   Necessarily, any two circles of unequal radii can intersect at most at two points.

You visualize two circles of unequal radii and, by manipulating them in imagination, you come to realize that a proposition as strong as (6) is true.

This example is interesting in that, although it is clearly plausible that the truth of (6) is worked out and worked out on the basis of the subject's understanding of the ingredient concepts, it is *implausible* to think that it is worked out via an *inference* from the relevant definitions. Rather, the working out takes place partly in the imagination, with the understanding supplying the relevant images, and the license to generalize and modalize the proposition that they appear to illustrate.[18]

In both of these cases, your justification for believing p relies on your *working p out* on the basis of your understanding, whether this working out be via inference from a definition of one of its ingredient concepts, or via the imagination, or perhaps in other ways as well.

It's not easy to fully specify this notion of 'working out'. But the crucial aspect of the phenomenon it points to is that the subject ends up with some grip, on the basis of reasoning in a broad sense, on *why* the proposition in question is to be believed, on the *grounds* for believing it.

Consider, though, by way of contrast, the famous Gettier thought experiment. In that case, you are told that Mr. Smith stands in a certain relation to a given proposition p. After contemplating the situation for a bit, it comes to seem to you that, in the situation as specified, Mr. Smith has a justified true belief that p, but does not know that p.

This process could be represented in one of two ways. It could be represented as your performing a person-level inference from

(7)   Mr. Smith stands in the Gettier relation to p

to

(8)   Mr. Smith has a justified true belief but does not know.

Or, it could be represented as your considering the conditional

(9)   If Mr. Smith stands in the Gettier relation to p, then Mr. Smith has a justified true belief but does not know

and its coming to seem true to you, leading you to assent to it.[19]

Either way, the crucial point is that, in this case, while you may have a good grip on why Mr. Smith has a justified true belief in the scenario as described, you *don't* have a good grip on *why* Mr. Smith does not *know*. It simply strikes you that he does not know.

There is an important sense in which the transition from (7) to (8), or the conditional in (9), is simply found to be 'primitively compelling' (although, of course, this need not imply that the transition or the proposition is concept-constituting: being found primitively compelling is a necessary condition for being concept-constituting, not sufficient for it). You can identify no premises from which you worked out that (9) is true. You can identify no definition of *knowledge* from which you deduced it. (The only definition of knowledge you are aware of is the JTB definition, and that predicts precisely the opposite conclusion.) Although you know in virtue of which features of the situation Mr. Smith has a justified true belief, you don't know in virtue of which features of the situation he doesn't *know* (philosophers have been arguing about that ever since the thought experiment was first put forward).

When (9) strikes you as true, you might develop some hypotheses about why it is true, hypotheses about the features of the contemplated scenario in virtue of which Mr. Smith does not know. You might think that it has to do with the fact that his reasoning involves false lemmas; or with the fact that the method by which he formed his belief could so easily have led to a false belief. And so on.

All these hypotheses, though, would have the status of conjectures. And even if every single one of them turned out to be false, this would not affect the probative value of the verdict elicited by the thought experiment. It would still count as a datum that anyone standing in the Gettier relation to p would have a justified true belief that p, but not know that p.

Similarly, in the Twin Earth case. You don't know in virtue of which features of the case it strikes you as true that Oscar's and Toscar's extensions of 'water' are non-overlapping. What you know is that it simply strikes you as true; and that fact sets off a search for the grounds of its truth.

This point is made even more vividly by Trolley examples.[20] When you contemplate the first Trolley case, the one where you sacrifice the one to save the five by flipping a switch that moves the trolley onto a side-rail, you might think you see that the moral is a consequentialist one: you have a duty to save the five, even if it involves sacrificing the one.

But that confidence is soon undermined by your reluctance, in the second variant of the thought experiment, to sacrifice the one to save the five where that act would involve actively throwing the large man standing next to you on the bridge onto the path of the oncoming trolley.

What, then, is the moral of the pair of thought experiments taken together? Is it that you are *required* to save the larger number under conditions where you can do so simply by letting someone die, but that it is *impermissible* for you to save the larger number if it requires you to actively kill someone?

We don't yet know what these pair of thought experiments show. Anything we say at this point would be conjectural, and subject to refutation by further considerations or further thought experiments. What we have is the raw *data* about what it is morally permissible to do under the two different scenarios.

Like the cases before them, this pair of Trolley cases illustrates that sometimes a proposition—in these cases, a conditional normative proposition—simply strikes you as true. You don't work it out from identifiable premises. You don't know *why* it is true. You don't know if there is a general principle that it exemplifies and which would predict the pattern of verdicts you are prepared to make.

All you have is that it vividly strikes you as true; and as such, you accept it. You treat it as a datum (defeasible, to be sure) that any acceptable theory of the topic should respect. In this respect, our intuitions about these cases resemble perceptions, and the verdicts based upon them resemble perceptual judgments. They are data awaiting proper explanation by a deeper theory.

A Role for Intuitions in Basis Accounts

Let us set aside for now the cases where an a priori justified proposition is believed because it is worked out. Let's look at cases where an a priori proposition is not worked out at all, but simply strikes you as true.

If we wish to say that, in these latter cases, your a priori justification for the proposition believed is given by your understanding of the concepts ingredient in the belief, how should we think about this? How could the understanding justify a proposition *other than* by showing it to follow from some premises (typically from a definition)? What could be the model for some *non-inferential* way in which our understanding of *knowledge* or *extension* could justify, respectively, the Gettier proposition, on the one hand, and the Twin Earth proposition, on the other?

Some philosophers, Ernest Sosa, for example, would have no great difficulty with this question. Since Sosa is, in effect, a Reliabilist about justification, he can simply say that 'we have a competence grounded in our understanding' for telling the true from the false in the particular domain under discussion. And it is that understanding-grounded reliability that explains (indeed constitutes) our justification.

However, since Reliabilism is a clearly inadequate view of epistemic justification, I cannot accept that answer. As a result, I face the problem of trying to say how our understanding of a proposition could *non-inferentially* justify our assent to that proposition. How could the relation between our understanding of p and our assent to p be analogous to the relation that obtains between our perception that p and our assent to p? This is the theoretical point at which *intuitions* seem to supply just what's needed in order to make Basis accounts work.

What I mean by 'intuition' I will explain in further detail below. For now, it will suffice to say that I intend to be invoking the classic (if still controversial) idea of an 'intellectual seeming'. This notion is to be sharply distinguished from any doxastic notion such as judgment, or an inclination to judge. It is to be thought of as the *intellectual* version of a sensory seeming (the sort of seeming that is caused in you by your vision, as when it visually seems to you that the cat is sleeping on the bed).

The sensory seeming is to be distinguished from the visual state that causes it. Two visual states may be identical, even as the sensory seemings that they cause are distinct. We know this most vividly from the case of aspect-seeing, as when one and the same diagram, and hence in the appropriate sense, one and the same visual state, sometimes seems to present a duck and sometimes a rabbit.

We see this phenomenon vividly in the intellectual case as well, as when a pun is experienced first with one meaning and then with another. For example:

(10)   I was wondering why that baseball was coming towards me so fast; then it hit me.

Most of us first hear (10) with the physical meaning of 'hit', and immediately thereafter with the cognitive meaning of 'hit'. This alternation between the two distinct meanings heard expressed (a phenomenon which rightly fascinated Wittgenstein) is not an alternation between states that have individuating sensory phenomenologies; it's an alternation between two intellectual impressions of which thought is being expressed.

We get a similar phenomenon in the syntactic case. Most people, when they first hear the garden-path sentence

(11) The horse raced past the barn fell.

hear it as ungrammatical. Eventually, though, they light on the passive sense of 'raced' and then experience the perfectly coherent thought that is expressed by the sentence under this grammatical guise.

These examples form part of the classical case for the involvement of intuitions, or intellectual seemings, in connection with ordinary cases of linguistic and syntactic understanding. And this no doubt explains why the idea that we manifest our syntactic and semantic competence through intuitions—about grammatical well-formedness, on the one hand, and analytic entailments, on the other—is hardly a new one.[21]

However, once we have made clear the distinction between Constitutive and Basis accounts of the epistemically analytic, and the difference between propositions that are believed because they are worked out, and those that simply strike us as true, we are in a position to see that, in addition to this standard observational evidence, there is a strong *theoretical* motivation, of a broadly internalist sort, for giving intuitions a role, even in what are meant to be understanding-based accounts. That role emerges when we ask, How does your understanding of p, in a case where your understanding does not supply you with a premise for inferring p, give you an epistemic basis for believing p?

It is hard to see what could count as an internalistically acceptable answer to this question, if not something along the following lines: The understanding of p, when appropriately prompted, supplies you with the intuition that p. If we were unable to provide an answer of this sort, we would be hard-pressed to say how the understanding of p could serve as an (internalistically recognizable) epistemic basis for believing p.

This, then, is part of the reason for why I have come to regard the avoidance of intuitions in the theory of the a priori as *futile*. The main stratagem by which intuitions were to be avoided was to be through understanding-based accounts of the a priori. However, it turns out that, once enough relevant distinctions have been made, the principal type of understanding-based account, the Basis version, will need to appeal to intuitions in order to tell a satisfying epistemological story.

Synthetic A Priori Propositions: Normative Truths

Be that as it may, there is an even stronger reason for doubting that the theory of the a priori can make do without appealing to intuitions—and that is that there are important cases of a priori justified belief that *cannot* be explained solely by the understanding that we have of them. To put it in Kantian terminology, there are *synthetic* a priori propositions. In particular, all *substantive* normative principles are synthetic a priori. I will illustrate my argument by focusing on the case of moral principles, but the argument is, I believe, a general one that applies to all substantive normative principles.

What do I mean by a 'substantive moral principle'? Let us agree that the minimal content of a moral judgment claiming that some act of type A is wrong (typically) expresses the speaker's distinctively moral disapproval of A, and (always) claims of A that it *merits* that distinctive sort of disapproval. I shall take this to be the uncontroversial minimal core of a concept like (morally) *wrong*.[22] *Mutatis mutandis* for the other canonical moral concepts.

A non-substantive, or trivial, moral proposition would then be an obviously epistemically analytic claim such as, for example,

(12)   If an act A is morally wrong, then it merits moral disapproval.

By contrast, a *substantive* moral principle would involve claiming that some particular act-type was morally wrong, as, for example, in:

(13)   Inflicting severe pain on babies just for fun is morally wrong.
(14)   Another person's suffering is a prime facie moral reason for someone to help relieve it.

Substantive moral claims can thus be represented as being of the following form:

(Moral Norm, MN)   Necessarily, if x is D, then x is M

where 'D' is a canonical descriptive term and 'M' is a canonical moral term.

Consider (13). Most of us believe (13). Indeed, most of us believe that it is as fully justified a proposition as we are likely to encounter;[23] and that it is justified a priori. The question of concern to me at the moment is: Does our justification for believing (13) rest solely on our understanding of its ingredient concepts?

Some philosophers are inclined to think that Moore (1903a) already showed us that the answer to this question is 'No' (see Darwall, Gibbard and Railton, 1992, Fine 2002). Although I agree with Moore's conclusion, I believe that the considerations he adduced in its favor are vulnerable; I hope to do a little better.

How did Moore argue for the claim that substantive moral principles could not be (in my terms) epistemically analytic? Without delving into the exegetical details, his most famous argument involves an appeal to a *restricted* version of the doctrine we have previously encountered as (Generalized Competent Dissent, GCD). The restriction is to *substantive moral* propositions:

(Moral Generalized Competent Dissent, MGCD)   For any substantive moral proposition p, it is possible for there to be someone who dissents from p while retaining full competence with p.

The weaknesses in Moore's argument should be apparent from our previous discussion.

For one thing, as we have seen, there is no general warrant to believe GCD. If there is warrant to believe MGCD, the special case where GCD is restricted to moral principles, we would need an explanation as to why. But Moore offers no such explanation.

Second, and as we have also already seen, merely establishing that a particular assent is not constitutive of understanding doesn't imply that our justification for that assent is not understanding-based, since it's possible that that justification is explained by a Basis model rather than by a Constitutive model.

For both of these reasons, Moore fails to justify the claim that our knowledge of moral principles cannot be explained by the understanding alone. In what follows, however, I will briefly supply an alternative argument for the claim that substantive moral principles are synthetic a priori.

Let's begin with the observation that, on either the Constitutive model or the Basis model, if a given proposition of the form MN were epistemically analytic, then mere reflection on the concepts *wrong* and *D* would suffice for you to justifiably believe that that instance of MN is true. However, mere reflection on the relevant concepts doesn't suffice for such belief.

To see why, suppose the opposite. Imagine that the concept that you would express by 'wrong' includes not only the minimal core that I previously outlined, according to which to call an act-type A wrong is to claim that A merits disapproval of the distinctively moral type, but also a *substantive* conception of which acts are wrong. For example, suppose it can be shown to follow from the concept that you express by 'wrong' (in the relevantly broad sense of 'follow'), that it is morally wrong to ignore someone else's pain if, at little cost to yourself, you could help relieve it.

About such a substantive concept, embodying a substantive view of which act-types count as wrong, it seems we can *always* competently ask:

(Concept Correctness Open Question) Yes, but is that the *correct* concept of wrong, the one that specifies those acts that are genuinely deserving of moral disapproval? We can all agree that act-type A is ruled wrong by *your* substantive concept of 'wrong'; but is it *genuinely* wrong?

Consider the contrast here with the concept *quadrilateral*. If someone said: 'According to my concept *quadrilateral*, a quadrilateral always has four sides', it wouldn't make any sense to ask, 'Yes, but is that the *correct* concept *quadrilateral*? Is that the concept that delivers the genuinely correct verdicts about how many sides quadrilaterals have?' (Of course, one could always ask whether a particular concept expressed by a word w is identical to the one that other members of one's community also express by w; but that is a different matter.)

By contrast, it always seems to make sense to ask, about any moral concept that embodies a *substantive* view about what counts as right and wrong, whether it is correct, whether it correctly reflects whatever moral facts there are about the rightness and wrongness of acts.[24]

Although the matter deserves a great deal more discussion than I can give it here, the argument I have offered seems not to be restricted to *moral* concepts but would appear to apply to any *normative* concept whatsoever, including those that are characteristic of the theories of rationality and justified belief.[25, 26]

If these considerations are correct, we cannot think of the a priori justified normative judgments that we are tempted to make as simply revealing to us some information that is already encoded within our canonical normative concepts.

Furthermore, if these a priori justified normative judgments are supported by intuitions, as they often seem to be, then those intuitions cannot be thought of as simply revealing to us the natures of our moral concepts (as on Basis accounts), but must be thought of more ambitiously, as revealing to us the true natures of moral right and wrong.

Fine (2002) would resist this last conclusion. He has maintained that Moore's Open Question Argument defeats not only the claim that normative truths are built into our moral *concepts*, but also the view that they are built into the very *natures* of the *properties* of right and wrong. Since Fine takes it that all metaphysically necessary truths are grounded in facts about the natures of the implicated properties, he concludes that moral truths cannot be regarded as metaphysically necessary but must be thought of as involving a *sui generis* notion of necessity, namely, *normative necessity*. This view of moral truths makes them analogous to nomological necessities, like laws of nature—that is to say, contingent from a metaphysical point of view.

This is quite a startling picture of moral truths and makes it very hard to see how we could have any a priori *knowledge* of them—via intuition, or in any other way.

It is, therefore, important to see that Fine's conclusion about moral properties is not supported by the version of Moore's Open Question Argument that I have been presenting here. My version applies exclusively to the normative *concepts*, asking whether any particular normative concept could encode substantive normative facts. This might equivalently be put by asking whether any particular normative concept correctly reflects the essence of the properties of right and wrong that are designated by our normative concepts.

What does follow from my version of Moore's argument is that, if intuition-backed moral knowledge is to be possible, there must be intellectual seemings whose justificatory power is not sourced in the understanding alone.

The acknowledgement of such non-understanding-sourced intuitions will sit ill with the theories of many philosophers, even of those who are not skeptical about intuitions. Intuition-friendly philosophers like Sosa, Goldman, and Pust, for example, all insist that intuitions ultimately derive whatever probative power they have from being sourced in the understanding (see Sosa 1998, 2007; Goldman 2007; Pust 2000).

However, if my argument works, it shows the need for an epistemic resource in the theory of the a priori that is not merely grounded in our conceptual understanding. Since I believe that it is independently plausible that that resource is provided by the rationalist notion of an intuition, or intellectual seeming, I take it to be an argument for the existence of such intuitions, ones whose probative power derives not merely from our understanding of concepts.

To put this point another way, we must recognize a distinction between a proposition that is *self-evident*—that is justifiably believable simply on the basis of being understood—and propositions that are *intuitive*—that is justifiably believable not merely on the basis of being understood but also because, when one considers them, one has the intellectual impression that they are true.

Interim Summary

I have argued that there are two distinct types of understanding-based accounts of a priori justification, Constitutive and Basis. While the first type of account relies on there being constitutive assents, the second one does not.

I further argued that both types of theory survive the invocation of the phenomenon of expert competent dissent, a phenomenon that is widely taken to undermine any understanding-based account of a priori justification.

However, I noted that a Basis model needs to rely on the notion of an intuition in order to provide a satisfactory epistemology of a priori justification.

And that, in any case, there are important instances of a priori justification that cannot be explained at all by understanding-based accounts.

I concluded that this establishes the need to recognize intuitions as a source of a priori warrant, alongside the understanding.

The Non-Uniformity of Sources of the A Priori

If the argument up to this point is correct, justification in the a priori domain has more than one source—some a priori justification is grounded in the understanding, while some is grounded in intuition.

Is this a plausible outcome? Shouldn't all a priori justification derive from a single source in much the way in which (as we are prone to think) all a posteriori justification derives (ultimately) from the single source of sensory experience?

That the a posteriori has a single source is secured trivially and by definition—the a posteriori just is justification that derives ultimately from experience. (That's not to deny, of course, that there are different subspecies of a posteriori justification—for example, inferential and perceptual.)

A priori justification, by contrast, has a merely negative characterization: it is that justification which is not a posteriori. And this means that there is no definitional guarantee that everything that is a priori will have the same epistemic source. For all that the notion of apriority speaks to, it is possible that some a priori justification has its source in the understanding and the rest in some other source, for example, in intuition.

Basic Skepticism about Intuitions: Phenomenology and Intellectual Seemings

But how could intuitions reveal to us the true natures of such properties as right and wrong, or of any other property for that matter? Isn't this just to postulate one mystery in order to solve another?

I understand well this type of skepticism about the justificatory power of intuitions; I used to endorse it myself.[27] But, as I've indicated, I've come to think that an appeal to intuitions is inevitable and that many of the misgivings that philosophers have about them are misguided. Obviously, there is a huge number of issues to be discussed; here I'll only be able to make a start on some of the most basic.

An intuition, as I understand it (following many others), is an intellectual *seeming*.[28] An intellectual seeming is similar to a sensory seeming in being a presentation of a proposition's being true; yet dissimilar to it in not having a sensory phenomenology.

It is also to be sharply distinguished from any species of judgment; it must be understood as pre-judgmental and pre-doxastic, if it is to be capable of serving as an *epistemic basis* for a judgment.

To illustrate, let's go back to the case of the Trolley problem about whether to throw the large man off the bridge in order to save the lives of the five innocents trapped below. In thinking about this case, it can come to very vividly seem to you that it would be wrong to throw him off the bridge. But we can also imagine that even while it so seems to you, you hesitate to make the judgment, wanting to assure yourself that you have not overlooked anything. Finally, satisfied, you make the judgment that it would be wrong. The state of its seeming wrong to you was intellectual, not sensory; yet evidently pre-judgmental and pre-doxastic. When the judgment finally came, it was based on that pre-judgmental seeming.

This, and many other intuitive judgments appear to instantiate this type of *three-step process*: you consider a scenario and a question about it; after sufficient reflection, a particular answer to that question comes to seem true to you, either because, as we saw earlier, you work out that it is true, or because, without working it out, it just comes to strike you as true; finally, you endorse this proposition.

Recently, however, a great deal of skepticism has been directed at the very existence of intellectual seemings in the sense invoked here. Skeptics say that when they try to introspect intellectual seemings they come up empty (Cappelen 2012, Deutsch 2015, and Williamson 2005). All they encounter, they say, is either the judgment itself, or, if you insist on something pre-judgmental, an *inclination to judge*. Williamson, for example, says:

Although mathematical intuition can have a rich phenomenology, even a quasi-perceptual one, for instance in geometry, the intellectual appearance of the Gettier proposition is not like that. Any accompanying imagery is irrelevant. For myself I am aware of no intellectual seeming beyond my conscious inclination to believe the Gettier proposition. Similarly, I am aware of no intellectual seeming beyond my conscious inclination to believe Naïve Comprehension, which I resist because I know better.   (2007a: 217)

It is certainly true that a vivid phenomenology is not ordinarily associated with the intuitions we have in response to thought experiments. But I don't believe that this observation gives us an adequate basis for being skeptical about intuitions, that it marks a distinction between intuitions and other undeniably real phenomena of conscious mental life.

Consider the very thing that the intuition skeptic is *not* skeptical about—namely, *occurrent judgment*. As I survey this room, there is a sense in which I am making dozens of judgments, and acquiring the corresponding beliefs. If this way of putting things seems somehow too 'active', then let's say that as I survey this room I *note* various things and *accept* various propositions and thereby acquire the corresponding beliefs.

But it would be false to say that each of those occurrent noticings, acceptances, or judgments has its own distinctive phenomenology, at least not if what we mean by 'phenomenology' is the type of phenomenal quality that is characteristic of sensation. Certainly, I can make various judgments without saying the words of a public language to myself (as John Broome seems to have been inclined to say at some point (see Broome 2013)).

Another interesting example of a conscious mental phenomenon that lacks a distinctive phenomenology is a phenomenon I have come to label 'taking'. I believe a strong case can be made for saying that what distinguishes person-level *inference* from mere *associative thinking* is that, in an inference, the transition from one thought to another is mediated by the thinker's *taking it* that the 'premise' thought supports the 'conclusion' thought (see Boghossian 2014). But it would be wrong to identify this taking with a mental state that has a distinctive phenomenology.[29]

Thus, the absence of a vivid phenomenology should not be regarded as decisive grounds against the existence of intellectual seemings.

Justification by Inclinations to Judgment

Well, perhaps there is no good reason *not* to believe in intellectual seemings; but what *positive* reason is there to believe in them? Why can't we do whatever needs doing simply with the notion of an 'inclination to judgment', as Williamson claims? Why do we need to recognize phenomenologically elusive states of conscious 'intellectual seemings' which are not themselves judgments, or inclinations to judge?

The main reason for being dissatisfied with any sort of doxastic substitute for intellectual seemings is that no such substitute could give us the means by which to explain, in any sort of internalistically acceptable way, how we could be *justified* in making the a priori judgments in question.

Consider again the Gettier scenario and the Gettier judgment that we end up with, that Mr. Smith has a justified true belief but does not know. This judgment, we believe, is strongly justified, indeed, so strongly justified that it is capable of refuting the very strongly entrenched JTB theory. Moreover, we take it to be justified a priori. Let us assume we are correct in these assumptions. How is the intuition skeptic, who believes only in inclinations to judgment, to explain these facts?

On the intuition-friendly story, the Gettier judgment is justified by the Gettier intuition: that Mr. Smith, in the circumstances as described, has a justified true belief but does not know is supported by its intellectually seeming to the thinker that Mr. Smith has a justified true belief but does not know. We shall shortly look at this story in greater detail. But it has an epistemic form that is familiar to us from the empirical case (the justification of judgment by sensory seemings).

But what can the intuition skeptic offer us?

He can try saying that your Gettier judgment is justified by your *inclination* to make it. But that wouldn't by itself be a good answer. Your being inclined to judge that p is not usually a good reason, all by itself, for your believing that p.

Here, once again, Reliabilism would be able to provide an easy solution. Suppose your being inclined to judge that p were, under the relevant conditions, a reliable means of arriving at the truth. Then, under the terms of Reliabilism, your judgment that p would be justified by your inclination, without there being any need to postulate intellectual seemings as the basis for the judgment that p.

Unfortunately, Reliabilism is false.[30] (It is striking how dramatically the landscape of epistemological issues would be affected if Reliabilism were a viable theory of epistemic justification.)

If we set Reliabilism aside, the only other conditions under which your inclination to judge that p would justify your judging that p would be if your inclination were based on its following, and on its seeming to you to follow, from some justified background theory of yours, that p.

If we apply this observation to the Gettier case, the only conditions under which your inclination to make the Gettier judgment could justify your making the Gettier judgment would be if it followed, and seemed to you to follow, from your background theory of knowledge, that Mr. Smith has a justified true belief but does not know.

The trouble (as we have already seen) is that your background theory of knowledge is presumably the JTB theory of knowledge. And far from its following from the JTB theory that Mr. Smith does not know, it is actually *inconsistent* with the JTB theory that Mr. Smith does not know. Indeed, the JTB theory is what gets refuted by the Gettier judgment.

So, how, on this account, could we be justified in making the Gettier judgment? However, if we are not justified in making the Gettier judgment, how could it be rational for us to have overthrown centuries of epistemological theorizing on its basis?

The problem here is a perfectly general one, as I hope is clear. Through thought experiments, and other exercises of the imagination and/or understanding, we arrive at (typically direct) a priori truths that can serve to refute previously well-established background theories.

The intuition-skeptic's story, that the a priori judgment flows from an antecedently justified background theory, is deeply problematic, because that background theory may not only not entail the judgment; it may actually be refuted by it.

Someone might believe this objection to the intuition-skeptic too hasty for the following reason. Admittedly, our intuitive judgment about the Gettier case does not derive from our *explicitly* held philosophical theory about knowledge, the JTB theory. But perhaps there is some *other* theory that we hold not explicitly, but *tacitly*, and that entails the Gettier judgment? When we react to the Gettier thought experiment with the Gettier judgment, might we not be manifesting our acceptance of this *tacit* theory?[31]

There are at least two reasons why this line of thought can't save the proposal on offer.

First, if appeal to such a tacit theory is to genuinely shore up an intuition-skeptical view, it had better be uncontroversial that the propositions of this tacit theory can themselves be justified without appeal to intuitions. However, if my previous discussion of the synthetic a priori status of normative propositions is correct, they cannot be.

Second, and putting this first objection to one side, we would still need to explain why we always trust the deliverances of the tacit theory *over* those of the explicit one. Why do we treat the putative Gettier truth as a *counterexample* to the JTB theory? Why not, rather, regard the thought experiment as showing that we hold a false *tacit* theory on the grounds that it has been shown to be in conflict with what the received view, the JTB theory, predicts?

Think of the corresponding issue as it might arise in the empirical sciences. If we discerned a conflict between an innately acquired and tacitly held *folk physics*, and an explicitly arrived at physical theory, we certainly wouldn't immediately privilege the folk physics. On the contrary, we would typically consider it refuted.[32] With what justification, then, do we privilege the tacit theory of knowledge over a theory that had been developed by such giants as Plato and Russell, and which had been accepted as received wisdom by countless generations of philosophers?

The fact that we (nearly) always privilege the intuition-supported judgment shows that we regard it as more strongly justified than its negation, a negation which is supported by all those explicit arguments.

But we don't yet have an explanation of why we would be right to do so, if we are restricted to appealing solely to the resources provided by the intuition-skeptic. It remains to show, of course, that we don't face a similar epistemological difficulty, if we help ourselves to the idea of an intellectual seeming. Unfortunately, that is a huge task which cannot be undertaken within the confines of the present volume and so will have to await another occasion.

Conclusion

Understanding-based accounts are plausible for a range of important cases of a priori justification. They come in two importantly different versions, neither one of which is defeated by the phenomenon of expert competent dissent.

However, the theory of the a priori cannot hope to make do without appeal to a notion of intuition or rational insight. This is so both because the Basis version of an understanding-based account needs to rely on it in spelling out how it proposes to do its epistemic work; but also because, more importantly, there are propositions that are synthetic a priori.[33]

Notes

1. This paper is published here for the first time.
2. In my sense, a person has 'understanding' of or 'competence with' a concept if he has mastery of the concept. If we think of concepts as individuated by their conceptual role, then a master of a concept would have a full grasp of the concept's individuative conceptual role. He wouldn't be like the subject in Burge's (1979) famous thought experiment, Burt, who has an incomplete understanding or faulty understanding of the concept *arthritis*, believing that arthritis can also occur in the thigh. Burge advocates saying that there is a notion of concept possession according to which Burt possesses the concept *arthritis* despite having a faulty grasp of it. I need not deny that claim. But I do need to insist that the sort of understanding that is presupposed by understanding-based accounts of a priori knowledge has to be the sort of 'full understanding' characteristic of the experts, rather than the sort of 'partial understanding' that may be possessed by ordinary folks. (Alternatively, you could take me to be talking about a priori knowledge involving propositions containing 'non-deferential' concepts.)

3. I shall work within a Fregean framework. I shall designate concepts by italicizing the English words that typically express them and propositional contents by italicizing the English sentences that typically express them.

4. The first point is entirely consistent with my previous commitments; the other two are not.

5. Later in the paper, when I discuss our a priori knowledge of normative propositions, I will explain why (3) and (4) may not ultimately be good candidates for understanding-based accounts; at this stage of the argument, though, this won't matter.

6. This was not clear in my (1996) but was clarified in my (2003b).

7. Why should these two types of explanation be seen as mutually exclusive? Suppose that S's understanding of p is constituted by S's disposition to assent to p. It would follow that S's understanding of p cannot serve as a good epistemic basis for S's assent to p, since, in general, S's disposition to assent to p cannot serve as an epistemic basis for her assent to p, let alone a good one.

8. An alternative version, favored, for example, by George Bealer (1998), would run the theory in terms of a subject's needing to have the *intuition* that instances of 'If A and B, then A' are true. I am open to this version of a conceptual-role semantics.

9. In my 2003b, this type of bridge principle is called the 'Meaning-Entitlement Connection.'

10. The qualification 'in the right way' is there to accommodate the possibility of deviant causal chains, a complication that need not detain us.

11. For present purposes, 'rejecting p' and 'dissenting from p' are to be taken to be equivalent to 'refusing to assent to p'.

12. A similar emphasis on the conceptual role's being 'underived' can be found in Schiffer 2013.

13. For concreteness I focus on a particular case, that of *and*. In his 2011, Williamson claims that I have retreated to this case having conceded defeat for Modus Ponens and other logical rules. I have no idea why he says that. Everything I say about conjunction could be adapted to the case of the other logical constants and their constitutive rules. In any case, the question under consideration is whether he has succeeded in devising a *general* recipe for defeating any proposed understanding–assent link. It's perfectly fair to assess his claim to have done so in the way that best exposes its weaknesses.

14. Williamson himself describes his relation to Naïve Comprehension along similar lines: 'Similarly, I am aware of...my conscious inclination to believe Naïve Comprehension, which I resist because I know better' (2007a: 217).

15. This is also argued for in Boghossian 2012.

16. It is important to see that a Basis view is not committed to any *particular* conception of the understanding of a concept.

17. While it is common for friends of the a priori to include examples involving knowledge as examples of a priori propositions that are covered by understanding-based accounts, we will later see a reason for doubting that any normative proposition falls under such an account. For now, I will go along with the common assumption.

18. Precisely how to describe the epistemology of such cases requires a lot more investigation than it has received.

19. Indeed, not only may (9) strike you as true, but so might its modalized, quantified counterpart: $\Box$ $(\forall x)$ $(\forall p)$ $[xGp \rightarrow xJTBp \land \neg xKp]$. Williamson (2007a) has disputed this characterization of the content of the proposition that's judged in this and other thought experiments. Limitations of space prevent me from discussing his objections here. I will just record my conviction that this standard representation of the judgment involved in thought experiments seems to me correct.

20. I will soon be arguing that normative propositions are not knowable a priori on the basis of the understanding alone. But this will not affect the use to which I am putting them here,

which is to illustrate the way in which some a priori propositions can simply strike us as true, without our working them out, without our having much of a sense of which features of the situation ground their truth.

21. I'm grateful to Barry Smith for emphasizing to me that it is the same notion of intuition that is at work in this connection as in connection with philosophical thought experiments.

22. By a moral judgment, I will always mean here a pure moral judgment that predicates of some act type, some canonical moral property such as 'right' or 'wrong,' 'good' or 'bad'. Judgments that predicate moral properties of individuals—as in 'Donald Trump is evil'— will be impure moral judgments whose truth will partly depend on that of the pure ones and partly on the truth of nonmoral judgments (about e.g. Donald Trump's biography).

23. A committed relativist about morality once publicly rejected my claim that we all believe (13) to be true and justified, by saying that she thought it depended on how much fun was at issue, drawing gasps from the room.

24. It might be thought that this argument presupposes a realist view of morality and that this limits its applicability. It's not clear to me how much of a realist view it presupposes, but certainly not more than I take to be true.

25. This is why I earlier said, in footnote 5, that propositions (3) and (4), involving the normative notions of knowledge and justification, may not ultimately be explicable by understanding-based accounts.

26. You might worry that if this argument locates any interesting division at all between concepts, it's not one between the normative and the non-normative. For isn't there a correctness open question about, for example, natural kind concepts, which are not in any obvious way normative concepts? I don't believe so: the sense of the open question in the two cases seems to me to be distinct. In the case of a normative concept, we can ask whether any of the purported truths yielded by the substantive normative concept is true. In the case of a natural kind concept, we can ask whether it 'carves nature at the joints', we are asking not whether the propositions it encodes are true, but rather whether they are nomological or counterfactual-supporting, or something along those lines.

27. See my (2003a). For another exposition of skepticism see Wright (2004).

28. See, for example, Bealer (1992). Some philosophers deny that intuitions are best understood as a species of seeming. John Bengson (2015), for example, thinks that intuitions should be thought of as presentations, rather than seemings. The difference between them is supposed to be that while the content of a seeming would be explicitly available to a subject, the content of a presentation need not be. I believe that, in this sense, presentations won't be able to epistemically justify a belief that is based upon them, but I won't go into this issue here.

29. In Ned Block's (1995) terminology, these states may be taken to be 'access conscious' without being 'phenomenal conscious'.

30. See Cohen (1984), Foley (1985), and Bonjour (1985).

31. Some who hold this view might be tempted by the thought that this tacit theory constitutes our grasp of the concept *knowledge*.

32. An example I learned from Gilbert Harman: humans seem innately to believe that an object (like a bomb) thrown from a moving object (like an airplane) will fall in a straight line. According to our best physical theories, however, such an object would move in a parabolic path in the direction in which the plane was moving when it released it.

33. I am grateful to John Bengson, Kit Fine, Yu Guo, Antonella Mallozzi, Jake Nebel, Stephen Schiffer, Susanna Siegel, Crispin Wright, and to audiences at the American University of Beirut, the NYU Seminar on Mind and Language, the Philosophical Society at the University of Oxford, and the 2016 Pro-Seminar for first-year PhD students at the Philosophy program at NYU, for helpful feedback on the material in this paper. This paper draws on some material from my 2017.

14

Reply to Boghossian on Intuition, Understanding, and the A Priori[1]

Timothy Williamson

In 'Intuition, Understanding, and the A Priori' (Chapter 13), Boghossian makes a Kantian-sounding division between the analytic a priori and the synthetic a priori.

Analyticity here is epistemic: Boghossian initially paraphrases 'epistemically analytic' as 'justifiably believable merely on the basis of being understood'. Correspondingly, 'synthetic' can be paraphrased as 'not justifiably believable merely on the basis of being understood'. He means understanding in the ordinary sense in which native speakers of a language fully understand what they express in it, at least when not deferring to experts (as they might in using natural kind terms). It is not the sense in which a linguist studying her own native language may painfully struggle to achieve a better theoretical understanding of it. Henceforth, I will use 'understand' for 'fully understand' in Boghossian's sense.

Boghossian contrasts epistemic analyticity with metaphysical analyticity, which concerns truth rather than understanding and picks up the old idea of truth in virtue of meaning. A significant point of agreement between us is our denial, for similar reasons, that there are metaphysically analytic truths. The sentence 'All squares are four-sided' expresses the proposition that all squares are four-sided, which is true because all squares *are* four-sided, just as the sentence 'Some dogs are spotted' expresses the proposition that some dogs are spotted, which is true because some dogs *are* spotted (Williamson 2007a: 48–72). It is not even clear that epistemic analyticity in Boghossian's sense entails truth, for truth is unnecessary for justification on his internalist view.

Boghossian holds that intuition is needed to explain synthetic a priori justification, for instance of normative truths. This is in striking contrast with his earlier work, where he rejected appeals to it as obscurantist (Chapter 2, originally Boghossian 2003a).

Boghossian also suggests that intuition is essentially involved in some analytic a priori justification too. More specifically, he divides the understanding-based justification characteristic of the epistemically analytic a priori into two types, labelled 'constitutive' and 'basis'. In the *constitutive* type, one's assent to a proposition is justified in virtue of the fact that one's understanding of it is partly constituted by one's disposition to assent to it. In the *basis* type, one's assent is justified in virtue of the fact that one's understanding of the proposition serves as a good epistemic basis

Debating the A Priori. Paul Boghossian and Timothy Williamson, Oxford University Press (2020).
© Paul Boghossian and Timothy Williamson.
DOI: 10.1093/oso/9780198851707.001.0001

for one's assent. Boghossian argues that the two types of justification are needed for different cases. In non-inferential justification of the basis type, he suggests, one's understanding of the proposition serves as a good epistemic basis for one's assent to it by supplying one with an intuition of that very proposition. There the role of understanding *involves* the role of intuition, rather than providing an alternative to it.

In Chapters 3, 5, and 7 (originally Williamson 2003, 2011, and 2012, respectively) and elsewhere (Williamson 2007a: 73–133), I argue that the connection between understanding and assent is too loose to support understanding-based justification of the types Boghossian postulates. As he recognizes, by itself the new-found role for intuition does not answer that challenge. He therefore spends much of the first half of the chapter responding to my critique, before invoking intuitions. Section 1 below answers his response. Section 2 turns to his appeal to intuitions, and argues that they cannot do the work for which he invokes them.

1. Understanding and Assent

Boghossian starts with the constitutive type of understanding-based justification. In such cases—if there are any—when all goes well one's assent to a proposition p is justified in virtue of the fact that one's understanding of p is partly constituted by one's disposition to assent to p. As he refines the account in the spirit of conceptual-role semantics, it makes having an *underived* or primitive disposition to assent to p a necessary condition for understanding p, for the relevant propositions p.

In my previous critique, I consider actual or possible people who came to understand p in the normal way but then developed sophisticated theoretical doubts about p, on the basis of which they now dissent from p, while still understanding p. These people are experts; their understanding of p is non-deferential. Boghossian concedes that such cases can arise. However, he rightly notes, dispositions can be retained while inhibited. Handcuffs may inhibit a prisoner's disposition to hit out. Similarly, an expert may retain the disposition to assent to p, while inhibiting it on theoretical grounds. Examples are common. Thus the mere combination of understanding with refusal to assent does not refute Boghossian's constitutive account in its current form. So far so good.

Naturally, in writing my original critique, I was well aware of the possibility of inhibited dispositions to assent, and addressed its relevance explicitly (Williamson 2003: 254; 2007a: 99–105). In particular, I argued that the expert may gradually lose even the *disposition* to assent to p, while still retaining understanding of p. After all, many acquired dispositions are *habits*, which can be lost as well as gained over time. Since having the underived disposition to assent to p entails having the disposition to assent to p, the expert lacks the underived disposition to assent to p but still understands p, and thus is a direct counterexample to Boghossian's present constitutive account.

The core of Boghossian's reply is his claim that once the expert loses her underived disposition to assent to p, it is no longer plausible that she still understands p. He treats her as if she had simply forgotten what proposition p is. He does not consider what the expert can still do, having lost the disposition to assent to p. She can still *remember* assenting to p; she knows just what it was like to exercise the disposition to do so. She can also *imagine* just what it is like to exercise the disposition, for others who still have it. She still expects *them* to assent to *p*. She feels to herself like someone who has painfully struggled free of the disposition to commit a common fallacy, or to reason according to the prejudices of the bigoted community in which she was reared. In these ways, her situation is very unlike that of 'an entirely unsophisticated person, a child, for example', to which Boghossian compares it. Unlike the child or unsophisticate, she can fluently converse with others when they assert *p*, perhaps explaining to them why, in her opinion, they are mistaken. By normal standards, she is exercising her native speaker competence with the language, in particular when she expresses *p*, not revealing her incompetence. The last thing she needs is a language lesson. Perhaps children and other unsophisticates who lack both the disposition to assent to *p* and the expert's abilities can also understand *p*, but one need not insist on that point just to give a counterexample to the claimed necessity of having an underived disposition to assent to *p* for understanding *p*, for the relevant propositions *p*.

Boghossian illustrates his argument with the example of 'and'-elimination, the inference from a conjunction to one or other of its conjuncts. However, I have already discussed that case in detail in Chapter 5 (originally Williamson 2011), arguing that a disposition to assent to all instances of 'and'-elimination is unnecessary for understanding conjunctions. Since Boghossian has not replied to that argument, there is no need to repeat it here. One can also argue for the same conclusion in a different way, pioneered by Paolo Casalegno (2004), which I defend in Chapter 7 (originally Williamson 2012) from Boghossian's criticisms in Chapter 6 (originally Boghossian 2012).

When we turn to the basis type of understanding-based justification, the dialectic differs slightly. In such cases—if there are any—when all goes well one's assent to *p* is justified in virtue of the fact that one's understanding of *p* serves as a good epistemic basis for one's assent to *p*. How can that be, if an expert can understand *p* without assenting to *p*, as Boghossian concedes?

Boghossian's answer is that the expert's understanding of *p* still provides her with a good justification for believing *p*, but her theoretical commitments prevent her from seeing it. However, given what has just been argued, we may assume that the expert understands *p* while having no disposition, derived or underived, to assent to *p*. In the key cases, she has no way of getting to *p* just by steps which strike her as cogent. Does *her* understanding of *p* provide her with a good justification for believing *p*? For her, such a justification is out of reach, not just out of sight.

Could Boghossian reply that, although the unorthodox expert's understanding of *p* provides *her* with no justification for *p*, the orthodox expert's understanding of *p* does provide *him* with a justification for *p*? Such a multiplication of understandings does not fit Boghossian's argument. The orthodox expert would no longer have a justification for *p* *because* he understands *p*, otherwise the unorthodox expert would also have that justification for *p*, since she too understands *p*. Rather, the orthodox expert would have a justification for *p* because he understands *p* *in a specific way*, in which the unorthodox expert does not understand *p*. But how are the relevant ways of understanding to be individuated? The obvious danger is that any difference in background beliefs will constitute a difference in ways of understanding, so that there will be understanding-based justifications of the basis type for all those background beliefs, making them all epistemically analytic. In any case, Boghossian treats understanding as something shared by competent non-deferential speakers, and denies it to the unorthodox expert who lacks the disposition to assent, so the envisaged response is not his.

Thus, to defend the basis type of understanding-based justification in the relevant cases, Boghossian will need strong arguments against the counterexamples of understanding p without being disposed to assent to p, just as he needs such arguments to defend the constitutive type of understanding-based justification. He has not supplied such arguments.

The failure of the required links between understanding and underived dispositions to assent vitiates Boghossian's appeal to intuitions with respect to the basis type of understanding-based justification, since the type lacks instances. However, that by itself does not destroy his case for intuitions, since he argues for them independently with respect to the synthetic a priori, for which he does not postulate understanding-based justification. Let us turn to that case.

2. Intuitions

What does Boghossian mean by 'intuition'? He says that intuitions are 'intellectual seemings'. He explains that 'An intellectual seeming is similar to a sensory seeming in being a presentation of a proposition's being true; yet dissimilar to it in not having a sensory phenomenology' (Chapter 13, p. 201). He adds that an intellectual seeming 'is also to be sharply distinguished from any species of judgment; it must be understood as pre-judgmental and pre-doxastic, if it is to be capable of serving as an *epistemic basis* for a judgment' (Chapter 13, p. 201). In characterizing intuitions as 'pre-judgmental and pre-doxastic', he is also denying that they are *dispositions* or *inclinations* or *temptations* to judge or believe, for a similar reason: 'Your being inclined to judge that p is not usually a good reason, all by itself, for your believing that p' (Chapter 13, p. 203).

According to Boghossian, many intuitive judgments are the outcome of a three-step process:

you consider a scenario and a question about it; after sufficient reflection, a particular answer to that question comes to seem true to you, either because...you work out that it is true, or because, without working it out, it just comes to strike you as true; finally, you endorse this proposition.   (Chapter 13, p. 202)

The intuition corresponds to the seeming true to you at the second step.

Boghossian envisages intuitions as playing a distinctive role in the epistemology of the a priori. However, the account in his paper does not predict that intuitions cannot play a similar role for what would normally be treated as a posteriori justification. His description of the three-step process covers a wide variety of cases. For instance, you consider the scenario that you receive an invitation to Donald Trump's birthday party, and this question about it: in the scenario, what should you do? After sufficient reflection, this answer to the question comes to seem true to you: you should ignore the invitation. It does so because, without working it out, it just comes to strike you as true. Finally, you endorse the proposition that you should ignore the invitation. But that does not seem a good candidate for a proposition belief in which is justified a priori.

One might postulate all sorts of unconscious inferences in such a case. However, on Boghossian's internalist conception of epistemic justification, what matters is what is explicitly available to the subject, which the unconscious inferences are not.

A more fundamental concern is whether any mental states meet Boghossian's job specification for intuitions. Consider his account of thinking about 'whether to throw the large man off the bridge in order to save the lives of the five innocents trapped below':

> it can come to very vividly seem to you that it would be wrong to throw him off the bridge. But we can also imagine that even while it seems to you, you hesitate to make the judgment, wanting to assure yourself that you have not overlooked anything. Finally, satisfied, you make the judgment that it would be wrong. The state of its seeming wrong to you was intellectual, not sensory; yet evidently pre-judgmental and pre-doxastic. When the judgment finally came, it was based on that pre-judgmental seeming. (Chapter 13, p. 202)

Clearly, in this case, the vivid seeming that it would be wrong precedes the judgment that it would be wrong. But why assume that it also precedes the *inclination* to judge that it would be wrong? Boghossian says 'you hesitate to make the judgment', which suggests that you are already set to make it, but hold off out of caution. In effect, you are disposed to make the judgment, but inhibit the disposition, temporarily. Before committing, you give yourself a final chance to check. Such processes are often conscious. In such a case, there may be nothing which could be the seeming except a consciously inhibited disposition to judge that it would be wrong to throw the man off the bridge. That is not pre-judgmental in the sense Boghossian requires, because he denies that judging p can be appropriately based on the disposition to judge p.

Of course, for all I have proved, in Boghossian's case you may also be in some further mental state which both presents the proposition that it would be wrong to throw the man off the bridge and precedes even the disposition to make that judgment. But how is one supposed to know whether one is in such a mysterious extra state? In my own case, for all introspection tells me, there is only the consciously inhibited disposition to judge.

Could Boghossian just postulate that we are in these mysterious extra states of intuiting? The trouble is that, given his internalism, any difference in justification presumably corresponds to a consciously available difference in mental state. Thus, if the difference between the presence and absence of the extra state of intuiting is not consciously available, it makes no difference to justification. Positing a consciously unavailable difference will not serve his purposes.

A similar problem arises for *unhesitating* judgments. For instance, a philosopher asks you to consider the scenario that on the street you pass a baby in a pram, and this question about it: should you throw the baby out of the pram? Obviously not; there is no need to pause for reflection—we might worry about someone who did. That the case is so much easier than the trolley problems debated by moral philosophers does not weaken its epistemic status; quite the opposite. But the intermediate step, which would correspond to the intuition, appears to be missing. At the conscious level, there is no intermediate stage of hesitation. In this case, the only consciously available mental state is the judgment itself, that you should not throw the baby out of the pram. It will not serve Boghossian's internalist purposes to postulate a consciously unavailable intermediate stage of intuiting.

The problem is not the availability of the *contents* of the alleged intuitions. They are the same as the contents of the ensuing explicit judgments. Even when one consciously resists the temptation to make the judgment, one is typically aware of the content of the judgment one is resisting the temptation to make. The problem is that, on Boghossian's account, in the relevant cases the justification to believe that content is sourced in a prior relation to it that is neither judging nor being tempted to judge, but intuiting. Thus, for the justification to meet his internalist standards, the intuiting relation itself must be accessible to the subject. But if it were, Boghossian would not need to resort to postulation. He could just tell us how to introspect the difference between intuitions and conscious temptations to judge in ourselves. He does no such thing.

When one examines Boghossian's arguments, one finds that the difference between intuitions and conscious temptations to judge is postulated, not found. In effect, he argues that, since internalism *must* be true, and cannot work without such a consciously accessible difference, there *must* be such a difference. But there is not. To postulate a consciously accessible difference is not to access it. His laudable desire to avoid obviously false psychological claims forces him to make intuitions so elusive to the subject that they cannot meet the internalist standard they were postulated to satisfy.

A further problem for non-doxastic intuitions is that their justificatory power is unclear. Why should they be impervious to all the usual distortions from ignorance and error, bigotry and bias? For instance, consistent Nazis' non-doxastic intuitions, if any, may well have pro-Nazi contents. On an internalist view of justification, can such intuitions help justify the Nazis in their beliefs? If so, can they also justify the Nazis in acting on those beliefs? If not, why not? Without answers to such questions, Boghossian's view cannot be fully assessed.

Epistemology is *hard*. No serious approach to epistemic justification is pain-free. Consequently, one should not simply dismiss such an approach on the basis of a handful of alleged counterexamples. One must compare the rival approaches over the full range of the phenomena to be understood, to assess which approach does best overall. That is not how Boghossian proceeds. Rather, he starts by dismissing Reliabilism, perhaps on the basis of alleged counterexamples such as Laurence Bonjour's. He uses the term 'Reliabilism' to cover a wide variety of externalist epistemologies, including my own knowledge-first theory as well as more traditional belief-first forms of reliabilism. Having eliminated the externalist competition once and for all, to his own satisfaction, he then considers how one might begin to develop an internalist alternative. But that is not how it works. There are well-developed externalist epistemologies. The onus is on internalists to do better. That requires a well-developed internalist alternative. The result of Boghossian's understandable caution is that he has not here provided one.

Note

1. This paper is published here for the first time.

15

Reply to Williamson on Intuition, Understanding, and the A Priori[1]

Paul Boghossian

In his 'Reply to Boghossian on Intuition, Understanding, and the A Priori' (Chapter 14) Williamson takes issue with the two main claims I make in Chapter 13.

The first of these claims is that there are two types of understanding-based justification, the Constitutive type and the Basis type. Williamson doesn't dispute the aptness of this distinction; rather, he rejects that there are any instances of either type.

The second claim he disputes is that intuitions, understood as *sui generis* states of intellectual seeming, must play a role in any adequate epistemology of the a priori.

Constitutive Accounts

Let's begin with Williamson's discussion of the Constitutive type of understanding-based justification, according to which your assent to a proposition, p, is justified in virtue of the fact that your understanding of p is partly constituted by your disposition to assent to p.

> (Understanding–Assent Link, UAL) To understand p, X must have an (underived) disposition to assent to p[2]

On this view, as it is often elaborated, your disposition to assent to p is part of the *conceptual role* of one of p's ingredient concepts.

In Chapter 13, I revisited a criticism of Williamson's well-known, expert-based recipe for generating counterexamples to any proposed UAL (see Williamson 2007a). I had previously hinted at this criticism in my 2012, but wanted here to develop it further.

According to a conceptual-role semantics, the dispositions to assent to p that are constitutive of understanding p are the dispositions that a thinker would find *primitively compelling*: that is, those that he would find compelling when considering p on its own and without the use of any collateral considerations.[3] In (UAL) above, I put this in terms of X possessing an *underived* disposition to assent to p; but it might be more revealing to use Peacocke's (1992) terminology: X's disposition to assent to p must be based on X's finding p primitively compelling.

Debating the A Priori. Paul Boghossian and Timothy Williamson, Oxford University Press (2020).
© Paul Boghossian and Timothy Williamson.
DOI: 10.1093/oso/9780198851707.001.0001

In the case of *conjunction*, for example, a conceptual-role theorist might identify your understanding of *and* in part with your finding it primitively compelling to infer *A* from *A and B* (Conjunction Elimination, CE). She will not identify your understanding of *and* with dispositions that you might find compelling as a result of other background beliefs; otherwise, she won't end up with only those dispositions that are genuinely constitutive of mastery of *and*. (Similarly, she might identify your understanding of *all* in part with your finding it primitively compelling to infer from *All Fs are Gs* to *This F is a G*. And so on for the other constants.)

This appeal to inferences or truths that are primitively compelling poses a prima facie problem for Williamson's recipe for generating a counterexample to any proposed UAL. His recipe depends on imagining an expert on, for example, *conjunction* who develops theoretical misgivings about CE and, as a result, comes to reject it. However, an expert who comes to reject CE as a result of theoretical considerations is an expert who comes to find CE *derivatively* uncompelling; and that is, of course, perfectly consistent with her continuing to find it primitively compelling.

In his reply, Williamson says that he anticipated this objection and dealt with it:

In my previous critique, I consider actual or possible people who came to understand *p* in the normal way but then developed sophisticated theoretical doubts about *p*, on the basis of which they now dissent from *p*, while still understanding *p*. These people are experts; their understanding of *p* is non-deferential. Boghossian concedes that such cases can arise. However, he rightly notes, dispositions can be retained while inhibited. Handcuffs may inhibit a prisoner's disposition to hit out. Similarly, an expert may retain the disposition to assent to *p*, while inhibiting it on theoretical grounds. Examples are common. Thus the mere combination of understanding with refusal to assent does not refute Boghossian's constitutive account in its current form. So far so good.

Naturally, in writing my original critique, I was well aware of the possibility of inhibited dispositions to assent, and addressed its relevance explicitly (Williamson 2003: 254; 2007a: 99–105). In particular, I argued that the expert may gradually lose even the *disposition* to assent to *p*, while still retaining understanding of *p*. After all, many acquired dispositions are *habits*, which can be lost as well as gained over time. Since having the underived disposition to assent to *p* entails having the disposition to assent to *p*, the expert lacks the underived disposition to assent to *p* but still understands *p*, and thus is a direct counterexample to Boghossian's present constitutive account.   (Chapter 14, p. 209)

Williamson's reasoning here is not appropriately responsive to the point I was making. Let me see if I can explain myself better.

On Williamson's description of the case, the expert, let's call her 'Vanna', comes to have serious theoretical doubts about p and so stops assenting to p, while retaining the disposition to assent to p. Later, she gradually loses even the disposition to assent to p.[4] All the while she retains her mastery of p. Williamson takes the possibility of this scenario to be sufficient to secure the counterexample he is after; however, it is *not* sufficient.

The reason is that, in general, you can lose a disposition to assent to p in one of two ways. On the one hand, you can lose the disposition to assent to p because, *all things considered*, p no longer seems plausible to you; on the other hand, you can lose the disposition to assent to p because, *independently of any other considerations*, p no longer seems plausible to you. (As we will see, Williamson's failure to draw this distinction will crop up again when we turn to the discussion of intuition later on in this chapter.)

To get a counterexample to the claim that CE is a UAL for *and*, you need a case where Vanna loses the disposition to assent to CE in the *second* of these two ways, without reliance on theoretical considerations, while retaining full mastery of *and*. Hence, merely emphasizing, as Williamson does, that Vanna loses not merely lose her practice of assenting to CE, but also her disposition to assent to CE, is not responsive to this point: it doesn't distinguish between the two ways in which Vanna might have come to lose her disposition to assent to CE, only one of which would constitute a counterexample to the view under consideration.

You might think, Well, what's the big problem? Why can't Williamson simply stipulate that, in addition to Vanna's coming to find CE objectionable on theoretical grounds, she also comes to find it utterly implausible when it is considered on its own and totally independently of the theoretical considerations she has developed?

Williamson is free to stipulate that, of course. What he isn't free to stipulate is that, when Vanna comes to find CE utterly implausible, when it is considered on its own and independently of any other considerations, she continues to retain full mastery of *and*, as opposed to mastery of some closely related concept.[5]

Williamson says,

> The core of Boghossian's reply is his claim that once the expert loses her underived disposition to assent to *p*, it is no longer plausible that she still understands *p*. He treats her as if she had simply forgotten what proposition *p* is. He does not consider what the expert can still do, having lost the disposition to assent to *p*. She can still *remember* assenting to *p*; she knows just what it was like to exercise the disposition to do so. She can also *imagine* just what it is like to exercise the disposition, for others who still have it. She still expects *them* to assent to *p*. She feels to herself like someone who has painfully struggled free of the disposition to commit a common fallacy, or to reason according to the prejudices of the bigoted community in which she was reared. In these ways, her situation is very unlike that of 'an entirely unsophisticated person, a child, for example', to which Boghossian compares it. Unlike the child or unsophisticate, she can fluently converse with others when they assert *p*, perhaps explaining to them why, in her opinion, they are mistaken.   (Chapter 14, pp. 209–10)

Some aspects of Williamson's response here are a bit mystifying. For example, simply to assert, as he does, that the expert who has lost her underived disposition to assent to p can still enjoy a number of p-involving propositional attitudes is, in the present context, simply to beg the question. Whether a person who has come to find p primitively uncompelling is still a master of p is the very question at issue.

If we set these question-begging claims to one side, how clear is it that Williamson has offered us a counterexample of the required type? To see that he hasn't, let us unpack his example in terms of the relevant parameters.

Initially, Vanna will understand perfectly well why folks are tempted to believe that *Mary ate the apple* follows from *Mary ate the apple and the pear*. She herself will still understand that it is hard to see how Mary could have eaten *both* the apple *and* the pear, yet failed to have eaten the apple. However, she will try to explain to the folks who care that, while this inference may seem entirely non-optional when considered on its own, it runs into trouble when it is applied in some remote theoretical domain, say, quantum mechanics.[6]

In the next stage, we are invited to imagine that Vanna comes to lose any sense even of initial plausibility for the claim that Mary's having eaten both the apple and the pear necessarily entails Mary's having eaten the apple. When she looks at this inference now, she feels no temptation to endorse it. She realizes, of course, that others are trained to make this inference; but she can no longer explain, to herself or to others, why this inference seems compelling.

Is it clear that later-stage Vanna, who can see no plausibility whatsoever in the claim that Mary's eating the apple and the pear entails Mary's eating the apple, still has the same concept of *and* that we do, as opposed to some closely related concept? It's certainly not clear to me.

If she were to say 'I completely understand why you are tempted by this inference, it's just that it runs into trouble when applied in quantum mechanics', that would be one thing. But when she says 'I have no idea why, apart from societal indoctrination, anyone would find this inference compelling', we have every right to question whether she is truly deploying the same concept as we are.

All these points are obscured by Williamson's stipulation that Vanna is an *expert* who understands *and* if anyone does. The stipulation is supposed to lull us into thinking that there is no way such a person could lose the concept *and*; anything she comes to think about *and* must be construed as an insight into *and* rather than a rejection of it. As Williamson is fond of saying, 'The last thing our expert needs is a language lesson.'

However, as I pointed out in my 2012, in the relevant sense, it is not insulting to Einstein's intelligence to point out to him that, in his Special Theory of Relativity, the word 'simultaneous' does not end up expressing the same concept (that of a two-place relation, rather than a three-place relation) that it did in the past.

The ineffectiveness of his example is obscured by Williamson's conflation of Vanna's finding CE primitively uncompelling with her losing the disposition to assent to CE. Since it is true that having an underived disposition to assent to CE entails having the disposition to assent to CE, and since it's clear that Vanna can come to lose the disposition to assent to CE, while still retaining mastery of *and*, it can look as though the example works.

However, as I've emphasized, Vanna can lose the disposition to assent to CE because she has come to find CE all-things-considered false, while still finding it primitively compelling; so merely securing that she has lost the disposition to assent to CE is not enough. We have to ask, Has Vanna lost the disposition to assent to CE because she finds it all things considered false, or because she finds it primitively false? If the former, it's irrelevant to its intended target; if the latter, it is unconvincing as a counterexample.

As I said in Chapter 13, to which Williamson is responding, if the expert's sophisticated considerations were really playing no role in persuading us that she continues to be a master of *and*, we ought to be able to describe a counterexample to CE in which such considerations are completely absent.

And the clearest way of doing that would be to describe someone with no sophisticated views about logic—a child, for example—*non-deferentially* acquiring *and* for the first time, while refusing to endorse CE. Such a child would all along refuse to see any plausibility at all in its following from *Mary ate the apple and the pear* that *Mary ate the apple* while still clearly being a master of *and.*

This, however, Williamson has not come close to doing. And there is every reason to believe it can't be done.

Casalegno Revisited

In this respect, Paolo Casalegno's (2004) recipe for generating counterexamples to proposed UALs is more promising than Williamson's, since Casalegno tries to make it plausible that an unsophisticate, indeed someone suffering from an inferential disability, could clearly understand *and* without having so much as the ability to perform CE inferences. Williamson mentions Casalegno's recipe with approval and has defended it in his 2012 against the objections to it that I laid out in my 2012. Let me take this opportunity to continue the debate.

Here, once again, is Casalegno's recipe:

Apart from this difficulty, the idea that, given a logical constant *C*, there is a well-defined set R of rules of inference such that a subject cannot be regarded as knowing the meaning of *C* unless she accepts the rules in R is intrinsically problematic. No matter how a rule of inference is chosen, it seems to me that we can imagine situations in which we would be disposed to say that a subject knows the meaning of *C* although the subject does not accept the rule in question. Suppose Mary suffers from a cognitive disability which makes her completely incapable of performing anything which could be counted as an inference. Nevertheless, she is able to use logically complex sentences to describe visually presented scenes. (I do not know whether this kind of cognitive disability has ever been observed; but it is no doubt conceivable.) For example, we can imagine that Mary, although unable to perform conjunction-introductions and conjunction-eliminations, would be able to assert, in appropriate circumstances, 'The box is red *and* the book is blue', or things like that. It seems to me that it would then be possible to say that, in spite of her disability, Mary knows the meaning of the word 'and'. At least: my intuition is that we would spontaneously adopt a homophonic translation for sentences such as 'The box is red and the book is blue' uttered by Mary; and wouldn't that be a way of acknowledging that, in Mary's mouth, the word 'and' has the same meaning it [has] for us?

(2004: 407)

What Casalegno is claiming, in other words, is that, for any rule, R, and constant, C, we can cook up a counterexample to the claim that inferring according to R is required for possession of C, by imagining someone who lacks the ability to infer with R but who nonetheless understands C because she uses it competently in sentences used to describe visually presented scenes.

There are several difficulties with this strategy for refuting a conceptual-role semantics for the logical constants.

First, recall that we are talking about 'full mastery' of a logical constant, the sort of mastery characteristic of experts, and not mere 'possession', which we might accord someone even if they fell short of full mastery. It's hard to reconcile someone's being an expert on logic with their suffering from severe inferential disabilities.

Second, the proposed strategy seems limited in its applicability. Even if we conceded that it produces a counterexample to the necessity of CE for mastery of *and*, how would this strategy work for the other logical constants? How would competence with the description of visually presented scenes be manifest for *if*, for example?

Third, it is important not to confuse the general idea of a conceptual-role semantics, which commits itself to there being UALs of some type or other, with the more specific idea of an inferential-role semantics, which commits itself to there being UALs that involve *inferences*. Casalegno's case raises an interesting question *within* conceptual-role semantics: should competent use of *and* to describe visually presented scenes also be regarded as necessary for mastery of *and*, in addition to whatever inferential abilities we may insist upon? The answer to this may well be 'yes'. But this would be a *contribution* to a conceptual-role semantics, not a refutation of it.

Fourth, notice how Casalegno's strategy proceeds. It questions whether an inferential competence is necessary for mastery of C by suggesting that a different *competence*, one involving using C to describe visually presented scenes, is sufficient. So, we haven't gotten away from the idea that some competence or other with C is necessary for mastery of C. Thus, even if we granted Casalegno's claim, we would still have it that *either* a UAL involving visually presented scenes, or one involving inference, is necessary. And it is hard to see what other kinds of competence might be relevant.

Finally, it is not out of the question that there might be more than one route to the mastery of a concept, as I pointed out in my 2011a. In his 2011 (Chapter 5, footnote 3) reply to me, Williamson responded to this suggestion dismissively:

In a footnote, Boghossian suggests that even if all understanding–assent links in the strict sense fail, 'A friend of epistemological analyticities might well be satisfied with the existence' of clusters of links of the form 'necessarily, anyone who understands w accepts S(w) or S′(w)...or S*(w)'. To be a genuine alternative, the latter must mean a disjunction of acceptances, not acceptance of a disjunction. Such a disjunctive link will not confer *a priori* status on knowledge of any one of the disjuncts (or on knowledge of their disjunction). Since Boghossian does not explain how it would serve his overall argumentative purposes, I discuss it no further.

(2011: 502)

Williamson's observations here take us away from what the focus of the discussion has been so far—namely, the existence of UALs—to the very different question of how such UALs might ground a priori justification, if they existed. As I have had occasion to note, Williamson has focused his fire exclusively on the existence of UALs and not on the nature of the bridge principles that might connect a particular UAL with the epistemic status of the assent it concerns.

It would take us too far afield to explore this issue in detail. Suffice it to say that, if it is at most a disjunction of acceptances that is necessary for mastery of a given concept, there are well-known ways to build a theory of a priori justification on that basis.

The idea I have in mind here is hardly without precedent. A similar possibility arose in connection with the description theory of proper names, when Searle (1958) proposed, contra Frege, that although there was no particular description that a subject need associate with a given name in order to count as understanding it, some cluster of descriptions in a disjunction of such clusters is necessary. Kripke (1980: 71–2) explains how that fact could be parlayed into saying that, if a particular cluster D* was the one that was associated with a given name by a given thinker, then D* would be a priori for that thinker.

Similarly, suppose that Mary's particular route to understanding w is through S*(w), as opposed to any of the other routes available to her. Then, by relativizing the notion of a priori status to individuals, we could say that S*(w) is a priori for Mary. This is hardly the place to delve into all the attendant complexities; I mean only to indicate in a general way that there is space for this possibility.

Basis Accounts

Williamson also seeks to refute Basis accounts of understanding-based a priori justification. In cases of a priori justified assent that is best explained by a Basis model, the understanding is not constituted by the assent in question, but rather serves as a good *epistemic basis* for it. But how can the understanding serve as such a basis, if an expert can understand p without assenting (or being disposed to assent) to it?

As Williamson rightly says, the answer I propose is that, even in such cases, the understanding does provide the requisite justification: it's just that the expert's theoretical misgivings preclude her from appreciating that justification. The expert has propositional justification for p, but can't convert it into a doxastic justification for p, a situation we are quite familiar with from other epistemic settings. Williamson objects:

However, given what has just been argued, we may assume that the expert understands *p* while having no disposition, derived or underived, to assent to *p*. In the key cases, she has no way of getting to *p* just by steps which strike her as cogent. Does *her* understanding of *p* provide her with a good justification for believing *p*? For her, such a justification is out of reach, not just out of sight.   (Chapter 14, p. 210)

Williamson's only argument against the existence of Basis-style explanations of a priori justification rests on his argument against the existence of UALs. Since we have found reason to reject that argument, we may continue to suppose that Vanna continues to find p primitively compelling, even as she has no disposition to assent to p, because she finds p derivatively uncompelling. This fits hand in glove with my description of Vanna as having propositional justification, but lacking the means to turn it into a doxastic justification. Hence, Williamson's case against Basis-style explanations also fails.

Intuitions and the A Priori

Let us turn to Williamson's discussion of my appeal to intuitions in the theory of the a priori. Williamson has two central complaints. First, that intuitions, on my account, even if they were conceded to exist, and were accorded justificatory power, cannot play a distinctive role in explaining a priori justification. Second, that it is doubtful that there are any mental states that fill the job description that I specify for intuitions. I will take these complaints in turn.

Williamson says that there is nothing in my account of intuitions that explains why intuitions are the source of distinctively a priori justification. He imagines you receiving an invitation from Donald Trump to his birthday party and having the direct and unmediated intuition that you should not accept it. And yet, he says, by ordinary standards, how to respond to a birthday invitation from Donald Trump is not an a priori matter.

Williamson's thought experiment is unrealistic. People don't tend to have unmediated *de re* moral intuitions about persons per se. They tend to have unmediated moral intuitions about their attributes or characters. If it were to seem true to me that I shouldn't accept an invitation from Trump, that would typically be grounded in my intuition that, other things being equal, I ought not to celebrate the birth of someone so evil (fill in your favorite Trump description). And *that* proposition *is* a priori.[7]

Well, perhaps most ordinary folks are as I say. But couldn't there be someone who did have a direct and unmediated intuition that he ought not to accept an invitation from Donald Trump, one that did not depend on any view about his character or attributes? And wouldn't it then follow that this person's empirical belief is justified by his intuition?

No, because the friend of the a priori need only have committed himself to its being a priori propositions that are (directly) justified by intuitions. An a priori proposition is a proposition—for example, *If it's sunny then it's sunny*—that *can* be justified non-perceptually. By contrast, an a posteriori proposition is one—for example, *It's sunny*—that *cannot* be justified non-perceptually. (This is not discussed in the chapter to which Williamson is responding; it is discussed in Boghossian (forthcoming).)

Is this a natural restriction or a merely ad hoc one? Why is intuition well suited for justifying only a priori propositions? Why is it a good way of justifying the moral *principle* I cited above, but not the empirical proposition that Trump is a pathological liar, or that I could levitate if I tried?

The answer is just what you would expect. Perceptions, being the product of a cognitive mechanism that is causally sensitive to facts about its environment, are well suited for justifying contingent propositions about the actual world. Intuitions, not being the product of such a causally sensitive mechanism, if they are well suited for justifying anything at all (not in dispute just now), are well suited for justifying propositions that are either necessary, or anyhow insensitive to the features of the actual world.[8] For promising examples of accounts along these lines, see McGinn (1975) and Peacocke (1993a), although there is much that remains to be worked out.

Intuitions or Inclinations to Judge?

Williamson's more important objection to my appeal to intuitions stems from his doubts that anything can fill the job description that I specify for them.

Williamson is perfectly happy to grant that, in responding with the judgment that p to a thought-experimental question, its seeming true to you that p will precede and explain your judging p. What he denies is that we have any reason to suppose that this seeming true that p is anything other than a *conscious inclination* to judge that p. By contrast, the intuitional picture holds that seemings true are quasi-perceptual states that precede and explain both the judgment *and* the inclination to judge. Hence, our disagreement may be pictured thus:

> *Williamson's picture*:   Thought-experimental scenario/question → Inclination to judge p → (which, when not defeated) → Judging p

> *Intuitional picture*:   Thought-experimental scenario/question → Intuition that p → (which, when not defeated) → Inclination to judge p → (which, when not defeated) → Judging p

How should we decide which picture is correct?

About the Trolley judgment that it would be wrong to throw the large man off the bridge, Williamson says,

> Of course, for all I have proved, in Boghossian's case you may also be in some further mental state which both presents the proposition that it would be wrong to throw the man off the bridge and precedes even the disposition to make that judgment. But how is one supposed to know whether one is in such a mysterious extra state? In my own case, for all introspection tells me, there is only the consciously inhibited disposition to judge.
>
> Could Boghossian just postulate that we are in these mysterious extra states of intuiting? The trouble is that, given his internalism, any difference in justification presumably corresponds to a consciously available difference in mental state. Thus, if the difference between the presence and absence of the extra state of intuiting is not consciously available, it makes no difference to justification. Positing a consciously unavailable difference will not serve his purposes.
>
> (Chapter 14, p. 212)

Searching his mind, Williamson finds only the conscious inclination to judge and no consciously available impression of truth that precedes that inclination and explains it. If we don't find such impressions via introspection, might we not have reason to *postulate* them? Williamson says that, even if a case could be made for postulating them, that path is not available to me, since, on my view, intuitions are needed to serve an internalist epistemological purpose, and so they need to be consciously available. His overall argument, then, goes like this:

1. To have reason to believe in a certain type of mental state, it must either be consciously available or reasonably postulated.
2. Intuitions are not consciously available (mere introspection does not reveal them).
3. Hence, to have reason to believe in intuitions, they must be reasonably postulated.
4. If a type of mental state is postulated, then it is not consciously available.
5. If a type of mental state is to serve an internalist purpose, it must be consciously available.
6. Hence, even if we had reason to believe in intuitions, they would not be able to serve an internalist purpose.

There is an enormous amount of interesting philosophy here that is worth discussing; in this reply, I will only be able to address a few central points.

categories are not mutually exclusive. Rather, what we need is a threefold distinction between those mental state types that are

(INT)   consciously available to introspection *without* theoretical guidance;

those that are

(INT+)   consciously available to introspection (typically) *only with* theoretical guidance;

and those that are

(MP)   merely postulated.[9]

Some non-representational phenomenal states—like pains or tickles—will impress themselves upon your attention without any help, just by the sheer strength and vivacity of their phenomenal properties.

However, in the case of experiences with representational content—the experience of blue, for example—their 'diaphanousness' can get in the way of introspecting them, as Moore (1903b) pointed out:

... the moment we try to fix our attention upon consciousness and to see *what*, distinctly, it is, it seems to vanish: it seems as if we had before us a mere emptiness. When we try to introspect the sensation of blue, all we can see is the blue: the other element is as if it were diaphanous... (450)

As Moore himself went on to observe, though:

Yet it [the sensation of blue] *can* be distinguished if we look attentively enough, and if we know that there is something to look for. (450)

Even with such phenomenal states as seeing blue, then, you might need guidance if you are to find them through introspection.

Many other mental state or event types fall into the INT+ category. Take, for example, occurrent judgments. We certainly don't believe in them simply because we stumble across them when we introspect. They can't be said to impress themselves upon our attention in the way that pains do. We believe in them in part because we know that there are states that play a specific type of role in the explanation of action. However, once we know what to look for, our occurrent judgments are readily introspectable.

In contrast with both of the preceding cases, there are such states as unconscious desires, states whose existence was established by Freud among others, that are merely postulated.

Intellectual impressions of truth belong to the INT+ category: they are consciously introspectable, though only if you know what to look for. What considerations might help us see that, in addition to conscious inclinations to judge, there are impressions of truth that precede such inclinations and help explain them?

It's obvious, I trust, that in standard empirical cases, we have the three-part impression–inclination–judgment structure outlined above. In a Müller–Lyer case, for example, there is the visual impression of the lines as being of unequal length; there is the consequent inclination to judge that they are unequal in length; and, for example, there is the visual impression of the lines as being of unequal length; there is the consequent inclination to judge that they are unequal in length; and, finally, there is the judgment that they are unequal in length. No one element can be reduced to the others, and, in particular, the impression can't be identified with the inclination to judge. This is obvious from the fact that, when I discover that the lines are not unequal in length, I lose both the judgment, and the inclination to judge, that they are; the impression, however, remains.

Williamson's view, then, is that in classical thought experiments, and in other a priori cases, with an exception being made for geometry, the impression element goes missing: in such cases, there is just the inclination to judge, and, if it is not inhibited, the judgment itself. As a result, there is no consciously available explanation for the inclination to judge. It must be experienced by the subject as coming out of nowhere.

However, this doesn't seem true to the phenomenology of intuitive responses to classical thought experiments. The conscious inclination to judge the Trolley proposition doesn't present itself as coming out of nowhere; rather, it presents itself as a response to its *seeming true* that you ought not to throw the large man off the bridge.

To see this, contrast your judgment in a Trolley case with that of Norman the clairvoyant, made famous by Laurence Bonjour (1985). In Bonjour's imagined scenario, Norman has a clairvoyant ability that he does not know about. One day, out of the blue, he finds himself with the inclination to believe that the President is in New York City. He has no consciously available evidence that bears on the President's whereabouts. His conscious inclination to belief is the product of his reliable clairvoyance, though Norman knows nothing about that. He just finds himself with that inclination; he can identify nothing on which it might be based.

Bonjour uses this example effectively against reliabilist theories of justification. But it is also useful for our purposes now, in illustrating what it would be like to come to be inclined to believe something out of the clear blue. If you ask Norman *why* he believes that the President is in NYC, he would say that he has no idea why. If you ask him if it *seems* true to him that the President is in NYC, he would say (exactly what Williamson says about thought experiments in general): 'Apart from the fact that I find myself inclined to believe it, there is no seeming.'

Williamson-type inclinations to believe, then, ones that are not based on anything, and in particular not on seemings, are hardly inconceivable. Indeed, they fit Norman's case perfectly. However, our typical responses to classical thought experiments are not like that. When we find ourselves inclined to judge that we ought not to throw the large man off the bridge, or that Mr. Smith has a justified true belief but does not know, these inclinations don't feel as though they are coming out of the blue in the way in which Norman's clairvoyant beliefs do. They present themselves as based on their seeming true. Thus, if we are to adequately capture how classical thought experiments work, we need to recognize not only conscious inclinations to judge but intellectual seemings as well, which would explain and justify those inclinations.

A second consideration in favor of the intuitional picture returns us to the observation that there are many cases where a proposition's seeming true survives the discovery that the proposition is false. For example, even after we discover that the Müller–Lyer lines are not unequal in length it still seems true that they are. And as Williamson acknowledges, this happens in a priori cases as well: even after we discover that Naïve Comprehension is false, it continues to seem true.

In the Müller–Lyer case, of course, the seeming true that survives the discovery that the lines are not unequal in length is neither the judgment that they are unequal in length, nor the inclination to judge that they are. Once I know that they are not unequal in length, I lose all inclination to judge that they are. What survives is just *the visual impression* of the lines, which continues to present them as being unequal in length, despite the fact that we now know they are not.

Why does the visual impression persist in depicting the lines as being of unequal length, despite our discovery that they are not? The answer, presumably, is that perception, being to a considerable degree modular, is not penetrable by the background knowledge about the length of the lines. Hence, the impression of inequality persists despite our discovery.

What about Naïve Comprehension? Here, too, there is a seeming that survives the discovery that it is false. Williamson thinks that he can account for this by claiming that the conscious inclination to believe Naïve Comprehension survives the discovery that it is false, the discovery serving only to inhibit its exercise.

As I've just been arguing, however, inclinations to believe tend not to work like that. They are cognitively penetrable and tend to disappear when their propositional objects are discovered to be false. In general, they are not like habits that are hard to shake. (The qualification allows that there might be some, perhaps very basic inclinations to judge, that are sticky—examples might include the inclination to believe that there is an external world, or that animals have propositional attitudes. But such special cases would not serve Williamson's purpose.)

The only good way to account for its continuing to seem that Naïve Comprehension is true, even after it is discovered to be false, is to recognize that there is an intuition of the truth of Naïve Comprehension, which, by virtue of being cognitively impenetrable, retains its misleading content.

The third argument in favor of recognizing intuitions is *epistemic* in nature. Since I've discussed it in Chapter 13, I won't rehearse it here at length. By internalist standards, it is not possible to explain the (very strong) justification that we have for typical a priori claims simply by invoking the fact that we are inclined to make them. In general, your being inclined to judge p is no justification for your judging p. On the other hand, as I've argued, p's seeming true to you is a very good candidate for providing at least prima facie justification for believing p.

In sum, it's quite clear that, in the types of contexts we have been looking at, in addition to the conscious inclination to judge, there is something pre-judgmental that behaves in just the way you would expect an impression of truth to behave.

Williamson also raises a question about the justificatory power of intuitions. He asks, 'Why should they be impervious to all the usual distortions from ignorance and error, bigotry and bias?' (Chapter 14, p. 213).

I do not provide a positive theory of the justificatory power of intuitions in my already lengthy essay for this volume. I do so in Boghossian (forthcoming), attempting to add to the excellent contributions made by such philosophers as Bealer (2000), Bengson (2015), and Chudnoff (2013). This is a rich area for epistemology, with much left to be studied and understood.

Apropos of the particular point that Williamson brings up, no one thinks (or anyhow should think) that just because visual perception is open to distortion by bias and bigotry (for examples, see Siegel (2017)) that it cannot be thought to provide prima facie justification for belief.[10]

Notes

1. This paper is published here for the first time.
2. This, of course, is overly simplified. Some UALs might involve inferences involving p rather than assents to it. What is meant will be clear in each case. The use of the expression 'underived' in this formulation will be further discussed below.
3. It should be reemphasized that 'understanding p' in the present context means 'full mastery of p' and not mere 'possession'.
4. Later on, I will be raising a question about Williamson's view that dispositions to assent to p can persist well after a thinker comes confidently to believe that p is false. For now, I will let it pass.
5. Williamson sometimes complains that this appeal to a 'closely related concept' is empty without a specification of what the alternative concept in question is. It's unclear what he is asking for. Obviously, we lack a word in English whose meaning is that concept. But we can, of course, specify the concept in question in terms of its conceptual role, one which will overlap with that for conjunction in certain respects, but deviate from it in others. (For an analogy, think here of the transition from a two-place concept of simultaneity to a three-place concept, necessitated by Einstein's Special Theory of Relativity.)
6. This, of course, is what some philosophers actually argued in the case of the distributive principles. See, for example, Putnam (1968).
7. Note, by the way, that this is a remark about the architecture of justification, not a remark about the psychological processes that lead to someone's making the moral judgment at issue, for a variety of reasons. For one thing, most of us will have automated our responses to various types of familiar situation so that we know what to think without having to run through an explicit inference in our heads. For discussion see Boghossian (2016).
8. Fixedly actually, in the terminology of Davies and Humberstone (1980).
9. Some of the material that follows overlaps with Boghossian (forthcoming).
10. Thanks to Ned Block, Christopher Peacocke, and Crispin Wright for helpful comments.

16

Boghossian on Intuition, Understanding, and the A Priori Once Again[1]

Timothy Williamson

This chapter highlights five of the key problem areas for Boghossian's 'Reply to Williamson on Intuition, Understanding, and the A Priori' (Chapter 15).

1. Losing Underived Dispositions

Since Boghossian has become more sympathetic to appeals to intuition, conditions on understanding bear less weight in his present account of justification for various principles, including logical laws, but they are still load-bearing. My general argument against understanding-based accounts has been that there are no understanding–assent links of the sort they require. My counterexamples to the alleged links are experts with the relevant term who come, on theoretical grounds, to refuse assent to instances of the principle at issue, while continuing to understand the term by normal standards.

As Boghossian refines his account, the proposed necessary condition on understanding is an *underived disposition* to assent. As is well known, something may retain a disposition to φ yet fail to φ when the occasion arises, because that underlying disposition is inhibited by another disposition. Thus there is no counterexample to the proposed necessary condition in an expert who retains the underived disposition to assent yet fails to assent when the occasion arises because that underived disposition is inhibited by a more theory-driven disposition to refuse assent.

I anticipated that response when I first presented my objection, and emphasized how the example must be specified to avoid it. Sometimes dispositions persist while inhibited, but sometimes they are genuinely lost. For instance, elasticity is a disposition; things can lose elasticity. Underived dispositions to assent can also be lost, even as a long-term effect of theorizing. For instance, consider a beginning student of mathematics who has an underived disposition to assent to any instance of '$n/n = 1$', including the instance '$0/0 = 1$'. Later, she calculates '$2 = 2 \times 1 = 2 \times (0/0) = (2 \times 0)/0 = 0/0 = 1$', and realizes that something is wrong. She learns to treat '$0/0$' as

Debating the A Priori. Paul Boghossian and Timothy Williamson, Oxford University Press (2020).
© Paul Boghossian and Timothy Williamson.
DOI: 10.1093/oso/9780198851707.001.0001

undefined. At first, she retains her underived disposition to assent to '0/0 = 1', but inhibits it when the question arises. After a while, however, she loses even the disposition to assent, as she settles into the correct way of thinking. This is not very different from someone giving up smoking: at first he retains the disposition to smoke, while inhibiting it; later, as he gets used to not smoking, he may lose even the disposition to smoke. Exactly the same can happen with the deviant expert, even when the disposition she loses is to reason *correctly* in some specific way. In the first flush of deviance, she retains the disposition to assent to any instance of the classical principle at issue, while inhibiting it on theoretical grounds in a subclass of cases. As she gets used to not assenting in those cases, she loses even the disposition to assent there. She has only the more cautious disposition to assent to instances outside the subclass, just as our mathematician comes to have only the more cautious disposition to assent to '$n/n = 1$' given '$n \neq 0$'. Thus I crafted my counterexamples to Boghossian's preferred understanding–assent links to lack even the underived disposition to assent.

Boghossian's final response confuses the issue in several ways.

First, he repeatedly drifts from the relevant question, whether the expert *lacks* an underived disposition to *assent*, to an irrelevant question, whether she *has* an underived disposition to *dissent*. By 'dissent' I mean a negative attitude, not mere failure to assent: in the simplest case, it is the difference between denial and non-assertion. For example, he considers the stipulation that the expert comes to find the rule of conjunction-elimination 'utterly implausible when it is considered on its own' (Chapter 15, p. 217). But it is enough for my purposes for the expert to *lack* an underived disposition to find the rule *plausible* (when it is considered on its own). Not finding something plausible does not amount to finding it implausible; one may have no primitive instinct on the matter, for or against. Similarly, he speaks of the expert finding the rule 'primitively false', but she can fail to find it primitively true (better: primitively valid) without finding it primitively false (better: primitively invalid). Lacking the underived disposition to assent is what it takes to violate the alleged necessary condition for understanding in the understanding–assent link at issue; having the underived disposition to dissent is an optional extra.

Second, Boghossian assumes that once the expert has lost the underived disposition to assent, she will have no insight into others' assent. For example, he imagines the expert saying about an instance of conjunction-elimination, 'I have no idea why, apart from societal indoctrination, anyone would find this inference compelling.' But it is often not hard to imagine what it is like to have a disposition without having it oneself. For example, I can imagine what it is like to have an underived disposition to smoke, even though I have no disposition to smoke. Similarly, an expert mathematician who lacks the underived disposition to accept the unrestricted rule '$n/n = 1$' may have a very clear idea why novices find the rule compelling. It is nothing to do with societal indoctrination; they have just picked up on an overgeneral pattern, in a way which usually gives good results. Our expert may take the same view of conjunction-elimination.

Third, Boghossian accuses me of failing to distinguish between two ways of losing a disposition to assent to *p*:

On the one hand, you can lose the disposition to assent to *p* because, *all things considered, p* no longer seems plausible to you; on the other hand, you can lose the disposition to assent to *p* because, *independently of any other considerations, p* no longer seems plausible to you.

(Chapter 15, pp. 215–16; his italics, except for '*p*')

Boghossian rightly insists that only the second way will do for my case. But that is what I have taken for granted all along. Indeed, his first way is not clearly a way of losing the disposition at all: a disposition can be retained while outweighed by others.

Once all Boghossian's red herrings have been removed, his main argument against my counterexamples is simply the claim that once the expert loses her underived disposition to assent to *p*, she no longer understands *p*. The danger with this strategy is that it violates normal standards for ascribing propositional attitudes. I relied on those standards in the long passage Boghossian quotes from me, where I contrast the expert's capacities with those of the child or unsophisticate; it is of course to be read as appended to the detailed descriptions of specific examples that I have supplied earlier in the book and elsewhere. I will not bore readers by repeating them. They are descriptions of the sort a normal person, not in the grip of a philosophical theory, would give of the deviant expert. Indeed, they have been widely accepted in responses to my earlier presentations of the examples. Most attempts to resist the larger philosophical morals I draw from them have avoided challenging the examples themselves, instead using the strategy of modifying the formulation of the understanding–assent links.

If my descriptions of the examples beg the question against Boghossian, as he alleges, they do so because he is in effect challenging normal standards for ascribing propositional attitudes. I could of course avoid that problem, by varying the descriptions to make them of the experts' attitudes to the relevant *sentences*, rather than the *propositions* they express, but by normal standards one would still be justified in then recovering the descriptions in propositional terms. Boghossian has provided no reason to suspect that those normal standards are incorrect.

Things are slightly complicated by Boghossian's stipulation:

. . . we are talking about 'full mastery' of a logical constant, the sort of mastery characteristic of experts, and not mere 'possession', which we might accord someone even if they fell short of full mastery.   (Chapter 15, p. 218)

Normal standards for propositional attitude ascription presumably line up with mere possession, in this sense, not with full mastery. For example, by normal standards, Putnam believed that elms were not beeches, even though for Boghossian he did not fully master the concepts *elm* and *beech*, because he lacked associated recognitional capacities. However, that does not help with my examples, because my experts *have* the sort of mastery characteristic of experts. In philosophical logic as elsewhere, unorthodoxy is not uncharacteristic of expertise.

Boghossian argues,

if the expert's sophisticated considerations were really playing no role in persuading us that she continues to be a master of *and*, we ought to be able to describe a counterexample to CE [conjunction-elimination] in which such considerations are completely absent.

(Chapter 15, p. 217)

He suggests that the best case of such an unsophisticate would be a child, who uses 'and' non-deferentially without ever having been disposed to accept CE, and doubts that such a child would count as a master of *and*. But the child is another red herring. The relevance of the expertise in my counterexamples is twofold. First, it blocks the objection that the protagonist is no expert. Second, it helps explain how the protagonist can be a fully paid-up member of the speech community, speaking the public language and interpretable in the normal way. By contrast, young children are paradigms of speakers who have *not* yet been fully inducted into the speech community. Boghossian seems to assume that if the expert's sophisticated considerations *do* play a role in persuading us that she continues to be a master of *and*, that must be because they override her persisting underived disposition to accept CE. That assumption is false. The twofold relevance of the expertise, just explained, is perfectly compatible with the entire absence of the underived disposition.

Thus Boghossian has cast no significant doubt on my counterexamples to his understanding–assent links. Strictly, then, there is no need at this point of another kind of counterexample, devised by Paolo Casalegno, which I also defended earlier in the book. However, Casalegno's counterexamples are very rewarding in their own right, so it is worth appraising Boghossian's further criticisms of them.

2. Casalegno's Counterexamples

Casalegno's cases involve a subject who competently uses logical constants in describing visually presented scenes, even though he cannot do sentence-to-sentence inferences with them.

Boghossian's first objection is that the cases do not involve 'full mastery' of the logical concept. This makes one wonder what Boghossian means by that technical terminology. The distinction between 'full mastery' and 'mere possession' is typically made by reference to the division of linguistic labour for natural kind terms. Tree experts use the words 'elm' and 'beech' autonomously, whereas laypeople like Putnam use the same words with deference to those experts. But Casalegno's cases do not involve deference. A whole community could use logical constants as he describes, with no distinction between experts and laypeople. His subjects are doubtless not expert logicians, but that should not disqualify them from full mastery. Indeed, as a matter of sociolinguistic fact, speakers of English do not defer to logicians in their use of logical constants in anything like the way they (sometimes) defer to botanists and zoologists in their use of natural kind terms. The debate about understanding–assent links is supposed to concern a kind of understanding much more widespread than academic expertise. Boghossian's grounds for denying full mastery seem to be just the inability to carry out the inferences at issue, but why is that crucial for full mastery? The obscurity of the phrase makes the question hard to answer. It also makes the point of seeking a theory of full mastery hard to see. To make progress, more insight is needed than one gains from Boghossian's peremptory rulings on particular cases.

Boghossian's second objection is that it is unclear how to generalize Casalegno's cases from conjunction to other logical constants. The generalization to other truth-functions is quite straightforward, as my discussion, and indeed Casalegno's, makes clear.

The subject can reel off many correct descriptions of the visually presented scenes in their language; it does not matter which truth-functions are taken as primitive. The same goes for quantifiers over suitably restricted domains. Boghossian gives 'if' as an example; whether 'if' is truth-functional is a contested question (Williamson 2020 argues that it is). In any case, Casalegno's agent might be able to make judgments like 'If I move this one up a bit, the pegs will all be in a straight line', referring to the visually presented scene, while still unable to perform modus ponens on sentences detached from perception, so a generalization can be made.

Boghossian's third objection is that 'the competent use of *and* to describe visually presented scenes' might 'also be regarded as necessary for mastery of *and*' (Chapter 15, p. 219), and so be incorporated into conceptual-role semantics, as an addition to some sort of inferential competence. In the form he specifies, the suggestion is a non-starter, since it makes mastery of *and* incompatible with blindness, but some more qualified version could be considered. Boghossian is clearly right that Casalegno's cases by themselves do not refute conceptual-role semantics; no one claimed otherwise. They refute only some specific implementations of that general approach. However, inferentialist accounts of the understanding of logical constants were *paradigms* of conceptual-role semantics, its most elegant, worked-out, and promising exemplars. Refuting them is not just 'a *contribution* to a conceptual-role semantics, not a refutation of it', in Boghossian's optimistic words (Chapter 15, p. 219). It is a major setback for the approach, short of a conclusive refutation. If the ability to use logical constants in describing visually presented scenes must be separately built into conceptual-role semantics, so must many other abilities, such as the ability to use them in describing situations presented by other senses, situations re-presented by memory, and so on. The danger is that the conceptual-role semantics becomes ever more ramshackle, an open-ended list, losing its theoretical unity and so much of its supposed explanatory power. Since the challenge does not affect referential semantics, conceptual-role semantics is liable to lag ever further behind its chief rival.

Boghossian's fourth objection is a variant of the third. He notes that Casalegno's cases involve the substitution of one kind of competence for another, so they do not break the link between competence and mastery. Indeed, having mentioned competence in describing visually presented scenes and inferential competence, he adds 'it is hard to see what other kinds of competence might be relevant'; the last paragraph lists some natural candidates. Indeed, the vagueness of the term 'competence' risks making the link between competence and mastery near-trivial: perhaps (full) mastery of a concept just is (full) competence to use it.

Finally, Boghossian gestures at a way to adjust understanding-based accounts of (some) a priori justification to the possibility that mastery of a given concept might take several different forms. He refers the reader to Kripke's regimentation of Searle's version of a descriptive theory of names, on which different speakers may associate the same name with different clusters of descriptions. He seems to have in mind clause (5): 'The statement, "If X exists, then X has most of the φ's" is known *a priori* by the speaker', where the φ's are 'those properties φ such that A [the speaker] believes "φX"' (Kripke 1980: 71). Of course, Kripke is just setting up Searle for refutation, and clause (5) is especially vulnerable to several of Kripke's counterexamples. The relativization of the cluster to the beliefs of a particular speaker excludes any role for community-wide consensus in eliminating rogue descriptions. As a starting point for an account of the a priori, it is discouraging, to say the least.

In short, Casalegno's counterexamples to Boghossian's earlier accounts stand. For now, the prospects for understanding-based accounts of justification, of either of the two types Boghossian distinguishes, are bleak.

3. Intuitions: Postulated or Found?

For Boghossian, intuitions are pre-doxastic intellectual seemings. I wrote that when one examines his arguments, 'the intellectual seemings turn out to be postulated, not found'. He *postulates* that we can find such intellectual seemings in ourselves, whenever his epistemological theory requires them. That is very different from our actually finding them in ourselves, on the required occasions. If his postulate is true, of course, then we *can* always find intellectual seemings in ourselves, but the antecedent is at issue. For what they are worth, the results of my own attempted introspection are quite at odds with Boghossian's postulate.

Boghossian takes me to be inferring 'not found' from 'postulated'. In reformulating my argument, he attributes to me the premise 'If a type of mental state is postulated, then it is not consciously available.' To that premise, he properly objects that 'postulated' and 'found' are not mutually exclusive: one might postulate a type of mental state on theoretical grounds and later, guided by the theory, find it in one's consciousness. I never suggested otherwise. Like Boghossian, I reject the quoted principle. Having pointed out that Boghossian postulates pre-doxastic intellectual seemings on theoretical grounds—he needs them to play a distinctive role in his internalist epistemology—I independently observed that many of us can find no such pre-doxastic intellectual seemings in ourselves. We can find conscious inclinations to judge, but they are not pre-doxastic, and Boghossian is very clear that they will not serve his theoretical purpose of justifying judgment: 'In general, your being inclined to judge p is no justification for your judging p' (Chapter 15, p. 225). He therefore postulates an intellectual seeming prior to the inclination to judge or believe.

Boghossian now tries to show that we *can* find pre-doxastic seemings in ourselves quite easily. He starts with perceptual seemings. According to him, in the Müller–Lyer illusion, once we learn that the two lines are the same length, although one still *seems* longer than the other, we lose the inclination to judge that it *is* longer. But that description of the case is unconvincing. Of course, my all-things-considered disposition is to judge that the two lines are the same length. But that is because a better source of information overrides the still felt visually-based inclination to judge that one line is longer. Without the latter, I have no visual impression or seeming that one is longer. Boghossian gives a natural explanation for the persistence of the visual impression:

perception, being to a considerable degree modular, is not penetrable by the background knowledge about the length of the lines. Hence, the impression of inequality persists despite our discovery.   (Chapter 15, p. 225)

Indeed, but a parallel explanation goes for the persistence of the felt inclination to judge the lines unequal. It is still there, like the fragility of the well-protected vase. If I forget about the background information for a moment, I revert to judging that one line is longer. Boghossian has not made plausible his key claim: that the visual impression is *more* persistent than the felt inclination to judge. Thus the Müller–Lyer illusion is an unhelpful analogy for Boghossian's purposes.

Of course, one could restrict the term 'inclination' to exclude stably overridden dispositions. But doing so would not help Boghossian. For a stably overridden disposition to judge is still not pre-doxastic in his required sense. If a disposition to judge *p* does not justify judging *p*, still less does a stably overridden disposition to judge *p*. Indeed, Boghossian's own diagram of his 'intuitional picture' shows that he admits the possibility of an inclination to judge *p* getting defeated and so not resulting in a judging of *p*. Surprisingly, he neglects to raise the possibility for the Müller–Lyer illusion.

Boghossian treats intellectual illusions, such as the Naïve Comprehension principle in set theory, as relevantly analogous to perceptual illusions. Even after Russell's Paradox has shown it to be inconsistent, it still seems true. Indeed, for all Boghossian has shown, whenever it still seems true to one, one still feels the inclination to accept it, which one uses Russell's bad news to stably override. Boghossian has not made plausible his key claim that these are separate mental states. Naïve Comprehension has an elegant, seductive shape, which continues to tempt us even when we know better. The illusion persists because we still lack a fully satisfying alternative picture of sets. When I temporarily picture sets according to one of the proposed alternatives, for instance one on which sets cannot be 'too large', Naïve Comprehension no longer even seems true, and I no longer feel even the inclination to accept it. Boghossian neglects to raise the possibility of defeated inclinations for Naïve Comprehension too.

Boghossian briefly offers another argument for the distinctness of intellectual seemings and felt inclinations to judge. He asserts that, in philosophical thought experiments, our inclinations to judgment 'present themselves as based on their seeming true' (Chapter 15, p. 224). Thus, if the felt inclinations just are the seemings, they in effect present themselves as based on themselves (perhaps under another guise), and so as circular, which would make the thought experiments intellectually vicious.

For all I know, Boghossian sometimes does feel his inclinations to judge to be non-circularly based on seemings. I have no such feeling about my inclinations to judge. They do *not* present themselves to me as based on their seeming true. When I ask 'Why am I inclined to judge *p*?', the answer 'Because *p* seems true to me' sounds forced and feeble, its explanans far too close to its explanandum to provide significant insight. It replaces a question of the form 'Why am I inclined to judge *p*?' with a question of the form 'Why does *p* seem true to me?', merely postponing the serious explanatory work by inserting a redundant middleman. What matters is why I favour *p* in the first place.

When Boghossian feels his inclinations to judge to be non-circularly based on seemings, the natural hypothesis is that he is experiencing them through the lens of his own epistemological theories. No doubt many philosophers experience their mental lives as vindicating their own widely divergent views. We need better evidence than that. Building a robust psychological theory on introspective foundations is much harder than Boghossian acknowledges: witness the history of psychology before the First World War.

In other cases, one unhesitatingly, confidently, and justifiably accepts *p*. On Boghossian's view, one must first, however briefly, have been in a pre-doxastic consciously accessible state where *p* seemed true to one but one had not yet felt an inclination to accept *p*. Even when I do my best to use his theoretical apparatus to identify such pre-doxastic seemings in myself, I find none. Many others are in the same boat. Are we negligent in our introspecting, or otherwise defective? Of course, if you accept his theory, and feel disposed to accept a verdict on a thought experiment, you will infer that you previously had a pre-doxastic intellectual seeming of it, but that hardly amounts to introspecting the seeming. To experience oneself as possessed by devils does not amount to genuinely introspective awareness of devils.

Many of us cannot find pre-doxastic intellectual seemings in ourselves, even with Boghossian's best help. The upshot is not just that we lack introspective evidence for his theory. His epistemology requires minimally competent agents to have *consciously accessible* pre-doxastic intellectual seemings. That we are unable to consciously access any such things is evidence that his epistemology is false.

4. Trump's Birthday Party

In my previous chapter, I mentioned that Boghossian's account of intuitions could apply to one's reaction to being invited to Donald Trump's birthday party, hardly an a priori matter. What Boghossian says in response embodies an intriguing view of human psychology:

> People don't tend to have unmediated *de re* moral intuitions about persons per se. They tend to have unmediated moral intuitions about their attributes or characters. If it were to seem true to me that I shouldn't accept an invitation from Trump, that would typically be grounded in my intuition that, other things being equal, I ought not to celebrate the birth of someone so evil (fill in your favorite Trump description). And *that* proposition *is* a priori. (Chapter 15, p. 221)

In effect, Boghossian is proposing an inferential model of the judgment that he should not accept the invitation. His postulated reasoning involves a combination of an a priori moral premise and an a posteriori non-moral premise. The moral premise is roughly that, other things being equal, anyone with such-and-such non-evaluative attributes is so evil that one ought not to celebrate their birth. The non-moral premise is that Trump has those non-evaluative attributes. The (defeasible) conclusion is that one ought not to celebrate Trump's birth by attending his birthday party. The moral premise is in effect a universal moral principle, though one may not have considered it before receiving the invitation. That premise is justified by a priori intuition, on Boghossian's account, while the second premise is justified by a posteriori empirical means, and the conclusion is inferentially justified a posteriori, because it is based on premises which are justified, one of them a posteriori.

In a footnote to the passage about Trump, Boghossian tries to clarify what he is saying about the inference:

...this is a remark about the architecture of justification, not a remark about the psychological processes that lead to someone's making the moral judgment at issue, for a variety of reasons. For one thing, most of us will have automated our responses to various types of familiar situation so that we know what to think without having to run through an explicit inference in our heads.   (Chapter 15, p. 226)

The explanation is rather puzzling, since on his account the justification comes from the intuition, which *is* psychological in nature. The agent's own doxastic justification is at stake, not just some propositional justification on offer irrespective of whether the agent takes it up. As Boghossian says in a piece to which he refers the reader for further discussion, 'You don't count as having reasoned well just because your conclusion follows from your premises' (2016: 50).

The footnote could easily be read as watering down Boghossian's internalist commitments. After all, automated responses sound suspiciously like the kind of thing an externalist might invoke. However, I assume that this passage is not intended to concede anything much to externalism. Instead, when he writes 'without having to run through an explicit inference in our heads', he still holds that there is an *implicit* inference, which we could in principle run through in our heads if we did have to (or something like that). Similarly, when he writes 'most of us will have automated our responses to various types of familiar situations', he holds that making the same response non-automatically is in principle available to us (or something like that). In what follows, I will assess Boghossian's account of the Trump case on the assumption that he still intends it in an internalist spirit.

Most people are unused to treating invitations to birthday parties or similar social events as raising serious moral issues. Accepting the putative moral premise is no mere automated response. Rather, the moral premise needs justifying, which for Boghossian requires an intellectual seeming. On his view, what people 'tend' to do in making such morally inflected decisions is to start by justifying a priori a universal moral principle, a task at which philosophers have toiled for millennia with no great success. If one decides more or less instantly not to accept the invitation, one must have justified the premises and reasoned to the conclusion very quickly, though still in a way accessible to consciousness, if the process is to meet the internalist requirements.

Perhaps Boghossian makes his daily decisions in the elaborate way he describes. Speaking for myself, I am not sure that I have ever justified a universal moral principle in my life, quickly or slowly, a priori or a posteriori. I suspect that I am not unusual in that respect. Indeed, the final judgment 'I ought not to attend Trump's birthday party' may well be *more* obvious than the a priori universal moral premise 'Other things being equal, anyone with such-and-such non-evaluative attributes is so evil that one ought not to celebrate their birth.' If the conclusion is epistemically better off than the conjunction of the premises, its justification does not all depend on them. Such cases are common.

Speaking for myself again, I rarely reach decisions by reasoning from general principles, at least, not in any way to which I have conscious access. When the decision is difficult, and there is plenty of time for reflection, I do not consciously reason; I simply procrastinate until one morning I wake up knowing what I am going to do.

When the decision is easier, or there is less time for reflection, I procrastinate less, without reasoning more. I doubt that I am unusual in that respect either.

People often *confabulate* post hoc rationalizations for their actions and judgments. They cite reasons in justification, but those reasons did not really mediate the original actions or judgments, even though it feels to them in retrospect as if they did. Indeed, the kind of inference Boghossian proposes is just the kind of thing one would come up with if one were confabulating a post hoc rationalization for one's assent to the conclusion. Trained philosophers tend to be well above average in their ability to confabulate post hoc rationalizations, which may be partly why they are so susceptible to highly intellectualized accounts of ordinary decision-making and judgment.

Once confabulated rationalizations are distinguished from originally mediating reasons, presumably Boghossian holds that the latter, not the former, are what doxastically justified the original assent to the conclusion. But he has not made it plausible that we ordinarily have conscious access to reasoning processes mediating apparently unreflective decisions and judgments. Of course, those decisions and judgments do not come from nowhere, but that does not mean that conscious reflection enables us to identify an implicit reasoning process by which we originally reached them, or even to be confident that they were reached by an inference from premises to conclusion, rather than a cognitive process of some other kind. Thus, by Boghossian's standards, most ordinary cases of apparently unreflective decisions and judgments may turn out to be unjustified.

Boghossian's demands for articulated justification look more appropriate for a PhD examination than they do for assessing the daily judgments of real people. But if most, perhaps all, of us fail Boghossian's examination, that does not mean that we can never know the difference between right and wrong. The point can be put in terms of psychologists' distinction between type 1 and type 2 thinking.[2] Type 1 thinking demands little of working memory and is not consciously reasoned; it is typically fast, automatic, and unreflective. Type 2 thinking demands much more of working memory and is consciously reasoned; it is typically slow, deliberate, and reflective. Type 2 thinking is built up out of components that involve type 1 thinking, as in the individual steps of a complex calculation, or facial recognition as an input to decision-making. When Boghossian insists on consciously accessible reasoning, he is in effect requiring type 2 thinking for the justification of beliefs. Given the reliance of type 2 thinking on type 1 thinking, that demand is unlikely to end well.

Presumably, a training in analytic philosophy helps one put on a show of meeting Boghossian's criteria, for one receives extensive practice in constructing explicit arguments. More generally, students of philosophy are encouraged to seek type 2 justifications for type 1 judgments. That may occasionally enhance the epistemic status of some of their beliefs. But even people with no such education know a lot: theories of justification that in effect reward type 2 thinking at the expense of type 1 thinking tend to disempower the ordinary knowledge on which all of us rely. Moreover, transferring the burden of judgment from type 1 to type 2 thinking is not always an improvement: for some tasks, the former may do better than the latter in integrating a wide variety of information (see Kornblith 2012 for examples).

Presumably, Boghossian does not intend to restrict justification to idealized beliefs: the subjects who judge on the basis of his kind of reasoning are not meant to form a narrow elite. That his criteria nevertheless have that effect is another indication that the range of conscious reasoning they require was postulated, not found.[3]

Boghossian has a second line of defence. At least for the sake of argument, he allows that someone might have 'a direct and unmediated intuition that he ought not to accept an invitation from Donald Trump, one that did not depend on any view about his character or attributes' (Chapter 15, p. 221). He suggests that he can still deny that the intuition would justify the corresponding belief. The idea is that only a priori propositions are (directly) justified by intuitions, where a priori propositions are those which can be justified non-perceptually. Since the proposition about Trump cannot be justified non-perceptually, it is not a priori, and so cannot be justified by intuition.

One may worry that applying the proposed criterion will be circular. For unless one already assumes that the proposition about Trump cannot be justified by intuition, why accept that it cannot be justified non-perceptually?

Even when the proposed criterion can be non-circularly applied, some of its results go contrary to Boghossian's purposes. Consider this proposition, where 'FLT' abbreviates a statement of Fermat's Last Theorem:

Trump-or-Fermat   Either one ought not to attend Trump's birthday party or FLT.

Trump-or-Fermat *can* be justified non-perceptually, in Boghossian's sense, by a mathematical proof of Fermat's Last Theorem followed by a final step of disjunction introduction. Thus Trump-or-Fermat is an a priori proposition in Boghossian's sense, and so *can* be justified by intuition, by his criterion. Now imagine someone who knows just enough mathematics to understand the statement of Fermat's Last Theorem, but has no idea of its established mathematical status. He happens to have a direct and unmediated intuition of Trump-or-Fermat (with no defeaters). By the criterion, he is thereby justified in believing Trump-or-Fermat.

When Boghossian comes to rationalize his criterion, he says this:

Perceptions, being the product of a cognitive mechanism that is causally sensitive to facts about its environment, are well suited for justifying contingent propositions about the actual world. Intuitions, not being the product of such a causally sensitive mechanism, if they are well suited for justifying anything at all (not in dispute just now), are well suited for justifying propositions that are either necessary, or anyhow insensitive to the features of the actual world.

(Chapter 15, p. 221)

One might expect such emphasis on the crucial significance of causally sensitive mechanisms to come from a supposedly discredited reliabilist, not from an internalist, for whom justification has nothing directly to do with such matters. Boghossian has some explaining to do.

5. Internalism and Bigotry

In my Chapter 14, I raised the concern that an account of justification based on how things seem to the subject is in danger of justifying bigoted beliefs, since they fit how things seem to the bigot. In his response, Boghossian addresses that concern only by saying that 'no one thinks (or anyhow should think) that just because visual perception is open to distortion by bias and bigotry [reference to Siegel 2017] it cannot be thought to provide prima facie justification for belief' (Chapter 15, p. 226).

The qualifier 'prima facie' may sound reassuring. Perhaps something will turn up to defeat the prima facie justifications for the bigoted beliefs. But Boghossian's internalism drastically restricts the scope for such defeat. If only consciously accessible mental states of the subject are available for that purpose, defeat must take the form of something like internal inconsistency or incoherence. The prima facie justification for a bigoted belief may be defeated by contrary seemings to the bigot. What if there is no such internal incoherence?

All this raises the spectre of the consistent Nazi, a familiar figure in metaethical debate, where it keeps cropping up because internalists have failed to deal with it effectively. Of course, in practice it is hard for *anyone*, including a Nazi, to be consistent. But a consistent Nazi is possible in principle, and so makes a legitimate example. His seemings and beliefs form a coherent whole; none of them is defeated by any of the others. Thus, on an internalist coherentist epistemology, the prima facie justification of the beliefs by the corresponding seemings becomes all things considered justification. For instance, on that view, since the consistent Nazi has the intuition that he ought to enslave or kill those who do not belong to a master race, and nothing in his other seemings and beliefs runs counter to that intuition, he is justified, all things considered, in his belief that he ought to enslave or kill those who do not belong to a master race.

Boghossian's claim that intuitions justify only a priori propositions offers little help here. For on what basis is he to deny a priori status to the proposition that the Nazi ought to enslave or kill those who do not belong to a master race? Doing so requires him to deny that the proposition can be justified non-perceptually. But that already assumes that the Nazi's intuition cannot justify. In any case, Boghossian's criterion has anomalous results, as explained in the previous section. Thus it cannot properly block the route from internalism to the consequence that the neo-Nazi is justified in his belief that he ought to enslave or kill those who do not belong to a master race.

If the same approach is applied to the justification of action as to the justification of belief, the view also implies that the consistent Nazi is justified, all things considered, in acting on his belief and enslaving or killing those who do not belong to a master race (in fact, since there is no master race, everyone counts as not belonging to a master race). After all, it is constitutive of a genuine belief that one has some disposition to act on it.

Surely no morally decent epistemology implies that the consistent Nazi is justified in believing that he ought to enslave or kill those who do not belong to a master race, and no morally decent philosophy of action implies that he is justified in going ahead and killing them. I am not attributing those consequences to Boghossian's own views. But an urgent, central challenge faces his internalist approach to justification, and others like it. To put it in terms of the example: how, if at all, does the internalist approach *not* imply that the consistent Nazi is justified in believing that he ought to enslave or kill those who do not belong to a master race—and justified in enslaving or killing them?[4,5]

Notes

1. This paper is published here for the first time.

2. Psychologists have substituted the terminology of 'type 1' and 'type 2' thinking for the earlier terminology of 'system 1' and 'system 2', in order to avoid the unintended implication that each type constitutes a single integrated system. See Evans and Stanovich 2013 for clarification and defence of the distinction by two leading dual-process psychologists.

3. There may be a similar explanation for Boghossian's difficulty in his 'Williamson on the Distinction between the A Priori and the A Posteriori Once Again' (Chapter 11) in coming to terms with my example of the role of perceptual pattern recognition in ordinary cases of following a mathematical proof.

4. Williamson 2019 discusses the problem of the consistent Nazi for epistemological coherentism in more detail.

5. Thanks to Jennifer Nagel and Amia Srinivasan for helpful comments on an early draft of this chapter.

17

Closing Reflections[1]

Timothy Williamson

One notable feature of real-life disputes between proponents of rival logics is how similar they are, methodologically, to other theoretical disputes. They may put in question the most fundamental principles of rational thought and discourse, but in practice they are neither markedly more nor markedly less rational than disputes over much less fundamental matters. Although some participants and commentators suggest that the parties are talking past each other, using the same words with different meanings, that suspicion is endemic to disputation in general.

In the period 1973–1980, when I was an undergraduate and graduate student at Oxford, Michael Dummett was in his prime. He made the dispute between classical and intuitionistic logic central to philosophical discussion. We were also brought up on Quine, both the Quine who held all logic to be revisable and the Quine who treated such revisions as changing the subject. Quine and Dummett can each be read as giving an understanding-based account of logical knowledge, though of very different kinds. Neither convinced me. I was never attracted by claims of a deep asymmetry between disputes in logic and theoretical disputes elsewhere. They did not fit my experience of such disputes in practice. Although equivocation sometimes occurred, resolving it left an irreducible residue of logical and philosophical disagreement. Some of my earlier publications touched on such issues (Williamson 1987/88, 1994). When invited to reply to Paul Boghossian on 'Blind Reasoning' for the 2003 Joint Session of the Aristotelian Society and the Mind Association in Belfast, I welcomed the opportunity to engage critically with a sophisticated understanding-based account of logical knowledge.

The Belfast encounter led me to develop my reflections on understanding-based accounts of more general kinds of knowledge, including philosophical knowledge, and on epistemological conceptions of analyticity like Boghossian's. That was one source of my book *The Philosophy of Philosophy* (Williamson 2007a). In it, I developed the beginnings of an alternative account of the epistemology of philosophy, which makes it much more similar to the epistemology of everyday judgments—for example, of counterfactual conditionals—than many philosophers like to think. From that perspective, the classification of such philosophical knowledge either as a priori or as a posteriori looked too crude to be helpful. It did not cut at the epistemological joints. That was the origin of my paper arguing that the distinction is shallow (Chapter 8), which sparked further exchanges in the dialogue between us.

Debating the A Priori. Paul Boghossian and Timothy Williamson, Oxford University Press (2020).
© Paul Boghossian and Timothy Williamson.
DOI: 10.1093/oso/9780198851707.001.0001

That was not my first discussion of the a priori. Much earlier, I had helped chip away at the stereotype of the a priori by arguing, against Gareth Evans (1979), that the phenomenon of contingent truths known a priori, famously uncovered by Kripke (1972), cannot be fully deflated as a trick with indexical operators such as 'actually'. I showed how we can know a priori that there is at least one believer, in a way quite different from those operative in the Kripkean examples (Williamson 1986).[2]

Boghossian locates the deep source of our disagreements over the epistemically analytic and the a priori in the contrast between his internalism and my externalism. What is the heart of epistemology? For him, it is justification within the inner world of appearances to a conscious subject. For me, it is an intelligent agent's knowledge of the outer world, including the agent.

Deep though the difference is, it does not play symmetric roles in our arguments. Boghossian's internalism imposes demanding constraints on the kind of solution he will accept to an epistemological problem. By contrast, my externalism consists mainly in the denial of internalism. Although I do have a positive account of knowledge, it does not constrict the resources available to epistemological theorizing in any way analogous to Boghossian's internalism. A case in point is our dispute over the a priori. My account of the examples at issue—for instance, about colour relations—assigned a key role to imagination. That is not a distinctively externalist resource; I described conscious processes, which internalists too could invoke. The externalism that so exercises Boghossian came in when I suggested that such cognitive uses of the imagination would have to be at least locally safe, or reliable, in order to provide knowledge. I said so not from any felt need to introduce externalist ideas at every turn, but simply in order to give the best available explanation of how such imaginative processes can sometimes provide knowledge, as they surely do. I could easily have stipulated that the protagonist of the example also entertained intellectual seemings of the kind most conducive to the sort of internalist justification centrally important to Boghossian, the sort which he attributes to the brain in the vat and perhaps the consistent bigot. I did not do so, because I took such justification to be too flimsy to bear the required epistemological weight.

As Boghossian emphasizes, he is offering no alternative positive account of the examples at issue. He wonders why I am so impatient for one. The reason is simple. I offered a sketch, however impressionistic, of the examples, available to someone who does not accept Boghossian's internalist constraints. While the internalist fails to offer an adequate competitor account, the examples constitute evidence—one source amongst many—in favour of externalism. It is the internalist who should be in a hurry.

More generally, Boghossian's skilful and ingenious deployment of the resources available to a conception of the mind more consonant with early modern philosophy than with contemporary psychology serves to make plain their poverty. Internalism confines epistemology to a superficial level of consciousness where most of the cognitive action is not. In doing so, it threatens to marginalize epistemology from the rest of philosophy, and indeed the rest of human inquiry.[3]

Our best chance of making progress in philosophy is by taking advantage of resources that have not already been around for centuries, while still employing more traditional resources too wherever appropriate. For epistemology, two new sources are salient. One is formal epistemology, which gives us the ability to explore the subtleties of complex epistemic situations more rigorously, applying the model-building methodology already characteristic of much natural and social science. The models may use the framework of Bayesian probability theory, or of epistemic logic, or some combination of the two.[4,5] The other salient new source is contemporary psychology, which offers far more realistic and more systematically tested accounts of the human mind than anything our shaky attempts at introspection can provide. That is not remotely to suggest that epistemology can be reduced to mathematics, or to psychology. It is neither, but has much to learn from both.

Neither formal epistemology nor contemporary psychology has an inherent bias in favour of externalism, or of internalism. As both fields develop, their theories may of course favour one side or the other, but that is in response to the emerging evidence, not dictated by preconceived methodological assumptions. In my view, the prospects for externalism are bright on both fronts, but there is still much to play for.[6] My sketchy comments on the epistemological role of the imagination, for example, cry out to be integrated with a properly articulated and tested psychological theory of the imagination.[7] Such methodologies have some hope of bypassing the trench warfare of internalists against externalists. If epistemology learns more from other disciplines, in the long run it will also have more to offer other disciplines in its turn.

Notes

1. This paper is published here for the first time.
2. For further discussion see Williamson 1988, a response to Oppy 1987, and more generally Hawthorne 2002.
3. For a critique from a slightly different angle of another internalist account of justification see Williamson 2007b. That piece would have been out of place in the present volume because its target is Robert Audi's theory.
4. See Williamson 2017 on model-building in philosophy.
5. Formal epistemology originated in subjective Bayesianism, a very different form of internalism from Boghossian's, but also one built around a norm of internal coherence. However, there is nothing inherently internalist about probabilities on evidence (Williamson 2000). By contrast, formal epistemic logic centred on knowledge from its beginnings (Hintikka 1962). I have used it to argue for externalist conclusions; see for instance Williamson 2014. When Nagel (forthcoming) appears, it will constitute a paradigm of epistemology informed by contemporary psychology, which it uses to argue for a broadly knowledge-first approach.
6. Williamson 2014 uses a model-building methodology to advance the case for externalism.
7. Harris 2000 and Byrne 2005 are good examples of promising work on the cognitive psychology of the imagination.

18

Closing Reflections

Paul Boghossian

Is philosophy a distinctive discipline, with its own domain, and its own a priori methods for investigating it; or is it just a speculative, more abstract cousin of the empirical sciences?

When I entered Princeton's graduate program in 1978, following an undergraduate degree in physics, Richard Rorty was in the process of completing his provocative book *Philosophy and the Mirror of Nature* (Rorty 1979). In it, Rorty argued that philosophy, especially of the analytic variety, depended for its viability on certain distinctions—particularly between the analytic and the synthetic, and the a priori and the a posteriori—which it had been busy undermining, thereby, in his view, turning its ingenuity against itself.

Rorty found analytic philosophy's demise a cause for celebration but to a novice graduate student, about to commit to a lifetime of studying the subject, it was disconcerting, to say the least. And yet it seemed to me that Rorty was more or less right about the dependence he was claiming, at least when it came to philosophy's most foundational issues, such as the nature of existence, essence, value, truth, logic, modality, rationality, among others. I couldn't see, for example, how to make sense of the philosophy book I had most admired as an undergraduate, Saul Kripke's *Naming and Necessity*, as an exercise in post-Quinean philosophy.

The rationalist conception of philosophy to which I was drawn does not, of course, require that nothing counts as a philosophical issue if it has an empirical dimension. That would be absurdly restrictive. For one thing, and as we have seen repeatedly throughout this volume, empirical evidence may always enter, often in very rich ways, in fixing the subject matter of a question to be answered by a priori means. In addition, there are certainly topics of philosophical interest in which empirical evidence may be relevant in other ways. If you wish to give an account of the nature of color concepts as they are deployed in perception (as is attempted in Boghossian and Velleman 1989, 1991) you may need to know a great deal about the science of colors and of color perception. If you wish to give an account of the nature of the imagination and of its capacity to justify empirical beliefs, you may need to know a great deal about the psychology of the imagination. Indeed, sometimes you may need to reconsider whether a particular topic is purely a priori: space and time provide striking examples of topics that were thought to be purely a priori until developments

Debating the A Priori. Paul Boghossian and Timothy Williamson, Oxford University Press (2020).
© Paul Boghossian and Timothy Williamson.
DOI: 10.1093/oso/9780198851707.001.0001

in physics forced a reconsideration. Rationalism about philosophy, then, isn't the view that philosophy *never* involves empirical evidence; it's rather the view that it needn't involve it; and that the most effective methods for studying its most foundational questions don't involve it.

Given these views, it came as something of a relief to discover that the distinctions that Quine and Rorty rejected could be saved from their critiques. One key moment involved the realization that philosophers had routinely conflated a dubious metaphysical notion of analyticity (truth in virtue of meaning) with a defensible epistemic notion (knowable to be true on the basis of grasp of meaning); and that the latter could be used, without invoking the former, to provide an account of at least some a priori knowledge. This was the view I first started exploring in 'Analyticity Reconsidered' (Boghossian 1996, reprinted here as Chapter 1) and that I pursued further in a number of subsequent papers.

One of these, 'Blind Reasoning' (2003a; Chapter 2) was slated for delivery at the Joint Session of the Aristotelian Society and the Mind Association in Belfast in July 2003, with a reply by Timothy Williamson. In that paper, my strategy had been to assume the existence of constitutive understanding–assent links—in the form of a conceptual-role semantics for the logical constants—so as to explore their potential for explaining our entitlement to basic logical inferences, inferences to which we seem to be entitled despite our not possessing a non-circular warrant for them. For these purposes, great precision in the correct formulation of a conceptual-role semantics was not required; of much greater moment was the question of the existence of the appropriate epistemic bridge principles connecting understanding–assent links with positive epistemic standing. In his reply, Williamson chose to devote much of his attention not only to the details of formulating a conceptual-role semantics but also to raising an ingenious new objection to the very possibility of understanding–assent links, his now famous argument from expert dissent. While I continued to ignore issues of detailed formulation, it was important to defend the possibility of understanding–assent links against his objections, the result being a number of further exchanges on this score.

Over the years, I came to change my mind about some central issues independently of Williamson's arguments. One of them stemmed from a growing awareness that one type of understanding-based account of the a priori—precisely the type that relied on understanding–assent links—was unlikely to yield an *internalistically* acceptable account of a priori justification without supplementation; and a commitment to some type of internalism about epistemic justification seemed to me then, as it continues to seem to me now, non-optional.

Another stemmed from the growing realization that understanding-based accounts were unlikely to yield explanations for the full range of a priori justification, in particular, for our knowledge of normative principles. Both of these realizations help explain the evolution of my attitude over these years towards the notion of *intuition*, from a hesitant skepticism to a cautious embrace.

As these remarks illustrate, our exchanges on particular problems—already quite broad in themselves—interacted with even broader background commitments. These background commitments, while not directly under discussion, conditioned and shaped our respective perceptions of the range of viable solutions to the problems which were.

Foremost among these background commitments concerns the conflict between externalism and internalism, most especially as it arises within epistemology, but also to some extent as it arises within meta-semantics. During the course of the debates, I was repeatedly struck by two points.

The first is the extent to which our divergent views on particular topics could be traced back to our divergent views about epistemic justification. Although Williamson occasionally professes open-mindedness on this issue, many of his arguments presuppose a broadly externalist, typically Reliabilist, conception of epistemic justification, a conception which I find impossible to accept. (To emphasize: what's at issue here is epistemic *justification*, not *knowledge*: it was common ground between us that, for the purposes of these exchanges, we would not presuppose a 'knowledge-first' epistemology.) For example, Williamson's central arguments against the importance of the a priori–a posteriori distinction will only seem plausible to someone with antecedent Reliabilist convictions.

The second point was how much *easier* many philosophical problems become on Reliabilist assumptions. What does justification have to do with truth, given that one can be justified in believing a false proposition? How does perception justify belief? How could the mere understanding of a proposition justify belief in that proposition? How could a mere intellectual impression justify belief in a general modalized proposition? All of these questions, and many others besides, which pose enormous challenges to internalists, become relatively easy on Reliabilist views.

Unfortunately, Reliabilism about epistemic justification is not plausible, and so this easy way out of those philosophical quandaries is blocked. As we can see from the intelligibility of skeptical scenarios in which you are surreptitiously envatted, the rational management of your beliefs is not, in the first instance, a matter of getting things right, much less a matter of getting them reliably right; it is about updating your beliefs in a way that is normatively appropriate, whether or not that results in true beliefs. A Reliabilist view of epistemic justification loses its subject matter just as fully as does a functionalist view of sensation: they both commit the mistake of conflating the normal effects of a property's instantiation with an account of that property's nature.

The externalism–internalism conflict in meta-semantics also plays an important background role in our debates. Williamson's social-externalist sympathies show up right at the start, in the debate in Belfast, in the form of his reliance on the claim that, by the sort of ordinary communal standards of competence exploited in a Burge-style thought experiment, it is sufficient for a subject to be competent in the use of a word 'C' for him to understand the concept C. Such a claim is clearly inhospitable to the conceptual-role semantics that I was presupposing in that symposium, a type of semantics that is much more appropriate for characterizing the understanding possessed by the experts to whom ordinary speakers defer (mastery), than for characterizing the understanding of ordinary speakers themselves.

Williamson's reliance on such weak communal standards of concept attribution continues through to the last of our exchanges, despite my insistence that I was talking about *mastery* of a concept, rather than mere *possession*. Williamson occasionally raises questions about how that distinction is to be understood. But that is not much of a mystery. The distinction I am invoking is *presupposed* by the very thought experiments—namely, Burge's—on which Williamson's social externalism is based. Those thought experiments, in which subjects are said to possess a given concept C despite understanding it *incompletely*, or *misunderstanding* it, because they defer to communal experts, depend on the idea that the conceptual role associated with C by the experts is both complete and fully correct, whereas those of ordinary speakers needn't be.

Furthermore, although I acknowledge the strength of the considerations that lead some philosophers to want to espouse externalist meta-semantical views, I believe we are some distance from fully understanding the difficulties, indeed paradoxes, to which an externalist individuation of concepts gives rise, and so should avoid writing as though the matter has already been decisively settled in their favor (see Boghossian 1994b, 2011b, in preparation).

The one mistake that, as it seems to me, everyone needs to avoid is antecedent commitment to some big 'system' (Naturalism, for example) in advance of a detailed exploration of particular issues. Whilst it can be impressive to construct a systematic view that contains mutually cohering answers to many central questions, we are better off developing careful, nuanced accounts of particular domains. The 'systems first' approach inevitably leads to procrustean maneuvers in which we are forced to chop off crucial aspects of common sense—qualia, normativity, the a priori, or what have you—in order to make the phenomena fit our preconceived picture. In the great battle of philosophical styles, represented by the two giants, David Lewis and Saul Kripke, both of whom I was privileged to have as teachers in graduate school, I side firmly with Kripke.

At the end of the day, what we most need is to encourage the attitude of intellectual humility gestured at in our preface: that all these competing ideas, about philosophy, and within philosophy, are just so many research programs which, despite philosophy's long history, are still in their early stages and deserve to be explored in a spirit of open-mindedness.

Bibliography

Bach, Kent. (1988). Burge's New Thought Experiment: Back to the Drawing Room. *Journal of Philosophy, 85*(2), 88–97.

Bach, Kent. (1999). The Myth of Conventional Implicature. *Linguistics and Philosophy, 22*(4), 327–66.

Barwise, Jon. (1977). *Handbook of Mathematical Logic.* North-Holland.

Bealer, George. (1992). The Incoherence of Empiricism. *Aristotelian Society Supplementary Volume, 66*(1), 99–138.

Bealer, George. (1998). A Theory of Concepts and Concepts Possession. *Philosophical Issues, 9,* 261–301.

Bealer, George. (2000). A Theory of the A Priori. *Pacific Philosophical Quarterly, 81*(1), 1–30.

Belnap, Nuel. (1962). Tonk, Plonk and Plink. *Analysis, 22*(6), 130–4.

Benacerraf, Paul. (1973). Mathematical Truth. *Journal of Philosophy, 70*(19), 661–79.

Bengson, John. (2015). The Intellectual Given. *Mind, 124*(495), 707–60.

Bird, Alexander. (1998). Dispositions and Antidotes. *Philosophical Quarterly, 48*(191), 227–34.

Block, Ned. (1995). On a Confusion about a Function of Consciousness. *Behavioral and Brain Sciences, 18*(2), 227–47.

Boghossian, Paul. (1989). The Rule-Following Considerations. *Mind, 98*(392), 507–49.

Boghossian, Paul. (1994a). Inferential-Role Semantics and the Analytic/Synthetic Distinction. *Philosophical Studies, 73*(2–3), 109–22.

Boghossian, Paul. (1994b). The Transparency of Mental Content. *Philosophical Perspectives, 8,* 33–50.

Boghossian, Paul. (1996). Analyticity Reconsidered. *Noûs, 30*(3), 360–91.

Boghossian, Paul. (1997). Analyticity. In B. Hale and C. Wright (eds), *A Companion to the Philosophy of Language* (pp. 331–68). Blackwell.

Boghossian, Paul. (2000). Knowledge of Logic. In Paul Boghossian and Christopher Peacocke (eds), *New Essays on the A Priori.* Clarendon Press.

Boghossian, Paul. (2001). How Are Objective Epistemic Reasons Possible? *Philosophical Studies, 106*(1/2), 1–40.

Boghossian, Paul. (2003a). Blind Reasoning. *Aristotelian Society Supplementary Volume, 77*(1), 225–48.

Boghossian, Paul. (2003b). Epistemic Analyticity: A Defense. *Grazer Philosophische Studien, 66*(1), 15–35.

Boghossian, Paul. (2008). Replies to Wright, MacFarlane and Sosa. *Philosophical Studies, 141*(3), 409–32.

Boghossian, Paul. (2009). Virtuous Intuitions: Comments on Lecture 3 of Ernest Sosa's A Virtue Epistemology. *Philosophical Studies, 144*(1), 111–19.

Boghossian, Paul. (2011a). Williamson on the A Priori and the Analytic. *Philosophy and Phenomenological Research, 82,* 488–97.

Boghossian, Paul. (2011b). The Transparency of Mental Content Revisited. *Philosophical Studies, 155*(3), 457–65.

Boghossian, Paul. (2012). Inferentialism and the Epistemology of Logic: Reflections on Casalegno and Williamson. *Dialectica, 66,* 221–36.

Boghossian, Paul. (2014). What is Inference? *Philosophical Studies, 169*(1), 1–18.

Boghossian, Paul. (2016). Reasoning and Reflection: A Reply to Kornblith. *Analysis*, 76(1), 41–54.

Boghossian, Paul. (2017). Postscript: Further Thoughts about Analyticity, 20 Years Later. In Hale Wright and Alexander Miller (eds), *A Companion to the Philosophy of Language, Second Edition* (pp. 611–18). Blackwell.

Boghossian, Paul. (forthcoming). Intuition and A Priori Justification. In Dylan Dodd and Elia Zardini (eds), *Beyond Sense? New Essays on the Significance, Grounds, and Extent of the A Priori*. Oxford University Press.

Boghossian, Paul. (in preparation). Transparency and Concepts.

Boghossian, Paul and Velleman, David. (1989). Color as a Secondary Quality. *Mind*, 98(January), 81–103.

Boghossian, Paul and Velleman, David. (1991). Physicalist Theories of Color. *Philosophical Review*, 100(January), 67–106.

Bonjour, Lawrence. (1985). *The Structure of Empirical Knowledge*. Harvard University Press.

Bonjour, Lawrence. (1998). *In Defense of Pure Reason: A Rationalist Account of A Priori Justification*. Cambridge University Press.

Boolos, George. (1971). The Iterative Conception of Set. *Journal of Philosophy*, 68(8), 215–31.

Brandom, Robert. (2000). *Articulating Reasons: An Introduction to Inferentialism*. Harvard University Press.

Broome, John. (2013). *Rationality through Reasoning*. Wiley-Blackwell.

Burge, Tyler. (1979). Individualism and the Mental. *Midwest Studies in Philosophy*, 4(1), 73–122.

Burge, Tyler. (1986). Intellectual Norms and Foundations of Mind. *Journal of Philosophy*, 83, 697–720.

Burge, Tyler. (1993). Content Preservation. *Philosophical Review*, 102, 457–88.

Byrne, Ruth. (2005). *The Rational Imagination: How People Create Alternatives to Reality*. MIT Press.

Cappelen, Herman. (2012). *Philosophy without Intuitions*. Oxford University Press.

Carnap, Rudolf. (1966). *Philosophical Foundations of Physics: An Introduction to the Philosophy of Science*. Basic Books.

Carroll, Lewis. (1895). What the Tortoise Said to Achilles. *Mind*, 4(14), 278–80.

Carston, Robyn. (2002). *Thoughts and Utterances: The Pragmatics of Explicit Communication*. Blackwell.

Casalegno, Paolo. (2002). The Problem of Non-conclusiveness. *Topoi*, 21, 75–86.

Casalegno, Paolo. (2004). Logical Concepts and Logical Inferences. *Dialectica*, 58, 395–411.

Casullo, Albert. (2003). *A Priori Justification*. Oxford University Press.

Casullo, Albert. (2012). Articulating the A Priori–A Posteriori Distinction. In *Essays on a Priori Knowledge and Justification*. Oxford University Press.

Casullo, Albert. (2013). Articulating the A Priori–A Posteriori Distinction. In Albert Casullo and Joshua C. Thurow (eds), *The A Priori in Philosophy*. Oxford University Press.

Casullo, Albert. (forthcoming). A Defense of the Significance of the A Priori–A Posteriori Distinction. In Dylan Dodd and Elia Zardini (eds), *Beyond Sense? New Essays on the Significance, Grounds, and Extent of the A Priori*. Oxford University Press.

Chisholm, Roderick. (1977). *Theory of Knowledge* (2nd edition). Prentice Hall.

Chudnoff, Elijah. (2013). *Intuition*. Oxford University Press.

Coffa, Alberto. (1991). *The Semantic Tradition from Kant to Carnap: To the Vienna Station*. Cambridge University Press.

Cohen, Stewart. (1984). Justification and Truth. *Philosophical Studies: An International Journal for Philosophy in the Analytic Tradition*, 46(3), 279–95.

Creath, Richard. (1992). Carnap's Conventionalism. *Synthese*, 93(1–2), 141–65.

Crossley, John, Ash, Christopher, Brickhill, Christopher, and Stillwell, John. (1972). *What Is Mathematical Logic?* Oxford University Press.

Darwall, Stephen, Gibbard, Allan, and Railton, Peter. (1992). Toward Fin de siècle Ethics: Some Trends. *The Philosophical Review*, *101*(1), 115–89.

Davies, M. and Humberstone, L. (1980). Two Notions of Necessity. *Philosophical Studies*, *38*(1), 1–30.

Deutsch, Max. (2015). *The Myth of the Intuitive: Experimental Philosophy and Philosophical Method*. MIT Press.

Devitt, Michael. (1995). *Coming to Our Senses: A Naturalistic Program for Semantic Localism*. Cambridge University Press.

Devitt, Michael. (2005). There is No a Priori. In Steup Matthias and Sosa Ernest (eds), *Contemporary Debates in Epistemology* (pp. 105–15). Blackwell.

Dummett, Michael. (1973). *Frege: Philosophy of Language*. Duckworth.

Dummett, Michael. (1975). Wang's Paradox. *Synthese*, *30*(3–4), 201–32.

Dummett, Michael. (1991). *The Logical Basis of Metaphysics*. Harvard University Press.

Elugardo, Reinaldo. (1993). Burge on Content. *Philosophy and Phenomenological Research*, *53*(2), 367–84.

Evans, Gareth. (1979). Reference and Contingency. *Monist*, *62*, 161–89.

Evans, Gareth. (1982). *The Varieties of Reference*. Ed. J. McDowell. Clarendon Press.

Evans, Jonathan and Over, David. (2004). *If*. Oxford University Press.

Evans, Jonathan and Stanovich, Keith. (2013). Dual-Process Theories of Higher Cognition: Advancing the Debate. *Perspectives on Psychological Science*, *8*(3), 223–41.

Field, Hartry. (1989). *Realism, Mathematics & Modality*. Blackwell.

Field, Hartry. (2005). Recent Debates about the A Priori. In Tamar Szabo Gendler and John Hawthorne (eds), *Oxford Studies in Epistemology* (vol. 1, pp. 69–88). Oxford University Press.

Fine, Kit. (2002). Varieties of Necessity. In Tamar Szabo Gendler. In John Hawthorne (ed.), *Conceivability and Possibility* (pp. 253–81). Oxford University Press.

Fodor, Jerry A. (1987). *Psychosemantics: The Problem of Meaning in the Philosophy of Mind*. MIT Press.

Fodor, Jerry A. (1994). *The Elm and the Expert*. MIT Press.

Fodor, Jerry A. and Lepore, Ernest. (1991). Why Meaning (Probably) Isn't Conceptual Role. *Mind and Language*, *6*(4), 328–43.

Fodor, Jerry A. and Lepore, Ernest. (1992). *Holism: A Shopper's Guide*. Blackwell.

Foley, Richard. (1985). What is Wrong with Reliabilism? *Monist*, *68*, 188–202.

Frege, Gottlob. (1879). Begriffsschrift, eine der arithmetischen nachgebildete Formelsprache des reinen Denkens. In J. van Heijenoort (ed.), Stefan Bauer-Mengelberg (trans.), *Frege to Gödel, A Source Book in Mathematical Logic, 1879–1931*. Harvard University Press.

Frege, Gottlob. (1950). *The Foundations of Arithmetic*. Northwestern University Press.

Frege, Gottlob. (1979). *Posthumous Writings*. (Hans Hermes, Friedrich Kambartel, Friedrich KaulbachPeter Long, and Roger White, trans.). Basil Blackwell.

Gödel, Kurt. (1947). What is Cantor's Continuum Problem? In *Kurt Gödel: Collected Works Vol. II* (pp. 254–70). Oxford University Press.

Goldberg, Sanford C. (2002). Do Anti-Individualistic Construals of Propositional Attitudes Capture the Agent's Conception? *Noûs*, *36*(4), 597–621.

Goldman, Alvin. (2007). Philosophical Intuitions: Their Target, Their Source, and Their Epistemic Status. *Grazer Philosophische Studien*, *74*(1), 1–26.

Grice, H. P. (1961). The Causal Theory of Perception, Part I. *Aristotelian Society Supplementary Volume*, *35*, 121–52.

Grice, H. P. (1989). *Studies in the Way of Words*. Harvard University Press.

Grice, H. P. and Strawson, P. F. (1956). In Defense of a Dogma. *Philosophical Review*, 65(2), 141–58.

Hale, Bob. (1987). *Abstract Objects*. Blackwell.

Hallett, Michael. (1984). *Cantorian Set Theory and Limitation of Size*. Clarendon Press.

Harman, Gilbert. (1967). Quine on Meaning and Existence I. The Death of Meaning. *Review of Metaphysics*, 21(1), 124–51.

Harman, Gilbert. (1973). *Thought*. Princeton University Press.

Harman, Gilbert. (1986a). *Change in View: Principles of Reasoning*. MIT Press.

Harman, Gilbert. (1986b). The Meanings of Logical Constants. In Ernest Lepore (ed.), *Truth and Interpretation: Perspectives on the Philosophy of Donald Davidson* (pp. 125–34). Blackwell.

Harman, Gilbert. (1994a). Doubts about Conceptual Analysis. In John O'Leary-Hawthorne and Michaelis Michael (eds), *Philosophy in Mind* (pp. 43–8). Kluwer Academic.

Harman, Gilbert. (1994b). Comments on Boghossian. Presented at the APA Symposium on Analytic Truth. Boston, MA.

Harman, Gilbert. (1996). Analyticity Regained? *Noûs*, 30(3), 392–400.

Harman, Gilbert. (1999). *Reasoning, Meaning, and Mind*. Clarendon Press.

Harman, Gilbert. (2003). The Future of the A Priori. *Journal of Philosophical Research*, 28, 23–34.

Harris, John. (1982). What's So Logical about the 'Logical' Axioms? *Studia Logica*, 41, 159–71.

Harris, Paul. (2000). *The Work of the Imagination*. Wiley-Blackwell.

Hawthorne, John. (2002). Deeply Contingent A Priori Knowledge. *Philosophy and Phenomenological Research*, 65, 247–69.

Hintikka, Jaakko. (1962). *Knowledge and Belief*. Cornell University Press.

Hintikka, Jaakko. (1999). The Emperor's New Intuitions. *Journal of Philosophy*, 96(3), 127–47.

Horwich, Paul. (2000). Stipulation, Meaning and Apriority. In P. Boghossian and C. Peacocke (eds), *New Essays on the A Priori* (pp. 150–69). Oxford University Press.

Huemer, Michael. (2001). *Skepticism and the Veil of Perception*. Rowman & Littlefield.

Hume, David. (1978). *A Treatise of Human Nature*. Oxford University Press.

Jackson, Frank. (1982). Epiphenomenal Qualia. *Philosophical Quarterly*, 32, 127–36.

Jackson, Frank. (1998). *From Metaphysics to Ethics: A Defence of Conceptual Analysis*. Clarendon Press.

Jenkins, Carrie and Masahi, Kasaki. (2015). The Traditional Conception of the A Priori. *Synthese*, 92, 2725–46.

Karttunen, Lauri and Peters, Stanley. (1979). Conventional Implicature. In David A. Dinneen and Choon-kyu Oh (eds), *Presupposition (Syntax and Semantics)* (vol. 11, pp. 1–56). Academic Press.

Kitcher, Philip. (1983). *The Nature of Mathematical Knowledge*. Oxford University Press.

Kitcher, Philip. (2000). A Priori Knowledge Revisited. In Paul Boghossian and Christopher Peacocke (eds), *New Essays on the A Priori* (pp. 65–91). Oxford University Press.

Kornblith, Hilary. (2012). *On Reflection*. Oxford University Press.

Kripke, Saul. (1972). Naming and Necessity. In Gilbert Harman and Donald Davidson (eds), *Semantics of Natural Language* (pp. 253–355). Reidel.

Kripke, Saul. (1979). A Puzzle about Belief. In A. Margalit (ed.), *Meaning and Use* (pp. 239–83). Reidel.

Kripke, Saul. (1980). *Naming and Necessity*. Blackwell.

Kroedel, Thomas. (2012). Implicit Definition and the Application of Logic. *Philosophical Studies*, 158(1), 131–48.

Lehrer, Keith. (1990). *Theory of Knowledge*. Routledge.

Lewis, David. (1970). How to Define Theoretical Terms. *Journal of Philosophy*, 67(13), 427–46.

Lewis, David. (1973). *Counterfactuals*. Blackwell.

Lewis, David. (1997). Finkish Dispositions. *Philosophical Quarterly, 47*(187), 143–58.

Lycan, William G. (1991). Definition in a Quinean World. In *Definitions and Definability: Philosophical Perspectives* (pp. 111–31). Springer.

Maddy, Penelope. (2007). *Second Philosophy: A Naturalistic Method*. Oxford University Press.

Maddy, Penelope. (2011). *Defending the Axioms: On the Philosophical Foundations of Set Theory*. Oxford University Press.

Malmgren, Anna-Sara. (2006). Is There a Priori Knowledge by Testimony? *Philosophical Review, 115*(2), 199–241.

Margolis, E. and Laurence, S. (2001). Boghossian on Analyticity. *Analysis, 61*(4), 293–302.

Martin, C. B. (1994). Dispositions and Conditionals. *Philosophical Quarterly, 44*(174), 1–8.

Martin, C. B. and Heil, John. (1998). Rules and Powers. *Noûs, 32*(12), 283–312.

McGee, Vann. (1985). A Counterexample to Modus Ponens. *Journal of Philosophy, 82*(9), 462–71.

McGee, Vann. (1997). How We Learn Mathematical Language. *Philosophical Review, 106*(1), 35–68.

McGee, Vann. (2000). Everything. In Gila Sher and Richard Tieszen (eds), *Between Logic and Intuition* (pp. 54–78). Cambridge University Press.

McGinn, Colin. (1975). 'A Priori' and 'A Posteriori' Knowledge. *Proceedings of the Aristotelian Society, 76*, 195–208.

Melis, Giacomo and Wright, Crispin. (forthcoming). Oxonian Scepticism about the A Priori. In Dylan Dodd and Elia Zardini (eds), *Beyond Sense? New Essays on the Significance, Grounds, and Extent of the A Priori*. Oxford University Press.

Moore, G. E. (1903a). *Principia Ethica*. Dover Publications.

Moore, G. E. (1903b). The Refutation of Idealism. *Mind, 12*(48), 433–53.

Nagel, Jennifer. (forthcoming). *Recognizing Knowledge: Intuitive and Reflective Epistemology*.

Oppy, Graham. (1987). Williamson and the Contingent A Priori. *Analysis, 47*, 188–93.

Parfit, Derek. (1984). *Reasons and Persons*. Oxford University Press.

Parsons, Charles. (1979). Mathematical Intuition. *Proceedings of the Aristotelian Society, 80*, 145–68.

Peacocke, Christopher. (1992). *A Study of Concepts*. MIT Press.

Peacocke, Christopher. (1993a). How Are A Priori Truths Possible? *European Journal of Philosophy, 1*, 2–175.

Peacocke, Christopher. (1993b). Proof and Truth. In John Haldane and Crispin Wright (eds), *Reality, Representation, and Projection* (pp. 165–90). Oxford University Press.

Peacocke, Christopher. (1998). Implicit Conceptions, Understanding and Rationality. *Philosophical Issues, 9*, 43–88.

Peacocke, Christopher. (2004). *The Realm of Reason*. Oxford University Press.

Peacocke, Christopher. (2008). *Truly Understood*. Oxford University Press.

Plantinga, Alvin. (1993). *Warrant: The Current Debate*. Oxford University Press.

Priest, Graham. (1995). *Beyond the Limits of Thought*. Cambridge University Press.

Prior, A. N. (1960). The Runabout Inference-Ticket. *Analysis, 21*(2), 38–9.

Pryor, James. (2000). The Skeptic and the Dogmatist. *Noûs, 34*(4), 517–49.

Pryor, James. (2001). Highlights of Recent Epistemology. *British Journal for the Philosophy of Science, 52*(1), 95–124.

Pryor, James. (2004). What's Wrong with Moore's Argument? *Philosophical Issues, 14*(1), 349–78.

Pust, Joel. (2000). *Intuitions as Evidence*. Taylor & Francis.

Putnam, Hilary. (1968). Is Logic Empirical? In Robert S. Cohen and Marx W. Wartofsky (eds), *Boston Studies in the Philosophy of Science: Proceedings of the Boston Colloquium for the Philosophy of Science 1966/1968* (pp. 216–41). Kluwer Academic.

Putnam, Hilary. (1975a). The Refutation of Conventionalism. In *Mind, Language and Reality: Philosophical Papers* (vol. 2, pp. 153–91). Cambridge University Press.

Putnam, Hilary. (1975b). The Meaning of 'Meaning'. *Minnesota Studies in the Philosophy of Science*, 7, 131–93.

Quine, W. V. (1936). Truth by Convention. In O. H. Lee (ed.), *Philosophical Essays for A. N. Whitehead* (pp. 90–124). Russell & Russell.

Quine, W. V. (1951). Two Dogmas of Empiricism. *Philosophical Review*, 60(1), 20–43.

Quine, W. V. (1953). *From a Logical Point of View: 9 Logico-Philosophical Essays*. Harvard University Press.

Quine, W. V. (1970). *Philosophy of Logic*. Harvard University Press.

Quine, W. V. (1976). *The Ways of Paradox, and Other Essays*. Harvard University Press.

Quine, W. V. (1981). *Theories and Things*. Harvard University Press.

Quine, W. V. (1986). Reply to Geoffrey Hellman. In *The Philosophy of WV Quine* (pp. 206–8). Open Court.

Ramsey, Frank. (1929). *Theories, in his Foundations: Essays in Philosophy, Logic, Mathematics and Economics* (ed. H Mellor). Routledge and Kegan Paul.

Rorty, Richard. (1979). *Philosophy and the Mirror of Nature*. Princeton University Press.

Rumfitt, Ian. (2000). 'Yes' and 'No'. *Mind*, 109(436), 781–823.

Russell, Bertrand. (1919). *Introduction to Mathematical Philosophy*. Dover Publications.

Salmon, Nathan. (1993). Analyticity and Apriority. *Philosophical Perspectives*, 7, 125–33.

Schechter, Joshua. (2010). The Reliability Challenge and the Epistemology of Logic. *Philosophical Perspectives*, 24(1), 437–64.

Schiffer, Stephen. (2003). *The Things We Mean*. Oxford University Press.

Searle, John. (1958). Proper Names. *Mind*, 67(266), 166–73.

Sextus Empiricus. (2000). *Outlines of Empiricism* (R. G. Bury, trans.). Harvard University Press.

Sgaravatti, Daniele. (2018). Experience and Reasoning: Challenging the A Priori/A Posteriori Distinction. *Synthese*. https://doi.org/10.1007/s11229-018-1718-7.

Shoenfield, Joseph. (1977). Axioms of Set Theory. In Jon Barwise and H. Jerome Keisler (eds), *Handbook of Mathematical Logic* (pp. 321–44). North-Holland.

Siegel, Susanna. (2012). Cognitive Penetrability and Perceptual Justification. *Noûs*, 46(2).

Siegel, Susanna. (2017). *The Rationality of Perception*. Oxford University Press.

Snowdon, Paul. (2010). On the What-It-is-Like-Ness of Experience. *Southern Journal of Philosophy*, 48(1), 8–27.

Sorensen, Roy. (2001). *Vagueness and Contradiction*. Clarendon Press.

Sosa, Ernest. (1998). Minimal Intuition. In Michael DePaul and William Ramsey (eds), *Rethinking Intuition* (pp. 257–69). Rowman & Littlefield.

Sosa, Ernest. (2007). *A Virtue Epistemology: Apt Belief and Reflective Knowledge*. Oxford University Press.

Stalnaker, Robert. (1968). A Theory of Conditionals. In Nicholas Rescher (ed.), *Studies in Logical Theory* (pp. 98–112). Blackwell.

Stalnaker, Robert. (1999). *Context and Content*. Oxford University Press.

Strawson, Peter. (1952). *Introduction to Logical Theory*. Methuen.

Strawson, Peter. (1971). *Logico-Linguistic Papers*. Taylor & Francis.

Street, Sharon. (2009). In Defense of Future Tuesday Indifference: Ideally Coherent Eccentrics and the Contingency of What Matters. *Philosophical Issues*, 19, 273–98.

Tolhurst, William. (1998). Seemings. *American Philosophical Quarterly*, 35(3), 293–302.

Wedgwood, Ralph. (2002). Internalism Explained. *Philosophy and Phenomenological Research*, 65(2), 349–69.

Williamson, Timothy. (1986). The Contingent A Priori: Has it Anything to Do with Indexicals? *Analysis*, 46, 113–17.

Williamson, Timothy. (1987/88). Equivocation and Existence. *Proceedings of the Aristotelian Society*, 88, 109–27.

Williamson, Timothy. (1988). The Contingent A Priori: A Reply. *Analysis*, *48*, 218–21.

Williamson, Timothy. (1994). *Vagueness*. Routledge.

Williamson, Timothy. (2000). *Knowledge and its Limits*. Oxford University Press.

Williamson, Timothy. (2001). Ethics, Supervenience and Ramsey Sentences. *Philosophy and Phenomenological Research*, *62*(3), 625–30.

Williamson, Timothy. (2003). Understanding and Inference. *Aristotelian Society Supplementary Volume*, *77*, 249–93.

Williamson, Timothy. (2005). Philosophical 'Intuitions' and Scepticism about Judgement. *Dialectica*, *58*(1), 109–53.

Williamson, Timothy. (2006). Conceptual Truth. *Aristotelian Society Supplementary Volume*, *80*, 1–41.

Williamson, Timothy. (2007a). *The Philosophy of Philosophy*. Blackwell.

Williamson, Timothy. (2007b). On Being Justified in One's Head. In John Greco, Alfred Mele, and Mark Timmons (eds), *Rationality and the Good: Critical Essays on the Ethics and Epistemology of Robert Audi* (pp. 106–22). Oxford University Press.

Williamson, Timothy. (2009). Reference, Inference, and the Semantics of Pejoratives. In Joseph Almog and Paolo Leonardi (eds), *The Philosophy of David Kaplan* (pp. 137–58). Oxford University Press.

Williamson, Timothy. (2011). Reply to Boghossian. *Philosophy and Phenomenological Research*, *82*, 498–506.

Williamson, Timothy. (2012). Boghossian and Casalegno on Understanding and Inference. *Dialectica*, *66*(2), 237–47.

Williamson, Timothy. (2013). How Deep is the Distinction between A Priori and A Posteriori Knowledge? In Albert Casullo and Joshua C. Thurow (eds), *The A Priori in Philosophy* (pp. 291–312). Oxford University Press.

Williamson, Timothy. (2014). Very Improbable Knowing. *Erkenntnis*, *79*, 971–99.

Williamson, Timothy. (2016). Knowing by Imagining. In Amy Kind and Peter Kung (eds), *Knowledge through Imagination* (pp. 113–23). Oxford University Press.

Williamson, Timothy. (2017). Model-Building in Philosophy. In Russell Blackford and Damien Broderick (eds), *Philosophy's Future: The Problem of Philosophical Progress* (pp. 159–73). Wiley-Blackwell.

Williamson, Timothy. (2019). Morally Loaded Cases in Philosophy. *Proceedings and Addresses of the American Philosophical Association*, *93*, 159–72.

Williamson, Timothy. (2020). *Suppose and Tell: The Semantics and Heuristics of Conditionals*. Oxford University Press.

Williamson, Timothy. (forthcoming a). More Oxonian Skepticism about the A Priori. In Dylan Dodd and Elia Zardini (eds), *Beyond Sense? New Essays on the Significance, Grounds, and Extent of the A Priori*. Oxford University Press.

Williamson, Timothy. (forthcoming b). Reply to Casullo's Defence of the Significance of the A Priori–A Posteriori Distinction. In Dylan Dodd and Elia Zardini (eds), *Beyond Sense? New Essays on the Significance, Grounds, and Extent of the A Priori*. Oxford University Press.

Wittgenstein, Ludwig. (1953). *Philosophical Investigations*. Blackwell.

Wright, Crispin. (1986). Inventing Logical Necessity. In Jeremy Butterfield (ed.), *Language, Mind and Logic*. Cambridge University Press.

Wright, Crispin. (2001). On Basic Logical Knowledge: Reflections on Paul Boghossian's 'How Are Objective Epistemic Reasons Possible?' *Philosophical Studies*, *106*(1–2), 41–85.

Wright, Crispin. (2004). Intuition, Entitlement and the Epistemology of Logical Laws. *Dialectica*, *58*(1), 155–75.

Yablo, Stephen. (1992). Review of Alan Sidelle, Necessity, Essence, and Individuation. *Philosophical Review*, *101*(4), 878–81.

Index

For the benefit of digital users, table entries that span two pages (e.g., 52–53) may, on occasion, appear on only one of those pages.

Printed and bound by CPI Group (UK) Ltd, Croydon, CR0 4YY